MVS JCL

Second Edition

Since 1981, Doug Lowe has written 22 computer books, 15 of them on IBM main-frame subjects ranging from MVS to CICS to VSAM. He has 17 years of data processing experience, and is widely respected for his ability to explain complex computer subjects in a clear, practical way. *MVS JCL (Second Edition)* is a revised edition of his 1987 bestseller, which has been used for training by programmers throughout the world.

MVS JCL

Second Edition

Doug Lowe

Mike Murach & Associates, Inc.

4697 W. Jacquelyn Avenue
Fresno, California 93722-6427 • (209) 275-3335

Development team

Editor: Anne Prince

Production director: Steve Ehlers

Related books

MVS TSO, Part 1: Concepts and ISPF, Doug Lowe
MVS TSO, Part 2: Commands and Procedures, Doug Lowe

VSAM: Access Method Services and Application Programming, Doug Lowe
VSAM for the COBOL Programmer, Doug Lowe

CICS for the COBOL Programmer, Part 1: An Introductory Course, Doug Lowe
CICS for the COBOL Programmer, Part 2: An Advanced Course, Doug Lowe

DB2 for the COBOL Programmer, Part 1: An Introductory Course, Steve Eckols
DB2 for the COBOL Programmer, Part 2: An Advanced Course, Steve Eckols

IMS for the COBOL Programmer, Part 1: Data Base Processing with IMS/VS and DL/I DOS/VSE, Steve Eckols
IMS for the COBOL Programmer, Part 2: Data Communications and Message Format Service, Steve Eckols

Structured ANS COBOL, Part 1: A Course for Novices, Mike Murach & Paul Noll
Structured ANS COBOL, Part 2: An Advanced Course, Mike Murach & Paul Noll

VS COBOL II: A Guide for Programmers and Managers, Anne Prince

MVS Assembler Language, Kevin McQuillen and Anne Prince

OS Utilities, Doug Lowe

10 9 8 7 6 5 4 3 2

ISBN: 0-911625-85-2

Library of Congress Cataloging-in-Publication Data

Lowe, Doug.
  MVS JCL / Doug Lowe. -- 2nd ed.
    p. cm.
  Includes index.
  ISBN 0-911625-85-2
  1. IBM MVS. 2. Job Control Language (Computer program language)
I. Title.
QA76.6.L675 1994
005.4'3--dc20   94-37779
                                              CIP

Contents

Expanded contents

Preface

MVS is IBM's most powerful operating system for mainframe computers. Thousands of computer installations use it to manage computer systems that cost millions of dollars and support hundreds or even thousands of users. And IBM continues to encourage more and more users of the smaller VSE operating system to convert to MVS. As a result, if you're involved in any type of programming activity on an IBM mainframe computer, odds are you're using MVS now or will be in the future.

One of the most difficult parts of learning how to use MVS is learning its job control language (JCL). It's difficult to learn it from the IBM manuals because they're *reference* manuals: They assume you already know JCL. That's why you need this book. It does what the IBM manuals don't do: It teaches MVS JCL in a way that's easy to understand and easy to put to practice.

But this book does much more than just show you how to code JCL statements: It explains the basics of how MVS works so you can then apply that understanding as you code JCL. With an operating system as complex as MVS, it's crucial that you have a basic understanding of how it works.

Who this book is for

This book is for anyone involved with any type of programming activity on an IBM mainframe running under MVS. If you're new to MVS, this book will help you approach a formidable operating system with confidence; if you have years of experience, this book will give you a solid understanding of the JCL facilities you've used all along. Whether you're an applications programmer, a systems programmer, or an operator, this book will teach you JCL facilities you'll use every day.

There have been three main versions of MVS: MVS/370, which ran on System/370 architecture machines (24-bit addressing); MVS/XA, which runs on the newer System/370-XA machines (31-bit addressing); and MVS/ESA, which runs on the newest Enterprise Systems Architecture machines. Each system is available with one of two Job Entry Subsystems: JES2 or JES3. This book applies to all MVS systems, and it teaches the important underlying differences between them. So whether your shop uses MVS/XA or MVS/ESA (or even if you still use MVS/370) and whether you use JES2 or JES3, this book is appropriate for you. (Incidentally, the examples in this book were tested under MVS/XA and JES2 running on a 3090 processor.)

The only prerequisite for this book is an elementary understanding of computers, which can come from an introductory-level data processing or programming class or experience working with a minicomputer or a microcomputer (like an IBM PC). The first chapters of this book—which experienced MVS programmers might want to skip—provide all the background information you need to learn JCL.

How to use this book

The organization of this book gives you many choices as to the sequence in which you study various features of MVS JCL. Table 1 shows the general plan of the book. The chapters in section 1 (chapters 1 through 4) provide the background information you need to understand before you can start learning JCL. Then, section 2 (chapters 5 through 7) presents the basics of coding MVS JCL. After you've read those two sections, you can read section 3, 4, or 5, depending on which subjects you're interested in: VSAM data management, non-VSAM data management, or program development and utilities.

You should read the chapters within the first three sections in order. In sections 4 and 5 (chapters 11 through 17), however, the chapters are independent of one another. So you can read them in any order you wish.

About the second edition

The second edition of this book has been thoroughly revised to cover the many new features that have been introduced in MVS since the first edition was published in 1987. In particular, you'll

Section	Chapters	Title	Prerequisite section
1	1-4	Introduction	(none)
2	5-7	Job Control Language	1
3	8-10	VSAM data management	2
4	11-14	Non-VSAM data management	2
5	15-17	Program development and utilities	2

Table 1

find coverage of ESA concepts, the Storage Management Subsystem (SMS), new JCL features for MVS/ESA such as the IF, ELSE, and ENDIF statements and the SET and INCLUDE statements, support for private procedure libraries, the ability to define VSAM files through JCL, and much more. In addition, many other improvements have been made throughout the book. For example, the presentation of the standard utility programs and the sort/merge program has been substantially expanded. Exercises have also been added to the end of each chapter for those who use the book for classroom instruction. These exercises are designed to let you apply the concepts presented in the chapter.

Conclusion

Whether you're new to MVS or have years of experience, this book is for you. It will teach you all the JCL facilities you're likely to use, whether you're an applications programmer, a systems programmer, or an operator. In addition, it will teach you the basics of how the MVS operating system works so you can use it with confidence. In short, this book will help you use MVS more effectively.

If this book doesn't teach you everything you need to know about MVS JCL, please let us know by filling out the postage-paid comment form at the back of the book. On the other hand, if this book is just what you've been looking for, we'd like to know that too. Either way, your response will help us continue to improve this book and future books as well. We look forward to hearing from you soon.

Doug Lowe
Fresno, California, September, 1994

Section 1

Introduction

Before you can learn how to use MVS, you need to understand its basic concepts. So, the four chapters in this section introduce you to the basic facilities of MVS. Chapter 1 is a general introduction to IBM mainframe data processing. Chapter 2 is more specific: It describes the various hardware components that make up a typical IBM mainframe computer. Chapter 3 presents some of the basic facilities provided by the MVS operating system. And chapter 4 teaches you how to use TSO/ISPF to create MVS jobs and submit them for processing.

Some of the material in this section (especially chapter 1) may be review for you, depending on your background. As a result, I suggest you review the objectives and terminology lists at the end of each chapter or topic to see whether you need to study it.

Chapter 1

An introduction to IBM mainframe data processing

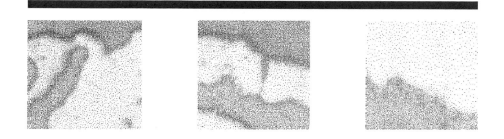

This chapter introduces you to the characteristics of data processing using IBM mainframe computers. Because many people have experience with computers that are quite different from mainframe computers, this chapter begins by examining the similarities and differences between mainframe computers and two other common types of computer systems: personal computers and minicomputers. Then, it describes some of the basic features provided by mainframe computer operating systems. Finally, it introduces the three major families of operating systems for IBM mainframe computers.

This chapter is designed for readers who have experience with computers, but not with mainframe computer systems. In other words, if you've used a personal computer or minicomputer system, this chapter will give you the background you need so you can start learning about MVS. If, on the other hand, your experience is with mainframe computers, IBM or not, this chapter will be mostly review. So feel free to skip it.

How mainframe computers compare with minicomputers and personal computers

Today, most computer systems used for business purposes can be divided into three classes: *personal computers*, *minicomputers*, and *mainframe computers*. Although these divisions are loosely based on the size of the computer systems, there are no hard and fast rules for deciding exactly where one category ends and the next begins. In other words, the categories overlap. As a result, the largest mini-computer systems are often larger than the smallest mainframe

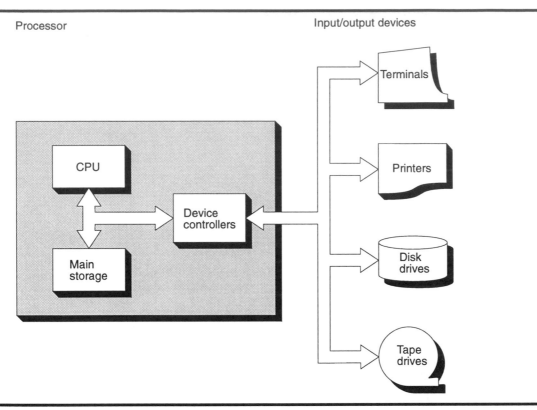

Processor   Input/output devices

Figure 1-1   The basic components of a modern computer system

computers. In addition, the boundaries are constantly changing. For example, the memory capacity of a typical personal computer today rivals that of a large minicomputer or a small mainframe computer of just a few years ago.

Several factors determine the "size" of a computer system. In particular, a computer's hardware configuration, the nature of its applications, and the complexity of its system software help classify the system as a personal computer, minicomputer, or mainframe.

Hardware configurations

Regardless of size, virtually all computers today consist of two basic types of components: *processors* and *input/output devices*. Figure 1-1 illustrates these components. As you can see, the processor consists of three parts: the *central processing unit*, or *CPU*, executes instructions; *main storage* or *main memory* stores instructions and data

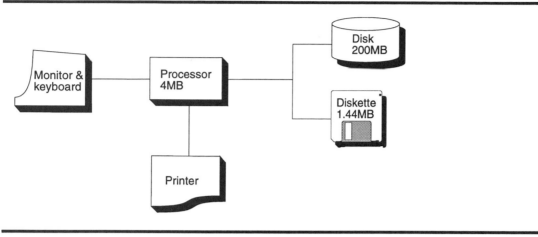

Figure 1-2   A typical personal computer configuration

processed by the CPU; and *device controllers* let the CPU and main storage connect to I/O devices. Input/output devices fall into two classes: those that provide input and output to the system, such as terminals and printers, and those that provide *secondary storage*, such as tape and disk drives.

Although all computer systems consist of these basic components, the way those components are combined for a particular computer system varies depending on the system's requirements. Now, I'll describe typical *configurations* of hardware equipment for personal computers, minicomputers, and mainframes.

Personal computer configurations   Personal computers, or *PCs*, are small, single user systems that provide a simple processor and just a few input/output devices. Figure 1-2 shows the configuration of a typical personal computer. This system consists of a processor with 4MB of main storage (one MB is about a million characters of data), a keyboard, a monitor, a printer, a diskette drive with a capacity of 1.44MB, and a 200MB hard disk. A personal computer such as this typically costs $1,000-4,000.

Although personal computers are by nature single-user systems, they can be connected to one another to form a *network*. Then, they can share resources such as printers and disk drives. With the right software, a network of personal computers can be used as an alternative to a minicomputer or a mainframe computer system.

Minicomputer configurations   Figure 1-3 shows a typical minicomputer configuration. Unlike personal computers, most minicomputers

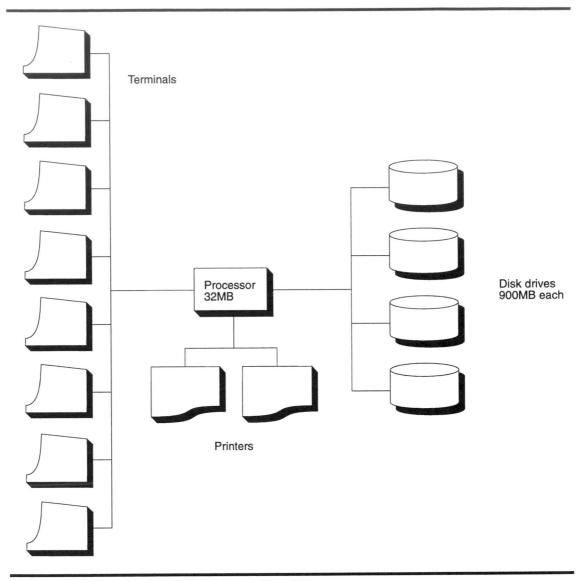

Figure 1-3   A typical minicomputer configuration

provide more than one terminal so that several people can use the system at one time. A system like this is sometimes called a *multi-user system*. The minicomputer configuration in figure 1-3 has 32MB of main storage, 8 terminals, two printers, and four disk drives each capable of storing 900MB, for a total storage capacity of 3.6GB (one GB is approximately one billion characters of data). Most minicomputer configurations cost between $20,000 and $100,000.

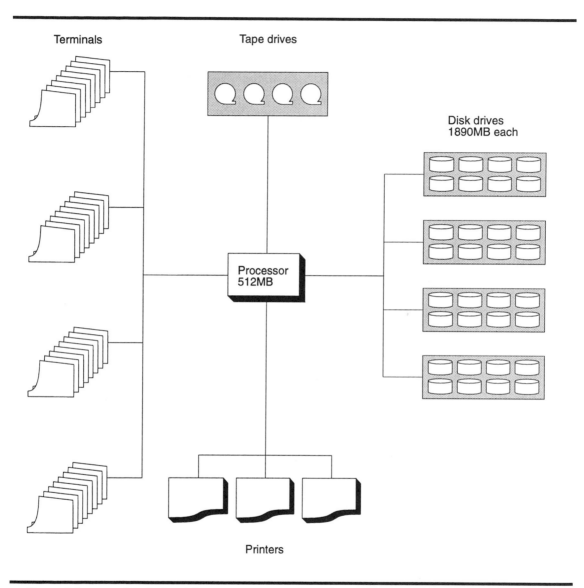

Terminals   Tape drives

Disk drives
1890MB each

Processor
512MB

Printers

Figure 1-4   A typical mainframe computer configuration

Mainframe configurations   Figure 1-4 shows a typical configuration for a mainframe computer. Although it consists of the same basic types of components as the personal computer and minicomputer, it has more I/O devices and larger storage capacities. For example, the configuration in figure 1-4 includes 32 disk drives, four tape drives, three printers, and a large number of terminals. The processor's main storage is 512MB, and the total disk capacity is more than 60GB. The cost of a system like this would be in the millions of dollars.

The System/360-370 family   Without doubt, the most popular family of mainframe computers ever is the System/360-370 family, introduced by IBM in 1964. The original System/360 was smaller than the smallest of today's personal computers, offering only 8 thousand bytes of main storage. Today, the largest member of the family can be configured with more than 260,000 times as much main storage: 2 *billion* bytes. You'll learn about the various components that make up a System/360-370 computer in the next chapter.

Applications

Another aspect of a computer's size is the nature of the *applications* for which it is used. In general, larger computers are used for a broader range of applications than are smaller computers. That's because the larger computers support more users, with more diverse needs, than do smaller computers.

To illustrate, consider a typical bank. Loan officers, who use specialized techniques to make sound decisions about loans, often use personal computers to make their calculations. Each branch may have a minicomputer or a network of personal computers to support a variety of needs for the individual branch. And the bank may have a centralized mainframe computer that supports all of the bank's branches, providing for an even broader range of needs. In other words, the bank uses personal computers for applications at the individual level, minicomputers or personal computer networks at the departmental or branch level, and mainframe computers at the corporate level.

Sometimes, computers of various sizes have similar applications that vary only in the volume of data processed. For example, a corner retail store may use a personal computer to manage its inventory, a larger retail store may use a minicomputer or a personal computer network for inventory management, and a large chain of retail stores may use a central mainframe computer for inventory management. All three stores use their computers for essentially the same function; it's the volume of data processed that distinguishes them.

System software

Yet another distinction among computers is the scope of its *system software*—that is, the programs that manage the computer system itself so that application programs can perform useful work. The cornerstone of system software is the *operating system*, which is a set of programs that directly controls the operation of the computer. Personal computers generally use a relatively simple operating system: Microsoft's MS-DOS or perhaps IBM's OS/2. Minicomputer systems generally have more complex operating systems to effectively manage a larger configuration of equipment. And mainframe computer systems have operating systems that are complex beyond imagination. The MVS operating system, the subject of this book, is among the most sophisticated and complex mainframe operating systems in use today.

One way to appreciate the increasing complexity of these operating systems is to consider the number of technical manuals that accompany them. MS-DOS, the most commonly used personal computer operating system, is thoroughly documented in a single manual. The operating system for a popular minicomputer system I've worked with is documented in about a dozen manuals. The subject of this book, the MVS operating system, has hundreds of manuals. In fact, IBM publishes a document called the *IBM System/370, 30xx, and 4300 Processors Bibliography*; in it is a 200-page section listing more than 10,000 publications related to the System/360-370 family. The printed documentation for MVS is so bulky that IBM now distributes it in electronic form. It requires more than 1.3 billion bytes of disk storage.

Another factor that indicates the complexity of an operating system is the need for specialized programmers to maintain it. Personal computers almost never require programmers to maintain their operating systems; instead, the end user learns how to use the operating system without help. Minicomputer systems are more complex; they sometimes require a programmer to keep the operating system working properly. Some minicomputer systems, however, don't require full-time programmers to maintain their operating systems.

In contrast, mainframe installations cannot function without a staff of *systems programmers* who work on a full-time basis to keep the system software in shape. The job of the systems programmers includes installing new system software, updating it to reflect changes made to the hardware or software configuration, optimizing it so that it runs efficiently, and correcting errors in the operating system.

In many ways, it's the complexity of the operating system that most clearly distinguishes mainframe computers from smaller computers. So, the next section introduces you to several basic facilities provided by mainframe computer operating systems.

Five characteristic features of mainframe operating systems

To help you understand the nature of mainframe operating systems, I'll now describe five basic characteristics common to most of them. As you read about these characteristics, you'll note that some of them are found on personal computer or minicomputer operating systems too, although not usually at the same level of sophistication as they're found on mainframes. The five characteristics are: virtual storage, multiprogramming, spooling, batch processing, and time sharing.

Virtual storage

In most computer systems, the processor's main storage is among the most valuable of the system's resources. As a result, modern mainframe computer operating systems provide sophisticated services to make the best use of the available main storage. Among the most basic of these services is virtual storage.

Simply put, *virtual storage* is a technique that lets a large amount of main storage be simulated by a processor that actually has a smaller amount of *real storage*. For example, a processor that has 128MB of real storage might use virtual storage to simulate 512MB of main storage. To do this, the computer uses disk storage as an extension of real storage.

The key to understanding virtual storage is realizing that at any given moment, only the current program instruction and the data it accesses needs to be in real storage. Other data and instructions can be placed temporarily on disk storage and recalled into main storage when needed. In other words, virtual storage operating systems transfer data and instructions between real storage and disk storage as they are needed.

Although the details of how virtual storage is implemented varies from one operating system to the next, the basic concept is the same. In chapter 3, you'll learn how virtual storage is implemented under MVS. Fortunately, though, virtual storage is largely transparent. From the user's point of view, virtual storage appears to be real storage.

Multiprogramming

Another feature common to all mainframe computers is *multiprogramming*. Multiprogramming means simply that the computer lets more than one program execute at the same time. Actually, that's misleading: At any given moment, only one program can have control of the CPU. Nevertheless, a multiprogramming system *appears* to execute more than one program at the same time.

The key to understanding multiprogramming is to realize that some processing operations—like reading data from an input device—take much longer than others. As a result, most programs that run on mainframe computers are idle a large percentage of the time waiting for I/O operations to complete. If programs were run one at a time on a mainframe computer, the CPU would spend most of its time waiting. Multiprogramming simply reclaims the CPU during these idle periods to let other programs execute.

Multiprogramming, like virtual storage, is mostly transparent: Each program appears to have exclusive use of the system. However, as you'll learn in chapter 3, the operating system facilities that enable multiprogramming are quite complicated.

Spooling

A significant problem that must be overcome by multiprogramming systems is sharing access to input and output devices among the programs that execute together. For example, if two programs executing at the same time try to write output to a printer, the output from both programs will be intermixed in the printout. One way to avoid this problem is to give one of the programs complete control of the printer. Unfortunately, that defeats the purpose of multiprogramming because the other program will have to wait until the printer is available.

To provide shared access to printer devices, *spooling* is used. Spooling manages printer output for applications by intercepting it and directing it to a disk device instead. Then, when the program is finished, the operating system collects its spooled print output and directs it to the printer. In a multiprogramming environment, each program's spooled output is stored separately on disk so that it can be printed separately.

Another benefit of spooling is that disk devices are much faster than printers. As a result, programs that produce spooled print output can execute faster than programs that access printers directly. The operating system component that actually prints the spooled output is multiprogrammed along with the application programs so that the printer is kept as busy as possible. But the application programs themselves aren't slowed down by the relatively slow operation of the printer.

Batch processing

If you've used an IBM personal computer, you're probably familiar with batch files, which contain a series of commands that are processed together as a batch. On a PC, batch files are an advanced facility that you use once in a while. On a mainframe computer, though, *batch processing* is the normal way of using the computer system, and has been for decades.

When batch processing is used, work is processed in units called *jobs*. A job may cause one or more programs to be executed in sequence. For example, one job may invoke the programs necessary to update a file of employee records, print a report listing employee information, and produce payroll checks. Another job might invoke a single program that copies the entire contents of a disk device to tape for backup purposes.

Job Control Language, or *JCL*, describes a job by providing information that identifies programs to be executed and data to be processed. JCL is a complex language that consists of several different types of statements with hundreds of different specifications. This book teaches you how to use an MVS system by creating jobs that consist of JCL statements. As a result, the focus of this book is on batch processing.

One of the problems that arises when batch processing is used is managing how work flows through the system. In a typical mainframe computer system, many users (perhaps hundreds) compete to use the system's resources. To manage this, the system's *job scheduler* processes each job in an orderly fashion. When a user submits a job to the system, that job is added to a list of other jobs, perhaps submitted by other users, that are waiting to be executed. As the processor becomes available, the job scheduling portion of the operating system selects the next job to be executed from this list.

In the process, the job scheduler can make decisions about the order in which jobs should be executed. In other words, jobs aren't necessarily executed in the order in which they're submitted. Instead, jobs with higher priority can be given preference over jobs with lower priority.

Time sharing

Batch processing was the only way to use mainframe computer systems in the early days of data processing when the primary input devices were card readers, which read decks of punched paper cards. As terminal devices became more and more common, users needed a more direct way to use the computer system. As a result, most modern mainframe computers provide time sharing facilities.

In a *time sharing* system, each user has access to the system through a terminal device. Instead of submitting jobs that are scheduled for later execution, the user enters commands that are processed immediately. As a result, time sharing is sometimes called *online processing*, because it lets users interact directly with the computer. For technical reasons, time sharing is sometimes called *foreground processing*, while batch job processing is called *background processing*.

Because of time sharing, mainframe computer systems have two faces: batch job processing and time sharing. In practice, you need to be familiar with both techniques of using your computer system. As a programmer, you'll use your computer's time sharing facilities most often to create, maintain, and store JCL statements and programs so they can be processed as jobs in background mode.

IBM mainframe operating systems

Now that you're familiar with some basic features of mainframe operating systems, I'll introduce you to the three major families of IBM mainframe operating systems: DOS, OS, and VM.

The DOS family of operating systems

DOS, which stands for *Disk Operating System*, was originally designed for small System/360 configurations that had limited processing requirements. Although DOS was first introduced in the mid-1960s, it has evolved significantly from its original version. As a result, today's DOS has little resemblance to the original DOS.

DOS today is commonly called *DOS/VSE*, or just *VSE*; VSE stands for *Virtual Storage Extended*, which refers to the particular way virtual storage is handled.

Although DOS/VSE has evolved into a respectable operating system, it's still most appropriate for smaller systems that don't have extensive processing requirements. For larger configurations, the OS family of operating systems is more appropriate.

The OS family of operating systems

OS, which stands for *Operating System*, was originally designed for installations that required the full range of processing possibilities available with the System/360. Originally, OS was intended to offer a smooth migration from DOS. But the two operating systems have evolved along different paths, so that they are now fundamentally incompatible with one another. As a result, a conversion from DOS to OS is a significant undertaking.

In the late 1960s and early 1970s, there were two versions of OS in widespread use, called *OS/MFT* and *OS/MVT*. They differed in the way they handled multiprogramming. MFT stood for *Multiprogramming* a *Fixed* number of *Tasks*; it preallocated a fixed number of *partitions* where user jobs could execute. Under MFT, the size of each partition remained constant, as did the number of jobs that could be multiprogrammed. In contrast, MVT, which stood for *Multiprogramming* a *Variable* number of *Tasks*, allocated storage to each program as it entered the system. Under MVT, each program was allocated a *region* of storage as it executed, and the number of programs that could be multiprogrammed depended on the storage requirements of each program and the total amount of available storage.

Neither MFT or MVT provided virtual storage; when virtual storage was developed in the early 1970s, MFT and MVT were replaced by *OS/VS1* and *OS/VS2*. OS/VS1 provided the same fixed partition structure of MFT, only in a virtual storage environment. Similarly, OS/VS2 provided a virtual storage version of the variable region structure of MVT. Both VS1 and VS2 provided a maximum of 16MB of virtual storage. There are still some shops around that use VS1 and VS2 today.

The current form of OS is called *MVS*, which stands for *Multiple Virtual Storage*. (Originally, MVS was called OS/VS2 Release 2 MVS; what was originally called OS/VS2 Release 1 is now sometimes called *SVS*, for *Single Virtual Storage*.) In MVS, each multiprogrammed job is given its own virtual storage address space, which can be up to 16MB or 2GB depending on which version of MVS you're using. The idea of multiple virtual address spaces is a bit confusing, so don't worry about it now. I'll explain it in more detail in chapter 3.

Today, there are three common versions of MVS. Because IBM periodically repackages MVS and gives it a different name to reflect the new packaging, it's easy to become confused. So, throughout this book, I'll say just MVS when it doesn't really matter what version of MVS you're using. If I'm referring specifically to an older version of MVS that limits a user's address space to 16MB, I'll call it *MVS/370*. To refer to the MVS versions that let user address spaces be up to 2GB, I'll say *MVS/XA* or just *XA*. And to refer to the newest versions of MVS, which let each job access more than one 2GB address space, I'll say *MVS/ESA* or just *ESA*.

The JCL facilities you'll learn how to use in this book apply most directly to MVS/XA and MVS/ESA systems. However, the basic forms of JCL statements haven't changed much since the original OS was introduced in the mid-1960s. As a result, much of what you learn in this book can be used on VS1, SVS, and MVS/370 systems as well.

The VM operating system

A third IBM operating system, called *VM*, takes a different approach to computer system management than DOS or OS. VM, which stands for *Virtual Machine*, uses a variety of techniques including virtual storage and multiprogramming to simulate more than one computer system (called a virtual machine) on a single real computer system. Within each simulated virtual machine, a more conventional operating system like VSE or MVS must be used. VM provides a special operating system, called *CMS* (for *Conversational Monitor System*), which lets a single terminal user use a virtual machine interactively.

At one time, it was not uncommon for MVS shops to use VM so they could create multiple MVS systems on a single processor. However, current IBM processors can be equipped with a feature called *PR/SM* (which stands for *Processor Resource/Systems Manager*), which does effectively the same thing much more efficiently. As a result, VM isn't used much any more. You'll learn a bit about PR/SM in the next chapter.

Discussion

The purpose of this chapter has been to orient you to the world of IBM mainframe data processing. As a result, you don't need to worry about many of the specifics this chapter presented; they'll be repeated in more detail in later chapters. Instead, I just want you to have a feel for what mainframe computer systems are about, especially in contrast to other types of computer systems you may have encountered.

Terminology

personal computer
minicomputer
mainframe computer
processor
input/output device
central processing unit
CPU
main storage
main memory
device controller
secondary storage
configuration
PC
network
multi-user system
application
system software
operating system
systems programmer
virtual storage
real storage
multiprogramming
spooling
batch processing
job
Job Control Language
JCL
job scheduler
time sharing
online processing
foreground processing

background processing
DOS
Disk Operating System
DOS/VSE
VSE
Virtual Storage Extended
OS
Operating System
OS/MFT
OS/MVT
partition
region
OS/VS1
OS/VS2
MVS
Multiple Virtual Storage
SVS
Single Virtual Storage
MVS/370
MVS/XA
XA
MVS/ESA
ESA
VM
Virtual Machine
CMS
Conversational Monitor System
PR/SM
Processor Resource/Systems
    Manager

Objectives

1. Distinguish among three types of computer systems: personal computers, minicomputers, and mainframe computers.

2. Describe these five features of mainframe computer operating systems: virtual storage, multiprogramming, spooling, batch processing, and time sharing.

3. Identify the three major families of IBM operating systems.

Chapter 2

An introduction to IBM mainframe systems

This chapter presents what you need to know about the hardware components that make up an IBM mainframe computer system. If you've had significant experience with IBM mainframe computers, you can probably skip this chapter because much of it will be review. If that's the case, review the terminology and objectives listed at the end to see if you should skip the chapter.

As you already know, a mainframe computer system is a large collection of computer hardware devices. Those devices fall generally into two categories: processors and input/output devices. After I describe the characteristics of IBM mainframe processors and I/O devices, I'll describe two typical configurations of mainframe computer equipment. That will give you an idea of how the various components can be used together.

Processors

As you know, the central components of mainframe computer systems are the processors. MVS runs on processors that are members of the System/360-370 family, a group of processors that has evolved over a period spanning nearly 30 years. The System/360-370 family includes the System/360 models of the mid-1960s, the System/370 models of the early 1970s, the 3030 models of the late 1970s, the 4300 and 3080 models of the early 1980s, and the 3090 systems of the late 1980s. Although the most recent members of this family are the ES/9000 systems, also known as *Enterprise systems*, many installations still run older 4300, 3080, and 3090 systems.

As IBM has developed new models of System/360-370 processors, it has used contemporary technologies to create better, faster, and cheaper machines. Although the older System/360 and System/370 models are obsolete, the current 4300, 3080, 3090, and ES/9000 processors are still generally called System/370s. That's because even though the technology has changed significantly, IBM has enhanced the basic operating characteristics of the processors in ways that have allowed the System/370 family to maintain a high degree of compatibility over its nearly 30 year life. And we can expect that future members of the System/370 family will maintain that compatibility as well.

Basic System/370 architecture

Figure 2-1 shows the basic arrangement of the subcomponents that make up a typical System/370-type processor. As you can see, the processor consists of three main parts: the CPU, main storage, and channels. From a general point of view, this basic configuration applies to all System/370-type computers, including the 4300, 303X, 308X, 3090, and ES/9000 computers. As you'll see in a moment, however, the arrangements of these basic components is more complex in processors with greater processing power.

As you know, the central processing unit, or CPU, contains the circuitry needed to execute program instructions that manipulate data stored in main storage, also called main memory. Although figure 2-1 doesn't show it, most System/370 processors use a special purpose high-speed memory buffer called a *cache* that operates between the CPU and main memory. This relatively small amount of storage operates at speeds even faster than the storage in main memory, so the overall speed of the processor is increased. Special circuitry constantly monitors accesses to main memory and keeps the most frequently accessed sections in the cache.

Certain System/370 processors also include an additional type of memory called *expanded storage*. Expanded storage is not directly available to application programs. Instead, it is used much as if it were a high-speed disk device. You'll learn more about the role of expanded storage in the next chapter.

Multiprocessing

In the more advanced models of the System/370 family, more than one CPU is included in the processor. In those *multiprocessor systems*, two or four processors share access to main memory; the

Processor

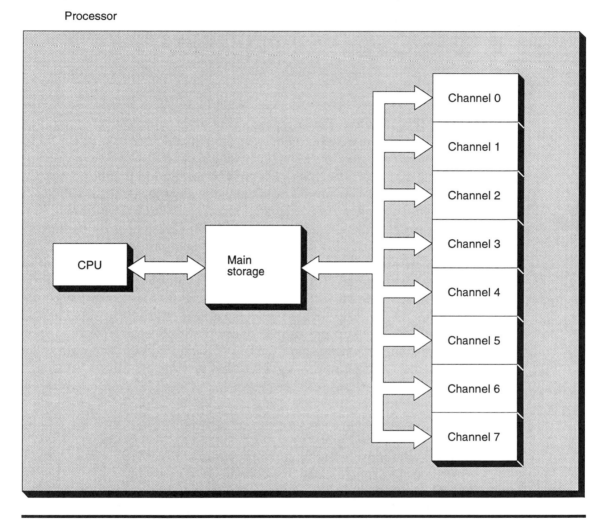

Figure 2-1   The basic architecture of the 370-series processor

operating system determines how each processor is utilized. Multi-processing provides two benefits. First, the overall instruction processing rate of the system is increased because two or more processors are available to execute program instructions. Second, the system's availability is increased because if one of the processors fails, the other can take over its work.

In multiprocessor configurations that contain four CPUs, the processor can be run in one of two modes: as a single four-CPU processor, or as two independent two-CPU processors. When operating as two independent processors, resources such as main storage and channels are split between the two processors. Depending on operational needs, the installation may switch from one mode to another.

PR/SM

At one time, multiprocessor configurations were considered exotic, and the facilities for managing them were often inadequate. So, many installations resorted to VM, an operating system designed to emulate multiple computer systems. VM could be configured to take advantage of multiple processors, but it didn't provide all of the controls needed to take full advantage of modern multiprocessor configurations.

To address this problem, current IBM multiprocessors include a feature called *Processor Resource/Systems Manager*, or *PR/SM*. PR/SM allows an installation to divide a multi-CPU processor into several *partitions*, or *LPARs*, each of which can function as an independent system. PR/SM can be configured so that a partition is reserved as a backup for a primary partition. If the primary partition fails, the backup partition can automatically take over the work that was being processed at the time of the failure. PR/SM also allows the I/O channels assigned to the various partitions to be reconfigured without disrupting work.

Channels

Perhaps the most interesting components of the 370 processors are the *channels*. The purpose of a channel is to provide a path between the processor and an I/O device. Figure 2-1 shows eight channels, numbered 0 through 7. As a result, there are eight different paths along which data can pass between the processor and I/O devices. Each channel can connect up to eight devices called *control units* that, as you'll learn later in this chapter, connect to I/O devices. As a result, the processor in figure 2-1 can support up to 64 control units. Depending on the processor and the device, a control unit may be housed within the processor's cabinet, the I/O device's cabinet, or in its own cabinet.

Actually, a channel is itself a small computer: It executes I/O instructions called *channel commands* that control the operation of the I/O devices attached to it. As a result, the channel frees the processor to execute other instructions. Since channel processing overlaps CPU processing, overall system performance is improved.

The basic channel design of the System/370 requires that I/O devices be connected to channels using heavy copper cables that can be no longer than 400 feet in length. These channels use a *parallel architecture*, which means that the cable transmits all of the bits that make up a byte simultaneously. To do that, the cable must have a separate wire for each bit—sixteen in all (the channel sends two bytes simultaneously)—plus additional wires for control signals. The result is that parallel channel cable is both heavy and expensive.

In 1990, IBM announced a new channel architecture, called *ESCON* (for *Enterprise System Connection*), that is based on fiber optic rather than copper cable. Fiber optic cable is not only 80 times lighter than copper cable, but it is also 50 times less bulky. ESCON will allow many data centers to replace literally tons of unmanageable copper cable with neatly organized runs of fiber optic cable.

Besides its reduced size and weight, ESCON provides two other advantages. First, it extends the 400-foot cable limit of standard channels to 26 miles. This lets installations locate disk devices on another floor or even in another building. Second, ESCON channels are nearly four times as fast as standard channels, transmitting data at 17MB per second rather than 4.5MB per second. This can reduce or eliminate the bottleneck encountered on many systems that use standard channels.

ESCON is still a new technology, one that most installations aren't yet using. It will become more and more common with time, however, particularly as processor speeds and disk capacities continue to grow and the 400-foot, 4.5MB per second limitations of standard channels become more and more unbearable.

Members of the System/370 family

To give you some perspective on the processing power of IBM processors, figure 2-2 lists several characteristics of the current System/370 processors. For each processor, I've listed the amount of main memory, the number of channels, and the number of CPUs that can be configured in the processor. Most of these values are ranges of numbers because the processors come in a variety of models that offer various features.

Figure 2-2 lists only the processors that were current when I wrote this book. Naturally, IBM continues to develop new processors. As a result, by the time you read this, IBM may have bigger and better processors that leave the ones listed in figure 2-2 obsolete. By the same token, most installations don't install new proces-

Processor	CPUs	Main memory	Max channels
4381	1 or 2	4-64MB	18
3084	4	32-128MB	48
3090	6	64-512MB	128
ES/9000	4-8	2,048MB	256

Figure 2-2   Recent members of the System/370 family

sors immediately after they're announced. So there are plenty of installations around that use older processors that aren't shown in figure 2-2, such as the 4381 and 303X models. Nevertheless, I think figure 2-2 gives you a good overview of the capabilities of IBM's major processor families.

Incidentally, the PC I'm using to write this book is in some ways more powerful than the least powerful processor I included in figure 2-2 for the first edition of this book. That was in 1987 when the entry-level processor was a 4361 with 1 CPU, 2 to 12MB of main memory, and from 1 to 6 channels. The PC I'm using to write the second edition of this book has 1 CPU, 20MB of main memory, and the rough equivalent of 2 processor channels—one "local bus" channel for my video card, plus the standard I/O bus channel for other devices.

Input/output devices

Input/output devices, or just I/O devices, are the devices that connect to a processor to provide it with input, receive output, or provide secondary storage. The common types of I/O devices found on IBM mainframes are (1) unit record devices, (2) magnetic tape devices, (3) direct access devices, and (4) telecommunications devices. There are other types of I/O devices besides these, but I won't cover them because they're for specialized uses. For each of the classes that are covered, I'll describe not only the individual I/O devices themselves, but also the control units that connect the I/O devices to processor channels.

Unit record devices

Unit record devices include two types of devices: card devices and printers. The term "unit record device" implies that each record processed by the device is a physical unit. In the case of card devices, each record is a punched card. As for printers, each record is a printed line. Unit record devices usually have built-in control units that attach directly to channels, so separate control units aren't required.

Card devices, which aren't commonly used anymore, come in three types: readers, punches, and reader/punches. A card reader is an input-only device: It can read data from punched cards, but can't punch data into blank cards. A card punch is just the opposite: It can punch data into cards, but can't read previously punched cards. A reader/punch combines the functions of a reader and a punch, and serves as both an input and an output device.

Unlike card devices, printers are in widespread use today; they provide the primary form of permanent output from the computer. There are a variety of different types of printers, but the most commonly used printers fall into two categories: impact printers and non-impact printers.

Impact printers produce printed output by striking an image of characters to be printed against a ribbon, which in turn transfers ink to the paper. The most common type of impact printer uses a train of characters that spins at high speed; when the correct character passes a print position, a hammer strikes the character against a ribbon to produce the printed text. Most impact printers operate in the range of 600 to 2,000 lines per minute.

Non-impact printers use laser technology to print text and graphic images. IBM's 3800 Printing Subsystem can print at rates of up to a remarkable 20,000 lines per minute. The actual speed of the 3800 printer depends on the size of each page and the number of lines per inch, because the 3800 transfers images to the paper an entire page at a time. For standard size paper (11X14) and normal print size (6 lines per inch), the 3800 prints 10,020 lines per minute. At that print rate, the 3800 can process more than a mile and a half of paper each hour.

Magnetic tape devices

A *tape drive* reads and writes data on a *magnetic tape* that's a continuous strip of plastic coated on one side with a metal oxide. Originally, most tape drives processed tape wrapped around an open reel much like an old-fashioned reel-to-reel tape recorder. Newer tape drives process tape that's sealed within a special *tape cartridge*. Either way, the concepts I'll present here apply.

How much data a reel or cartridge of tape can contain depends on the length of the tape and the *density* used to record the data. Density is a measurement of how many bytes are recorded in one

Figure 2-3   How records are blocked on a tape

inch of tape. Tape densities for standard reel tapes are usually 1600 or 6250 *bytes per inch* (*bpi*). Cartridge tape drives can record data using much higher densities.

Data records are normally written to tape in groups called *blocks*, as shown in figure 2-3. Here, five records are stored together as a single block. As you can see, empty spaces called *gaps* are required to separate blocks from one another. The larger the block, the less the amount of wasted space on a tape. However, there's an extra cost involved when blocking is used: A buffer is required in main storage to contain the entire block. As a result, the larger the block, the more main storage that's required to contain it.

Tape processing has one serious drawback: It must be sequential. In other words, to read the 50,000th record on a tape, the first 49,999 records must be read first. As a result, tape is ill-suited for applications that require direct access to stored data. Instead, tape is most often used for off-line storage of large quantities of data, especially data that serves as a backup for online data on DASD devices.

To attach a tape drive to a processor, a control unit is required. For some models, the control unit is inside one of the tape drives. For other models, it's in a separate cabinet. Depending on the model, the controller can attach up to four or eight tape drives.

Direct access devices

The official IBM term for a *disk drive* is *direct access storage device*, or *DASD*. Because DASDs allow direct and rapid access to large quantities of data, they've become a key component of mainframe systems. They're used not only to store user programs and data, but also to store programs and data for operating system functions.

Disk drives read and write data on a *disk pack* (sometimes called a *volume*). A disk pack, shown in figure 2-4, is a stack of metal platters coated with a metal oxide material. Data is recorded on both sides of the platters.

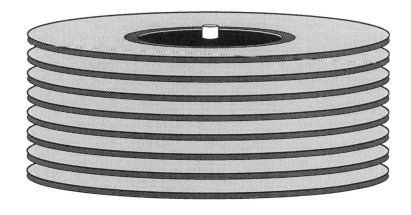

Figure 2-4   A disk pack

Most of IBM's older DASDs used removable disk packs, but the newer IBM DASDs use a disk pack that is fixed in a permanent, sealed assembly inside the drive. Nonremovable disk packs have two advantages over removable packs: they're faster and they're more reliable. Because speed and reliability are important requirements of online applications, DASDs with nonremovable packs are well suited for today's mainframe systems.

Tracks and cylinders   Data is recorded on the usable surfaces of a disk pack in concentric circles called *tracks*, as figure 2-5 shows. The number of tracks per surface varies with each device type. For example, the surface in figure 2-5 has 808 tracks, numbered from 0 to 807. A disk pack with 19 usable surfaces, each with 808 tracks, has a total of 15,352 tracks.

Figure 2-6 shows a side view of an *access mechanism*, or *actuator*, the component that reads and writes data on the tracks of a disk pack. As you can see, the actuator has one read/write head for each recording surface. When the actuator moves, all of its heads move together so they're all positioned at the same track of each recording surface. As a result, the disk drive can access data on all of those tracks without moving the actuator.

The tracks that are positioned under the heads of the actuator at one time make up a *cylinder*. As a result, there are as many tracks in a cylinder as there are usable surfaces on the pack, and there are as many cylinders in a pack as there are tracks on a surface. So a pack that has 19 surfaces, each with 808 tracks, has 808 cylinders, each with 19 tracks.

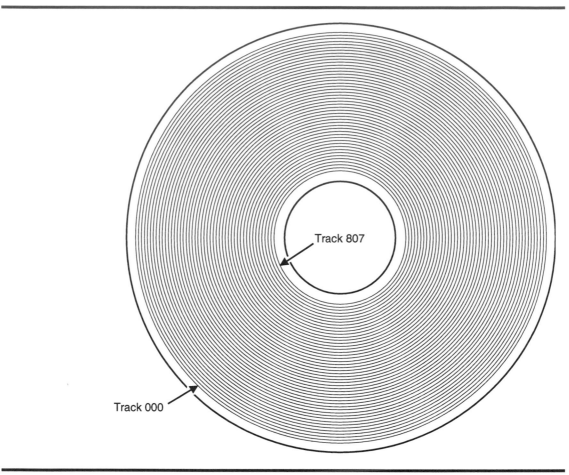

Figure 2-5   Tracks on a disk surface

Device capacity and data format   Figure 2-7 presents some characteristics of the various IBM DASD units supported by MVS systems.
Frankly, many operating characteristics of DASD units, such as how
fast the disk pack rotates or how fast data is transferred, just aren't
significant to most programmers. What is relevant is the capacity of
each device: the maximum number of bytes per track, the number of
tracks per cylinder, the number of cylinders per drive, and the total
capacity of the drive. That's the information shown in figure 2-7.

     To fully understand the information in figure 2-7, you need to
know a little about the format in which data is stored. IBM manu-
factures two basic types of disk drives that store their data in different formats. All of the drives listed in figure 2-7 are *count-key-data*
(*CKD*) devices, which store data in variable-length blocks. Another

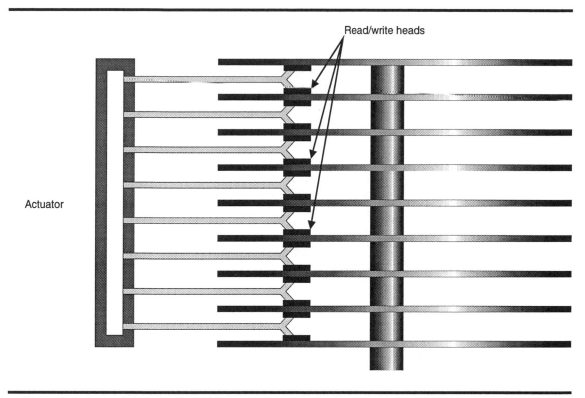

Read/write heads

Actuator

Figure 2-6   Side view of a DASD actuator

type of device, called *fixed-block architecture (FBA)* devices, stores data in fixed-length blocks of 512 bytes each. Since FBA devices aren't supported under MVS, I won't mention them again. (If you understand the details of how disk drives work on a PC, you understand FBA devices. CKD devices work surprisingly differently.)

Figure 2-8 shows how data is stored on a CKD device. Here, each data block is preceded by a *count area* and a *key area*. (The count area is required; the key area is optional.) Because the disk revolves counterclockwise, the read/write head encounters the count and key areas before the data area. The count area contains the information needed to locate and process the key and data areas.

One of the problems with CKD devices is that the data capacity of each track depends on the size of the blocks used to store the data. That's because gaps are required to separate the count, key, and data areas, just as gaps are required on magnetic tape. When smaller areas are used, more blocks of data can be stored on each track. But when more blocks are stored, more gaps are used, so the total capacity of the track is reduced.

Device	Max bytes per track	Tracks per cylinder	Cylinders per volume	Total bytes per volume
3330	13,030	19	404	100MB
3330-11	13,030	19	808	200MB
3350	19,069	30	555	317MB
3375	35,616	12	1,918	819MB
3380	47,476	15	885	630MB
3380-E	47,476	15	1,770	1,260MB
3380-K	47,476	15	2,655	1,890MB
3390-1	56,664	15	1,113	946MB
3390-2	56,664	15	2,226	1,892MB
3390-3	56,664	15	3,339	2,838MB
3390-9	56,664	15	10,017	8,514MB

Figure 2-7   Capacities of IBM DASD units supported by MVS

The total capacity for each drive shown in figure 2-7 is the maximum capacity for the device. That assumes that all of the data in each track is stored in a single block; if more than one block is stored per track (and that's usually the case), the capacity is reduced because of the additional gaps required to separate the blocks.

Control units   Each type of DASD device requires two kinds of control units to attach it to a processor channel. The first, called a *string controller*, attaches a group of DASDs of the same type; the resulting group is called a *string*. The number of devices that can be connected on one string depends on the device type; for 3390-model disks, up to 32 drives can be connected in one string.

The second kind of control unit, called a *storage control*, connects up to eight strings of DASD units to a channel. The most common type of storage control is the 3990, which attaches two DASD strings. If both strings consist of 3390 drives, up to 64 drives can be connected to a single 3990.

Figure 2-9 shows how a 3990 storage control might be used to control two strings of 3390 DASDs, each containing 16 drives. As you can see, the 3990 connects to the processor through channel connections; the 3390 DASDs, in turn, connect to the 3990.

The 3990 storage control provides high-speed *cache storage* that acts as a buffer between the processor and the actual disk units.

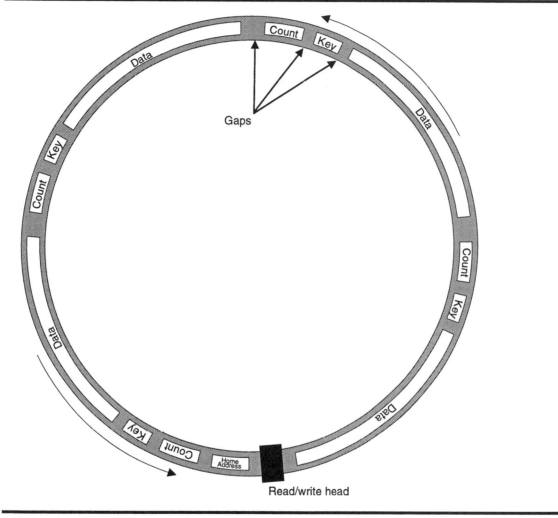

Figure 2-8   Count-key-data format

Special circuitry keeps track of what disk data is accessed most frequently and tries to keep that data in the cache storage. Then, when that data is referenced, it can be read directly from cache; the DASD unit doesn't have to be accessed at all. Depending on the 3990 model, the size of the cache can range from 32MB to 1,024MB. Obviously, cache storage in the storage control significantly improves a system's overall performance.

In addition, the 3990 storage control can support more than one channel connection to the processor. This enables several simultaneous disk operations to be processed at once. The smallest 3990

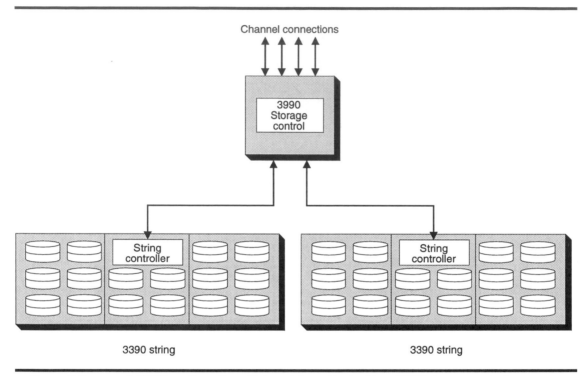

Channel connections

3990
Storage
control

String
controller

String
controller

3390 string   3390 string

Figure 2-9   A 3390 configuration with two strings attached to a 3990 storage control

models support up to four standard channel connections, and the
largest can support 16 standard channel connections or 128 ESCON
channel connections.

Data communications equipment

Data communications equipment lets an installation create a *data
communications network* (or *telecommunications network* or just *network*) that lets users at *local terminals* (terminals at the computer site)
and *remote terminals* (terminals that aren't at the computer site)
access a computer system. Now, I'll briefly describe the components of a data communications network, with emphasis on the
most common type of terminals used on IBM mainframe networks:
the 3270 Information Display System.

Elements of a data communications network   Figure 2-10 shows
the basic components that make up a data communications network. Basically, five elements make up the network: (1) a host

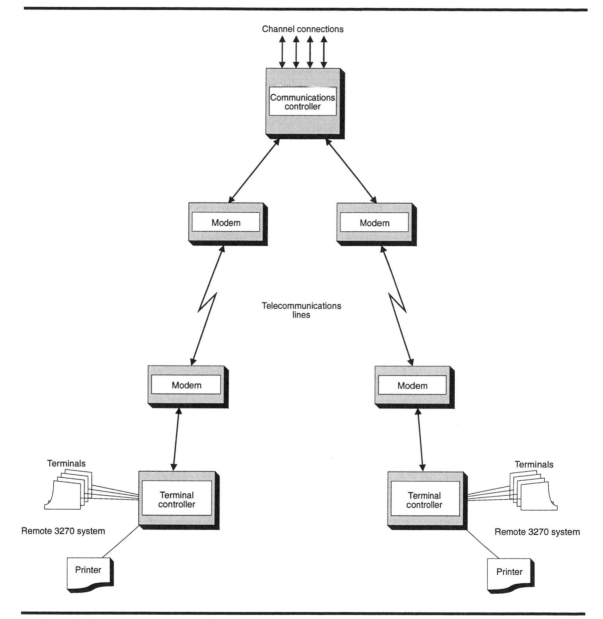

Figure 2-10   Components of a data communications network

system, (2) a communications controller, (3) modems, (4) telecommunications lines, and (5) terminal systems.

At the center of the network is the host system, a System/370 processor.   The control unit that attaches to the host system's channels is called a *communications controller*; it manages the communications functions necessary to connect remote terminal systems via *modems* and *telecommunications lines*. A modem is a device that translates digital signals from the computer equipment at the sending end (either the host or remote system) into audio signals that are transmitted over the telecommunications line, which can be a telephone line, a satellite link, or some other type of connection. At the receiving end of the line, another modem converts those audio signals back into digital signals.

Although the terminal systems in figure 2-10 are connected remotely via telecommunications lines and modems, that's not a requirement. If the terminal system is located close enough to the host system, the modems and telecommunications lines can be eliminated. Then, the terminal system is connected directly to the communications controller or one of the host processor's channels.

Whether attached locally or remotely, the most commonly used terminal system on IBM mainframes is the 3270 Information Display System. Because you're likely to use a 3270 terminal as you learn how to use Job Control Language, it's important that you have a basic understanding of its components and how they work together.

The 3270 Information Display System   The *3270 Information Display System* is not a single terminal, but rather a subsystem of terminals, printers, and controllers that attach to a host computer system remotely through a communications controller and telecommunications lines or locally through a communications controller or direct attachment to a channel. A typical 3270 controller (a 3274) controls up to 32 terminals and printers and can be connected to a processor either directly or remotely over a telecommunications network that consists of modems and telephone lines. The two remote 3270 systems in figure 2-10 each include one controller, four terminals, and one printer.

Because of the enormous popularity of the 3270 system, many manufacturers besides IBM offer compatible terminals, printers, and controllers. And most manufacturers of minicomputers and personal computers offer *emulator programs* that allow their computers to mimic 3270 devices. As a matter of fact, I did much of the work for this book using an emulator program running on a desktop PC. Because of cost advantages and additional benefits, it's becoming more and more common to see such products in use in 3270 networks.

Two typical mainframe configurations

With such variety in the types of IBM mainframe processors and I/O devices, the number of possible system configurations is endless. As a result, one IBM mainframe configuration is likely to be different from

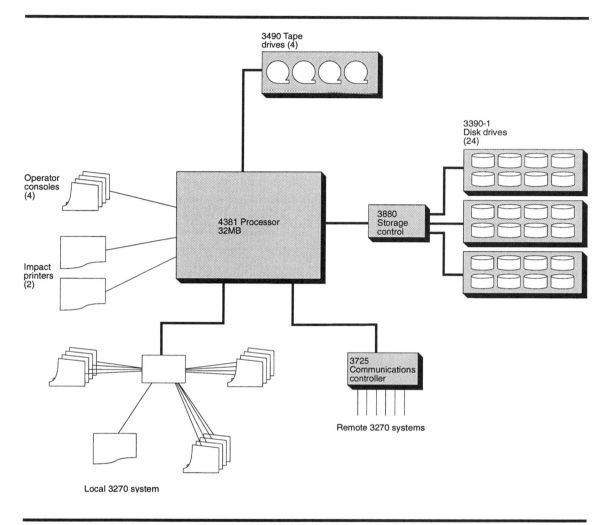

Figure 2-11   A small mainframe configuration

another, even though the two systems might be used for similar purposes. Now, I'll present two typical, though hypothetical, mainframe configurations. By studying these configurations, you'll get a better understanding of how the various hardware components I've already described might be used together in an actual computer system.

A small mainframe computer configuration

Figure 2-11 represents a small mainframe computer system built around a 4381 processor. Before I describe the individual components of this system, I want to be sure you realize that the term "small" is relative. When compared with a personal computer system or most minicomputer systems, this configuration is huge. But by mainframe standards, it's safe to call this a small configuration.

For direct access storage, the configuration in figure 2-11 uses three strings of 3390 model 1 DASDs, each containing eight drives. As a result, the system has a total of 24 disk drives. Since each 3390 model 1 has a capacity of 946MB, the total DASD capacity of this system is about 22 billion bytes.

As you know, 3390s are fixed-media DASDs; their disk packs cannot be removed. To provide a way to create backup copies of data on the 3390s, a string of four 3490 tape drives is used.

The four operator consoles let system operators control the operation of the system. Some of the consoles might be dedicated to specific tasks, such as managing the tape drives or controlling the two high-speed impact printers that are used as the primary printing devices for the system.

A local 3270 system, directly attached to the 4381 processor, provides 12 terminals and one printer; its terminals are used by the programming staff, who are based in the same building that houses the computer. The 3725 communications controller allows remote 3270 systems to access the system via telephone lines. The terminals attached to the remote systems, which aren't shown in figure 2-11, are used by data-entry clerks and other end users.

A medium-sized 3090 configuration

Figure 2-12 shows a medium-sized mainframe configuration, based around a 3090 processor that contains 256MB of main memory. The processor is partitioned into two independent systems, known as the A-side and the B-side. Two 3990 storage controls are used to attach four strings of 3390-2 disk drives. The total DASD capacity of this configuration is about 121 billion bytes. As in the 4381 configuration, the tape drives—in this case, 16 of them—are used mostly to create backup copies of DASD data.

The 3090 system in figure 2-12 includes two local 3270 systems, eight operator consoles, three 3211 line printers, and a 3800 printing subsystem. In addition, two communications controllers are attached to the processor to support remote users. If the communications controllers are fully equipped, this system could conceivably support hundreds or even thousands of terminal users.

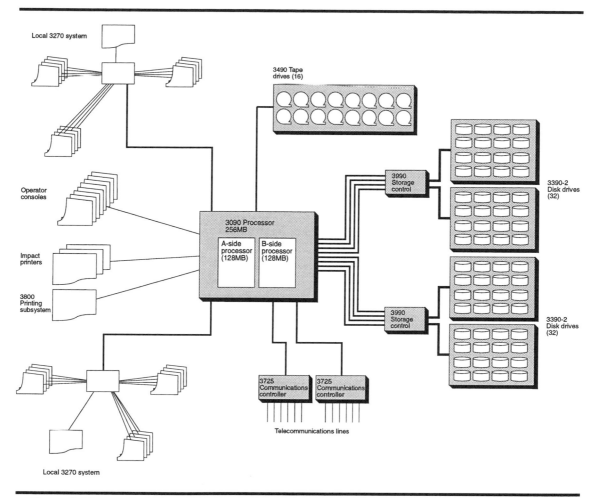

Figure 2-12   A medium-sized mainframe configuration

Discussion

Quite frankly, I've described the characteristics of IBM hardware components in more detail than you really need to know to understand JCL. So, if you're struggling with some of the concepts in this chapter, particularly with the internal operation of processors and the complexity of large configurations, don't worry about it. As long as you understand the basic ideas this chapter presents, you're ready to move on to the next chapter, where you'll learn about the basics of the MVS operating system.

Terminology

Enterprise system	DASD
cache	disk pack
expanded storage	volume
multiprocessor system	track
Processor Resource/Systems	access mechanism
Manager	actuator
PR/SM	cylinder
partition	count-key-data
LPAR	CKD
channel	fixed-block architecture
control unit	FBA
channel commands	count area
parallel architecture	key area
ESCON	string controller
Enterprise System Connection	string
unit record device	storage control
impact printer	cache storage
non-impact printer	data communications equipment
tape drive	data communications network
magnetic tape	telecommunications network
tape cartridge	network
density	local terminal
bytes per inch	remote terminal
bpi	communications controller
block	modem
gap	telecommunications line
disk drive	3270 Information Display System
direct access storage device	emulator program

Objectives

1. Identify the three basic components of a System/370 processor.

2. Explain why the track capacity of a disk drive depends on the size of the blocks that are stored on the drive.

3. Describe how controllers are used to connect DASD units to processor channels.

4. List the elements of a data communications network.

Chapter 3

MVS concepts and terminology

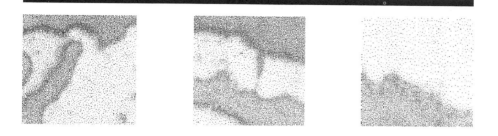

Topic 3   How MVS manages user jobs

Jobs and Job Control Language
Job Entry Subsystems
How JES2 and JES3 process jobs
> How a job is entered into the system
> How a job is scheduled for execution
> How a job is executed
> How a job's output is processed
> How a job is purged
> Two alternative ways to allocate data sets

Job output

Topic 4   Understanding a complete MVS system

System generation and initialization
> System generation
> System initialization

System data sets
Subsystems and other MVS facilities
> TSO and ISPF
> Telecommunications
> CICS
> IMS
> DB2
> RACF
> SMF
> Language translators, the linkage editor,
>   and the loader
> Utility programs

Now that you've learned about the various types of hardware devices that make up a mainframe computer configuration, you're ready to learn how the MVS operating system manages those devices. As a result, this chapter's four topics explain the basic concepts of MVS. At the same time, they introduce and explain many of the terms that are used to describe MVS facilities. In topic 1, you'll learn about two basic MVS functions: virtual storage and multiprogramming. In topic 2, you'll learn about the facilities MVS provides for managing user data, particularly data that resides on disk devices. In topic 3, you'll learn how a job is typically processed by MVS. And in topic 4, you'll see the complete set of components that makes up an MVS system.

Topic 1

Virtual storage and multiprogramming

In chapter 1, you learned that virtual storage and multiprogramming are important components of modern mainframe operating systems. Simply put, virtual storage is a facility that simulates a large amount of main storage by treating DASD storage as an extension of real storage. In other words, when virtual storage is used, the processor appears to have more storage than it actually does.

As for multiprogramming, it's a facility that lets two or more programs use the processor at the same time. The key to understanding multiprogramming is realizing that most programs spend most of their time waiting for I/O operations to complete. So while one program waits for an I/O operation, the CPU can execute instructions for another program.

Under MVS, as you'll soon learn, the concepts of virtual storage and multiprogramming are closely related. In a way, virtual storage and multiprogramming are the same thing under MVS. To understand why this is so, you first need to know about the important concept of address spaces.

Address spaces

Main storage consists of millions of individual storage locations, each of which can store one character, or *byte*, of information. To refer to a particular location, you use an *address* that indicates the storage location's offset from the beginning of memory. The first byte of storage is at address 0, the second byte is at address 1, and so on. Each successive byte of main storage has an address that's one greater than the previous byte of storage.

An *address space* is simply the complete range of addresses—and, as a result, the number of storage locations—that can be accessed by the computer. The maximum size of a computer's address space is limited by the number of digits that can be used to represent an address. To illustrate, suppose a computer records its addresses using six decimal digits. Such a computer could access storage with addresses from 0 to 999,999. So the computer's address space could contain a maximum of one million bytes of storage. (Of course, computers actually record their addresses using binary digits rather than decimal digits.)

The original System/370 processors used 24-bit binary numbers to represent addresses (a *bit* is the binary equivalent of a digit). Since the largest number that can be represented in 24 bits is about 16 million (abbreviated 16M), an address space on a System/370 cannot contain more than 16M bytes of storage. Because this 16MB address space limitation severely restricted the capabilities of the System/370, IBM replaced it in the early 1980s with a new architecture known as *370-XA*. 370-XA processors can operate in *370 mode* using standard 24-bit addresses or in *XA*, or *Extended Architecture, mode* using 31-bit addresses. In XA mode, the largest address that can be represented—and therefore the largest address space that can be used—is about 2 billion, or 2G.

In the late 1980s and early 1990s, IBM extended this architecture even further with the introduction first of *ESA/370*, then *ESA/390*. These designs utilize the same 31-bit addresses that 370-XA uses, but they extend the architecture in other ways. For example, ESA/390 allows the use of high-speed fiber-optic channels known as ESCON.

As you might guess, MVS/370 was designed to operate on System/370 processors that utilize 24-bit addresses, and MVS/XA was designed to operate on 370-XA processors that use 31-bit addresses. MVS/ESA also uses 31-bit addresses, but runs only on ESA/370 and ESA/390 processors.

One way to think of virtual storage is that it lets the computer push its address space to the maximum allowed by the address format, even if the amount of real storage installed on the processor is less than the maximum. So, in 370 mode, virtual storage can simulate a 16MB address space, even if only 4MB or 8MB of real storage is actually installed. That's precisely how virtual storage worked on older System/370 operating systems such as OS/VS1 and OS/VS2 SVS. Under MVS, however, the concept of virtual storage is taken one step further.

Multiple virtual storage

MVS not only simulates more storage, but it also uses real storage to simulate several address spaces, each of which is independent of the others. In fact, MVS derives its name from this technique: MVS stands for *Multiple Virtual Storage*.

To understand multiple virtual storage, consider figure 3-1. Here, you can see that real storage and areas of DASD storage called *page data sets* are used in combination to simulate several virtual storage address spaces; in this example, four address spaces are

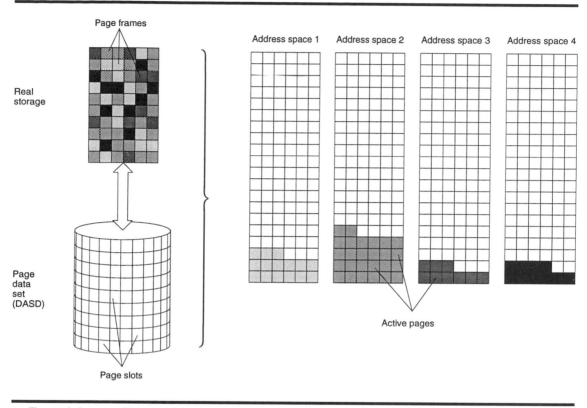

Page frames

Address space 1   Address space 2   Address space 3   Address space 4

Real
storage

Page
data
set
(DASD)

Active pages

Page slots

Figure 3-1   The concept of virtual storage under MVS

simulated. Each of these address spaces provides an entire 16MB range of addresses (2GB on an XA or ESA processor). As a result, to refer to a particular byte of virtual storage under MVS, you need to know two things: (1) the address, which identifies a specific byte of storage within a 16MB or 2GB address space, and (2) the address space to which the address applies.

When multiple virtual storages are used, the total amount of virtual storage that can be simulated is almost limitless, because MVS can create an almost unlimited number of address spaces. However, the size of an address (24 bits or 31 bits) still limits the size of each individual address space to 16MB or 2GB. And various factors such as the speed of the processor and the amount of real storage installed effectively limit the number of address spaces that can be simulated.

Although an MVS system can support more than one address space at a time, I want to be sure you realize that the CPU can access only one of them at a time. When the CPU is accessing instructions and data from a particular address space, that address space is said to be in control of the CPU. So the program in that address space will continue to execute until MVS intervenes and places the CPU in control of another address space.

Multiple virtual storage is how MVS implements multiprogramming. In short, each background job or time sharing user is given its own address space. So each job or user can access up to 16MB or 2GB of virtual storage independently of any other job or user on the system at the same time. To pass control from one job or user to another, MVS simply transfers control of the CPU to the other job's or user's address space. Then, the CPU can access instructions and data in that address space until MVS is ready to pass control to a job or user in yet another address space.

Paging   As I've already mentioned, the total amount of virtual storage that can be used under MVS is almost unlimited. As a result, the amount of real storage present on a particular machine is nearly always less than the amount of virtual storage being used. To provide for the larger virtual storage, MVS treats DASD as an extension of real storage.

To understand this, look again at figure 3-1. MVS divides virtual storage into 4K sections called *pages*. Data is transferred between real and DASD storage one page at a time. As a result, real storage is divided into 4K sections called *page frames*, each of which can hold one page of virtual storage. Similarly, the DASD area used for virtual storage, called a page data set, is divided into 4K *page slots*, each of which holds one page of virtual storage.

When a program refers to a storage location that isn't in real storage, a *page fault* occurs. When that happens, MVS locates the page that contains the needed data on DASD and transfers it into real storage. That operation is called a *page-in*. In some cases, the new page can overlay data in a real storage page frame. In other cases, data in a page frame has to be moved to a page data set to make room for the new page. That's called a *page-out*. Either way, the process of bringing a new page into real storage is called *paging*.

Notice in figure 3-1 that at any given moment, page frames in real storage contain pages from more than one address space. That's what the various shades and patterns in real and virtual storage represent. MVS keeps track of what pages are in what page frames by maintaining tables that reflect the current status of real storage and of each address space. The real storage frames that contain those tables can't be paged out; they must always remain in real storage as long as their associated address spaces are active.

Expanded storage   Most newer System/370 processors include a special type of memory known as *expanded storage*. Expanded storage improves the efficiency of virtual storage operations by acting as a large buffer between real storage and the page data sets. Simply put, when a virtual storage page must be paged out, the processor moves the page's contents to expanded storage. This transfer occurs at CPU speeds rather than at DASD speeds, so the operation is almost instantaneous. Pages are written to the actual page data set only when expanded storage becomes full.

The amount of expanded storage on a processor varies depending on the processor model. The largest ES/9000 processors can be configured with as much as 8GB of expanded storage. Most installations don't need that much expanded storage for normal paging operations, but as you'll see in a moment, large amounts of expanded storage can provide additional benefits when MVS/ESA is used.

Swapping   Depending on the amount of real storage a system has and the types of jobs it's processing, MVS can efficiently multiprogram only a certain number of jobs at once. So, using a process called *swapping*, MVS periodically transfers entire address spaces in and out of virtual storage so they are temporarily unavailable for processing. When an address space is *swapped out*, its critical pages—the ones that contain the tables that keep track of the location of each virtual storage page for the address space—are written to a special data set called a *swap data set*. Later, when the system can accommodate the job again, the address space is *swapped in* so it can be processed again.

Figure 3-2 should help you understand swapping. Here, four address spaces are currently swapped in; the shading indicates the address space that's currently in control. Four additional address spaces are swapped out. They can't compete for virtual storage or the CPU until they're swapped in.

You can think of swapping as the same thing as paging, only at a higher level. Rather than move small 4K pieces of virtual storage in and out of real storage, swapping effectively moves entire address spaces in and out of virtual storage. Because paging occurs only for address spaces that are currently in virtual storage, paging does not occur for address spaces that are swapped out.

Program modes   A program within an address space may run in one of two modes: *real mode* and *virtual mode*. These modes simply indicate whether or not a program is subject to the paging and swapping processes I've just described. Paging and swapping

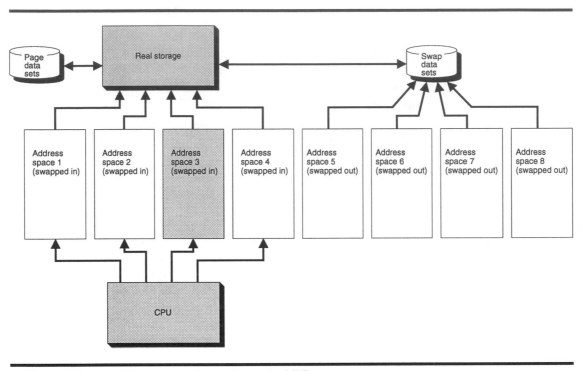

Figure 3-2   The concept of swapping under MVS

operate only for programs that run in virtual mode. Programs that operate in real mode aren't paged or swapped.

Why are some programs allowed to operate in real mode? Consider how the operating system must operate: The parts of the operating system that are responsible for managing virtual storage cannot themselves be subject to the paging process. In other words, those parts must be *resident* in real storage all the time. Those parts of the operating system must run in real mode, so they're *non-pageable* and *non-swappable*. Similarly, certain other programs, particularly those that communicate directly with channel devices or those that have critical time dependencies, must run in real mode. Most programs, however, run in virtual mode.

How MVS/370 address spaces are organized

Now that you understand that each job or user on an MVS system executes in a separate address space, you're ready to learn how MVS/370 organizes data within each address space. (I'll describe MVS/XA and ESA address spaces, which are similar, in a moment.)

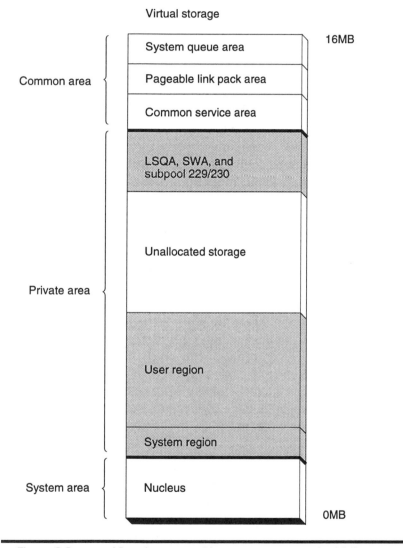

Virtual storage

Figure 3-3 Virtual storage address space areas under MVS

At the outset, you should realize that some of the storage within an address space is required for various components of the operating system, some of the storage is required by the program or programs run by the job or user, and some of the storage is simply unallocated.

Figure 3-3 shows how a typical MVS/370 address space is organized. Here, you can see that the address space is divided into three basic areas: the system area, the private area, and the common area. I'll describe the system and common areas first; then, I'll describe the private area.

The system and common areas   The *system area* and the *common area* are the portions of the address space that contain operating system programs and data. These areas are shared by all of the address spaces on the system. In other words, the system area and the common area are the same for each address space.

The system area resides at the low end of the address space. It contains the MVS *nucleus*, which among other things controls the operation of virtual storage paging and swapping. The entire system area must be resident at all times, so it operates in real mode: It can't be paged or swapped.

The common area, at the high end of the address space, contains additional components of the operating system. In particular, three important operating system components are in the common area: the system queue area, the pageable link pack area, and the common service area. The *system queue area*, or *SQA*, contains important system tables and data areas that are used by programs residing in the nucleus; like the system area, the SQA is fixed in real storage. The *common service area*, or *CSA*, contains information that's similar to information in the SQA but that doesn't have to be fixed in real storage; the CSA, unlike the SQA, is pageable.

The *pageable link pack area*, or *PLPA*, contains operating system programs that don't have to be fixed in real storage in the nucleus (the PLPA can also contain user programs that are heavily used). As its name implies, the pageable link pack area is not fixed in real storage.

The private area   The private area is the portion of an address space that contains data that's unique for each address space. Within each job's or user's private area, there are three basic areas. At the bottom of the private area is the *system region*, an area of storage used by operating system programs that provide services for user programs running in the private area.

At the top of the private area are three local system areas that contain information that applies only to the private area of a particular address space. The *local system queue area*, or *LSQA*, contains tables used to control the private area, including the tables needed to manage the private area's virtual storage. (It's the LSQA that's written to the swap data set when an address space is swapped out.) The *scheduler work area*, or *SWA*, contains tables used to manage the execution of jobs and programs within the private area. The third system area, called *subpool 229/230*, contains additional system information.

The rest of the private area, which comprises most of the address space, is either unallocated or allocated to a *user region*. It's in

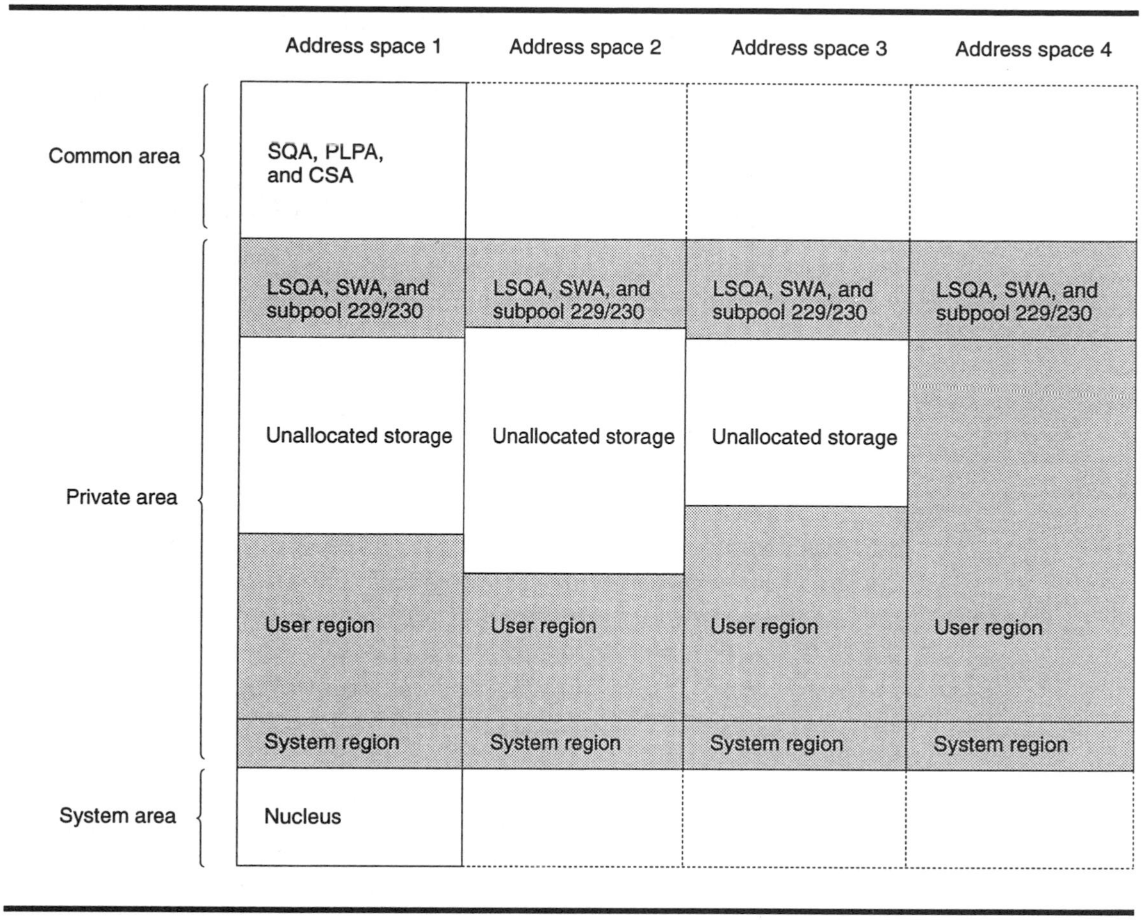

Figure 3-4   Virtual storage address space areas for multiple address spaces under MVS

the user region that your program or programs actually execute. The size of the user region varies depending on the amount of storage required by the program being executed. If necessary, the user region can allocate all of the storage between the system region and the LSQA, SWA, and subpool 229/230. On most MVS systems, that amounts to about 10MB to 12MB.

As I said earlier, the system area and the private area are accessible to all address spaces, but the private area is unique to each address space. That way, critical components of MVS that reside in the system area and the common area are available at all times, no matter which address space currently has control of the CPU. To understand this, consider figure 3-4. Here, you can see that four address spaces share the system and common areas and retain unique private areas. If the system and common areas weren't shared in this way, that information would have to be duplicated in each address space. (As in figure 3-3, the shading indicates storage allocated from the private area. In address space 4, all of the available storage in the private area has been allocated.)

Address space organization under MVS/XA and MVS/ESA

As I mentioned earlier, newer models of System/370 family processors provide an addressing mode in which 31-bit addresses rather than 24-bit addresses can be used. One of the major problems IBM faced when making this change was keeping these new processors compatible with the old processors. In other words, programs written with 24-bit addresses must still be able to run properly on processors that provide 31-bit addresses.

To provide that compatibility and still reap the benefits of 31-bit addressing, processors that use 31-bit addresses and the operating systems that support them provide a full 2GB address space, but they include special provisions for addresses below 16MB. In short, the first 16MB of an address space can be accessed using 31-bit or 24-bit addresses. So 24-bit programs can run unchanged, still restricted by the 16MB limitation, while 31-bit programs can use the full 2GB address space.

Because of this arrangement, the layout of an XA or ESA address space is different than you might expect. Figure 3-5 illustrates the layout of an address space under MVS/XA or ESA. The first thing to notice is that the address space is logically divided at the 16MB line. For the sake of clarity, I placed the 16MB line at about the halfway point in the figure; in an actual address space, 16MB is less than one one-hundredth of the total address space.

Under XA or ESA, there is no system area; instead, the MVS nucleus is combined with the other operating system data in the common area. As a result, an XA or ESA address space has two types of areas: the common area contains the operating system and is common to all address spaces, and the private area contains the data that's unique to each job's or user's address space, including the program that's being executed. In addition, an XA or ESA address space provides two sections of each area: one below the 16MB line, the other above it. So, in figure 3-5, the private area resides below the 16MB line, and the *extended private area* resides above it. Similarly, the common area is below the 16MB line, and the *extended common area* is above it.

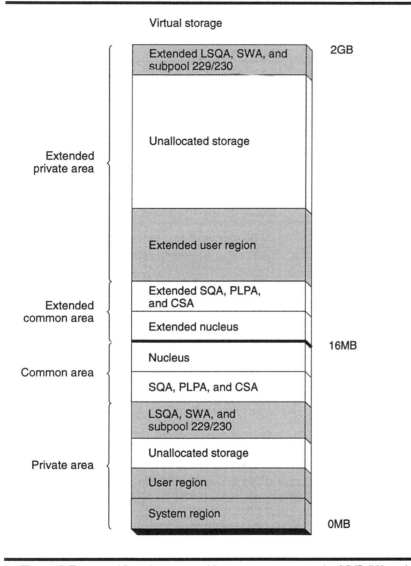

Figure 3-5   Virtual storage address space areas under MVS/XA and MVS/ESA

Notice the peculiar arrangement of the common area and the extended common area, which bracket the 16MB line. The nucleus occupies the highest locations of storage below the 16MB line, while the *extended nucleus* occupies the lowest locations above 16MB. As a result, the nucleus and the extended nucleus occupy a continuous range of addresses that cross the 16MB line. The system queue area (SQA), pageable link pack area (PLPA), and common service area (CSA) also have two parts each: one below and one above the 16MB line.

It might seem as if splitting the private areas by placing the common areas between them would cause problems for large programs that require virtual storage allocated for an *extended user region* (the portion of the user region that resides above 16MB). But that's not the case. Programs that use space from the extended user region treat both parts of the user region as if they were one continuous area. In any event, few programs use all of the private area available under MVS, let alone require space in the extended private area above 16MB.

MVS/ESA dataspaces and hiperspaces

Although MVS/ESA uses the same basic address space layout as MVS/XA, ESA extends the multiple address space concept another step further. As with MVS/XA, each job or user is assigned a separate 2GB address space. However, ESA also lets a job or user create one or more additional 2GB address spaces that can be used to hold large amounts of data. Thus, a job or user has access to an almost unlimited amount of storage.

Depending on the requirements of the application, the additional address spaces created for data storage can be one of two types: *dataspaces* or *hiperspaces*. One difference between dataspaces and hiperspaces is how their contents are managed. The contents of dataspaces are managed directly by user-written programs. But the contents of hiperspaces are managed by MVS/ESA, and they're made available to application programs in 4KB units. Another difference between dataspaces and hiperspaces is where they reside. Dataspaces reside in normal virtual storage and are subject to paging and swapping operations. But hiperspaces reside only in expanded storage and are never brought into real storage. Thus, hiperspaces provide a unique way to take advantage of a processor's expanded storage.

Hiperspaces are used by a new MVS/ESA feature called *hiperbatch*, which can be used to improve the performance of certain types of batch jobs. To do that, hiperbatch copies entire data sets into hiperspace where they can be accessed concurrently by several batch jobs. The details of setting up a hiperbatch environment are beyond the scope of this book. However, the good news is that once a hiperbatch environment is set up, application programs can access the data in a hiperspace as if the data was stored in an ordinary DASD data set. In other words, hiperbatch is transparent to application programs and the JCL that invokes them.

Discussion

To use MVS effectively, you need a basic understanding of how virtual storage and multiprogramming work together. However, I want you to realize that the information I presented in this topic, though complex, is really just an overview. If you've grasped the notion that each user or job under MVS is given a separate address space of 16MB or 2GB, then you're ready to move on to the next topic.

Terminology

byte	non-pageable
address	non-swappable
address space	system area
bit	common area
370-XA	nucleus
370 mode	system queue area
XA mode	SQA
Extended Architecture mode	common service area
ESA/370	CSA
ESA/390	pageable link pack area
Multiple Virtual Storage	PLPA
page data set	system region
page	local system queue area
page frame	LSQA
page slot	scheduler work area
page fault	SWA
page-in	subpool 229/230
page-out	user region
paging	MVS/XA
expanded storage	MVS/ESA
swapping	extended private area
swap-out	extended common area
swap data set	extended nucleus
swap-in	extended user region
real mode	dataspace
virtual mode	hiperspace
resident	hiperbatch

Objectives

1. Describe how MVS implements virtual storage and multiprogramming.

2. Describe the three basic areas of an MVS/370 address space.

3. Describe how an MVS/XA or ESA address space differs from an MVS/370 address space.

Topic 2

How MVS manages user data

MVS provides a variety of facilities that let you manage data that resides on tape, DASD, and other I/O devices. Because data management is among the most important functions MVS provides, all of the chapters in sections 3 and 4 stress it. Even so, you need a basic understanding of MVS data management facilities from the start. So, this topic introduces you to the basic concepts of MVS data management: how data sets are stored on tape and DASD, how data sets are processed by user jobs and programs, and how a new feature of MVS/ESA called the Storage Management Subsystem affects the way data sets are managed. Before I get into that discussion, however, I want you to be aware of the distinction between VSAM and non-VSAM data management.

VSAM and non-VSAM data management

There are two rather different data management environments that coexist under MVS: *VSAM* and *non-VSAM*. VSAM, which stands for *Virtual Storage Access Method*, was announced in the early 1970s. It was supposed to eventually replace the older non-VSAM data management functions, which are essentially the same today as they were in the mid-1960s when they were originally developed.

Unfortunately, VSAM wasn't able to meet all of a typical installation's data management needs. As a result, VSAM and non-VSAM data management facilities coexist on today's MVS systems. Because VSAM and non-VSAM data management coexist, I'll occasionally distinguish between VSAM and non-VSAM functions in this topic and throughout the rest of this book.

Until the release of MVS/ESA, one of the important differences between VSAM and non-VSAM data management was that you could make most of the specifications necessary to create a non-VSAM file using standard JCL facilities. In contrast, you had to create a VSAM file using a utility program called Access Method Services. The Storage Management Subsystem of MVS/ESA, however, lets you bypass Access Method Services and define VSAM data sets using JCL. You'll learn how to use the Storage Management Subsystem in chapter 9 and Access Method Services in chapter 10. And you'll learn how to code JCL specifications for non-VSAM files throughout this book.

How data sets are stored

Before I describe how data sets are actually processed, I'll describe the mechanisms MVS uses to keep track of the data it stores. Those mechanisms include labels, catalogs, and data set organizations.

Before I continue, though, I want to define a basic term: *data set*. A data set is simply a collection of related data that is managed as a unit by MVS. Within a data set, data is organized into smaller units called records, which can be processed individually by application programs. In other words, a data set is the same as a *file*.

MVS label processing

When a data set is stored on disk or tape, MVS normally identifies it with special records called *labels*. To access a data set identified by labels, you supply information in JCL statements that MVS compares with the label information. That way, you can be sure that the correct data set is processed.

DASD labels   There are two types of DASD labels: volume labels and file labels. Figure 3-6 is a simplified example of labels on a DASD unit. You can refer to it as I describe the format of DASD labels.

All DASD volumes must contain a *volume label*, often called a *VOL1 label*. The VOL1 label is always in the same place on a disk volume: the third record of track 0 in cylinder 0. The VOL1 label has two important functions. First, it identifies the volume by providing a *volume serial number*, or *vol-ser*. Every DASD volume must have a unique six-character vol-ser. Second, the VOL1 label contains the disk address of the VTOC.

The *VTOC*, or *Volume Table of Contents*, is a special file that contains the file labels for the data sets on the volume. These labels, also called *Data Set Control Blocks*, or *DSCBs*, have several formats, called Format-1, Format-2, and so on. The first DSCB in figure 3-6 is a Format-4 DSCB; it describes the VTOC itself.

Each Format-1 DSCB in a VTOC describes a data set by supplying the data set's name, DASD location, and other characteristics. Figure 3-7 gives the rules for forming an MVS data set name. And figure 3-8 shows you how to avoid some common naming errors. Each group of characters separated by periods in a data set name is called a *qualifier*. As you'll see in a moment, the first qualifier in a name, called the *high-level qualifier*, often has special significance.

Space is allocated to DASD files in areas called *extents*; each extent consists of one or more adjacent tracks. When a file is initially

Disk volume

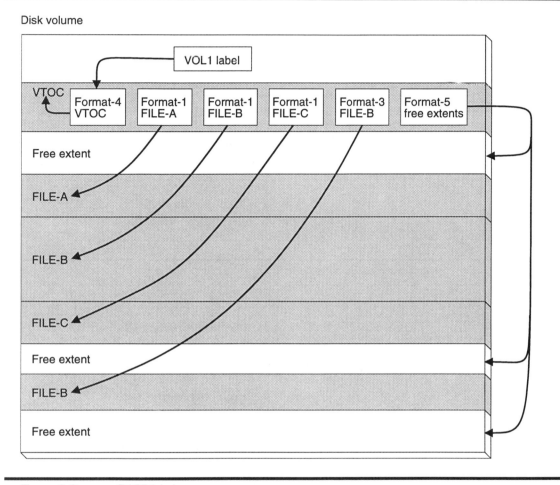

Figure 3-6   DASD labels

created, one extent, called the *primary extent*, is allocated to it. As additional records are written to the file, however, that extent might not be large enough. So MVS tries to automatically allocate additional extents, called *secondary extents*, for the file.

A Format-1 DSCB has room to define three extents for a file: the primary extent and two secondary extents. If the file requires more than three extents, a Format-3 DSCB is created; it contains room for thirteen additional secondary extents. As a result, a file can contain up to sixteen extents: three defined in the Format-1 DSCB, and thirteen defined in the Format-3 DSCB. In figure 3-6, you can see that a Format-3 DSCB for FILE-B defines additional extents. (For simplicity, figure 3-6 doesn't show the individual file extents.)

Length	1 to 44 characters (standard).
	1 to 35 characters (generation data group).
	Only the first 17 characters are used for tape data sets.
Characters	The 26 letters (A-Z).
	The 10 digits (0-9).
	The 3 national characters (@, #, and $).
	The period (.).
	Other special characters should be avoided.
Qualifiers	Data set names with more than eight characters must be broken into qualifiers that each contain between one and eight characters. Separate qualifiers from one another with periods. The periods are counted in the overall length of the data set name.
First character	The first character of each qualifier must be a letter or national character.
Last character	The last character of a data set name should not be a period.

Figure 3-7   Rules for forming data set names

Format-5 DSCBs contain information about *free extents*, that is, sections of the disk volume that aren't allocated to files. Each format-5 DSCB can define up to 26 free extents; if the volume has more than 26 free extents, more than one Format-5 DSCB is used. The Format-5 DSCB in figure 3-6 defines three free extents.

If you're using ISAM files, you should also know about the Format-2 DSCB. This DSCB contains information about the index of an ISAM file. You'll learn how indexes work later in this topic, and you'll learn about ISAM files in chapter 13.

For non-VSAM files, VTOC labels contain information that describes the files' characteristics, such as their organization, the size of their blocks and records, and so on. Normally, this information is obtained from JCL specifications when the file is created. For VSAM files, however, the VTOC plays a less important role: VTOC labels simply record the DASD space occupied by VSAM files. The characteristics of those files are stored in catalog entries. (I'll describe catalogs in a moment.)

Tape labels   Unlike DASD volumes, labels are optional on tape volumes. Most tapes have *standard labels*; that is, they have volume and file labels that conform to MVS conventions. Alternatively, a tape can have *non-standard labels* or no labels at all. If standard labels are used, the VOL1 label assigns a six-character vol-ser to the tape, just as it does for a DASD volume. File labels on tape, however, are different than they are on DASD.

Invalid data set names	Valid data set names
ACCOUNTS.RECEIVABLE.FILE (Second segment too long.)	ACCOUNTS.RECEIVBL.FILE
AR.TRANS.1994 (Third segment starts with a digit.)	AR.TRANS.Y1994
AR.TRANS.APR+MAY.Y94 (Third segment contains an invalid character.)	AR.TRANS.APR.MAY.Y94
INVMAST. (Name ends with a period.)	INVMAST

Figure 3-8   Invalid data set names with valid alternatives

To illustrate tape file labels, figure 3-9 shows the arrangement of labels on a tape volume that contains two files. As you can see, the labels are stored along with the files rather than together as in a DASD volume's VTOC. At the start of a tape file is a *file-header label* (*HDR1*). The HDR1 label is followed by the file's data. At the file's end is an *end-of-file label* (*EOF1*). The actual layout of a tape is a little more complicated than this, but figure 3-9 shows all you really need to know at this point.

Catalogs

MVS provides a comprehensive *catalog* facility that records the location of files so that you don't have to specify the vol-ser of the volume that contains the file. Considering that many MVS installations have hundreds of DASD volumes and thousands of data sets, cataloging is a must. It would be impractical to keep track of the locations of that many files manually.

Under MVS, there are two types of catalogs as shown in figure 3-10: *master catalogs* and *user catalogs*. Each MVS system has just one master catalog and an unlimited number of user catalogs. The master catalog contains entries that identify system data sets; that is, data sets that are required for the operating system to function. In contrast, the user catalogs contain entries that identify user data sets that contain user data. In addition, each user catalog must be defined in the master catalog.

An MVS installation can create catalogs using any of three formats. Catalogs of the oldest format, called *OS catalogs* or *CVOLs*, aren't used much anymore. (CVOLs didn't distinguish between

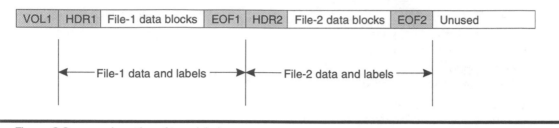

| VOL1 | HDR1 | File-1 data blocks | EOF1 | HDR2 | File-2 data blocks | EOF2 | Unused |

←—————File-1 data and labels—————→←————File-2 data and labels————→

Figure 3-9   Location of tape labels

master and user catalogs.) When VSAM was announced in the early 1970s, one of its major benefits was a comprehensive catalog facility that could easily be used to manage the growing number of data sets typical of a large MVS installation. This new facility used *VSAM catalogs* that were based on the master/user catalog structure.

Unfortunately, the VSAM catalog structure contained fundamental weaknesses that led IBM to develop yet another catalog structure, called the *Integrated Catalog Facility*, or *ICF*. ICF catalogs are functionally similar to VSAM catalogs, but they have a different internal format. Today, most larger installations have fully converted to ICF catalogs, though some smaller installations still use VSAM and CVOL catalogs.

All files managed by VSAM must be cataloged in a VSAM or ICF catalog. For VSAM files, the catalog contains not just information that locates the file, but information that specifies the file's characteristics as well. Since that information for non-VSAM files is stored in the data set labels in the VTOC, non-VSAM files don't have to be cataloged. Still, cataloging a non-VSAM file in a VSAM or ICF catalog makes the file easier to locate later on because you don't have to remember the vol-ser of the volume that contains the file. If your installation uses the Storage Management Subsystem under MVS/ESA, *all* data sets have to be cataloged.

As I mentioned earlier, the high-level qualifier of a data set name can have special significance. That's because it normally indicates the catalog in which the file is defined. For example, a data set named MMA2.CUSTOMER.MASTER is cataloged in the user catalog indicated by MMA2.

In some cases, the high-level qualifier and the user catalog name are the same. More often, though, the high-level qualifier is an *alias* of the actual name. (An alias is simply an alternate name for something; in this case, a user catalog.) For example, MMA2 might be an alias for a

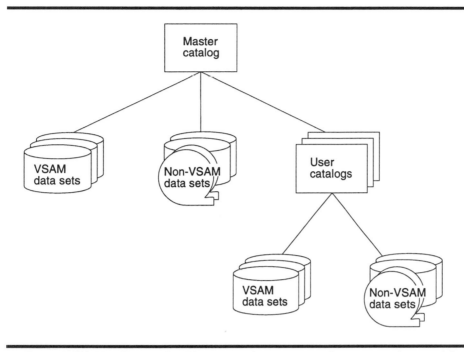

Figure 3-10   The relationships among the master catalog, user catalogs, and data sets

catalog named VCAT.MPS800. Then, MMA2.CUSTOMER.MASTER
would be cataloged in the catalog named VCAT.MPS800. By using
aliases, files with different high-level qualifiers can be cataloged in the
same user catalog.

Data set organization

Within a data set, data can be organized in one of several ways
depending on how the data will ultimately be processed. The
variety of data set organizations that can be used under MVS fall
into two categories: non-VSAM and VSAM.

Non-VSAM data set organization   MVS, apart from VSAM,
provides four basic ways of organizing data stored in data sets:
physical sequential, indexed sequential, direct, and partitioned.
When *physical sequential organization* is used, records are stored one
after another in consecutive sequence. Sometimes, a data element
within each record contains a key value that's used to sequence the
records in the file in a particular order. For example, figure 3-11
shows a simple 10-record employee file in sequence by employee
social security number.

Disk location	Social security number	First name	Middle initial	Last name	Employee number
1	213-64-9290	Thomas	T	Bluestone	00008
2	279-00-1210	William	J	Colline	00002
3	334-96-8721	Constance	M	Harris	00007
4	498-27-6117	Ronald	W	Garcia	00010
5	499-35-5079	Stanley	L	Abbott	00001
6	558-12-6168	Marie	A	Littlejohn	00005
7	559-35-2479	E	R	Mendez	00006
8	572-68-3100	Jean	D	Glenning	00009
9	703-47-5748	Paul	M	Collins	00004
10	899-16-9235	Alice		Lee	00003

Figure 3-11   An employee file with sequential organization by social security number

A sequential file can reside on just about any type of I/O device that can be attached to an MVS system, including tape drives, card readers and punches, and printers. In fact, physical sequential is the *only* file organization that's allowed for those devices, because by nature they require data to be processed in a sequential manner, one record after the next.

Physical sequential organization is appropriate for a DASD file when the file's records don't have to be retrieved at random. When a DASD file is processed sequentially, access from one record to the next is fast. But a disadvantage of sequential files is that records have to be processed one at a time from the beginning, as if the file resided on tape.

In contrast, a file with *indexed sequential organization* is set up so that records can be accessed sequentially *and* randomly, depending on processing requirements. To do that, an indexed sequential file includes an *index* that relates key field values to the locations of their corresponding data records. Figure 3-12 illustrates how the sequential file in figure 3-11 would appear with indexed sequential organization. Here, each entry in the index relates a *key* value to the location of a corresponding data record. Using this scheme, records can be retrieved sequentially or randomly.

In a file with *direct organization*, each record can be accessed at random. However, a direct file doesn't use an index to enable random processing. Instead, you have to know a record's disk location to access it randomly. Direct files aren't commonly used for user applications because of the programming complexities involved in calculating disk addresses.

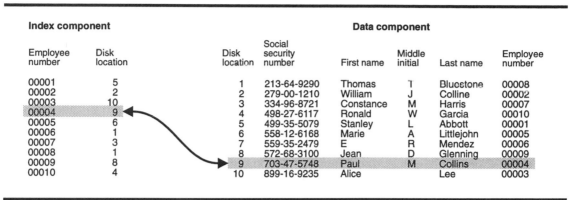

Index component			Data component				
Employee number	Disk location	Disk location	Social security number	First name	Middle initial	Last name	Employee number
00001	5	1	213-64-9290	Thomas	T	Bluestone	00008
00002	2	2	279-00-1210	William	J	Colline	00002
00003	10	3	334-96-8721	Constance	M	Harris	00007
00004	9	4	498-27-6117	Ronald	W	Garcia	00010
00005	6	5	499-35-5079	Stanley	L	Abbott	00001
00006	1	6	558-12-6168	Marie	A	Littlejohn	00005
00007	3	7	559-35-2479	E	R	Mendez	00006
00008	1	8	572-68-3100	Jean	D	Glenning	00009
00009	8	9	703-47-5748	Paul	M	Collins	00004
00010	4	10	899-16-9235	Alice		Lee	00003

Figure 3-12   An employee file with indexed sequential organization

A particularly interesting type of MVS file organization is *partitioned organization*. A *partitioned data set* (sometimes called a *PDS* or a *library*) is divided into one or more *members*, each of which can be processed as if it were a separate physical sequential file. To keep track of the members in a PDS, each member's name is stored in a directory. Although members of a PDS are usually processed individually, the entire library can be processed as a unit. Figure 3-13 shows a PDS with three members, each containing COBOL source code.

Of the four non-VSAM file organizations, the most important are physical sequential and partitioned; indexed sequential and direct aren't used as commonly because their functions are better handled by VSAM files. Physical sequential organization provides the basic support you need to process data on any type of device other than DASD. And partitioned data sets are widely used by MVS to store important operating system information, as well as by programmers to store libraries of programs in various stages of development.

VSAM data set organizations   Under VSAM, there are three basic types of file organizations you can use. An *entry-sequenced data set*, or *ESDS*, is similar to a physical sequential file. Its records can be accessed only in the order in which they were created. Unlike physical sequential data sets, however, an ESDS can reside only on a DASD unit. A *key-sequenced data set*, or *KSDS*, is like an indexed sequential data set. It lets you process records sequentially or randomly based on a key value. KSDS is the file organization used

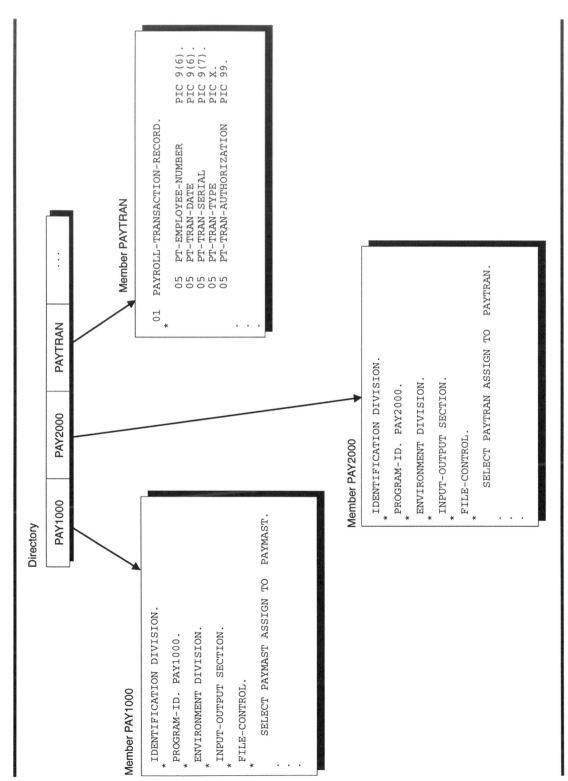

Directory

PAY1000	PAY2000	PAYTRAN	. . .

Member PAYTRAN

```
01  PAYROLL-TRANSACTION-RECORD.
*
    05  PT-EMPLOYEE-NUMBER        PIC 9(6).
    05  PT-TRAN-DATE              PIC 9(6).
    05  PT-TRAN-SERIAL            PIC 9(7).
    05  PT-TRAN-TYPE              PIC X.
    05  PT-TRAN-AUTHORIZATION     PIC 99.
*
        . . .
```

Member PAY1000

```
IDENTIFICATION DIVISION.
*
PROGRAM-ID.  PAY1000.
*
ENVIRONMENT DIVISION.
*
INPUT-OUTPUT SECTION.
*
FILE-CONTROL.
*
    SELECT PAYMAST ASSIGN TO   PAYMAST.
        . . .
```

Member PAY2000

```
IDENTIFICATION DIVISION.
*
PROGRAM-ID.  PAY2000.
*
ENVIRONMENT DIVISION.
*
INPUT-OUTPUT SECTION.
*
FILE-CONTROL.
*
    SELECT PAYTRAN ASSIGN TO   PAYTRAN.
        . . .
```

Figure 3-13   A partitioned data set with three members

for the vast majority of user data sets under MVS. A *relative-record data set*, or *RRDS*, is similar to a direct data set. It lets you retrieve a record by specifying its location relative to the start of the file.

How data sets are processed

Now that you know about the basic techniques MVS uses to store data sets, you're ready to see how user jobs and application programs process those data sets. In general, an application program that's part of a user job goes through three phases as it processes a data set: allocation, processing, and deallocation.

Allocation

When you request access to an existing data set, MVS uses information you provide in your JCL along with information in the data set label and catalog to locate the data set. Similarly, if you're creating a new data set, MVS uses the information you provide to locate and set aside space for the data set. The process of locating an existing data set or space for a new data set and preparing the system control blocks needed to use the data set is called *allocation*.

Under MVS, allocation occurs at three levels: first, a unit (device) is selected and allocated; then, a volume is allocated; and finally, a data set on that volume is allocated. The way MVS allocates units, volumes, and data sets affects how you request them, so you need a basic understanding of how allocation works at each level.

How MVS allocates units When you request access to a data set, MVS determines which *unit*, or device, the data set resides on or will reside on. Then, that unit is allocated to your job. Before I explain how MVS determines which unit to allocate, I want you to realize that in some cases, allocating a unit to your job means that no other jobs on the system can use that unit until your job is finished with it. Usually, that happens when you allocate devices like tape drives that, by their nature, can't be shared. In contrast, a DASD unit is sharable, so it can be allocated to more than one job at once.

How MVS selects an appropriate unit for your allocation depends on how you request the unit. The simplest, but least used, way to request a unit is to specify the unit's device address. Each device in a system has a unique three-digit hexadecimal address, so requesting a unit by address causes the device at that address to be allocated.

Instead of specifying a particular device address, you're more likely to request a unit by specifying a *generic name* or a *group name*. Both have a similar effect: They indicate that you want one of a group of devices rather than a particular device. From that group, MVS uses various criteria to select the most appropriate unit to allocate. A generic name is an IBM-supplied name that indicates a device type, like 3350 or 3380; all of the devices of a particular type are included when you specify a generic name.

A group name, sometimes called an *esoteric name*, is a more flexible way to group devices. Each installation creates its own group names and associates specific devices with each name. One group name, SYSALLDA, is always available. It identifies every DASD unit on the system. Almost all MVS installations define a group named SYSDA, which identifies the direct access devices that are available for general usage. Similarly, most MVS shops define a group named TAPE, which identifies all of the installation's tape drives, regardless of their type. You'll have to check with your installation to find out what other group names besides SYSALLDA, SYSDA, and TAPE you can use.

How MVS allocates volumes   There are two ways to request a volume. When you use a *specific volume request*, you identify a particular volume by specifying its vol-ser or letting MVS obtain the volume identification from a catalog. When you use a *non-specific volume request*, you don't specify a vol-ser. Instead, you let MVS select the volume on which a new data set will be created (non-specific volume requests aren't valid for existing data sets).

If you issue a specific volume request, MVS searches all of the devices that match the unit you requested. If it finds the volume, that volume and unit are allocated to your job. If MVS doesn't find the volume, it selects one of the units and instructs the operator to mount the volume on that unit. When the operator has mounted the volume, the unit and the volume are allocated to your job.

In the case of DASD with non-removable volumes (3350, 3375, 3380, or 3390), each unit always has the same volume mounted. As a result, coding a specific volume request for one of these DASDs is similar to requesting a specific unit by specifying its device address. In most cases, though, you're better off specifying a vol-ser than a unit address.

How MVS allocates data sets   Once the unit and volume for an existing data set have been allocated, the data set's file labels are read to ensure that the requested data set exists. For a new data set, file labels are created and, if the data set resides on DASD, space is allocated to the data set and the VTOC is updated to indicate the allocation. To allocate a new data set, you must supply the characteristics of the data such as the data set's organization, record and block size, and the amount of space the data set will require.

An important specification that determines how a non-VSAM data set is allocated is the file's *disposition*. Disposition, coded in the JCL statement that identifies the file, indicates whether the file already exists or is being created. In addition, for an existing file, disposition indicates whether the file can be shared by other jobs or should be allocated for exclusive use (DASD only). If you code a disposition for a VSAM file, it's ignored unless you're running under MVS/ESA and SMS is activated.

Another important factor that influences how a non-VSAM data set is allocated is whether the file is permanent or temporary. A *permanent data set* is one that existed before the job began or will be retained after the job ends. In contrast, a *temporary data set* is one that is created and deleted within a single job. A permanent file must always be given a data set name, but a temporary file doesn't have to have a name.

Processing

Once a data set (along with its unit and volume) is allocated, application programs can process it. To do that, special operating system facilities called access methods are used.

How the access methods process data sets   An *access method* is an interface between an application program and the physical operations of storage devices. When you code an I/O instruction in an application program, you actually invoke an access method, which in turn issues the proper I/O instructions to access the I/O device. Access methods relieve you of having to handle the complex technical details of using I/O devices and maintaining data sets in the correct format.

Access methods can be divided into three categories: basic, queued, and VSAM. A *basic access method* provides the lowest level of support for a data set type. In particular, the *Basic Sequential Access Method*, or *BSAM*, provides low-level support for sequential data sets, the *Basic Indexed Sequential Access Method*, or *BISAM*, provides low-level support for indexed sequential files, and the *Basic Direct Access Method*, or *BDAM*, provides low-level support for direct files.

The *queued access methods* provide a higher level of support for sequential and indexed sequential files. They let you process those files on a sequential basis in an efficient way by providing sophisti-cated processing techniques that anticipate your next I/O operation. For sequential files or members of partitioned data sets, the *Queued Sequential Access Method*, or *QSAM*, is used; the *Queued Indexed Sequential Access Method*, or *QISAM*, is used for indexed files. There is no queued access method for direct data sets.

VSAM provides access method support for its key-sequenced, entry-sequenced, and relative-record data sets. Under VSAM, techniques similar to those used by both basic and queued access methods are used.

Open processing Before a program can issue I/O instructions for a file, it must issue an OPEN instruction to establish a connection between a program, a data set, and an appropriate access method. For non-VSAM files, that connection is made through a special control block called a *Data Control Block*, or *DCB*. For VSAM files, a control block called the *Access method Control Block*, or *ACB*, has a similar function. Both the DCB and the ACB are simply tables in storage that contain vital information about the status of a data set as it's processed. The main purpose of OPEN processing is to initial-ize the DCB or ACB.

When a data set is opened, DCB/ACB information comes from one of three sources: the data set's label or catalog entry, the JCL, and the program itself. Usually, as little information as possible is specified in the program. That way, the program doesn't have to be changed whenever a minor change is made to the characteristics of the data set.

You can use any of several *open modes* when you open a data set. In *input mode*, records can be read but not written to the data set; the file must exist before it's opened in this mode. In *output mode*, records can be written but not read. If the file doesn't exist, a new one is created; if it already exists, the records are added to the end of the file. In *I/O mode*, records can be both read and written; the file must already exist. And there are other open modes that provide other ways to process files.

I/O requests When a program issues instructions to perform I/O operations on a data set, those instructions are processed by one of the access methods. In general, there are four kinds of I/O operations you can issue: read a record, write a record, update (or rewrite) a record, and delete a record. During processing, most access methods handle blocking and deblocking so that the program processes one record at a time, even though the data is stored in blocks that may consist of more than one record. The access method also maintains other elements of a data set's structure, such as the index of an indexed sequential data set or a VSAM key-sequenced data set.

CLOSE processing   When a program is finished processing a data set, it issues a CLOSE instruction to disconnect itself from the file. If a file is not properly closed, you may not be able to OPEN it the next time you need to process it. I want to be sure you realize, though, that closing a file does not deallocate it. As a result, an application program can open and close a data set several times without worrying about the file being allocated and deallocated each time.

Deallocation

Just as data sets must be allocated before they can be processed, they must be *deallocated* after they are processed. You don't have to do anything explicitly to deallocate a file; each file is automatically deallocated when a job is finished with it. However, there is one important factor you can influence when a data set is deallocated: the file's disposition.

Disposition indicates what MVS does with a non-VSAM file when it's deallocated. The disposition of a temporary file indicates whether the file should be retained until the end of the job or deleted immediately. For a permanent file, disposition indicates whether the file should be kept or deleted. In addition, a permanent file's disposition indicates whether an entry for the file should be retained in the master catalog or a user catalog. Once again, if you specify a disposition for a VSAM file, it's ignored unless you're running under MVS/ESA and SMS is activated.

Storage Management Subsystem

One of the most significant new features of MVS is an automated storage management system called the *Storage Management Subsystem*, or *SMS*. (The official name for SMS is *DFSMS*, but most people drop the DF and refer to it simply as SMS.) SMS removes many of the manual procedures that are associated with managing data sets, such as determining which volume a data set should be stored on, calculating the amount of space to allocate to the data set, and determining when a data set is no longer needed and can therefore be deleted or moved to off-line storage.

When you create a data set under SMS, you assign that data set to a pre-defined *storage class*. SMS uses the storage class to select an appropriate volume on which to store the data set. As a result, the storage class frees you from determining the volume that will be used for the data set.

A data set's *management class* determines how long the data set will be kept online and how often it will be backed up. For example, one management class might be used for data sets that should be retained indefinitely and backed up every day, and another class might be used for data sets that should be backed up only once a week and can be deleted if they haven't been accessed in 60 days.

A data set's *data class* determines the characteristics of the data set: its organization, record format, and default space allocation. For example, one class might be set up for creating data sets that will contain COBOL source statements and another class might be set up for creating VSAM key-sequenced data sets.

The various settings that are allowed for storage class, management class, and data class vary from one installation to the next. In addition, an installation can set up *automatic class selection*, or *ACS, routines*, that automatically pick the storage class, management class, and data class for all new data sets. These ACS routines are often set up so that they analyze the data set name to determine which class to assign to the data set. For example, if the low-level qualifier of the data set name is COBOL, the ACS routine could assign the COBOL data class to the data set.

Besides the use of JCL parameters to specify a data set's storage class, management class, and data class, the most significant JCL change that results from SMS is the ability to create VSAM data sets using JCL statements. Without SMS, you must invoke the Access Method Services program to create VSAM data sets.

Discussion

By now, you should realize that the data management facilities of MVS involve complicated relationships among many system components. So don't worry if you don't understand all of the details this topic presents. If you're familiar with the techniques MVS uses to store data sets (labels, catalogs, and data set organizations) and the steps by which a data set is processed (allocation, processing, and deallocation), you're ready to read on.

Terminology

VSAM	label
non-VSAM	volume label
Virtual Storage Access Method	VOL1 label
data set	volume serial number
file	vol-ser

VTOC
Volume Table of Contents
Data Set Control Block
DSCB
qualifier
high-level qualifier
extent
primary extent
secondary extent
free extent
standard labels
non-standard labels
file-header label
HDR1
end-of-file label
EOF1
catalog
master catalog
user catalog
OS catalog
CVOL
VSAM catalog
Integrated Catalog Facility
ICF
alias
physical sequential organization
indexed sequential organization
index
key
direct organization
partitioned organization
partitioned data set
PDS
library
member
entry-sequenced data set
ESDS
key-sequenced data set
KSDS
relative-record data set
RRDS
allocation

unit
generic name
group name
esoteric name
specific volume request
non-specific volume request
disposition
permanent data set
temporary data set
access method
basic access method
Basic Sequential Access Method
BSAM
Basic Indexed Sequential Access
    Method
BISAM
Basic Direct Access Method
BDAM
queued access method
Queued Sequential Access Method
QSAM
Queued Indexed Sequential Access
    Method
QISAM
Data Control Block
DCB
Access method Control Block
ACB
open mode
input mode
output mode
I/O mode
deallocation
Storage Management Subsystem
SMS
DFSMS
storage class
management class
data class
automated class selection routine
ACS routine

Objectives

1. Describe MVS label processing for tape and DASD files.

2. Distinguish between master and user catalogs.

3. List and describe four non-VSAM file organizations and three VSAM file organizations.

4. Describe the factors that influence unit, volume, and data set allocation.

5. List three basic and two queued access methods and indicate what file organization each supports.

6. Explain how OPEN processing affects a file's DCB or ACB.

7. Indicate how disposition influences deallocation.

Topic 3

How MVS manages user jobs

Now that you know about the basic MVS facilities of virtual storage, multiprogramming, and data management, you're ready to learn about the MVS facilities that manage the execution of jobs. Among those facilities are services that read and store jobs, select jobs for execution based on the relative importance of each job, allocate resources to jobs as they execute, and process printed output produced by jobs. Collectively, the functions performed by those services are usually referred to as *job management*.

As you work with MVS and learn how to use Job Control Language, it's critical that you have an understanding of how MVS job management handles your jobs. If you don't, much of what MVS does for you will seem confusing or mysterious. As a result, this topic describes the basic concepts of MVS job management. First, I'll explain what a job is and how JCL specifies its processing requirements. Next, I'll explain how an MVS component called the Job Entry Subsystem has overall responsibility for job management. Then, I'll describe the phases that a job goes through as it's processed. Finally, I'll show you a sample of the output that results from a simple job and explain each of its components.

Jobs and Job Control Language

Simply put, a *job* is the execution of one or more related programs in sequence. Each program to be executed by a job is called a *job step*. To illustrate, suppose you want to process a job that executes two programs: the first sorts a customer file into customer name sequence, and the second prints a report that lists customers by name. That's a two step job because two programs are required. When you submit a job to be processed by MVS, the job is treated as a whole. The job begins with the execution of the first program and continues until the last program has finished executing, unless an unforeseen error condition occurs.

Job Control Language, or *JCL*, is a set of control statements that provide the specifications necessary to process a job. Obviously, the purpose of this book is to teach you JCL. As a result, we'll consider JCL in depth in later chapters. For now, though, I want you to know about three basic JCL statements that are present in nearly every job: JOB, EXEC, and DD. The first statement of any job is a JOB

```
//SYDOEJ    JOB   USER=SYSDOE,PASSWORD=XXXXXXXX
//          EXEC  PGM=IEBGENER
//SYSPRINT  DD    SYSOUT=A
//SYSUT1    DD    DSN=SYDOE.COPYLIB.COBOL(OPENITEM),DISP=SHR
//SYSUT2    DD    SYSOUT=A
//SYSIN     DD    DUMMY
```

Figure 3-14   JCL statements for a job that prints a library member

statement. It provides information that identifies the job, such as the job's name and your name. For each job step in the job, an EXEC statement indicates the name of the program to be executed. Following an EXEC statement, a DD statement is normally required for every file that's processed by the program.

To illustrate, figure 3-14 shows a simple one-step job. The purpose of this job is to copy data from a file to a printer. As you can see, the first statement in the job is a JOB statement. It names the job (SYDOEJ) and indicates my user-id (SYDOE) and password. Then, an EXEC statement specifies that the program for the job's only step is named IEBGENER; that's the name of a program provided by IBM that copies files.

Four DD statements are used in this job. The first, named SYSPRINT, is a printed listing of informational messages produced by the IEBGENER program; the specification SYSOUT=A tells MVS to direct the file to a printer along with the rest of the job's printer output. The second, SYSUT1, identifies the file I want to copy to the printer. It's a member of a partitioned data set that's named SYDOE.COPYLIB.COBOL; the member itself is named OPENITEM. The next DD statement, SYSUT2, is for the output file. It specifies SYSOUT=A just like the SYSPRINT file. So it too will be included with the job's printer output. The last DD statement, SYSIN, is required in case you need to give the IEBGENER program special instructions. Since I don't have any special instructions for IEBGENER in this job, I just coded DUMMY.

As simple as this job is, there's probably much about it that you don't understand at this point. That's OK. The point here isn't to learn how to code JCL; you'll learn that later. I just want you to see a typical job now so you'll become acquainted with the basic JCL statements: JOB, EXEC, and DD.

Job Entry Subsystems

To process a job like the one in figure 3-14, an important component of MVS called the *Job Entry Subsystem* is used. Simply put, the Job Entry Subsystem is the MVS component that keeps track of jobs that enter the system, presents them to MVS for processing, and sends their spooled output to the correct destination, normally a printer.

To fully understand MVS Job Entry Subsystems, you must understand that the original versions of OS did not provide a Job Entry Subsystem. On those systems, an operating system component called the *job scheduler* provided a relatively crude form of job entry and spooling. Because the MVS job scheduler was inadequate for most installation's needs, a program called *HASP*, which stood for *Houston Automatic Spooling Program*, was used at most installations. HASP, which itself ran as a user job, duplicated many of the functions of the job scheduler, but it provided more efficient operation and comprehensive control than the job scheduler alone.

Although HASP became the norm at most installations, some shops used another program, called *ASP*, or *Asymmetric Multiprocessing System*. ASP was designed particularly for installations that used more than one processor. For those shops, it provided excellent control of job processing in a multiprocessing environment. ASP, like HASP, ran as a user job and duplicated many functions of the job scheduler.

When MVS was announced, IBM integrated the functions performed by HASP and ASP into the operating system by providing the Job Entry Subsystem. Because both HASP and ASP had strong footholds at large IBM shops, yet were incompatible with one another, two versions of JES were announced: *JES2* and *JES3*. Basically, JES2 is the equivalent of HASP, and JES3 is the equivalent of ASP. The job scheduler itself was dropped, and many operating system components related to job scheduling were rewritten to accommodate JES2 and JES3. As a result, the overhead inherent with HASP/ASP processing is eliminated under JES2/JES3.

Although you should know whether your shop uses JES2 or JES3, it doesn't really matter in most cases. For typical jobs that don't have unusual processing requirements that depend on the unique characteristics of JES2 or JES3, both Job Entry Subsystems provide essentially the same functions: They let you enter a job into the system, they decide when your job should be processed, they pass your job to MVS for processing, and they deliver your job's printed output to the correct destination. With that in mind, I'll describe JES2 and JES3 job processing in more detail.

1. The job is submitted.

2. The job is selected for execution.

3. The job is executed.

4. The job's output is processed.

5. The job is purged.

Figure 3-15   How an MVS job is processed

How JES2 and JES3 process jobs

Figure 3-15 describes the life cycle of a typical job under JES2 and JES3. Each job follows a predictable series of steps: The job is submitted, selected for execution, and executed; its output is processed; and the job is purged. Now, I'll describe each of those steps in detail.

How a job is entered into the system   In the early days of the System/360-370, the phrase "entering a job into the system" meant that a system operator removed a deck of cards containing a job's JCL and data from a file cabinet, placed the cards into a card reader, and pressed the card reader's "start" button. The card reader, which was under control of a system program called a *reader task*, read the cards, which were placed in a system file on DASD called the *job queue*. From the job queue, the job would be selected for execution by the job scheduler.

Although many installations still have a card reader and may use it occasionally, it's no longer the predominant way to enter a job into the system. Rather than create the job using punched cards, a programmer today uses a display terminal to create the JCL and data for the job. In the process, the job stream is stored in a file on a DASD unit. At this point, the job has not been entered into the system. Even though it resides on a DASD unit that's attached to the system, MVS (or, more accurately, JES2 or JES3) doesn't know about the job.

To enter, or *submit*, the job into the system, the terminal user issues a SUBMIT command. That causes JES2 or JES3 to read the job stream from the DASD file and copy it to a job queue, which is a part of a special DASD file called the *JES spool*. Even though the job originated from DASD rather than cards, the process is essentially the same as if a card reader was used. In fact, the JES component that processes the input job stream is called an *internal reader*.

Job class	Characteristics
A	The job will execute within 15 minutes of submission.
B	The job will execute within 30 minutes of submission.
C	The job will execute within 1 hour of submission.
D	The job will execute overnight.
H	The job is held until released by an operator.
L	The job will execute within 15 minutes of submission; each step is limited to 1 minute execution time.
T	The job requires tape processing.

Figure 3-16   Typical job class assignments

In some cases, a facility called *Remote Job Entry*, or *RJE*, is used as an alternative way to submit jobs. Originally, RJE provided a way to use an *RJE station*—a special facility that consisted of a card reader, card punch, and a printer—to enter jobs from a remote location; the RJE stations were connected to the computer system via telephone lines. Today, most RJE stations are themselves separate computer systems that include a facility to emulate (mimic) a card reader, card punch, and printer. When you send a job stream to an MVS system using RJE, JES2/JES3 treats the job as if it originated at a local card reader or an internal reader.

How a job is scheduled for execution   As I've already mentioned, MVS does not necessarily process jobs in the order in which they are submitted. Instead, JES examines the jobs in the job queue and selects the most important jobs for execution. That way, JES can prioritize its work, giving preference to more important jobs.

JES uses two characteristics to classify a job's importance, both of which can be specified in the job's JCL: *job class* and *priority*. Of the two, job class is more significant. If two or more jobs of the same class are waiting to execute, the JES scheduler selects the one with the higher priority.

Each job class is represented by a single character, either a letter (A-Z) or a digit (0-9). Job classes are assigned based on the processing characteristics of the job. To illustrate, figure 3-16 shows the characteristics of seven typical job class assignments. Job classes A through D classify jobs based on how quickly they must be scheduled for execution. Class A jobs execute within 15 minutes, class B jobs within 30 minutes, class C jobs within an hour, and class D jobs are scheduled for overnight execution. Class H jobs are held. That means they won't be scheduled at all until a system operator explicitly releases the job for execution. Class L jobs, like class A jobs, are scheduled within 15 minutes. In addition, class L jobs add the restriction that each job step can use no more than one minute of CPU time. Finally, class T is reserved for jobs that require tape volumes to be mounted. By placing those jobs in a special class, the system operators have better control over tape processing.

Bear in mind that the job class assignments in figure 3-16 are only an example. Each installation makes its own job class assignments, so the job classes your installation uses will certainly be different.

At this point, it's not essential that you understand the details of how jobs are selected for execution. But I do want you to know about a special type of program called an *initiator*, because that knowledge will help you understand not only job scheduling, but MVS multiprogramming as well. An initiator is a program that runs in the system region of an address space that's eligible for batch job processing. (Not all of the address spaces on an MVS system can process batch jobs, so they don't all have initiators.) Each initiator can handle one job at a time. It examines the JES spool, selects an appropriate job for execution, executes the job in its address space, and returns to the JES spool for another job.

The number of active initiators on a system and, as a result, the number of address spaces eligible for batch job processing determines the number of batch jobs that can be multiprogrammed at once. Initiators (and their address spaces) can be started when MVS is activated. And, they can be started or stopped by an operator while MVS is running. That way, an installation can vary the number and type of active initiators to meet changing processing needs.

Each initiator has one or more job classes associated with it; it executes jobs only from those classes. That way, an installation can control how many jobs of each class can be executed simultaneously, and in what combinations. To illustrate, figure 3-17 shows the job classes associated with six initiators. Because there's only one initiator associated with class A, only one class A job can execute at a time. Jobs of other classes can execute in various combinations. (Once again, the job classes in use at your installation are undoubtedly different from the classes described here.)

Within a job class, initiators select jobs for execution based on their priorities, which can range from 0 to 15. Jobs with higher priority values are selected for execution before jobs with lower priority values. As a result, a class A job with priority 13 will be

Initiator	Eligible job classes
1	A
2	B, C, D, H, L, T
3	B, C, D, H, L, T
4	B, C
5	B, C
6	C

Figure 3-17   An example of how job classes are assigned to initiators

executed before a class A job with priority 10. If two or more jobs have the same class and priority, they're executed in the order in which they were submitted.

How a job is executed   Figure 3-18 shows how a job is executed once an initiator has selected it for execution. As you can see, the initiator and several other MVS programs run in the system region. (In topic 1 of this chapter, you learned that the system region is a part of the private area of a user's address space.) The first thing an initiator does after it selects a job for execution is invoke a program called the *interpreter*. The interpreter's job is to examine the job information passed to it by JES and create a series of control blocks in the scheduler work area (SWA), a part of the address space's private area. Among other things, these control blocks describe all of the data sets the job needs.

After the interpreter creates the SWA control blocks, the initiator goes through three phases for each step in the job. First, it invokes *allocation routines* that analyze the SWA control blocks to see what resources (units, volumes, and data sets) the job step needs. If the resources are available, they're allocated so the job step can process them. Next, the initiator builds a user region where the user's program can execute, loads the program into the region, and transfers control to it. As the user program executes, it uses the control blocks for the resources allocated to it. When the program is completed, the initiator invokes *unallocation routines* that release any resources used by the job step.

That, in a nutshell, is how a job is executed. For each job step, three activities occur: first, resources are allocated; second, a region is created and the program is loaded and executed; third, resources are released. This process continues until there are no more job

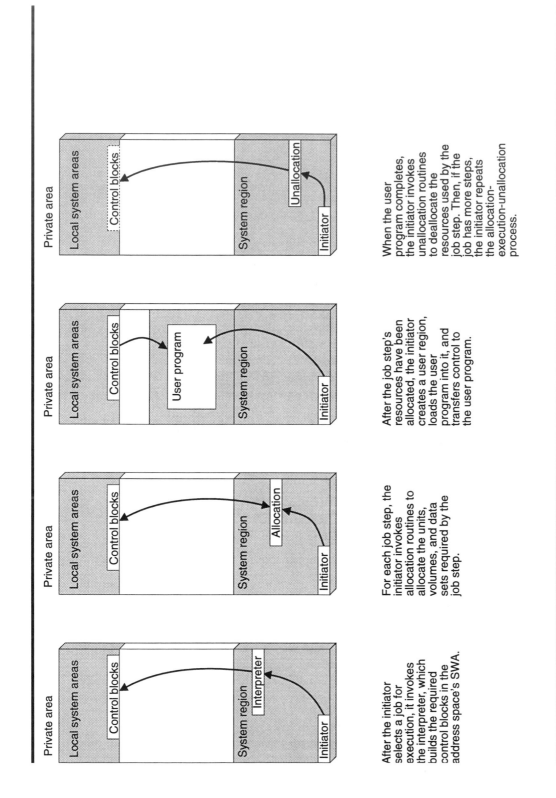

After the initiator selects a job for execution, it invokes the interpreter, which builds the required control blocks in the address space's SWA.

For each job step, the initiator invokes allocation routines to allocate the units, volumes, and data sets required by the job step.

After the job step's resources have been allocated, the initiator creates a user region, loads the user program into it, and transfers control to the user program.

When the user program completes, the initiator invokes unallocation routines to deallocate the resources used by the job step. Then, if the job has more steps, the initiator repeats the allocation-execution-unallocation process.

Figure 3-18   Data set allocation and job step execution

steps to process. Then, the initiator releases the job and searches the spool again for another job of the proper class to execute.

As a user's program executes, it can retrieve data that was included as part of the job stream and stored in the JES spool. Input data processed in this way is called *SYSIN data* or *in-stream data*; the user's program treats the data as if it was read from a card reader. Similarly, the user's program can produce output data that's stored in the JES spool; the program treats the data, called *SYSOUT data*, as if it was written to a card punch or, more commonly, a printer. SYSOUT data is held in a *SYSOUT queue* until it can be processed by JES2/JES3.

How a job's output is processed Like jobs, SYSOUT data is assigned an *output class* that determines how the output will be handled. Most likely, an output class indicates which printer or printers can be used to print the output. In some cases, an output class specifies that the output not be printed; instead, it's held so that you can view it from a display terminal. Common output classes are A for standard printer output, B for standard card punch output, and Z for held output. (Held output stays on the SYSOUT queue indefinitely; usually, output is held so that it can be examined from a TSO terminal.)

A single job can produce SYSOUT data using more than one output class. For example, you might specify that job message output—that is, MVS and JES information relating to your job—be produced using class A. Similarly, you might specify class A for output produced by one or more of your programs. Then, all of that class A output is gathered together and printed as a unit. However, you might specify class D for some of your job's spooled output. Then, the class D output will be treated separately from the class A output.

JES lets you control how SYSOUT data is handled in other ways besides specifying output classes. For example, you can specify that output be routed to a specific printer, or you can specify that two or more copies of the output should be produced or that the output should be printed on special forms rather than on standard paper. Throughout this book you'll learn about various ways of handling SYSOUT data.

How a job is purged After the job's output has been processed, the job is purged from the system. Simply put, that means that the JES spool space the job used is freed so it can be used by other jobs. And any JES control blocks associated with the job are deleted. Once a job has been purged, JES no longer knows of its existence. To process the job again, you return to step 1: submit the job.

Two alternative ways to allocate data sets   In the job processing steps I've just described, data sets are allocated to jobs by MVS on a step-by-step basis. MVS allocates data sets before it executes your program, and it deallocates them when your program is completed. This method of data set allocation is often called *job-step allocation*. There are two other ways in which data sets can be allocated, however. The first, called JES3 allocation, is used only on JES3 systems. The second, called dynamic allocation, is used on both JES2 and JES3 systems, primarily by time sharing users.

When *JES3 allocation* is used, JES3 examines a job's JCL and allocates some or all of the units, volumes, and data sets the job requires *before* the job is scheduled for execution. Then, when the job executes, the MVS allocation routines are used to allocate the data sets that weren't pre-allocated by JES3. The advantage of JES3 allocation is that JES3 knows the allocation needs of all the jobs submitted for execution. As a result, it can avoid scheduling jobs together if they have conflicting resource requirements. Another advantage of JES3 allocation is that initiators, and their address spaces, aren't tied up during allocation. So the overall efficiency of the system is increased.

In a sense, *dynamic allocation* is the opposite of JES3 allocation. Rather than allocate resources before the job is scheduled and its programs are executed, dynamic allocation doesn't allocate data sets until an executing program requests that they be allocated. In other words, dynamic allocation allocates data sets *after* normal step allocation rather than before it.

The main user of dynamic allocation is TSO, the MVS time sharing facility. TSO lets you, as a terminal user, allocate data sets whenever you need them and deallocate them when you don't need them any more. The key to understanding this is realizing that MVS treats each TSO terminal session (from LOGON to LOGOFF) as a single job step. As a result, step allocation can be used only for data sets that are required for the duration of your terminal session. Dynamic allocation is used for data sets that you need only during part of your terminal session.

Job output

Now that you've seen how MVS and JES work together to process your job, look at figure 3-19. It shows the complete output produced for the job in figure 3-14. (This output was produced on a JES2 system. Output under JES3 is similar.) As I describe each portion of this job output, you should relate it to the job processing steps I've just described to get a better understanding of MVS and JES job management.

```
*START JOB 2697 SYDOEJ   1   001 001 LOCAL   ROOM   11.48.09 AM 01 NOV 93 PRT15   SYS2 START A*
*START JOB 2697 SYDOEJ   1   001 001 LOCAL   ROOM   11.48.09 AM 01 NOV 93 PRT15   SYS2 START A*
*START JOB 2697 SYDOEJ   1   001 001 LOCAL   ROOM   11.48.09 AM 01 NOV 93 PRT15   SYS2 START A*
*START JOB 2697 SYDOEJ   1   001 001 LOCAL   ROOM   11.48.09 AM 01 NOV 93 PRT15   SYS2 START A*
*START JOB 2697 SYDOEJ   1   001 001 LOCAL   ROOM   11.48.09 AM 01 NOV 93 PRT15   SYS2 START A*
*START JOB 2697 SYDOEJ   1   001 001 LOCAL   ROOM   11.48.09 AM 01 NOV 93 PRT15   SYS2 START A*
*START JOB 2697 SYDOEJ   1   001 001 LOCAL   ROOM   11.48.09 AM 01 NOV 93 PRT15   SYS2 START A*
*START JOB 2697 SYDOEJ   1   001 001 LOCAL   ROOM   11.48.09 AM 01 NOV 93 PRT15   SYS2 START A*
```

The first page of a job's output is a separator page produced by the Job Entry Subsystem. Although its format varies, it normally includes the job name and number, as well as information the operator uses to deliver the printed output properly.

Figure 3-19   Output from the job in figure 3-14 (part 1 of 7)

```
        J E S 2   J O B   L O G   --   S Y S T E M   S Y S 2   --   N O D E   N J E $ G D C

11.44.52 JOB 2697  ICH70001I SYDOE      LAST ACCESS AT 11:42:13 ON MONDAY, NOVEMBER 1, 1993
11.44.52 JOB 2697  $HASP373 SYDOEJ      STARTED - INIT 15 - CLASS A - SYS SYS2
11.44.53 JOB 2697  IEF403I SYDOEJ -     STARTED - TIME=11.44.53
11.44.55 JOB 2697  -                                              --TIMINGS (MINS.)--            ----PAGING COUNTS----
11.44.55 JOB 2697  -JOBNAME  STEPNAME PROCSTEP   RC   EXCP   CONN  TCB   SRB  CLOCK   SERV  PG  PAGE  SWAP  VIO  SWAPS
11.44.55 JOB 2697  -SYDOEJ                       00     18     69  .00   .00    .0     671   1    0     0    0     1
11.44.55 JOB 2697  IEF404I SYDOEJ - ENDED - TIME=11.44.55
11.44.55 JOB 2697  -SYDOEJ   ENDED.  NAME-                     TOTAL TCB CPU TIME=   .00   TOTAL ELAPSED TIME=   .0
11.44.55 JOB 2697  $HASP395 SYDOEJ      ENDED

------ JES2 JOB STATISTICS ------

   01 NOV 93 JOB EXECUTION DATE

          13 CARDS READ

          91 SYSOUT PRINT RECORDS

           0 SYSOUT PUNCH RECORDS

           5 SYSOUT SPOOL KBYTES

        0.05 MINUTES EXECUTION TIME
```

> The job log is a record of JES2 messages written to the operator's console, as well as the operator's reply where appropriate.

> The job statistics provide summary information about the system resources used by the job.

Figure 3-19   Output from the job in figure 3-14 (part 2 of 7)

```
1 //SYDOEJ  JOB USER=SYSDOE,PASSWORD=                              JOB 2697
2 //       EXEC PGM=IEBGENER
3 //SYSPRINT DD  SYSOUT=A
4 //SYSUT1   DD  DSN=SYDOE.COPYLIB.COBOL(OPENITEM),DISP=SHR
5 //SYSUT2   DD  SYSOUT=A
6 //SYSIN    DD  DUMMY
```

> The JCL listing indicates the JCL statements as they were processed by the job.

Figure 3-19   Output from the job in figure 3-14 (part 3 of 7)

```
ICH70001I SYDOE    LAST ACCESS AT 11:42:13 ON MONDAY, NOVEMBER 1, 1993
IEF236I ALLOC. FOR SYDOEJ
IEF237I JES2 ALLOCATED TO SYSPRINT
IEF237I 1A0  ALLOCATED TO SYSUT1
IEF237I 118  ALLOCATED TO SYS00178
IEF237I JES2 ALLOCATED TO SYSUT2
IEF237I DMY  ALLOCATED TO SYSIN
IEF142I SYDOEJ - STEP WAS EXECUTED - COND CODE 0000
IEF285I   JES2.JOB02697.S0000101                     SYSOUT
IEF285I   SYDOE.COPYLIB.COBOL                         KEPT
IEF285I   VOL SER NOS= TS0005.
IEF285I   ICFCAT.VSTOR02                              KEPT
IEF285I   VOL SER NOS= STOR02.
IEF285I   JES2.JOB02697.S0000102                      SYSOUT
U11-604 ***************************************************************
U11-605 *
U11-606  CA ELEVEN (CARTS) - AUTOMATED RERUN AND TRACKING SYSTEM - VERSION 1.3.2
U11-605 *
U11-610 JOBNAME=SYDOEJ   ,ACTION EXIT (U11ACTEX) DECIDED NOT TO TRACK
U11-605 *
U11-604 ***************************************************************
IEF373I STEP /       / START 93305.1144
IEF374I STEP /       / STOP  93305.1144 CPU    0MIN 00.06SEC SRB    0MIN 00.00SEC VIRT   100K SYS   248K EXT   12K SYS   8824K
IEF375I JOB /SYDOEJ / START 93305.1144
IEF376I JOB /SYDOEJ / STOP  93305.1144 CPU    0MIN 00.06SEC SRB    0MIN 00.00SEC
```

The message log shows system messages concerning the execution of job steps and the allocation and deallocation of data sets. The installation may tailor this output to provide additional information.

Figure 3-19   Output from the job in figure 3-14 (part 4 of 7)

```
DATA SET UTILITY - GENERATE                                          PAGE 0001

IEB352I WARNING : OUTPUT RECFM/LRECL/BLKSIZE COPIED FROM INPUT

PROCESSING ENDED AT EOD
```

This is the output listing for the SYSPRINT data set, which specified SYSOUT=A.

Figure 3-19   Output from the job in figure 3-14 (part 5 of 7)

```
*
 01  OPEN-ITEM.
*
    05  OI-INVOICE-NUMBER                  PIC 9(6).
    05  OI-STATUS-CODE                     PIC X.
        88  OI-ACTIVE-ACCOUNT              VALUE "A".
        88  OI-BAD-DEBT                    VALUE "B".
    05  OI-INVOICE-DATE.
        10  OI-INVOICE-MONTH               PIC 99.
        10  OI-INVOICE-DAY                 PIC 99.
        10  OI-INVOICE-YEAR                PIC 99.
    05  OI-SEARCH-KEY                      PIC X(5).
    05  OI-CUSTOMER-NUMBER.
        10  OI-CUSTOMER-NUMBER-2           PIC 99.
        10  OI-CUSTOMER-NUMBER-4           PIC 9(4).
    05  OI-PURCHASE-ORDER-NUMBER           PIC X(25).
    05  OI-INVOICE-AMOUNTS                 COMP-3.
        10  OI-PRODUCT-TOTAL               PIC S9(5)V99.
        10  OI-CASH-DISCOUNT               PIC S9(5)V99.
        10  OI-INVOICE-SUBTOTAL            PIC S9(5)V99.
        10  OI-SALES-TAX                   PIC S9(5)V99.
        10  OI-FREIGHT                     PIC S9(5)V99.
        10  OI-INVOICE-TOTAL               PIC S9(5)V99.
    05  OI-PAYMENT-CREDIT-DATA             COMP-3.
        10  OI-DISCOUNTS-TAKEN             PIC S9(5)V99.
        10  OI-SUM-OF-PAYMENTS             PIC S9(5)V99.
        10  OI-SUM-OF-CREDITS              PIC S9(5)V99.
        10  OI-BALANCE-DUE                 PIC S9(5)V99.
```

This is the output listing for the SYSUT2 data set, which specified SYSOUT=A.

Figure 3-19   Output from the job in figure 3-14 (part 6 of 7)

```
*END JOB 2697 SYDOEJ 1 001 001 LOCAL    ROOM    11.48.10 AM 01 NOV 93 PRT15    SYS2 END A*
*END JOB 2697 SYDOEJ 1 001 001 LOCAL    ROOM    11.48.10 AM 01 NOV 93 PRT15    SYS2 END A*
*END JOB 2697 SYDOEJ 1 001 001 LOCAL    ROOM    11.48.10 AM 01 NOV 93 PRT15    SYS2 END A*
*END JOB 2697 SYDOEJ 1 001 001 LOCAL    ROOM    11.48.10 AM 01 NOV 93 PRT15    SYS2 END A*
*END JOB 2697 SYDOEJ 1 001 001 LOCAL    ROOM    11.48.10 AM 01 NOV 93 PRT15    SYS2 END A*
*END JOB 2697 SYDOEJ 1 001 001 LOCAL    ROOM    11.48.10 AM 01 NOV 93 PRT15    SYS2 END A*
*END JOB 2697 SYDOEJ 1 001 001 LOCAL    ROOM    11.48.10 AM 01 NOV 93 PRT15    SYS2 END A*
```

The last page of the job output, like the first, is a separator page.

Figure 3-19   Output from the job in figure 3-14 (part 7 of 7)

The first page of the job output in figure 3-19 is called a *separator page*. It's simply an identifying page inserted by JES2 to help the system operator identify the listing when it comes off the printer. If you'll turn to the last part of figure 3-19, you'll see that it's a separator page, too. In other words, the output for each job is bracketed by separator pages: one at the beginning and one at the end. What comes between the separator pages is a collection of SYSOUT data of a particular class. Usually, that includes messages and job information produced by MVS and JES, as well as printed output produced by your programs.

Part 2 of figure 3-19 shows two sections of information produced by JES. The first, called the *job log*, is a listing of the messages produced by JES2 as your job executed. These messages are also displayed on the JES2 operator's console. Notice that two of the messages are prefixed by the code $HASP, a carryover from the days when JES2 was known as HASP. The job log is the first thing you'll normally look at when you examine a job's output, because it tells you whether your job ran successfully or not. In figure 3-19, the job ran successfully, so there aren't any error messages here.

After the job log are the JES2 *job statistics*, a collection of mildly useful information about your job's execution such as how many input "cards" were read, how many records were printed or punched, how much spool space was used, and your job's total execution time.

The next page of the job listing, part 3 in figure 3-19, is a listing of the JCL that was processed for your job. In this case, it's just a listing of the JCL I submitted for the job. You'll learn later in this book how JCL from other sources can appear here too.

After the JCL listing is the *message log*, shown in part 4 of figure 3-19. These are messages produced by MVS—not JES2—as your job executes. If you study the messages near the top of the listing, you can see how the execution of this job's one step follows the sequence I presented in figure 3-18. Each of these messages is labeled with a seven character identifier that begins with the letters IEF, a standard code that indicates that the messages were produced by the MVS job scheduler. Message IEF236I indicates that the next messages specify what devices were allocated for the job step. Then, the IEF237I messages describe the allocations for the job step. Message IEF142I indicates that the job step—that is, the program IEBGENER—was executed successfully. And finally, the IEF285I messages were produced when the resources needed by the job step were deallocated. For each step in your job, you'll find messages in this sequence: allocation (IEF237I), execution (IEF142I), and deallocation (IEF285I). If errors occur, you'll find other messages as well.

Besides the standard IEF messages, the message log also includes information that varies from one installation to the next. In figure 3-19, there is one group of that kind of information, set off by lines of asterisks. These lines indicate that a rerun and tracking system is installed, but that the system was not used to track this job.

The job in figure 3-19 produced two SYSOUT data sets: one containing informational messages produced by the IEBGENER program (identified by the SYSPRINT DD statement), the other containing the printed version of the data set copied by IEBGENER (identified by the SYSUT2 DD statement). Part 5 of figure 3-19 shows the SYSPRINT data set; as you can see, it shows the messages produced by IEBGENER. The warning message simply indicates that the input file (a member of a partitioned data set with 80-byte records) and the output file (a JES2 SYSOUT file with 132-byte records) have different record lengths. That's nothing to worry about. The last IEBGENER message indicates that processing ended when the end of data (EOD) condition was reached for the input file. Part 6 of figure 3-19 is the second SYSOUT data set, a copy of the input that was read from the partitioned data set.

Discussion

As you learn how to code JCL statements, the concepts this topic presents will provide the perspective you need to understand how MVS, along with JES2 or JES3, process the statements you code. Although general perspective is essential at this point, details aren't. So as long as you've grasped the basic ideas of how jobs are processed, you're ready to continue on to the last topic of this chapter where you'll learn about the variety of components that make up a complete MVS system.

Terminology

job management	ASP
job	Asymmetric Multiprocessing
job step	System
Job Control Language	JES2
JCL	JES3
Job Entry Subsystem	reader task
job scheduler	job queue
HASP	submit
Houston Automatic Spooling	JES spool
Program	internal reader

Remote Job Entry
RJE
RJE station
job class
priority
initiator
interpreter
allocation routines
unallocation routines
SYSIN data
in-stream data
SYSOUT data
SYSOUT queue
output class
job-step allocation
JES3 allocation
dynamic allocation
separator page
job log
job statistics
message log

Objectives

1. Distinguish between a job and a job step.

2. Identify the basic functions of the JOB, EXEC, and DD JCL statements.

3. Describe the basic function of a Job Entry Subsystem.

4. Describe the operation of each of the following job processing steps:
   a. submission
   b. scheduling
   c. execution
   d. output processing
   e. purging

5. Explain how JES3 allocation and dynamic allocation differ from standard step allocation.

6. Given sample job output, identify each of its components.

Topic 4

Understanding a complete MVS system

So far, the information I've presented in this chapter has related to basic MVS concepts. Now, in the last topic of this chapter, I'm going to broaden your understanding of how the MVS facilities you already know work together in a typical MVS system. In particular, you'll learn about two important activities that are required to establish a working MVS system: system generation and system initialization. Then, you'll learn about the DASD files that are required to support MVS. And finally, you'll learn about a variety of subsystems and other facilities you're likely to find on your MVS system.

System generation and initialization

As I said, system generation and initialization are activities that are required to establish a working MVS system. *System generation* is the process of creating an MVS system, and *system initialization* is the process of starting a previously generated MVS system. Both system generation and initialization are the responsibility of the systems programming staff, so unless you're a systems programmer, you don't have to worry about the overwhelming details of these activities. You'll better understand MVS, however, if you have a basic idea of how system generation and initialization work.

System generation   When an installation purchases the MVS operating system, IBM sends the basic components that make up MVS on a series of tapes, called *distribution libraries*. System generation, only a part of the overall process of installing MVS from the distribution libraries, selects and assembles the various components an installation needs to create a working MVS system. To control system generation, often called *sysgen*, a systems programmer codes special *macro instructions* that specify how the MVS components from the distribution libraries should be put together.

Interestingly, an installation must already have a working MVS system before it can generate a new one. That's because an existing MVS system is required to execute the sysgen macro instructions. Fortunately, most installations perform sysgen to upgrade to a newer version of MVS or to make changes to their current version. So they can use their current version of MVS to execute the sysgen.

For installations that don't already have an MVS system because they're converting from another operating system, such as DOS/VSE, the system installation process includes setting up a small, limited function MVS system that can execute the sysgen for the complete, full function MVS system.

The macro instructions a systems programmer codes for a sysgen fall generally into two categories. The first category of macro instructions define the system's hardware configuration. They're needed because MVS must know about every I/O device that's attached to the system. As a result, whenever a new I/O device is installed, the system must be generated again. (Actually, MVS lets you do a smaller, less time consuming type of sysgen called an *iogen* to change the I/O device configuration.)

The second category of macro instructions in a sysgen indicate which options of the operating system should be included. In particular, these instructions indicate whether JES2 or JES3 is used, what optional access methods are installed, and so on.

The output from sysgen is a series of *system libraries* that contain, among other things, the executable code that makes up the operating system. Later in this topic when I describe system data sets, you'll learn about the system libraries produced by sysgen.

System initialization   Once an MVS operating system has been generated, it can be used to control the operation of the computer system. To begin a system initialization, the system operator uses the system console to start an *Initial Program Load*, or *IPL*. That causes the computer system to clear its real storage and begin the process of loading MVS into storage from the system libraries. System initialization is a complicated process that I won't describe in detail. Just realize that when system initialization is complete, MVS is ready to process your work.

During system initialization, many options can be selected to affect how MVS will operate. In fact, the systems programmers and operators have more influence over MVS at initialization time than they do during sysgen. Initialization options come from one of two sources: the system operator or a special system library called SYS1.PARMLIB. By specifying options in SYS1.PARMLIB, MVS can be initialized with little operator intervention.

System data sets

As I mentioned, the result of a sysgen is a series of system libraries that contain the various components that make up the operating system. These libraries, along with other files, make up the *system data sets* that are required for MVS to operate properly. As I describe some of the more important system data sets, notice that the name of each begins with SYS1. That's the standard identifier for a system data set.

Some of the system data sets I'll describe here must be placed on a key DASD volume known as the *system residence volume*; the volser of the system residence volume is usually *SYSRES*. When an operator begins a system initialization, he or she must identify the device address of the system residence volume; that's how IPL is able to locate the system data sets it needs to begin.

SYS1.NUCLEUS   *SYS1.NUCLEUS* is a partitioned data set that contains, among other things, the MVS nucleus program. The members of SYS1.NUCLEUS that contain the nucleus are created during sysgen. During system initialization, those members are brought into main storage and control is given to the nucleus. SYS1.NUCLEUS always resides on the system residence volume.

One of the members of SYS1.NUCLEUS contains a pointer to the master catalog. That's important because the system data sets are cataloged there. So, once the master catalog is available, the system data sets that aren't on the system residence volume can be located.

SYS1.PARMLIB   *SYS1.PARMLIB*, as I've already mentioned, plays a key role during system initialization. It contains about 30 members that specify various options MVS is to use as it is initialized. Although some information is placed in SYS1.PARMLIB automatically by sysgen, most of the SYS1.PARMLIB options are coded directly by the systems programmer. In addition, during initialization, the system operator can change the options specified in SYS1.PARMLIB.

SYS1.LINKLIB and SYS1.LPALIB   Two partitioned data sets, *SYS1.LINKLIB* and *SYS1.LPALIB*, contain executable programs that are either a part of the operating system or are written by users. There's an important difference between the two libraries. As its name indicates, SYS1.LPALIB is the library that contains modules that are a part of the link pack area (LPA). During system initialization, all of the members of SYS1.LPALIB are read into virtual storage in the link pack area. As a result, they're always available in storage for any program that needs them. Heavily used portions of the operating system, such as access methods, are usually placed in SYS1.LPALIB. In contrast, programs in SYS1.LINKLIB are not read into storage until they're required.

SYS1.MACLIB   *SYS1.MACLIB* is a partitioned data set that contains the macro instructions that are a part of MVS. That includes not only the macro instructions that are used for sysgen, but also the macro instructions that provide a standard interface to the operating system's facilities, particularly the access methods. Unless you're an assembler language programmer, you probably won't use SYS1.MACLIB.

SYS1.PROCLIB   *SYS1.PROCLIB* is a partitioned data set whose members, called *procedures*, contain JCL statements. JCL procedures are best suited for jobs that are used over and over again. By placing those jobs in the procedure library, each user can use the procedure rather than code the job's JCL statements again. You'll learn how to use and create procedures in chapter 7.

SYS1.CMDLIB   *SYS1.CMDLIB* is a partitioned data set that contains the program modules that implement various TSO commands you can enter from a TSO terminal. If you use TSO, you'll frequently use the commands stored in this data set.

Page and swap data sets   As you learned in the first topic of this chapter, MVS uses *page data sets* to hold individual pages of virtual storage when they are paged out of real storage. And, when an entire address space is swapped out of virtual storage, some of its pages are stored in a *swap data set*. Typically, eight or ten page data sets are provided with a total capacity of about 250 to 300MB. One of the page data sets is used for the PLPA (pageable link pack area), another for all other common areas, and a third is optionally used as a backup copy of the PLPA and common area page data sets. The remaining page data sets are used for private address spaces.

As for swap data sets, an installation typically provides three or four, with a total capacity of about 20 to 30MB. Of course, the number and size of page and swap data sets can vary dramatically from one installation to the next. I've given numbers here just for the sake of perspective.

Other system data sets   There are many other system data sets besides the ones I've described here. You already know about one: the master catalog. Two other data sets are used to diagnose problems within MVS: *SYS1.LOGREC* contains information about hardware problems, and *dump data sets* (named SYS1.DUMP00, SYS1.DUMP01, and so on) contain *storage dumps* that record the contents of virtual storage when an MVS system component fails. In addition, most of the MVS subsystems and facilities I'll describe next require their own system data sets.

Subsystems and other MVS facilities

So far in this chapter, I've discussed facilities that are a direct part of the MVS operating system or its job entry subsystems, JES2 and JES3. In addition, though, a complete production MVS system contains a variety of other software products. As a result, in addition to being familiar with the critical components of MVS itself, you also need to know about the other IBM software products that make up a complete system.

Some of the facilities I'll describe here are considered to be subsystems. Strictly speaking, a *subsystem* is a software product that operates in its own address space under the control of MVS. What it does within the address space, however, is of no concern to MVS. Within an address space, a subsystem may provide services that duplicate services provided by the operating system. For example, two of the subsystems you'll learn about here provide multiprogramming facilities that duplicate the multiprogramming facilities provided by MVS.

Every MVS installation has a *primary subsystem* that you already know about: it's the job entry subsystem, JES2 or JES3. In other words, JES2 and JES3 both run in their own address space. And, they provide services that are normally associated with an operating system: job management and spooling.

Frankly, the distinction between a subsystem and a component of MVS is more technical than practical. Some of the components I'll describe aren't subsystems, but they provide important services and have as broad a scope as a subsystem. So don't worry much about the distinction.

TSO and ISPF   *TSO*, which stands for *Time Sharing Option*, is a subsystem that lets terminal users invoke MVS facilities interactively. TSO does this by treating each terminal user as a job. In fact, when you log on to TSO, TSO creates a JCL stream and submits it to JES2/JES3 for processing. Each TSO user is given a unique address space and can allocate data sets and invoke programs just as a batch job can.

ISPF, which stands for *Interactive System Productivity Facility*, runs as a part of TSO and takes advantages of the full-screen capabilities of 3270 terminals. You'll most likely use a part of ISPF called *PDF*, or *Program Development Facility*, as you develop programs and job streams. In chapter 4, you'll learn enough about ISPF to create jobs and submit them for processing.

Telecommunications   For a system to support any terminal devices, local or remote, it must include a *telecommunications (TC) access method*.

Although you can write assembler language programs that use TC access method services directly, you're more likely to use them through another IBM software product that's designed to manage terminal processing, such as TSO. Although there are other, lower function TC access methods, most MVS installations use the most powerful TC access method: the *Virtual Telecommunication Access Method*, or *VTAM*. VTAM is actually a part of a comprehensive telecommunications product called *SNA*, which stands for *System Network Architecture*.

VTAM is considered to be a subsystem because it runs in its own address space. As a result, VTAM is able to provide centralized control over all of the terminal devices attached to an MVS system. Each VTAM terminal device is allocated to the VTAM address space. *VTAM application programs*, which run in other address spaces, communicate with those terminal devices indirectly: They issue requests to VTAM, which in turn services the request for the appropriate terminal. TSO and other telecommunications programs like CICS/VS and IMS DC, which you'll learn about in a moment, are themselves VTAM application programs.

CICS   CICS (*Customer Information Control System*) works with VTAM to support large networks of terminals that can run interactive application programs written in a variation of the COBOL programming language. CICS runs in its own address space and provides multiprogramming within its address space. In other words, CICS manages the execution of many application programs that communicate with terminal devices; multiprogramming within a CICS address space is transparent to, and subordinate to, the multiprogramming operation of MVS itself.

IMS   IMS (*Information Management System*) consists of two components: DL/I and Data Communications. The *DL/I* component of IMS lets users set up and maintain complex hierarchical data bases that can be processed by application programs run as batch jobs.

If the optional *Data Communications* component of IMS (*IMS DC*) is used, you can code interactive application programs that use IMS data bases and communicate with terminals. Like CICS, IMS DC implements its own multiprogramming that's transparent to MVS. IMS DC multiprogramming is more like MVS multiprogramming than CICS multiprogramming, however. The *IMS control region* (in its own address space) schedules application programs for execution in *dependent regions* (also in separate address spaces). The control region also manages communication between the application programs, data bases, and terminals.

DB2   Like IMS, *DB2* (which stands for *DataBase 2*) is a database management system. It manages relational databases that can be accessed using *SQL* (*Structured Query Language*). Depending on an installation's needs, DB2 may or may not be set up so that an independent address space is utilized to manage concurrent access to DB2 data.

Unlike IMS, DB2 does not provide its own online environment. Instead, online DB2 programs are generally written so that they run under CICS.

RACF   An important consideration in any MVS installation is maintaining adequate security so data can't be accessed by unauthorized users. To provide that security, most installations use a comprehensive security package called *Resource Access Control Facility*, or *RACF*. RACF identifies both users and resources, such as data sets. Then, whenever a user attempts to access a resource, RACF ensures that the user has the correct authority. RACF is not a subsystem, but rather a set of routines stored in the PLPA that are invoked by a user's address space whenever needed.

SMF   Another important consideration in most MVS installations is the ability to keep track of which users are using the system so that they can be properly billed. *System Management Facility*, or *SMF*, monitors jobs as they execute and records information such as the amount of CPU time used, the amount of DASD I/O that was performed, the number of print records that were created, and so on. This information is recorded in special data sets so that it can be used as the basis for billing.

Language translators, the linkage editor, and the loader   *Language translators* are the programs that convert source programs into *object modules*. One language translator, the assembler, is supplied as a part of MVS. Other language translators, like the COBOL, PL/I, and FORTRAN IV compilers, are separate products. The purpose of the language translators is to reduce the programming time required to prepare a working object program. As a result, they all print diagnostic (error) listings to help the programmer correct clerical errors. In addition, they often provide debugging tools to help the programmer test the program.

The *linkage editor* program, supplied as a part of MVS, converts object modules into executable programs called *load modules* that can be loaded into virtual storage and executed. The *loader* program is like the linkage editor except that instead of creating a permanent load module, the loader program creates a temporary load module, executes it, and then deletes it. The loader is used mostly during program testing. In chapter 15, you'll learn how to code jobs that use these program development facilities.

Utility programs   Certain routine processing functions, such as copying files and sorting records within a file, are common to most computer installations. As a result, MVS provides a set of general purpose *utility programs* (or *utilities*) to perform those functions. When you invoke a utility program, you can supply parameters to specify the exact processing it should do. In topic 3 of this chapter, you saw a job that used the most basic MVS utility program: IEBGENER, which produces a copy of a data set. In chapter 16, you'll learn more about this utility as well as other utilities that come with MVS.

Discussion

Now that you've learned about the process of system generation and initialization, the system data sets required for an MVS system to operate, and the various subsystems and components that make up a complete MVS system, you have the perspective you need to learn how to use MVS. Remember, however, that the purpose of this topic is to provide just that: perspective. You don't *have* to know any of the information this topic presented to code JCL statements. So don't spend a lot of time struggling with subjects that may have confused you, like how CICS manages multiprogramming or why IMS DC requires several address spaces. As long as you have the perspective this topic presented, you're ready to move on to chapter 4, where you'll learn how to use TSO/ISPF to create and maintain members that contain JCL statements.

Terminology

system generation	SYS1.NUCLEUS
system initialization	SYS1.PARMLIB
distribution library	SYS1.LINKLIB
sysgen	SYS1.LPALIB
macro instruction	SYS1.MACLIB
iogen	SYS1.PROCLIB
system library	procedure
Initial Program Load	SYS1.CMDLIB
IPL	page data set
system data set	swap data set
system residence volume	SYS1.LOGREC
SYSRES	dump data set

storage dump
subsystem
primary subsystem
TSO
Time Sharing Option
ISPF
Interactive System
    Productivity Facility
PDF
Program Development Facility
telecommunications access method
TC access method
Virtual Telecommunication Access
    Method
VTAM
SNA
System Network Architecture
VTAM application program
CICS
Customer Information Control System
IMS
Information Management System

DL/I
IMS Data Communications
IMS DC
IMS control region
dependent region
DB2
Database 2
SQL
Structured Query Language
Resource Access Control
    Facility
RACF
System Management
    Facility
SMF
language translator
object module
linkage editor
load module
loader
utility program
utility

Objectives

1. Distinguish between system generation and system initialization.

2. Identify the general contents of each of these system data sets:
    a. SYS1.NUCLEUS
    b. SYS1.PARMLIB
    c. SYS1.LINKLIB
    d. SYS1.LPALIB
    e. SYS1.MACLIB
    f. SYS1.PROCLIB
    g. SYS1.CMDLIB

3. Describe the functions of:
    a. TSO
    b. VTAM
    c. CICS
    d. IMS and IMS DC
    e. DB2
    f. RACF
    g. SMF

**Chapter
4**

How to use ISPF to create job streams and submit them for processing

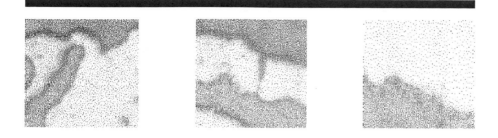

In chapter 3, you learned that TSO is an MVS component that lets terminal users access MVS facilities. ISPF, which runs under the control of TSO, provides a powerful and comprehensive program development environment that includes a full-screen text editor and facilities to manage background job processing. In this chapter, you'll learn how to use ISPF's full-screen editor to create and maintain job streams. And, you'll learn how to use ISPF's background job management facilities to submit those jobs, monitor their progress, and display their output.

Since you don't have to know how to use TSO and ISPF to understand the chapters that follow, you can skip this chapter for now and come back to it when you're ready to enter a job. I think it's best to read this chapter now, though, so you'll be able to apply the skills this chapter teaches as you learn JCL.

Incidentally, not all MVS installations use ISPF for text entry. For example, some installations use an IBM product called CMS (the Conversational Monitor System) for text entry. And some installations use text editors developed by third-party software suppliers. Of course, you need to learn how to use the text editor that's available at your installation. If that's not ISPF, I suggest you skip this chapter altogether and review some introductory material for your text editor instead.

Basic skills for working with ISPF

Before you can use ISPF to create a job stream, you need to learn some basic skills for working with it. First, you need to know how to access ISPF. Then, you need to become familiar with the format of the ISPF panels, and you need to know how to use the ISPF menus and PF keys to perform functions within ISPF. Finally, you need to know how to terminate ISPF.

How to access ISPF   Although the exact procedures you use to access ISPF vary from one installation to the next, three things must always happen. First, you must establish a session between your terminal and TSO. Second, you must identify yourself to TSO. And third, you must start ISPF. Typically, the first two steps are combined by entering a single LOGON command that both connects and identifies you to TSO. Once you've gained access to TSO, you usually start ISPF by entering this command:

    ISPF

As I said, though, logon procedures vary. So find out from your supervisor the exact procedures used to access ISPF.

Once you've accessed ISPF, you'll see the *primary option menu* shown in figure 4-1. As you can see, ISPF provides many functions. In this chapter, I describe just two of them: the edit option and the OUTLIST utility, which lets you examine job output.

The format of ISPF panels   The format of all ISPF display screens, called *panels*, is similar. In particular, the top two lines of all panels are reserved for system information, the third line is optionally used to display error messages, and the remainder of the screen (including line 3 if no message is displayed) is used to display data. In addition, this graphic:

    ===>

is used to indicate fields where you can enter data. (You don't always have to enter data in these fields, though.)

The first line of each panel contains a title. For example, the title in figure 4-1 is this:

    ISPF/PDF PRIMARY OPTION MENU

In addition, the right-hand side of line 1 is often used to display a short message. During an edit operation, for example, the current line and column numbers are displayed in this area. And short error messages are often displayed there, too.

```
--------------------- ISPF/PDF PRIMARY OPTION MENU ---------------------
OPTION  ===>
                                                     USERID  - SYDOE
      0  ISPF PARMS  - Specify terminal and user parameters   TIME  - 10:38
      1  BROWSE      - Display source data or output listings  TERMINAL - 3278
      2  EDIT        - Create or change source data            PF KEYS - 24
      3  UTILITIES   - Perform utility functions
      4  FOREGROUND  - Invoke language processors in foreground
      5  BATCH       - Submit job for language processing
      6  COMMAND     - Enter TSO command or CLIST
      7  DIALOG TEST - Perform dialog testing
      8  LM UTILITIES- Perform library administrator utility functions
      9  IBM PRODUCTS- Additional IBM program development products
     10  SCLM        - Software Configuration and Library Manager
      C  CHANGES     - Display summary of changes for this release
      S  SDSF        - Spool Display and Search Facility
      T  TUTORIAL    - Display information about ISPF/PDF
      X  EXIT        - Terminate ISPF using log and list defaults

Enter END command to terminate ISPF
```

Figure 4-1   The ISPF primary option menu

You use the second line to enter commands to be processed by ISPF. For a menu screen, the command area is identified like this:

```
OPTION ===>
```

For other screens, the command area looks like this:

```
COMMAND ===>
```

In either case, you can enter a variety of ISPF commands in the command area.

The third screen line is normally blank, although it contains data when you're using the edit option. Whenever a short error message appears in line 1, you can obtain a longer version of it in line 3 by entering HELP in the command area or by pressing the PF1 or PF13 keys.

How to use ISPF menus   ISPF menus are easy to use. To select a menu option, you simply enter the option's number or letter in the command area. For example, to select the edit option from the primary option menu, you enter 2, like this:

```
OPTION ===> 2
```

When you press the enter key, ISPF displays the first panel of the edit function.

PF key	Command	Meaning
PF1/13	HELP	Has two functions: (1) invokes an online tutorial that displays information about how to use various ISPF functions; (2) when a short error message is displayed on line 1, causes a longer error message that includes additional information to be displayed on line 3.
PF3/15	END	Returns to the previous panel.
PF4/16	RETURN	Returns directly to the primary option menu.
PF7/19	UP	Moves the screen window towards the beginning of the member.
PF8/20	DOWN	Moves the screen window towards the end of the member.
PF10/22	LEFT	Moves the screen window left.
PF11/23	RIGHT	Moves the screen window right.

Figure 4-2   Default meanings for commonly used PF keys

Many of ISPF's primary functions lead to additional menus. For example, if you select option 3 (utilities), the next panel displayed is another menu with additional functions. You can easily bypass the second menu screen by specifying both options at the primary menu, using a period to separate the selections. For example, if you enter this response at the primary option menu:

```
OPTION ===> 3.8
```

the utilities menu isn't displayed. Instead, option 8 of the utilities menu is automatically selected. (Option 3.8 is the OUTLIST utility, which I'll describe later in this chapter.)

How to use PF keys   Besides entering commands in the command area, you can also control certain ISPF functions using the program function (PF) keys. Figure 4-2 shows the default meanings of the more commonly used PF keys. These defaults may be changed at your installation, so be sure to find out what function each key performs on your system.

Notice that each of the PF key assignments are duplicated. For example, PF1 and PF13 have the same meaning. The reason for this is simple. All 3270 terminals have either 12 or 24 function keys. To operate PF1 through PF12 on either type of terminal, two key strokes are required (ALT and the appropriate key). On terminals with 24 function keys, however, only one keystroke is required to operate PF13 through PF24. By duplicating the PF key assignments, then, users with 24 keys can use PF13 through PF24 to cut down on keystrokes, while users with just 12 PF keys still have access to all the functions.

Many of the PF keys described in figure 4-2 are self explanatory; others will be discussed later in this chapter. Now, I'll explain two of them: PF3/15 and PF4/16.

PF3/15, called the end key, terminates an ISPF function. Whenever you've completed processing an ISPF function and wish to return to the previous menu, use PF3/15.

PF4/16, called the return key, is similar in function to the end key. The difference is that PF4/16 returns you directly to the primary option menu, bypassing any intermediate panels.

You can also use PF4/16 to move directly from one option to another. You do this by entering an equal sign followed by the desired primary option selection in the command area, like this:

```
OPTION ===> =3.2
```

Then, when you press PF4/16, ISPF takes you directly to option 3.2. It's the same as returning to the primary option menu, then selecting option 3.2, but it requires only one step.

How to terminate ISPF   To terminate ISPF, you select option X from the primary option menu. That returns you directly to TSO. To access ISPF again, enter the ISPF command. Or, to log off, enter this command:

```
LOGOFF
```

This command ends your TSO session. After you've logged off, you'll have to log on to access ISPF again.

How to use the ISPF editor

The ISPF *edit option* lets you enter data and store it in a library member. In addition, it lets you retrieve data from a library member and make changes to it. The ISPF editor provides many advanced features that make it a powerful tool. For now, though, I'm just going to show you the most basic elements of the editor. You can learn about the more advanced features from other sources.

How to start an edit session   To access ISPF's edit option, you select option 2 from the primary option menu. ISPF then displays the edit entry panel, shown in figure 4-3. On it, you enter the name of the data set you want to process. And, if it's a partitioned data

```
------------------------------- EDIT - ENTRY PANEL -------------------------------

  COMMAND ===>

  ISPF LIBRARY:
     PROJECT ===> SYDOE
     GROUP   ===> TEST        ===>           ===>           ===>
     TYPE    ===> CNTL
     MEMBER  ===> SYDOEJ            (Blank or pattern for member selection list)

  OTHER PARTITIONED OR SEQUENTIAL DATA SET:
     DATA SET NAME   ===>
     VOLUME SERIAL   ===>            (If not cataloged)

  DATA SET PASSWORD ===>            (If password protected)

  PROFILE NAME      ===>            (Blank defaults to data set type)

  INITIAL MACRO     ===>            LMF LOCK   ===> YES     (YES, NO, or NEVER)

  FORMAT NAME       ===>            MIXED MODE ===> NO      (YES or NO)
```

Figure 4-3   The edit entry panel

set, you enter the name of the member within it. For the purposes of this discussion, I'll assume partitioned data sets are being used. In figure 4-3, I shaded the entries I made.

ISPF uses a more restrictive naming convention than MVS does. Under ISPF, library names consist of three components: project, group, and type. In practice, the project component of a library name is often your user id. The group name is a name you make up to identify the contents of the library. And type indicates the type of data stored in the member, such as COBOL source code, JCL statements, and so on. Figure 4-4 shows some common ISPF library types. To form the MVS data set name for the library, ISPF simply combines the project, group, and type components. So, in figure 4-3, I'm accessing a data set named SYDOE.TEST.CNTL.

After the three components of the library name, you specify the name of the member you wish to process. In figure 4-3, I specified SYDOEJ as the member name. If a member named SYDOEJ exists, ISPF retrieves it for editing. If not, ISPF creates a member using that name. The library itself must already exist, however. Contact your supervisor to find out what library to use or how to create your own library.

Type	Meaning
ASM	Assembler language source code
CLIST	Command procedure containing TSO commands
CNTL	Job stream containing JCL statements
COBOL	COBOL source code
DATA	Uppercase text data
FORT	FORTRAN source code
OBJ	Executable object module
PLI	PL/I source code
TEXT	Upper and lowercase text data

Figure 4-4   Common data set types

In this case, the member I specified doesn't exist. So, ISPF displays the panel shown in figure 4-5. If the member did exist, the display would be similar, but would include data from the member. In either case, the edit display consists of three distinct areas. The top two lines of the screen form the *heading area*; in it, you can enter commands that invoke various editing functions. The leftmost six columns of lines 3 through 24 form the *line command area*. In it, you can enter *line commands* that affect specific lines. The rest of the panel is the *screen window*; in it, data from the member you're editing is displayed. Since figure 4-5 shows an editing session for a new member, no data is displayed in the screen window.

How to edit data   Figure 4-6 shows the edit data display after I've keyed data into it and pressed the enter key. To enter data in the screen window, you just key in the characters you want in the positions you want. You can use the terminal's cursor control keys to move the cursor around the screen. If you want to change the text displayed on the screen, just type the new data over the old. When you're finished, press the enter key. As you can see in figure 4-6, ISPF removed the blank lines I didn't key in and replaced the apostrophes in the line command area with line numbers.

Once you've filled a screen, you'll need to scroll down to be able to enter more data. That's where the PF keys come in. If you'll look back to figure 4-2, you'll see that PF7 and PF8 scroll backwards and forwards through the source member. At the right-hand side of line

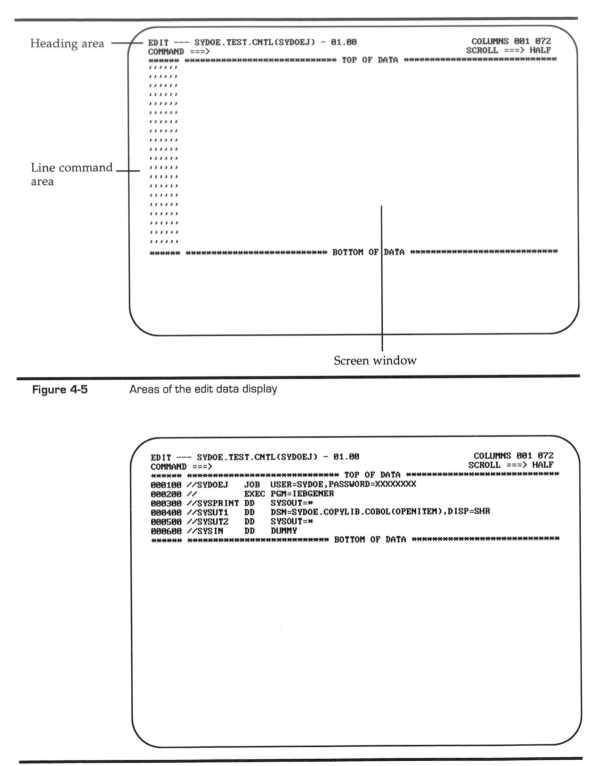

Heading area

Line command area

Screen window

Figure 4-5   Areas of the edit data display

Figure 4-6   The edit data display after data has been entered

Inserting lines

I	Insert a single line following this line.
I*n*	Insert *n* lines following this line.

Deleting lines

D	Delete this line.
D*n*	Delete *n* lines starting with this line.
DD	Delete the block of lines beginning with the first DD command and ending with the second DD command.

Repeating lines

R	Repeat this line.
R*n*	Repeat this line *n* times.
RR	Repeat a block of lines.
RR*n*	Repeat a block of lines *n* times.

Copying and moving lines

C	Copy this line.
C*n*	Copy *n* lines.
CC	Copy a block of lines.
M	Move this line.
M*n*	Move *n* lines.
MM	Move a block of lines.
A	Copy or move lines after this line.
A*n*	Repeat the copy or move *n* times after this line.
B	Copy or move lines before this line.
B*n*	Repeat the copy or move *n* times before this line.

Figure 4-7   Basic line commands

2 is a field labeled SCROLL; in it, you can specify how many lines to scroll each time you use PF7 or PF8. You can specify PAGE or HALF to scroll a full or half page of data at a time. Or, you can enter a number to specify how many lines to scroll. For example, if you change the scroll amount to 20, the display moves forward 20 lines each time you press PF8. In figure 4-6, the scroll amount is HALF.

As I mentioned, the line command area lets you enter commands that affect individual lines. Figure 4-7 shows the most useful of the line commands. As you can see, you can use line commands to delete lines, insert new lines, repeat lines, and move or copy lines. Figure 4-8 shows how to use the I and D line commands to insert and delete lines. In part 1, I entered the shaded line commands: The D command will delete line 300, and the I2 command will insert two lines following line 500. In part 2, you can see the

```
EDIT --- SYDOE.TEST.CNTL(SYDOEJ) - 01.00                    COLUMNS 001 072
COMMAND ===>                                               SCROLL ===> HALF
****** ***************************** TOP OF DATA ****************************
000100 //SYDOEJ    JOB  USER=SYDOE,PASSWORD=XXXXXXXX
000200 //          EXEC PGM=IEBGENER
D00300 //SYSPRINT DD   SYSOUT=*
000400 //SYSUT1    DD   DSN=SYDOE.COPYLIB.COBOL(OPENITEM),DISP=SHR
I20500 //SYSUT2    DD   SYSOUT=*
000600 //SYSIN     DD   DUMMY
****** ***************************** BOTTOM OF DATA *************************
```

Figure 4-8   Using the I and D line commands (part 1 of 2)

```
EDIT --- SYDOE.TEST.CNTL(SYDOEJ) - 01.00                    COLUMNS 001 072
COMMAND ===>                                               SCROLL ===> HALF
****** ***************************** TOP OF DATA ****************************
000100 //SYDOEJ    JOB  USER=SYDOE,PASSWORD=XXXXXXXX
000200 //          EXEC PGM=IEBGENER
000400 //SYSUT1    DD   DSN=SYDOE.COPYLIB.COBOL(OPENITEM),DISP=SHR
000500 //SYSUT2    DD   SYSOUT=*
'',''''
'',''''
000600 //SYSIN     DD   DUMMY
****** ***************************** BOTTOM OF DATA *************************
```

Figure 4-8   Using the I and D line commands (part 2 of 2)

Commands to locate specific lines or text

LOCATE line-number	Moves the screen window directly to the indicated line.
FIND text	Searches for the specified text, beginning with the current line. If the text contains commas or spaces, enclose it in apostrophes.
FIND text FIRST	Searches for the specified text, beginning with the first line of the member.

Commands to store and retrieve data in other members

COPY member-name	Retrieves data from the specified member; use an A or B line command to specify where the data should be placed. If you omit member-name, ISPF displays a panel that lets you enter a library and member name.
MOVE member-name	Same as COPY, but the input member is deleted.
CREATE member-name	Creates a member; use the C or M line command to specify which lines should be placed in the new member. If you omit member-name, ISPF displays a panel that lets you enter a library and member name.
REPLACE member-name	Same as CREATE, but if the specified member already exists, it's replaced.

Commands to terminate edit

END (PF3/15)	Save changes and return to the edit entry panel.
RETURN (PF4/16)	Save changes and return to the primary option menu.
CANCEL	Return to the edit entry panel without saving changes.

Figure 4-9   Useful primary commands

results of these two commands: Line 300 is gone, and there are two blank lines following line 500.

To copy or move lines, you must enter two commands. First, enter a C or M line command to mark the lines you want to copy or move. If you want to copy or move more than one line, specify a number after C or M or use CC/MM in pairs to mark a range of lines. Then, use an A or B command to mark the location where you want the copied or moved lines placed. If you use the A line command, the lines are placed after the line you specify; if you use the B line command, the lines are placed before the line you specify.

Besides line commands, you can also enter *primary commands* in the command area. Figure 4-9 shows some basic primary commands. Using them, you can locate specific lines or text, store and retrieve data in other members, and terminate the edit option.

How to terminate an edit session The usual way to end an editing session is to press the end key (PF3/15). When you do this, ISPF saves your changes in the library member and returns to the entry panel, where you can specify another member to edit. If you use PF4/16 instead, your changes are saved and you're returned to the primary option menu.

If you want to terminate the edit session without saving your changes, you can enter the CANCEL primary command in the command area. CANCEL returns you to the edit entry panel without copying your edited member back to the library. So any changes you made to the member are lost.

How to manage background job processing

Once you've used the editor to enter the JCL statements and data for a job, you can use ISPF job processing facilities to submit the job for processing in a batch address space. Then, you can use the OUTLIST utility to monitor the job's progress, display the job's output, and route the job's output to a printer or delete it altogether.

How to submit a job There are several ways to submit a job for batch processing under ISPF. The easiest way is to enter a SUBMIT command while you're editing the member that contains the job stream. The SUBMIT command writes the entire member to an internal reader, which places the job in the JES spool so it will be scheduled and executed. There aren't any options to specify on the SUBMIT command, so just enter the word SUBMIT as a primary command.

ISPF acknowledges your submitted job by displaying a message like this near the bottom of the screen:

```
JOB SYDOEJ(JOB02697) SUBMITTED
***
```

Here, SYDOEJ is the name of the job, and JOB02697 is the job identifier used to uniquely identify the job (more than one job can have the same name). I suggest you write down the job identifier each time you submit a job, because you may need to refer to it later.

Notice the three asterisks that appear under the message. Three asterisks are displayed whenever ISPF invokes a function that displays data on the screen in a line-by-line format rather than using ISPF's full-screen display facilities. The three asterisks simply mean that you must press the enter key to continue.

How to use the OUTLIST utility To monitor a job's progress and control its output, you use the OUTLIST utility. To invoke the OUTLIST utility, first invoke the utilities menu (option 3 from the

```
------------------------- OUTLIST UTILITY -------------------------
OPTION  ===>

     L - List job names/id's via the TSO status command
     D - Delete job output from SYSOUT hold queue
     P - Print job output and delete from SYSOUT hold queue
     R - Requeue job output to a new output class
     blank - Display job output

  FOR JOB TO BE SELECTED:
     JOBNAME ===> SYDOEJ
     CLASS   ===>
     JOBID   ===>

  FOR JOB TO BE REQUEUED:
     NEW OUTPUT CLASS ===>

  FOR JOB TO BE PRINTED:                     (A for ANSI   )
     PRINTER CARRIAGE CONTROL ===>           (M for machine )
                                             (Blank for none)
```

Figure 4-10   The Outlist utility entry panel

primary option menu). Then, select option 8. Alternatively, you can just key in 3.8 from the primary option menu. And if you want to go directly from the editor to the OUTLIST utility, enter =3.8 and press PF4/16.

Figure 4-10 shows the OUTLIST entry panel. As you can see, the OUTLIST utility provides five functions. You invoke four of them using a one-letter option code: L, D, P, or R. The fifth option is invoked by leaving the option field blank.

If you select option L, ISPF invokes a TSO function that examines the JES spool for jobs you submitted. For each job it finds, it displays the job's name, identifier, and status, like this:

```
JOB SYDOEJ(JOB02697) ON OUTPUT QUEUE
***
```

Here, the job SYDOEJ has completed execution and its output is waiting in the JES spool. Again, the three asterisks mean you must press the enter key to return to ISPF.

To display a job's output, you must enter the job's name and, if there's more than one job with the same name, the job identifier. In figure 4-10, I entered SYDOEJ as the job name. Figure 4-11 shows how ISPF displays the job's output using its browse facility (option 1 from the primary option menu). This facility is similar to the edit

```
 BROWSE - SYDOE.SPF201.OUTLIST -------------------- LINE 000000 COL   001 080
 COMMAND ===>                                          SCROLL ===> PAGE
 ************************************ TOP OF DATA ******************************
 1                    J E S 2   J O B   L O G  --  S Y S T E M   S Y S 2  --  N O
 0
  11.44.52 JOB 2697  ICH70001I SYDOE    LAST ACCESS AT 11:42:13 ON MONDAY, NOVE
  11.44.52 JOB 2697  $HASP373 SYDOEJ    STARTED - INIT 15 - CLASS A - SYS SYS2
  11.44.53 JOB 2697  IEF403I SYDOEJ - STARTED - TIME=11.44.53
  11.44.55 JOB 2697  -                                             --TIMINGS
  11.44.55 JOB 2697  -JOBNAME  STEPNAME PROCSTEP    RC   EXCP   CONN     TCB
  11.44.55 JOB 2697  -SYDOEJ                        00     18     69     .00
  11.44.55 JOB 2697  IEF404I SYDOEJ - ENDED - TIME=11.44.55
  11.44.55 JOB 2697  -SYDOEJ    ENDED.  NAME-EATON RM 2S324      TOTAL TCB CPU
  11.44.55 JOB 2697  $HASP395 SYDOEJ    ENDED
 0------ JES2 JOB STATISTICS ------
 -    01 NOV 93 JOB EXECUTION DATE
 -           13 CARDS READ
 -           91 SYSOUT PRINT RECORDS
 -            0 SYSOUT PUNCH RECORDS
 -            5 SYSOUT SPOOL KBYTES
 -         0.05 MINUTES EXECUTION TIME
          1 //SYDOEJ   JOB USER=SYDOE,PASSWORD=
          2 //         EXEC PGM=IEBGENER
          3 //SYSPRINT DD  SYSOUT=*
```

Figure 4-11   A browse panel displaying job output

option, but it doesn't let you change data. You can, however, use the scrolling PF keys (PF7/19 and PF8/20) to move forward and backward through the output listing. And, because each print line is longer than 80 characters, you can use PF10/22 and PF11/23 to scroll right and left. In addition, you can use the LOCATE and FIND commands to search for specific lines or text.

After you've displayed a job's output, you may want to obtain a printed copy of it. There are two ways to do that. First, you can select the P option and direct the output to a particular printer. Or, you can use the R option to change the job's output class from a held class to a class associated with a particular printer. If you don't need a printed copy of the job's output, you can delete it using the D option.

Discussion

As I said at the start, this chapter gives you just enough information to start using ISPF so you can enter and submit jobs. Naturally, there's much more to learn about ISPF. So experiment a bit, and turn to other materials for more information. The IBM manual *Interactive System Productivity Facility/Program Development Facility Program Reference* describes all of the facilities available from ISPF. In addition, my book *MVS TSO, Part 1: Concepts and ISPF* explains how to use ISPF editing facilities as well as many other facilities of ISPF and TSO. Nevertheless, the small introduction to ISPF this chapter provides should be enough to get you started.

Terminology

primary option menu
panel
edit option
heading area
line command area
line command
screen window
primary command

Objective

Use ISPF facilities to create a JCL member, submit it for background processing, and display the resulting job output.

Exercises

1. Find out the procedures used at your installation to log on and access ISPF, including your TSO user-id and password.

2. Use the ISPF editor to create a library member that contains the following JCL statements (find out from your supervisor or instructor the details for coding the JOB card and the library and member name to use):

    ```
    //jobname   JOB   USER=user-id,PASSWORD=xxxxxxxx
    //          EXEC  PGM=IEBGENER
    //SYSPRINT DD    SYSOUT=*
    //SYSUT1    DD    *
    This is a sample test file.
    This is a sample test file.
    This is a sample test file.
    This is a sample test file.
    This is a sample test file.
    /*
    //SYSUT2    DD    SYSOUT=*
    //SYSIN     DD    DUMMY
    ```

3. Submit the job created in exercise 2 for processing.

4. Use the OUTLIST utility to view the results of your job. If the job did not execute because of a JCL error, use the ISPF editor to correct the mistake and resubmit the job.

Section 2

Job Control Language

The three chapters in this section present a complete professional subset of MVS Job Control Language. In chapter 5, you'll learn how to use the basic forms of the basic MVS JCL statements to perform tasks that are required for just about every job you code. In chapter 6, you'll build on what you learn in chapter 5 by learning how to use specific MVS facilities to manage job and program execution, data set allocation, and SYSOUT processing. Finally, in chapter 7, you'll learn how to use and create pre-coded segments of JCL called *procedures*.

This section represents the core of the entire book, and chapter 5 is the core of this section. As a result, I suggest you invest as much time as it takes to master all of the material in chapter 5 before you move on to chapters 6 and 7. The benefits will be well worth the extra time that's required.

**Chapter
5**

Basic MVS Job Control Language

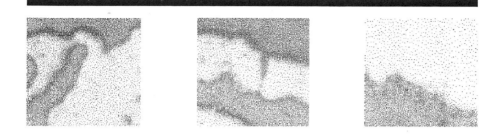

In this chapter, you'll learn how to use a basic subset of MVS Job Control Language. Topic 1 explains the rules you must follow when coding JCL statements. Then, topic 2 shows you how to code the JCL statements that make up the basic subset. To be sure you understand how those statements work together, topic 3 illustrates them in two real-life job streams.

Don't think that because this chapter presents a "subset" of JCL, you won't learn anything of substance. The JCL statements you learn to code in this chapter are the ones you'll use most often as you develop jobs for production. In addition, the information presented in this chapter will serve as a foundation for what's in the chapters that follow. So be prepared to spend a lot of time studying this chapter. You need to master it.

Topic 1

How to code JCL statements

In chapter 3, you saw a simple job stream that used the IEBGENER program to copy the contents of a library member to a printer. The JCL for that job included a JOB statement to identify the job, an EXEC statement to invoke the IEBGENER program, and several DD statements to identify the data sets processed by IEBGENER. To properly code those statements, you must follow certain rules that govern punctuation, syntax, and so on. In this topic, you'll learn about those general rules so you'll be prepared to learn how to code actual JCL statements in the next topic.

Figure 5-1 presents an overview of the most commonly used JCL statements. You already know the basic functions of the first three: JOB, EXEC, and DD. You'll learn about the next three statements—delimiter, null, and comment—in this chapter. As for the other statements, you'll learn about them in chapters 6 and 7. As a result, by the time you've completed the chapters in this section (chapters 5 through 7), you'll have learned how to use all of the JCL statements in figure 5-1.

Before I begin, I want you to realize that besides the JCL statements shown in figure 5-1, you can also include *JES2* or *JES3 control statements* in your jobs, depending on whether your installation uses JES2 or JES3. Simply put, these control statements supply information that's processed directly by the job entry subsystem. I'll explain the rules for coding JES2 and JES3 control statements in chapter 6.

The basic format of a JCL statement

JCL statements are coded in 80-byte records, as if they were punched into 80-column cards. Although cards aren't typically used any more, JCL retains the 80-character card image format. That way, JCL statements can easily be edited using 3270 terminals, most of which also have an 80-character per line format. And even though they're usually entered at a terminal and stored in a DASD file, JCL statements are still commonly called cards.

Although JCL statements use an 80-character format, only 72 of the 80 characters are available to code JCL. The last eight columns of each record—columns 73 through 80—are reserved for an optional sequence number. If you use the ISPF editor to create and maintain JCL, the sequence numbers may or may not be automatically placed in each record. Either way, it doesn't matter.

Statement	Purpose
JOB	Identifies a job and supplies accounting information.
EXEC	Identifies a job step by indicating the name of the program to be executed.
DD	Identifies a data set to be allocated for the job step.
delimiter (/*)	Marks the end of an in-stream data set.
null (//)	Marks the end of a job.
comment (//*)	Provides comments.
PROC	Marks the beginning of a procedure.
PEND	Marks the end of a procedure.
INCLUDE	Copies statements from another library member into the job.
IF/THEN/ELSE/ENDIF	Provides conditional execution of a job step.
JCLLIB	Identifies a private procedure library.
SET	Sets default values for symbolic variables.
OUTPUT	Supplies options for SYSOUT processing.

Figure 5-1   JCL statements

Within the 72 characters available in each record, you code JCL in a relatively free-form manner with just a few restrictions. Each JCL statement is divided into several fields, which are summarized in figure 5-2. Because the format in figure 5-2 is a bit obscure, figure 5-3 shows how the IEBGENER job presented in chapter 3 uses the JCL statement fields.

The identifier field   The *identifier field* identifies a record as a JCL statement. For most JCL statements, the identifier field occupies the first two character positions and must contain two slashes (//). There are two exceptions. First, the delimiter statement has a slash in column 1 and an asterisk in column 2 (/*). Second, the identifier field for a comment statement is three characters long: The first two columns contain slashes and the third contains an asterisk(//*). You'll learn about the delimiter and comment statements in topic 2 of this chapter.

The name field   The *name field* associates a name with a JCL statement. It's always required on a JOB statement, where it supplies a name for your job. It's optional on EXEC and DD statements, but it's usually coded on DD statements. In figure 5-3, the name field for the JOB statement is SYDOEJ; for the four DD statements, the names

---

Basic format of JCL statements

```
identifier [name] [operation] [parameters] [comments]
```

Explanation

identifier	Two slashes starting in column 1. Exceptions: (1) for a delimiter statement, /* starting in column 1; (2) for a comment statement, //* starting in column 1.
name	One to eight alphanumeric or national characters, starting with a letter or national character. Must begin in column 3 if coded.
operation	A valid operation code, such as JOB, EXEC, or DD. Must be preceded and followed by a space.
parameters	One or more parameters, depending on the operation. Individual parameters are separated from one another by commas, with no intervening spaces.
comments	Comments may follow the parameters, preceded by one space and not extending beyond column 71.

Figure 5-2   JCL statement fields

are SYSPRINT, SYSUT1, SYSUT2, and SYSIN. I didn't code a name field on the EXEC statement. The name field is not allowed on a delimiter, comment, or null statement.

If you code a name field, it must begin in column 3, right after the identifier field. It consists of from one to eight characters, which may be letters, numbers, or national characters (#, @, and $). The first character of a name must be a letter or a national character.

The operation field   The *operation field* follows the name field and specifies the statement's function. Delimiter, comment, and null statements don't have an operation field; their unique identifier fields indicate their functions.

The operation field can be coded anywhere on the card, as long as it's separated from the name field by at least one blank. Usually, though, I start the operation field in column 12. That leaves room for the two-character identifier field, an eight-character name field, and one space. And the listing is a bit easier to read if all the operation fields are lined up.

The parameters field   The *parameters field* begins at least one position after the end of the operation field and can extend into column 71; I usually start the parameters field in column 17 whether I'm coding a JOB, EXEC, or DD statement. That way, the parameters for each JCL statement line up. Within the parameters field, you code one or more *parameters* that supply information that influences how the statement is

```
  Identifier field   Operation    Parameters
         Name        field        field
         field
           |           |            |
           |           |            |
//SYDOEJ      JOB  USER=SYSDOE,PASSWORD=XXXXXXXX
//            EXEC PGM=IEBGENER
//SYSPRINT    DD   SYSOUT=*
//SYSUT1      DD   DSN=SYDOE.COPYLIB.COBOL(OPENITEM),DISP=SHR
//SYSUT2      DD   SYSOUT=*
//SYSIN       DD   DUMMY
```

Figure 5-3   JCL fields used in a sample IEBGENER job

processed. Learning how to code JCL is largely a matter of learning how to code parameters correctly. That's because there are just a few different types of statements, but most of them have dozens of parameters that can be coded in many different ways.

When a parameters field consists of more than one parameter, you separate the individual parameters with commas. MVS assumes that the parameters field is complete when it encounters a space, so don't include a space by accident. If you need to include a space as part of a parameter value, you must enclose the parameter value in apostrophes.

A parameter may be one of two types: positional or keyword. A *positional parameter* must occur in a specific position within the parameters field. In other words, MVS interprets the meaning of a positional parameter based on its position in the parameters field. If you need to omit a positional parameter, you may need to account for the missing parameter by coding an extra comma. You'll see many examples of this later, so don't let it confuse you now.

Most JCL parameters are *keyword parameters*. When you code a keyword parameter, you don't have to worry about its position in the parameters field. Instead, you identify the parameter by coding a keyword followed by an equals sign and a value, like this:

```
UNIT=SYSDA
```

Here, UNIT is the keyword; the value SYSDA is associated with the UNIT parameter. When you code a JCL statement that has more than one keyword parameter, you can code the parameters in any order you wish. However, keyword parameters must always come after any required positional parameters.

Some JCL parameters require *subparameters,* which are individual specifications within a single parameter. You code subparameters in much the same way as you code the entire parameters field: positional subparameters first, followed by keyword parameters in any order; if you omit positional subparameters, you may have to account for them by coding extra commas. The entire subparameter list must usually be enclosed in parentheses, like this:

```
DCB=(DSORG=PO,LRECL=80,BLKSIZE=6160)
```

Here, DCB is a keyword parameter; the subparameter list includes three keyword subparameters: DSORG, LRECL, and BLKSIZE. If there's only one subparameter, the parentheses are optional. So

```
DCB=(DSORG=PO)
```

is equivalent to

```
DCB=DSORG=PO
```

Although it looks unusual to omit the parentheses, it's perfectly acceptable.

Here's an example of a keyword parameter that requires positional subparameters:

```
DISP=(,DELETE)
```

Here, DISP is the keyword parameter and DELETE is the second of two positional subparameters. Since I omitted the first parameter, I coded a comma to mark its place. Parentheses are required in this case.

The comments field   Following the parameters field, you can code a brief comment in the *comments field.* The comments field begins in the position after the space that marks the end of the parameters field and ends in column 71. MVS ignores what you code here, so you can record any comments you wish. Frankly, I don't find much use for placing comments in the comments field. Usually, such comments just state the obvious. And there's not enough room in the comments field to code a useful comment.

How to continue JCL statements

Often, you won't be able to fit all the parameters you need to code on a single 80-character line. When that happens, you'll have to continue the statement onto one or more additional lines.

Coding continuation lines can be a source of confusion, but it's easy if you follow a few simple rules. First, break the parameter field after the comma that follows a parameter or subparameter.

Example 1

```
//SYSUT2   DD   DSNAME=MMA2.COPYLIB.BACKUP,DISP=(NEW,CATLG),UNIT=SYSDA,
// VOL=SER=MPS800,SPACE=(CYL,(10,5,2)),DCB=DSORG=PO
```

Example 2

```
//SYSUT2   DD   DSNAME=MMA2.COPYLIB.BACKUP,DISP=(NEW CATLG),
//              UNIT=SYSDA,VOL=SER=MPS800,
//              SPACE=(CYL,(10,5,2)),
//              DCB=DSORG=PO
```

Figure 5-4   Two examples of continuing a JCL statement

Second, code slashes in columns 1 and 2 of the following line. And third, code the next parameter or subparameter beginning anywhere in columns 4 through 16. There are three common mistakes to avoid: (1) don't forget to code the trailing comma on the continued line; (2) don't forget to code the slashes in columns 1 and 2 of each continuation line; and (3) don't mistakenly align the continued parameter field with non-continued parameter fields in column 17. If you make any of these mistakes, MVS won't recognize your continuation line and your job won't be processed.

Figure 5-4 shows two examples of a DD statement continued beyond the first line; DD statements are the ones you'll continue most often because they usually have the most parameters. In example 1, I coded as many parameters on each line as I could. In example 2, I coded just one or two parameters per line. If you have to continue a JCL statement, I think it's more readable if you code one or two parameters per line.

There's one case where you'll have to code a special character in column 72 to continue a statement. That's when you're continuing the comments field rather than the parameters field. To do that, you have to code a non-blank character in column 72; any character will do, but most people use an X. Frankly, the rules for continuing a JCL statement when a comments field is involved are a bit confusing. So I suggest that you use the comment statement (//*) for longer comments rather than continuing a comments field from line to line.

Guidelines for coding JCL statements

By its very nature, JCL is a cryptic language. There's nothing you can do to change that, so the best you can do is to avoid making your JCL more confusing than it needs to be. If you follow the simple recommendations I've made in this topic, like coding just one or two parameters per line and aligning the operation and parameters fields of each statement, you'll take a big step toward that end.

It's a good idea to begin your jobs with a group of comment statements that document the job as thoroughly as possible. Your installation may have standards that require this, so be sure to find out. In any event, the documentation should include your name, the date you created the job, and a description of what each job step does and any special processing requirements it may have. These comments should be updated whenever the job is modified.

Terminology

JES2 control statement
JES3 control statement
identifier field
name field
operation field
parameters field
parameter
positional parameter
keyword parameter
subparameter
comments field

Objectives

1. Describe the basic format of a JCL statement.

2. Distinguish between positional and keyword parameters.

3. Describe how to code subparameters.

4. Describe how to continue JCL statements onto additional lines.

Topic 2

Basic JCL statements

In this topic, you'll learn how to code six basic job control statements: JOB, EXEC, DD, delimiter, comment, and null. These six basic statements are all you'll need to code for most of the jobs you develop. And although you won't learn all of the parameters you can code on a JOB, EXEC, or DD statement here, you'll learn the ones you'll use most often.

How to identify a job: the JOB statement

The JOB statement, which must always be the first JCL statement coded for a job, has three basic functions. First, it identifies a job to MVS and supplies a *job name* that MVS uses to refer to the job. Second, it supplies accounting information so that MVS can determine who is responsible for the job and, if necessary, who should be billed for the computer resources the job uses. And third, it supplies various options that influence or limit how the job is processed.

Figure 5-5 shows a simplified format for the JOB statement, and figure 5-6 shows four sample JOB statements that will help you see how the parameters are coded. As you can see, there are two positional parameters: accounting information and programmer name. In addition, there are several keyword parameters. So, if you omit the accounting information but code the programmer name, you'll have to precede the programmer name with a comma. However, if you omit both positional parameters, you don't have to code any commas before the first keyword parameter.

Of all the JCL statements, the JOB statement is the one whose required format varies the most from one installation to the next. That's because MVS provides several ways for an installation to tailor the JOB statement so it provides appropriate accounting information. For example, one computer system I used required the accounting information parameter, while another did not; instead, it used the USER and PASSWORD parameters to authorize my job. In any event, you'll have to find out exactly how you must code the JOB statement at your installation.

How to select a job name   You must always code a name on the JOB statement; the name you supply becomes the job name MVS uses to identify your job. Your job name does not have to be unique. If two or

---

The JOB statement

```
//jobname   JOB [ accounting information ] [ ,programmer name ]
                [ ,USER=user-id ]
                [ ,PASSWORD=password ]
                [ ,NOTIFY=user-id ]
                [ ,MSGCLASS=class ]
                [ ,MSGLEVEL=(stmt,msg) ]
```

Positional parameters

accounting information	May or may not be required, depending on the installation. For JES2 installations, see figure 5-7 for format.
programmer name	May or may not be required, depending on the installation. If required, the installation may dictate a specialized format.

Keyword parameters

USER	May be required to specify the user-id of the user who submitted the job.
PASSWORD	May be required to supply a password that authorizes access to the system.
NOTIFY	Optional; specifies a TSO user to be notified when the job completes.
MSGCLASS	Optional; specifies a single-character output class to be used for the job's message output.
MSGLEVEL	Optional; controls the amount of system messages produced for the job. See figure 5-9 for details.

Figure 5-5   The JOB statement

more active jobs have the same name, they can be distinguished by the *job identifier* (or *job number*), which is unique for all active jobs.

Depending on the installation and how you use the system, there may be rules that govern how you can form job names. Often, the first two to four characters of a job name have to match an account number assigned to you by your installation. For example, suppose your account number is MMA385 and your installation requires that the first three characters of the job name match the first three characters of the account number. Then, job names like MMACOPY or MMAXB14 would be acceptable under that scheme.

If you're submitting a job from TSO or ISPF, you should follow a rigid format for creating job names: your TSO user-id followed by a single alphanumeric character. For example, the TSO user-id I used to test the examples in this book is SYDOE. So, throughout this book, you'll see job names like SYDOEA and SYDOEM. The reason

---

Example 1

```
//PAY4OB1   JOB   MMA2AB14,'206-LOWE'
```

Account number MMA2AB14, programmer name 206-LOWE.

Example 2

```
//PAY4OB2   JOB   (MMA2AB14,206),LOWE,MSGCLASS=A,MSGLEVEL=(0,0)
```

Account number MMA2AB14, room 206, programmer name LOWE. The job output will be printed using class A, and only the JOB statement will be printed (unless errors occur).

Example 3

```
//MMA2P4B2  JOB   USER=SYDOE,PASSWORD=XXXXXXXX
```

TSO user-id SYDOE, password XXXXXXXX.

Example 4

```
//SYDOEB    JOB   NOTIFY=SYDOE
```

TSO user SYDOE will be notified when the job finishes.

Figure 5-6   Examples of JOB statements

for this restriction is simple; ISPF requires it in order to use the OUTLIST utility to monitor your job's progress and manage its output. So if you don't follow this job naming convention, you may not be able to control your job from ISPF.

The accounting information parameter   The accounting information parameter is an installation-dependent positional parameter that supplies information used to determine who's responsible for the job and how its billing should be handled. Usually, this parameter consists of several positional subparameters, the first of which is normally an account number.

Figure 5-7 shows the default format for the accounting information parameter under JES2. I say *default* format because it's a relatively simple matter for an installation to change the format by adding, deleting, or rearranging subparameters as needed. Under JES3, there is no default accounting information format, so the installation must tailor it according to its needs. In either case, be sure to find out from your installation how to code the accounting information parameter, if you need to code it at all.

The accounting information parameter (JES2 only)

`(pano,room,time,lines,cards,forms,copies,log,linect)`

Subparameters

Note: The subparameters are positional, so code a comma for each omitted subparameter.

pano	One to four alphanumeric characters representing the programmer's account number.
room	One to four alphanumeric characters representing the programmer's room number.
time	A one- to four-digit number representing an estimate of the job's execution time in minutes.
line	A one- to four-digit number representing an estimate, in thousands of lines, of the number of lines the job writes to SYSOUT data sets.
cards	A one- to four-digit number representing an estimate of the number of cards the job punches to SYSOUT data sets.
forms	One to four alphanumeric characters representing an installation-defined form identifier that specifies the forms used to print the job's SYSOUT data sets.
copies	A one- to three-digit number that specifies how many copies of the job's SYSOUT data sets should be printed.
log	If N, the job is not printed. If any other character or if omitted, the job log is printed.
linect	A one- to three-digit number that specifies how many lines should be printed on each page of the job's SYSOUT data sets.

Figure 5-7   JES2 format for the JOB statement accounting information parameter

If only one subparameter is required in the accounting information parameter, you can omit the parentheses. For example, the statement

`//SYDOEA   JOB   MMA2B5AC`

includes an accounting information parameter with just one subparameter: an eight character account number (MMA2B5AC).

The programmer name parameter   The programmer name parameter is another JOB statement parameter that may or may not be required at your installation. And if it's required, the value you specify may or may not be important. At some installations, you have to code the programmer name parameter in a particular way to identify yourself. At others, the value you code is used for documentation.

In any event, you must enclose the programmer name field in apostrophes if it contains special characters or spaces. For example,

```
15.16.16 JOB 5969 $HASP165 SYDOEA ENDED AT MVSPS1 CN (00)
***
```

Figure 5-8   A message like this is delivered to your TSO terminal when your job completes if you code the NOTIFY parameter on the JOB statement

'205-BILL' is enclosed in apostrophes because of the hyphen. Periods aren't considered special characters in this case, so 205.BILL doesn't need apostrophes. If the programmer name field includes an apostrophe, as in O'Reilly, you'll have to code two consecutive apostrophes and enclose the entire name in apostrophes, like this: 'O''Reilly'.

The USER and PASSWORD parameters   In chapter 3, you learned that RACF is a security manager that controls access to MVS resources. If your job processes resources that are protected by RACF, you must be authorized by RACF to use those resources. Two JOB statement parameters let you identify yourself to RACF: USER and PASSWORD. The USER parameter specifies your RACF user-id, which is usually the same as your TSO user-id. Similarly, the PASSWORD parameter supplies a RACF password that's valid for the user-id you specify; it's usually the same as your TSO password. (A third RACF-related parameter, GROUP, isn't often needed. So I won't cover it here.)

If you submit a batch job from TSO, your RACF user-id and password are automatically passed on to the batch job. So, you don't have to specify USER and PASSWORD on a JOB statement submitted from TSO.

The NOTIFY parameter   If you submit a job from a TSO terminal, you can code the NOTIFY parameter on the JOB statement so that you'll automatically be notified when the job completes. For example, suppose you code this JOB statement:

```
//SYDOEA JOB NOTIFY=SYDOE
```

When the job completes, a message like the one in figure 5-8 will be sent to your TSO terminal. If you're working under ISPF, you'll have to press the enter key to return to the ISPF panel that was displayed when the message arrived. And if you aren't logged on to TSO when the message arrives, you'll receive the message when you log on.

The MSGCLASS and MSGLEVEL parameters   As you already know, MVS lists JCL statements and produces various system messages as your job executes. The MSGCLASS and MSGLEVEL parameters let you manage that output. MSGCLASS lets you specify

---

The MSGLEVEL parameter

`MSGLEVEL=(stmt,msg)`

Explanation

stmt   A single decimal digit that specifies how JCL statements should be printed, as follows:

          0   Print only the JOB statement.

          1   Print only JCL statements, including those that come from procedures.

          2   Print only JCL statements submitted through the input stream; don't print statements from procedures.

msg   A single digit that specifies how system messages should be printed, as follows:

          0   Print step completion messages only; don't print allocation and deallocation messages unless the job fails.

          1   Print all messages.

Figure 5-9   The JOB statement MSGLEVEL parameter

an output class that's associated with your job's message output. For example, if you specify MSGCLASS=A, your job's message output is assigned to output class A. (At most shops, that means the output will be printed on one of the installation's high-speed printers on standard computer paper.) If you omit the MSGCLASS parameter, MVS assigns a default. Usually, the default message class is A, but for jobs submitted from a TSO terminal, the default message class might be a held output class. At my installation, the default for TSO submitted jobs is class X, a held class.

The MSGLEVEL parameter lets you specify the type of messages you want included in your output. MSGLEVEL has two positional subparameters:

`MSGLEVEL=(stmt,msg)`

The first, stmt, controls which JCL statements appear in the JCL statement listing. The second, msg, controls the amount of message output that appears in the message log. Figure 5-9 shows the values you can code for each subparameter.

If you omit MSGLEVEL, a default value is used. At most installations, the default is MSGLEVEL=(1,1), which causes all of the JCL and system messages to be printed. Normally, that's what you want, so you can omit the MSGLEVEL parameter altogether.

For a production job that produces pages of JCL and message output, however, you may want to specify MSGLEVEL=(0,0). Then,

---

The EXEC statement

```
//stepname EXEC PGM=program-name [ ,PARM=information ]
```

Positional parameter

PGM   Specifies the name of the program to be executed for this job step.

Keyword parameter

PARM   Optional; specifies information that's passed to the program.

Figure 5-10   The EXEC statement

only the JOB statement will be printed, and the allocation and deallocation messages will be printed only if the job fails.

How to identify a job step: the EXEC statement

An EXEC statement is required to identify the program executed by each step in a job. Figure 5-10 shows the basic format of the EXEC statement, and figure 5-11 shows three examples of how it's typically coded.

The stepname field of an EXEC statement is optional, but you should code it in any job that has more than one step. Since system messages refer to job and step names, coding a step name will help you identify the source of errors indicated by such messages. In addition, coding a meaningful step name helps document the function of the job step.

The PGM parameter   In the PGM parameter, you specify the name of the program you want to execute for the job step. Actually, the name you specify is the name of a member of a partitioned data set. The member must be a load module; that is, a module that's been link-edited and is ready to execute. In example 1 of figure 5-11, the program name is PAY5B10, in example 2 it's IEBDG, and in example 3 it's HEWL.

Normally, the program you specify must be a member of a system load library, such as SYS1.LINKLIB. In chapter 6, however, you'll learn how to use a private library to execute a program that doesn't reside in SYS1.LINKLIB or one of the other system libraries.

One other point about the PGM parameter: I want to be sure you realize that it's a positional parameter even though it has the form of a keyword parameter. So code it as the first parameter on the EXEC statement.

Example 1

```
//PAYLIST    EXEC PGM=PAY5B10
```

Execute the program named PAY5B10. The step name is PAYLIST.

Example 2

```
//DATAGEN    EXEC PGM=IEBDG,PARM='LINECT=0050'
```

Execute the program named IEBDG, passing 'LINECNT=0050' as a parameter to
the program. The step name is DATAGEN.

Example 3

```
//LINKED     EXEC PGM=HEWL,PARM='LET,MAP,XREF'
```

Execute the program named HEWL, passing 'LET,MAP,XREF' as a parameter to
the program. The step name is LINKED.

Figure 5-11   Examples of the EXEC statement

The PARM parameter   In the PARM parameter, you can code
information that can be accessed by the program you specify in the
PGM parameter. That kind of information is usually used to influence the way the program works. For example, many IBM-supplied
programs, like utilities, compilers, and the linkage editor, use
PARM information to set various processing options. User programs can use this facility, too.

In the PARM field, you code information in a form that's expected by the program that will receive the information. As a result,
there aren't any JCL rules that govern the format of this information
other than the rules of punctuation you must follow for any parameter value. So, if the PARM field contains special characters like
commas, spaces, parentheses, and so on, you should enclose the
entire field in apostrophes. As a result, the PARM values in examples 2 and 3 of figure 5-11 are both enclosed in apostrophes.

How to allocate a job's data sets: the DD statement

As you know, before a job step's program is executed, any data sets
the program will process are allocated. To describe the data sets that
must be allocated, you code DD (data definition) statements. Normally, you code one DD statement for each data set your program
will process. You code the DD statements *after* the EXEC statement
that identifies the job step.

The DD statement is the most complicated of the JCL statements. Figure 5-12 shows three simple formats of the DD statement that let you allocate in-stream data sets (data sets that are included in the job stream along with JCL statements), SYSOUT data sets (data sets that are directed to a JES-managed printer), and DASD data sets (data sets that reside on disk). Later in this book, you'll see these formats expanded; these are just the basic forms of the DD statement.

There's one thing each of the DD statement formats have in common: each requires a *ddname*. The ddname is a one- to eight-character symbolic name that the processing program uses to refer to the file. In a COBOL program, the ddname is the name specified in the ASSIGN clause of the file's SELECT statement. In an assembler language program, it's the name specified in the DDNAME parameter on the file's DCB or ACB macro. Other programming languages have similar facilities to specify a file's ddname.

It's crucial at this point for you to realize that the ddname is *not* necessarily the actual name of the file as indicated in the file's label. Instead, the ddname is an intermediate name that lets a program refer to the file without using its actual data set name. That way, the program can be used to process different files, as long as the files have similar formats. (There's no rule that says the data set name and the ddname can't be the same. But they usually aren't.)

The DD statement for in-stream data sets

In chapter 3, you learned that you can include *in-stream data sets* along with JCL statements in a job stream. JES copies the in-stream data to a spool volume, from which your processing program can retrieve the data as it executes. The in-stream data is in the form of 80-byte card images, and your program treats the data as if it was a standard sequential (QSAM) file read from a card reader.

Figure 5-13 shows portions of three job streams that use in-stream data sets. Example 1 shows the typical way of coding in-stream data. First, a DD * statement indicates that the records that follow are data for the in-stream data set. The ddname on the DD * statement associates the in-stream data set with the file referred to by the program; no data set name is required because the file will reside in JES spool space. Following the data, a *delimiter statement* (/*) marks the end of the data. The delimiter statement is optional in this case. If you omit it, the next JCL statement (// in columns 1 and 2) would indicate the end of the in-stream data set.

Normally, a delimiter statement or a subsequent JCL statement marks the end of the in-stream data set. What if you want to include

The DD statement for in-stream data sets

```
//ddname DD  ┌ *    ┐
             { DATA }
             └      ┘
             [ ,DLM=xx]
```

The DD statement for SYSOUT data sets

```
//ddname DD SYSOUT=x
```

The DD statement for DASD data sets

```
//ddname    DD   DSNAME=data-set-name
                 ,DISP=(status,normal-disp,abnormal-disp)
            [ ,UNIT=unit ]
            [ ,VOL=SER=vol-ser ]
            [ ,SPACE=unit,(primary,secondary,dir) ]
            [ ,DCB=(option,option...) ]
```

Explanation (in-stream format)

* or DATA   Indicates that in-stream data follows. If you code an asterisk, the next JCL state-
             ment ends the data. If you code DATA, you must include a delimiter statement to
             end the data.

DLM   Specifies the characters that identify a delimiter statement. If omitted, slash-
             asterisk (/*) is the default.

Explanation (SYSOUT format)

SYSOUT   Specifies a one-character output class to be associated with the SYSOUT data set. If
             you code an asterisk, the output class you specified in the MSGCLASS parameter of
             the JOB statement is used.

Explanation (DASD format)

DSNAME   Specifies the file's data set name.

DISP   Specifies the file's status and normal and abnormal disposition. See figure 5-15 for
             valid subparameters.

UNIT   Specifies a unit address, generic name, or group name that identifies the device
             where the file resides. Not required for cataloged data sets.

VOL=SER   Specifies the six-character vol-ser of the volume that contains the file. Not required
             for cataloged data sets.

SPACE   Specifies the DASD space to be allocated for the file. Unit indicates the unit of
             measure: CYL for cylinders, TRK for tracks, block size for blocks. Primary indi-
             cates the amount of space to be initially allocated to the file, and secondary
             indicates the size of each secondary extent. Dir indicates the number of directory
             blocks to allocate for a partitioned data set.

DCB   Specifies options to be used for the file's data control block. See figure 5-18 for
             valid options.

Figure 5-12   Three formats of the DD statement

Example 1

```
//INVTRAN   DD    *
A00101005995CH445
A00103010030CH445
A00272001950CJ550
A00301015395CH445
A00311011231CJ550
A00560089331CH445
/*
```

Example 2

```
//SYSUT1    DD    DATA
//STEP1     EXEC  PGM=INV1040
//INVLSTA   DD    SYSOUT=A
//INVLSTB   DD    SYSOUT=A
/*
```

Example 3

```
//SYSIN     DD    DATA,DLM=##
//INVTRAN   DD    *
A00101005995CH445
A00103010030CH445
A00272001950CJ550
A00301015395CH445
A00311011231CJ550
A00560089331CH445
/*
##
```

Note: The shading indicates the records that are processed as data for the in-stream data set.

Figure 5-13   Three ways of coding in-stream data

JCL statements as a part of the in-stream data? That's where the DD DATA statement comes in. Simply put, if you specify DATA instead of an asterisk, you *must* code a delimiter statement to mark the end of your data. That way, JCL statements can be read as data. Example 2 in figure 5-13 shows how the DD DATA statement works. Here, the shaded records are read as in-stream data.

The DLM parameter lets you change the two-character code used to represent the delimiter statement. You might need to do that if your in-stream data set has records with /* in columns 1 and 2. Although that's an unlikely situation, it's possible. Example 3 in figure 5-13 shows you how to use the DLM parameter.

Although I don't recommend it, you can omit the DD statement for in-stream data altogether if the program expects the ddname to be SYSIN. That's because when MVS encounters data that it doesn't recognize as JCL or JES2/JES3 statements, it automatically generates a SYSIN DD statement to treat the data as an in-stream data set. Even if the expected ddname is SYSIN, however, I think it's a good idea to code the DD statement.

The DD statement for SYSOUT data

You also learned in chapter 3 that JES2 and JES3 let a program produce *SYSOUT data sets* that are collected in JES spool space before they are actually printed. By coding the SYSOUT parameter on a DD statement, you indicate that a file is a SYSOUT data set and should be processed by JES2/JES3.

The SYSOUT parameter also specifies the output class associated with the SYSOUT data set. For example, the DD statement

```
//SYSPRINT DD     SYSOUT=A
```

specifies that the data set identified by the ddname SYSPRINT is a JES SYSOUT file with output class A.

Usually, class A is associated with an installation's standard printer devices. When you specify class A, your output will usually be printed by a 3800 Printing Subsystem or a high-speed impact printer on standard computer forms. SYSOUT data sets can also be routed to card punch devices; the standard SYSOUT class for punched output is B. And if you specify a held output class, your output isn't immediately printed, so it can be displayed from a TSO terminal.

If you code an asterisk instead of an output class in the SYSOUT parameter, the output class defaults to the class you specified in the MSGCLASS parameter of the JOB statement. That way, the SYSOUT data will be printed along with the job's message output. I usually code SYSOUT=* and omit the MSGCLASS parameter. That way, the installation's default output class applies to my entire job. (At my installation, the default output class is X—a held output class—for jobs submitted from a TSO terminal.) Later, if I want to change the output class for the entire job, I just add a MSGCLASS parameter to the JOB statement. Because this gives me the most flexibility in handling SYSOUT data, most of the SYSOUT data sets you'll see in this book specify SYSOUT=*.

The DD statement for DASD data sets

As you can see in figure 5-12, the format of the DD statement for DASD data sets is more complex than the formats for in-stream or SYSOUT data. Actually, the format is even more complex than it might at first appear. That's because the parameters in figure 5-12 can be coded in various combinations, depending on whether the data set is new or old, temporary or permanent, and cataloged or uncataloged. And, of course, there are many other DD statement parameters that I haven't included in figure 5-12. In particular, I haven't included the parameters you can use with the Storage Management Subsystem under MVS/ESA. You'll learn about those parameters in chapters 6 and 9. In this chapter, I'll assume that you're not using SMS.

Figure 5-14 shows four examples of the DD statement for DASD data sets. Example 1 shows you how to allocate an existing cataloged data set. Example 2 shows you how to allocate an existing data set that isn't cataloged. Example 3 shows you how to create a new data set. And example 4 shows you how to allocate a temporary data set that's used by a single job step; it doesn't require a data set name. Example 1 is the only DD statement format that's valid for VSAM files. Since they're always cataloged, it's not necessary to specify UNIT and VOLUME parameters as in example 2. And unless you're using SMS, you create a VSAM file using Access Method Services rather than JCL.

The DSNAME parameter   The DSNAME parameter is always required for a permanent data set. It supplies the data set name as it's stored in the data set's label (that is, in the Format-1 DSCB in the VTOC) or in the file's catalog entry. In figure 5-14, examples 1, 2, and 3 specify the data set name SYDOE.INVNTORY.MASTER. Notice that the periods can be included in the data set name without enclosing the entire parameter in apostrophes.

For a temporary data set, the DSNAME parameter is optional. If you code it, you must follow a special format, which I'll explain in chapter 6 when I describe in detail how to use temporary data sets. If you omit DSNAME for a temporary data set as in example 4 in figure 5-14, MVS generates a unique name for you.

To refer to a member of a partitioned data set, you code a standard data set name followed by the member's one- to eight-character name in parentheses. For example, consider this DSNAME parameter:

```
DSNAME=SYDOE.TEST.COBOL(ORD1100)
```

Here, the member named ORD1100 in a partitioned data set named SYDOE.TEST.COBOL is allocated. When you refer to a PDS member

Example 1

```
//INVMAST   DD    DSNAME=SYDOE.INVNTORY.MASTER,DISP=SHR
```

Allocate an existing cataloged data set named SYDOE.INVNTORY.MASTER for shared access.

Example 2

```
//INVMAST   DD    DSNAME=SYDOE.INVNTORY.MASTER,DISP=SHR,
//                UNIT=SYSDA,VOL=SER=MPS8BV
```

Allocate an existing uncataloged data set named SYDOE.INVNTORY.MASTER for shared acess. The data set resides on a SYSDA-class volume named MPS8BV.

Example 3

```
//INVMAST   DD    DSNAME=SYDOE.INVNTORY.MASTER.DISP=(NEW,CATLG),
//                UNIT=SYSDA,VOL=SER=MPS8BV,
//                SPACE=(CYL,(10,2)),
//                DCB=(DSORG=PS,RECFM=FB,LRECL=100,BLKSIZE=3100)
```

Allocate a new cataloged data set named SYDOE.INVNTORY.MASTER on the SYSDA-class volume named MPS8BV. The file will have 10 cylinders of primary space and 2 cylinders of secondary space, it will have physical sequential organization, and fixed-length blocked records (100-byte records, 3100-byte blocks).

Example 4

```
//WORK01    DD    UNIT=SYSDA,VOL=SER=MPS800,
//                SPACE=(CYL,(1,1))
```

Allocate a temporary data set on the SYSDA-class volume named MPS800, using 1 cylinder of primary and 1 cylinder of secondary space. No name is required since the file will be created and deleted within a single job step.

Figure 5-14   Examples of DD statements for DASD data sets

in this way, the entire library is allocated to your job step, but only the member you specify is processed by the job step's program. In fact, the program doesn't even have to know it's processing a PDS; it can process the member as if it were a sequential data set.

Incidentally, you can abbreviate the DSNAME parameter as DSN. Throughout this book, I'll use the full DSNAME form of the parameter. In actual practice, however, I often write DSN instead.

The DISP parameter   The DISP parameter has three positional subparameters: status, normal disposition, and abnormal disposition. Figure 5-15 shows the values you can code for each of the three

Status

NEW	The data set does not exist and should be created.
OLD	The data set exists and should be allocated for exclusive use.
SHR	The data set exists and should be allocated for shared use.
MOD	The data set is allocated for exclusive use and is positioned at the end of the data, so additional records may be added after the last record. If you also code VOL=SER, the data set must exist.

Normal and abnormal disposition

DELETE	The data set is deleted. If it was retrieved from the catalog, it is also uncataloged.
KEEP	The data set is retained.
CATLG	The data set is retained and a catalog entry is made.
UNCATLG	The data set is retained, but its catalog entry is removed.
PASS	Normal disposition only. The data set is retained for use by a later job step.

Default values

status	If omitted, MVS assumes NEW.
normal disposition	Depends on the value specified or assumed for status: if NEW, normal disposition is DELETE; if OLD, SHR, or MOD, normal disposition is KEEP.
abnormal disposition	Takes on the value specified or assumed for normal disposition.

Figure 5-15   Subparameters of the DISP parameter

DISP subparameters, describes each option, and explains how MVS selects default values for subparameters you omit. And figure 5-16 shows six examples of the DISP parameter.

Status specifies whether the file is new (NEW), an existing file to which you want exclusive access (OLD), an existing file you want to access and allow others to access too (SHR), or an existing file to which you want to add records (MOD). *Normal disposition* specifies what the system should do with the data set if the job step ends normally; you can keep the file (KEEP), delete it (DELETE), catalog it (CATLG), uncatalog it (UNCATLG), or retain it for use by a subsequent job step (PASS). *Abnormal disposition* specifies what to do if your program fails; you can specify any of the values you can specify for normal disposition except PASS.

The default values MVS assumes for the DISP subparameters can be confusing, but if you'll keep in mind three simple rules, you'll be able to remember how the defaults are assigned. First, if you omit the status subparameter, MVS assumes NEW. Second, if you omit the normal disposition subparameter, the default depends on the status subparameter: if it's NEW, the default is DELETE; otherwise, it's KEEP. In other words, the default is to delete new files and keep existing files. Third, if you omit the abnormal disposition subparameter, it takes on whatever value you specify or let default for normal disposition.

Because of the way these defaults work, it's common to omit the DISP parameter altogether for a file you want to create and delete in the same job step. Omitting the DISP parameter altogether is the same as coding DISP=(NEW,DELETE,DELETE).

To allocate an existing data set, you'll normally code just the status subparameter, letting the normal and abnormal disposition subparameters assume default values. Example 1 in figure 5-16 shows this; here, an existing file is allocated for shared access, so other jobs can access the file too. Because I omitted the disposition subparameters, both assume KEEP as their default value.

Example 2 in figure 5-16 shows how to request exclusive access to an existing data set. When you allocate a data set in this way, no other job can allocate the data set until your job step ends.

The MOD subparameter, shown in example 3 in figure 5-16, is like OLD except that it causes MVS to establish file positioning after the last record in the file. That way, if the program writes any records to the file, they're added to the end of the file. If you specify MOD for a file that doesn't exist, MVS creates a file as if you had specified NEW. (The defaults for normal and abnormal disposition, however, remain KEEP.)

To create a new data set (non-VSAM), you specify NEW as the status and you code a normal disposition subparameter to indicate how you want the data set retained, as in example 4 in figure 5-16. Here, the file is retained and cataloged. If you specify KEEP instead of CATLG, the file is retained but no catalog entry is made. If you omit the status subparameter altogether, NEW is assumed.

In example 5 of figure 5-16, I specified DELETE as the normal disposition. DELETE removes a data set from the DASD volume's VTOC and uncatalogs it if it was cataloged. If you specify UNCATLG instead of DELETE, the file's catalog entry is removed, but the file remains on disk so you can retrieve it later as an uncataloged data set. (It's unusual to uncatalog but not delete a cataloged data set, so you probably won't use UNCATLG often.) The PASS disposition is used mostly for temporary data sets, so I'll describe it in more detail in chapter 6 when I show you how to use temporary data sets.

Example 1

`DISP=SHR`   Allocate an existing data set for shared access; normal and abnormal disposition default to KEEP.

Example 2

`DISP=OLD`   Allocate an existing data set for exclusive access; normal and abnormal disposition default to KEEP.

Example 3

`DISP=MOD`   If the data set exists, extend it; otherwise, create it. Access is exclusive; normal and abnormal disposition default to KEEP.

Example 4

`DISP=(NEW,CATLG)`   Allocate a new data set and catalogs it; abnormal disposition defaults to CATLG.

Example 5

`DISP=(OLD,DELETE)`   Allocate an existing data set and delete it; abnormal disposition defaults to DELETE.

Example 6

`DISP=(,KEEP,DELETE)`   Allocate a new data set and keep it if the job step ends normally; if the job step ends abnormally, delete the data set.

Figure 5-16   Examples of the DISP parameter

Example 6 shows how to specify an abnormal disposition. Here, I omitted the status specification, so NEW is assumed. If the job step completes normally, the data set is retained (KEEP); if the job step ends abnormally, the data set is deleted (DELETE). If you omit the abnormal disposition subparameter, the normal disposition you specify (or allow to default) is used if the job step fails.

For VSAM files, you specify just the status subparameter; you don't specify a normal or abnormal disposition subparameter. That's because VSAM files are always cataloged, and they're created and deleted by the VSAM utility program, Access Method Services. In most cases, you'll code the DISP parameter for a VSAM file like this:

`DISP=SHR`

That way, the file can be shared by other jobs. When you define a

VSAM file using Access Method Services, you can specify an option that controls the level of sharing allowed for the file. You'll learn about that in chapter 10.

If your installation has installed and activated SMS, you can also create and delete VSAM files using JCL. In that case, you can code the normal and abnormal disposition subparameters, and you can code NEW for the status subparameter. See chapter 9 for more information.

For a temporary data set that's used only by a single job step, you can omit the DISP parameter altogether and MVS uses a default of (NEW,DELETE). That way, the data set will be created and deleted in the same job step. In chapter 6, when I describe temporary data sets in more detail, you'll learn about other DISP options for temporary data sets.

The UNIT and VOLUME parameters   The UNIT and VOLUME parameters work together to specify the location of a data set. UNIT indicates the device where the data set resides, and VOLUME indicates the vol-ser of the data set's volume. You specify UNIT and VOLUME when you're creating a new data set or when you're retrieving an existing uncataloged data set. For a cataloged data set, the unit and volume information is stored in the catalog, so you don't need to code it in the JCL.

You can code the UNIT parameter in one of three ways, which correspond to the three ways MVS allocates units that I described in chapter 3. First, you can specify a device address, such as UNIT=301. Here, the unit at address 301 will be allocated. As a general rule, it's not a good idea to specify an actual device address in a UNIT parameter.

Second, you can use a generic name that identifies a particular type of device. For example, if you specify UNIT=3380, a 3380 device can be used.

Third, you can specify a group name that identifies devices that belong to categories set up by the installation. SYSDA and TAPE are commonly used group names. SYSDA typically refers to any DASD unit that's available for public use, and TAPE refers to any available tape drive. Your installation probably has other group names you can use, so be sure to find out what they are.

If your installation has installed SMS, it may have set up a UNIT default. In that case, you can omit the UNIT parameter altogether if the default setting is appropriate.

The VOLUME parameter lets you specify which volume you want to allocate for your data set. That's called a *specific volume request*. For a new data set, the VOLUME parameter is optional; if you omit it, MVS scans the eligible volumes based on how you code the UNIT parameter to determine which volume is best to contain your file. That's called a *non-specific volume request*.

On the VOLUME parameter, you specify a volume serial number, like this:

```
VOLUME=SER=MPS800
```

Here, the vol-ser is MPS800. Usually, you abbreviate the VOLUME parameter, like this:

```
VOL=SER=MPS800
```

The effect is the same. If you code the VOLUME parameter, you should always code the UNIT parameter too.

The SPACE parameter   For a new non-VSAM data set, you must code the SPACE parameter to tell MVS how much primary and secondary space to allocate to the data set. The SPACE parameter format shown in figure 5-12 is confusing; it has two positional subparameters, and the second subparameter itself has three positional subparameters. That's why two sets of parentheses are required.

The first subparameter of the SPACE parameter indicates the unit of measure used for the space allocation. Most often, you'll allocate space in terms of cylinders (CYL) or tracks (TRK). For example, in the SPACE parameter

```
SPACE(CYL,(10,1))
```

the unit of allocation is cylinders.

For small files, you can allocate space in terms of blocks. In that case, you supply the size of each block as the unit of measure, like this:

```
SPACE(800,(500,100))
```

Here space is allocated in terms of 800-byte blocks.

The second SPACE subparameter indicates how much space to allocate to the data set. It has three positional subparameters that specify primary, secondary, and directory space. The primary allocation indicates how many units of space to allocate for the data set's primary extent. If the file requires more space than that, up to 15 secondary extents can be allocated, each as large as the secondary amount you specify.

The directory allocation is only for partitioned data sets. It indicates how large the library's directory should be. The directory allocation ignores the unit of measure you specify and allocates the directory instead in units called *directory blocks*, each of which is

Example 1

SPACE=(CYL,(10,2))   Primary: 10 cylinders
                                       Secondary: 2 cylinders

Example 2

SPACE=(TRK,(5,2))   Primary: 5 tracks
                                       Secondary: 2 tracks

Example 3

SPACE=(800,(500,100))   Primary: 500 800-byte blocks
                                       Secondary: 100 800-byte blocks

Example 4

SPACE=(CYL,(4,1,5))   Primary: 4 cylinders
                                       Secondary: 1 cylinder
                                       Directory: 5 blocks

Figure 5-17   Examples of the SPACE parameter

large enough to define 21 members. So if you expect the library to hold 40 members, allocate two directory blocks.

Figure 5-17 shows four examples of the SPACE parameter. Examples 1, 2, and 3 allocate primary and secondary space in terms of cylinders, tracks, and blocks. The maximum amount of space allowed by the SPACE parameter in example 1 is 40 cylinders: one 10 cylinder primary extent and 15 two-cylinder secondary extents. For example 2, the maximum is 35 tracks: one 5-track primary extent and 15 two-track secondary extents. And for example 3, the maximum is 2,000 800-byte blocks: one 500-block primary extent and 15 100-block secondary extents. Example 4 shows a SPACE parameter for a partitioned data set. It allows 19 cylinders of primary and secondary space and a directory that can accommodate 105 entries.

For installations that have installed and activated SMS, the SPACE parameter can be used in conjunction with the AVGREC parameter to specify a file's space requirements more precisely. See topic 3 of chapter 6 for details.

The DCB parameter   The last DD statement parameter I'll describe in this chapter is the DCB parameter. It lets you specify file characteristics that are stored in the file's Data Control Block. You code the DCB parameter only for new files; for existing files, the information is retrieved from the data set label. In addition, you don't have to

`DSORG=xx`	Specifies the data set's organization, as follows:	
	PS	Physical sequential
	PO	Partitioned
	DA	Direct
	IS	Indexed sequential
`RECFM=n`	Specifies the format of the file's records, as follows:	
	F	Fixed length, unblocked
	FB	Fixed length, blocked
	V	Variable length, unblocked
	VB	Variable length, blocked
	VBS	Variable length, blocked, spanned
	U	Undefined
`LRECL=n`	Specifies the length of the file's records.	
`BLKSIZE=n`	Specifies the length of the file's blocks; for FB, BLKSIZE is normally a multiple of LRECL.	

Figure 5-18   Commonly used DCB subparameters

code the DCB parameter for a new file if your application program supplies the required information.

Figure 5-18 shows four commonly-used DCB subparameters. They're keyword subparameters, so you can code them in any order you wish. The DSORG subparameter specifies the organization of the data set: sequential (PS), partitioned (PO), direct (DA), or indexed sequential (IS).

The RECFM subparameter specifies how the file's records are formatted. Most often, you'll code FB or VB, meaning that the file has fixed- or variable-length blocked records. The LRECL subparameter specifies the length of the file's records, and the BLKSIZE subparameter specifies the length of the file's blocks.

There aren't any default values for the DCB subparameters, but their values are often supplied from the processing program rather than from the DD statement. So, when you code a DD statement to create a data set, you need to code only the DCB subparameters that aren't specified in the program you're executing. Often, the program supplies all of the DCB information except block size, so you'll need to specify BLKSIZE in the DD statement's DCB parameter.

Figure 5-19 shows four examples of the DCB parameter. In example 1, a sequential file with fixed-length 133-byte unblocked records is defined. In example 2, the file is a PDS with blocked records; each record is 80 bytes long and 10 records fit in each block (10 X 80 = 800). Example 3 shows how to specify variable-length blocked records. Here, LRECL specifies the *maximum* record length

---

Examples 1

```
DCB=(DSORG=PS,RECFM=F,LRECL=133)
```

> Sequential file with fixed-length 133-byte unblocked records.

Example 2

```
DCB=(DSORG=PO,RECFM=FB,LRECL=80,BLKSIZE=800)
```

> Partitioned data set with fixed-length 80-byte records in 800-byte blocks.

Example 3

```
DCB=(RECFM=VB,LRECL=500,BLKSIZE=6160)
```

> Variable-length records up to 500 bytes in 6160-byte blocks. DSORG supplied by program.

Example 4

```
DCB=BLKSIZE=3200
```

> Block size is 3200 bytes; other DCB information supplied by program.

Figure 5-19   Examples of the DCB parameter

(500 bytes) and BLKSIZE specifies the block size (6160 bytes). Example 4 shows that if you code just one DCB subparameter, you can omit the parentheses.

Incidentally, the RECFM, LRECL, and BLKSIZE subparameters can be coded as separate DD statement parameters. Thus, example 3 in figure 5-19 could be coded like this:

```
RECFM=VB,LRECL=500,BLKSIZE=6160
```

Here, the DCB parameter is omitted and the subparameters are coded separately. The effect is the same. (Note that DSORG can *not* be coded as a separate parameter; it must be coded as part of a DCB parameter.)

How to mark the end of a job: the null statement

The *null statement* consists of slashes in columns 1 and 2 and no other data in the rest of the record. The purpose of a null statement is to mark the end of a job. It's not required, however, so you probably won't ever use it. If you have more than one job in an input stream, the end of one job is implied by the beginning of the next. And the end of the last job is implied by the end of the input stream.

How to document a job: the comment statement

You can use *comment statements* to place comments in your job. They can be helpful to clarify a confusing JCL statement or just to identify the purpose and operation of a job. Comment statements begin with two slashes and an asterisk starting in column 1, like this:

```
//* THIS IS A COMMENT
```

The entire comment statement is ignored, but it's printed along with the JCL listing.

As I mentioned in topic 1 of this chapter, it's a good idea to include comment statements in your jobs to indicate who wrote the job and when and to explain what the job's steps do. If you use comment statements, be sure to code them after the JOB statement since the JOB statement must always be the first JCL statement of a job.

Discussion

At this point, you've been introduced to the basic formats of the important JCL statements. To help you get a better idea of how these statements are used in actual jobs, the next topic presents two complete production jobs. As you read topic 3, many of the questions you have now may be answered. So move on now to topic 3, and return to this topic if you're still not sure about how each JCL statement and parameter works.

Terminology

job name
job identifier
job number
ddname
in-stream data set
delimiter statement
SYSOUT data set
status

normal disposition
abnormal disposition
specific volume request
non-specific volume request
directory blocks
null statement
comment statement

Objectives

1. Code a valid JOB statement using the format required by your installation.

2. Code an EXEC statement to invoke a program and pass a parameter value to it.

3. Code the JCL and data for an in-stream data set. The data may or may not include JCL statements.

4. Code a DD statement for a SYSOUT data set.

5. Code a DD statement for the following DASD data sets:
    a. An existing cataloged data set
    b. An existing uncataloged data set
    c. A new non-VSAM data set

Exercises

To answer the questions for these exercises, refer to the following job stream:

```
//SYDOEA    JOB  USER=SYDOE,PASSWORD=XXXXXXXX
//EXTRACT   EXEC PGM=EGAX401
//SYSPRINT  DD   SYSOUT=A
//X401LST   DD   SYSOUT=A
//X401CUST  DD   DSN=EGA.CUSTOMER.MASTER,DISP=SHR
//X401INV   DD   DSN=EGA.CUSTOMER.INVOICE,DISP=SHR
//X401DET   DD   DSN=EGA.CUSTOMER.DETAIL,DISP=SHR
//X401CRED  DD   DSN=EGA.CUSTOMER.CREDIT,DISP=SHR
//X401PARM  DD   *
001000
//X401EXTR  DD   DSN=EGA.CUSTOMER.EXTRACT,DISP=(NEW,CATLG),
//              UNIT=SYSDA,VOL=SER=TS0001,
//              SPACE=(CYL,(20,10)),
//              DCB=(DSORG=PS,RECFM=FB,LRECL=600,BLKSIZE=3600)
//REPORT    EXEC PGM=EGAX402
//SYSPRINT  DD   SYSOUT=A
//X402IN    DD   DSN=EGA.CUSTOMER.EXTRACT,DISP=(OLD,DELETE)
//X402LIST  DD   SYSOUT=A
```

1. How many job steps are there in this job?

2. Which data set is created as output by one job step and deleted by another?

3. What DASD volume is the data set mentioned in exercise 2 created on?

4. What is the ddname of the data set that is allocated to process in-stream data?

Topic 3

Two complete job streams

This topic presents two complete MVS jobs that use the JCL you
learned in topic 2. To make sure you understand these jobs and the
JCL elements they use, I'll explain each job statement by statement.
The first is a relatively simple job that invokes a program to post a
file of transaction records against a master file; both files are VSAM
files. The second job is a bit more complex. It invokes several application programs to produce reports extracted from two master files:
an accounts receivable file and a customer file. The job makes heavy
use of non-VSAM files.

A transaction-posting application

Figure 5-20 presents a system flowchart for a job that uses a file of
customer transaction records to update a file of customer master
records. Both files are VSAM files. A third VSAM file is used to
accumulate any transaction records that contain incorrect data. The
post-customer-transactions program (CM3000) produces three print
files: a transaction journal that lists the transactions individually, a
transaction summary report that highlights important summary
data, and an error listing. Figure 5-21 shows the ddnames that the
CM3000 program uses to refer to those data sets. Figure 5-21 also
shows the data set names for each of the data sets.

The JCL for the job   Figure 5-22 shows the JCL for the transaction-
posting job. Although it's straightforward, I'll explain each statement to be sure you understand it.

1. The JOB statement provides the job name for the job: CM3000.
    To submit this job from a TSO terminal, you should use a job
    name that conforms to TSO naming conventions instead (user-id
    followed by a single character).

2. The EXEC statement invokes the application program named
    CM3000. The step name here is POST.

3. The CUSTTRAN DD statement allocates the customer trans-
    action file (SYDOE.CUSTOMER.TRANS). Because it's a VSAM
    file, I specified DISP=SHR.

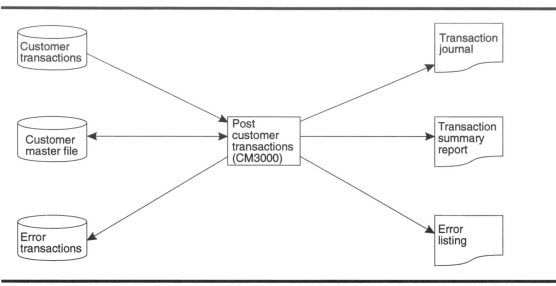

Figure 5-20   System flowchart for the transaction-posting application

ddname	Data set name
CUSTTRAN	SYDOE.CUSTOMER.TRANS
CUSTMAST	SYDOE.CUSTOMER.MASTER
ERRTRAN	SYDOE.CUSTOMER.TRANS.ERRS
TRANJRNL	(SYSOUT data set)
TRANSUM	(SYSOUT data set)
ERRLIST	(SYSOUT data set)

Figure 5-21   Data set requirements for the transaction-posting application

4. The CUSTMAST DD statement allocates the customer master file (SYDOE.CUSTOMER.MASTER). It too is a VSAM file, so I specified DISP=SHR.

5. The ERRTRAN DD statement allocates the VSAM transaction error file, named SYDOE.CUSTOMER.TRANS.ERRS. Again I specified DISP=SHR.

6. The TRANJRNL DD statement allocates the transaction journal SYSOUT data set. The output class defaults to the job's message class, so all the job's output is printed together.

```
1  //CM3000    JOB   USER=SYDOE,PASSWORD=XXXXXXXX
2  //POST      EXEC  PGM=CM3000
3  //CUSTTRAN  DD    DSNAME=SYDOE.CUSTOMER.TRANS,DISP=SHR
4  //CUSTMAST  DD    DSNAME=SYDOE.CUSTOMER.MASTER,DISP=SHR
5  //ERRTRAN   DD    DSNAME=SYDOE.CUSTOMER.TRANS.ERRS,DISP=SHR
6  //TRANJRNL  DD    SYSOUT=*
7  //TRANSUM   DD    SYSOUT=*
8  //ERRLIST   DD    SYSOUT=*
```

Figure 5-22   JCL for the transaction-posting application

7. The TRANSUM DD statement allocates the transaction summary report SYSOUT data set.

8. The ERRLIST DD statement allocates the error listing SYSOUT data set.

A report-preparation application

Figure 5-23 is the system flowchart for a report-preparation application that uses the JCL elements this chapter has presented. Here, the first application program (AR7100) creates a file with data from two master files (a customer file and an accounts receivable file). Before this program can be run, the receivables file, stored in invoice number sequence, must be sorted into invoice number within customer number sequence. Then, AR7100 can match records from the sorted receivables file with records from the customer file, which is already stored in customer number sequence. The sorting will be done by an IBM-supplied utility program called SORT.

The output of the AR7100 program is the dunning file, which is used to produce customer statements and three reports. Two of the reports (an overdue-invoices report and an aged-trial-balance report) are prepared in the dunning file's original sequence: invoice within customer. Because both of these reports are prepared from the same file, a single program (AR7200) is used so the file is read just once.

The other two output files the application produces require that the dunning file be sorted into a different sequence: invoice within customer number within state. So after the SORT program is run,

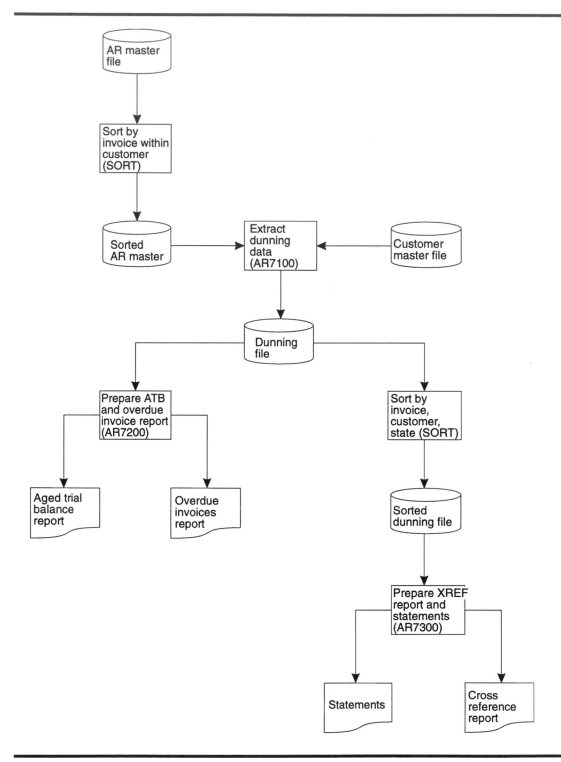

Figure 5-23   System flowchart for the report-preparation application

Step name	Program	ddname	Data set name
SORT1	SORT	SYSOUT SORTIN SORTOUT SORTWK01 SYSIN	(SYSOUT data set) SYDOE.ACCOUNT.MASTER SYDOE.ACCOUNT.MASTER.SORT (temporary work file) (in-stream data set)
AR7100	AR7100	ARSORT CUSTMAST DUNNING	SYDOE.ACCOUNT.MASTER.SORT SYDOE.CUSTOMER.MASTER SYDOE.DUNNING.FILE
AR7200	AR7200	DUNNING ATB OVERDUE	SYDOE.DUNNING.FILE (SYSOUT data set) (SYSOUT data set)
SORT2	SORT	SYSOUT SORTIN SORTOUT SORTWK01 SYSIN	(SYSOUT data set) SYDOE.DUNNING.FILE SYDOE.DUNNING.FILE.SORT (temporary work file) (in-stream data set)
AR7300	AR7300	DUNSORT XREF STMTS	SYDOE.DUNNING.FILE.SORT (SYSOUT data set) (SYSOUT data set)

Figure 5-24   Data set requirements for the programs invoked by the report-preparation application

AR7300 uses the sorted dunning file to prepare a cross-reference listing and the customer statements. Again, both output files are prepared by a single program so the dunning file is read just once.

Figure 5-24 lists the data sets required by each program invoked by the report-preparation job. For each file, I've listed the ddname and the data set name or an indication if the file is an in-stream data set, a temporary work file, or a SYSOUT data set. Only the names of the data sets that exist outside of the job are important. In this case, that's the customer master file and the accounts receivable master file. The names of the other files—for example, the sorted dunning file—aren't as important because they're created and deleted within a single job.

The JCL for the job   Figure 5-25 shows the JCL for the report-preparation job. To be sure you understand it, I'll describe it in detail.

1. The JOB statement assigns the job name: SYDOEA

2. The first EXEC statement invokes SORT, a system utility that sorts data sets. The step name is SORT1.

```
1    //SYDOEA    JOB    USER=SYDOE,PASSWORD=XXXXXXXX
2    //SORT1     EXEC   PGM=SORT
3    //SYSOUT    DD     SYSOUT=*
4    //SORTIN    DD     DSNAME=SYDOE.ACCOUNT.MASTER,DISP=SHR
5    //SORTOUT   DD     DSNAME=SYDOE.ACCOUNT.MASTER.SORT,DISP=(NEW,KEEP),
     //                 UNIT=SYSDA,VOL=SER=MPS800,
     //                 SPACE=(CYL,(1,1)),
     //                 DCB=(DSORG=PS,RECFM=FB,LRECL=400,BLKSIZE=3200)
6    //SORTWK01 DD      UNIT=SYSDA,VOL=SER=MPS800,
     //                 SPACE=(CYL,(1,1))
7    //SYSIN     DD     *
     SORT    FIELDS=(16,5,CH,A,1,5,CH,A)
     /*
8    //AR7100    EXEC   PGM=AR7100
9    //ARSORT    DD     DSNAME=SYDOE.ACCOUNT.MASTER.SORT,DISP=(OLD,DELETE),
     //                 UNIT=SYSDA,VOL=SER=MPS800
10   //CUSTMAST DD      DSNAME=SYDOE.CUSTOMER.MASTER,DISP=SHR
11   //DUNNING   DD     DSNAME=SYDOE.DUNNING.FILE,DISP=(NEW,KEEP),
     //                 UNIT=SYSDA,VOL=SER=MPS800,
     //                 SPACE=(CYL,(1,1)),
     //                 DCB=(DSORG=PS,RECFM=FB,LRECL=400,BLKSIZE=3200)
12   //AR7200    EXEC   PGM=AR7200
13   //DUNNING   DD     DSNAME=SYDOE.DUNNING.FILE,DISP=OLD,
     //                 UNIT=SYSDA,VOL=SER=MPS800
14   //ATB       DD     SYSOUT=*
15   //OVERDUE   DD     SYSOUT=*
16   //SORT2     EXEC   PGM=SORT
     //SYSOUT    DD     SYSOUT=*
     //SORTIN    DD     DSNAME=SYDOE.DUNNING.FILE,DISP=(OLD,DELETE),
     //                 UNIT=SYSDA,VOL=SER=MPS800,
     //SORTOUT   DD     DSNAME=SYDOE.DUNNING.FILE.SORT,DISP=(NEW,KEEP),
     //                 UNIT=SYSDA.VOL=SER=MPS800,
     //                 SPACE=(CYL,(1,1))
     //                 DCB=(DSORG=PS,RECFM=FB,LRECL=400,BLKSIZE=3200)
     //SORTWK01 DD      UNIT=SYSDA,VOL=SER=MPS800,
     //                 SPACE=(CYL,(1,1))
     //SYSIN     DD     *
     SORT    FIELDS=(43,2,CH,A,1,5,CH,A,50,5,CH,A)
     /*
17   //AR7300    EXEC   PGM=AR7300
18   //DUNSORT   DD     DSNAME=SYDOE.DUNNING.FILE.SORT,DISP=(OLD,DELETE),
     //                 UNIT=SYSDA,VOL=SER=MPS800
19   //XREF      DD     SYSOUT=*
20   //STMTS     DD     SYSOUT=*
```

Figure 5-25   JCL for the report-preparation application

3. The SORT program writes output messages to a SYSOUT data set named SYSOUT.

4. The input file—that is, the file to be sorted—is defined by the SORTIN DD statement. Here the accounts receivable master file is specified: SYDOE.ACCOUNT.MASTER. Because this is an existing cataloged file, only the data set name and disposition are specified.

5. The output file, named SYDOE.ACCOUNT.MASTER.SORT, is identified by the SORTOUT DD statement. In the DD statement, I specified unit, volume, space, and DCB information in addition to the data set name and disposition. One cylinder of primary space is allocated on a SYSDA device named MPS800. The file is physical sequential with fixed blocked records; each record is 400 bytes long and each block is 3200 bytes long. The file is kept but not cataloged.

6. The SORT program requires work space on a DASD device. So, the SORTWK01 DD statement defines a temporary data set by specifying just unit, volume, and space information. No data set name is required since the file is deleted when the SORT program ends. Because I omitted the DISP parameter, MVS assumes (NEW,DELETE).

7. The SYSIN DD statement defines an in-stream data set that contains a control statement that specifies which input positions to sort on. Don't worry about how this statement is coded. Following the control statement, a delimiter statement (/*) marks the end of the SYSIN data set.

8. The EXEC statement for the AR7100 job step invokes the application program named AR7100. This program extracts data from the sorted accounts receivable master file and the customer master file to create the dunning file. AR7100 requires three data sets, identified by the ddnames ARSORT, CUSTMAST, and DUNNING.

9. The ARSORT DD statement defines the sorted accounts receivable master file. The data set name I specified here is the same as the data set name I specified in the SORTOUT DD statement in the first job step. The file isn't needed after this job step, so it's deleted. Since the file isn't cataloged, I specified the UNIT and VOL=SER parameters. And, since the file already exists, SPACE and DCB information isn't needed.

10. The CUSTMAST DD statement identifies the customer master file, an existing cataloged data set.

11. The DUNNING DD statement defines the output file created by the AR7100 program. Because this file is new, I specified unit, volume, space, and DCB information. The file is kept but not cataloged.

12. The EXEC statement for the AR7200 step invokes the application program named AR7200, which creates the aged-trial-balance and overdue-invoices reports. AR7200 requires three data sets, with ddnames DUNNING, ATB, and OVERDUE.

13. The DUNNING DD statement identifies the dunning file. Here, I coded DISP=OLD since the file was created in the previous job step. Normal disposition defaults to keep, so the file can be processed again in a subsequent job step.

14. The ATB DD statement specifies that the aged-trial-balance report is a SYSOUT data set.

15. The OVERDUE DD statement specifies that the overdue-invoices report is a SYSOUT data set too.

16. The SORT2 step invokes the SORT program again. Like the SORT1 step, DD statements for message output (SYSOUT), sort input (SORTIN), sort output (SORTOUT), a work file (SORTWK01), and a control statement (SYSIN) are provided. Notice that the dunning file is deleted when the job step ends. It's not required after this step.

17. The AR7300 step invokes the third application program, AR7300. It processes the sorted dunning file and produces a cross-reference listing and customer statements.

18. The sorted dunning file, created in the SORT2 step, is processed and deleted.

19. The cross-reference listing is a SYSOUT data set.

20. The statements are also a SYSOUT data set.

Discussion

The examples I presented in this topic are typical of the ones you'll code as you work in an MVS shop. Because you need to know how to code jobs like these, I tried to avoid simple, trivial examples. Nevertheless, as you'll learn in the chapters that follow, MVS jobs can be much more complex than the ones shown in this topic.

Two things should be made clear by these jobs. First, the bulk of your JCL coding involves DD statements. Although there are a few other options you can code on JOB and EXEC statements, those statements are normally coded as they are in this chapter. But there's much more to learn about the DD statement.

Second, the report-preparation job invoked a utility program (SORT) that required additional control statements placed in an in-stream data set. That's typical of many MVS jobs. So even though there's much to learn about MVS JCL, you also need to know about utility control statements. You'll learn about several MVS utility programs later in this book.

In the chapters that follow, you'll learn additional JCL parameters and statements that let you use many advanced functions of MVS. Those chapters build on what's in this chapter, though. So be sure you've mastered what's in this chapter before you move on.

Objective

Given complete specifications for a job, code its JCL using the statements presented in this chapter.

Exercise

Using the following system flowchart and data set requirements, code the JCL necessary to execute the specified job. Allocate 20 cylinders of primary space and 10 cylinders of secondary space to each output data set.

System flowchart

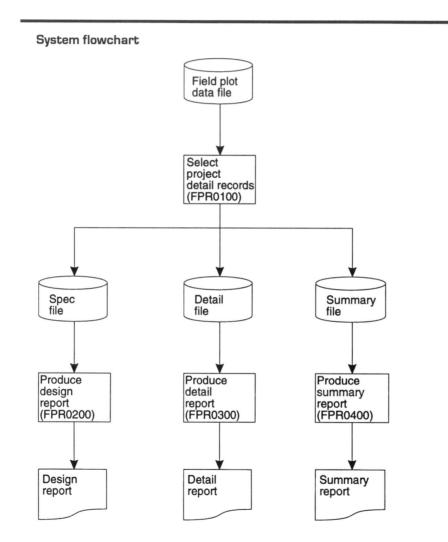

Data set requirements

Step name	Program	ddname	Data set name
FPR0100	FPR0100	FLDPLOT	SYDOE.FPR.PLOT
		SPECFILE	SYDOE.FPR.SPECFILE
		DETAIL	SYDOE.FPR.DETAIL
		SUMMARY	SYDOE.FPR.SUMMARY
FPR0200	FPR0200	SPECFILE	SYDOE.FPR.SPECFILE
		DSGNRPT	SYSOUT
FPR0300	FPR0300	DETAIL	SYDOE.FPR.DETAIL
		DETLRPT	SYSOUT
FPR0400	FPR0400	SUMMARY	SYDOE.FPR.SUMMARY
		SUMMRPT	SYSOUT

Chapter 6

Expanding the basic subset

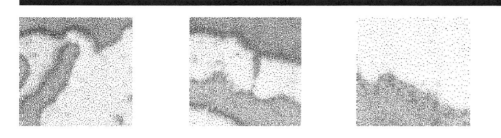

In chapter 5, you learned the basic forms of the basic JCL statements. With them, you can create jobs of considerable complexity. Even so, you've learned only a small fraction of JCL's full capabilities. In this chapter, then, you'll build on the foundation you learned in chapter 5 by learning additional JCL parameters and coding techniques.

Besides standard JCL statements, this chapter also introduces several JES2 and JES3 control statements. You'll find that many of them duplicate the functions provided by standard JCL statements. When you can code either a JCL parameter or a JES2/JES3 parameter for the same function, I suggest you use the JCL parameter. That way, you'll reduce the number of statements you need to code, and you'll simplify your job streams. Nevertheless, it pays to know about the JES2/JES3 statements even when they duplicate JCL functions. And some of the JES2/JES3 parameters you'll learn about in this chapter have no JCL statement parallels.

This chapter has four topics. Topic 1 presents an overview of the JES2/JES3 control statements along with the rules you must follow when you code them. Topic 2 presents the JCL and JES2/JES3 facilities that let you manage the way your programs and jobs are scheduled and executed. Topic 3 presents additional ways to allocate data sets. And topic 4 presents advanced techniques for processing SYSOUT data sets. Although you can read topics 2, 3, and 4 in any order you wish, you should read topic 1 first so you'll know how to code the JES2/JES3 control statements the other topics present.

Topic 1

How to code JES2/JES3 control statements

Besides standard JCL statements, your job streams can include JES2 or JES3 control statements that influence the way the Job Entry Subsystem processes your job. Before you can learn how to use JES2/JES3 statements, you must learn a few simple rules to follow when you code them. That's what you'll learn in this topic.

Figure 6-1 presents the most commonly used JES2 and JES3 control statements and describes their functions. The set of control statements that's available at your installation depends on which Job Entry Subsystem your shop uses. If your installation uses JES2, you can use only the JES2 control statements. Likewise, JES3 users can use only the JES3 control statements. Although the statements have different formats, the JES2 and JES3 control statements I present in this book have similar functions. (I won't cover all of the statements in figure 6-1 in this book; I'll just describe the ones I think are the most useful.)

The basic format of JES2/JES3 control statements

Figure 6-2 gives the rules for coding JES2 and JES3 control statements. To begin with, the JES control statements follow rules that are similar to the rules for coding JCL statements. There are three main differences; (1) JES2/JES3 statements use a different identifier field in the first columns of each statement; (2) JES2/JES3 statements don't have a name field; and (3) JES2/JES3 statements follow different continuation rules.

The identifier field for a JES2 control statement is the same as for a JCL delimiter statement: a slash in column 1 and an asterisk in column 2 (/*). For JES3 control statements, the identifier field is the same as for a JCL comment statement: a slash in columns 1 and 2 and an asterisk in column 3 (//*). The only exceptions are the /*SIGNON and /*SIGNOFF statements, which have the same format as they do with JES2, and the //**PAUSE statement, which is coded with two slashes and two asterisks.

JES2 statements

/*JOBPARM option,option...

>   Specifies processing options for a job. See topic 2, figure 6-7.

/*MESSAGE message

>   Sends a message to the operator.

/*NETACCT account-no

>   Specifies the job account number.

/*NOTIFY user-id

>   Notifies the specified user when the job is completed. Same as the NOTIFY parameter on the JOB statement.

/*OUTPUT code,option,option...

>   Specifies SYSOUT processing options. See topic 4, figure 6-36.

/*PRIORITY priority

>   Specifies the job priority. Same as the PRTY parameter on the JOB statement. If coded, this statement must be placed *before* the JOB statement.

/*ROUTE {XEQ|PRINT} node

>   Routes the job for execution or printing to a specific JES2 node.

/*SETUP volume,volume...

>   Instructs the operator to mount the specified tape volumes prior to job execution.

/*SIGNOFF

>   Ends a remote job session. This statement may be placed anywhere in the job stream.

/*SIGNON   REMOTEnnn [password] [new-password] [password2]

>   Begins a remote job entry session. REMOTE*nnn* begins in column 16; *password* begins in column 25; *new-password* begins in column 35; *password2* begins in column 73. If coded, this statement must be the first statement in the job stream.

/*XEQ node

>   Routes the job to *node* for execution. Same as /* ROUTE XEQ.

/*XMIT node [DLM=xx]

>   Transmits data to another JES2 node. DLM specifies the delimiter; if omitted, /* is assumed.

Figure 6-1   JES2 and JES3 control statements (part 1 of 2)

JES3 statements

`//*DATASET DDNAME=ddname,option,option...`

Supplies data for an in-stream data set. This statement must be placed immediately before the first record of the in-stream data. The data is terminated by an //*ENDDATASET statement.

`//*ENDDATASET`

Indicates the end of an in-stream data set. This statement must be placed immediately after the last record of the in-stream data.

`//*ENDPROCESS`

Indicates the end of a series of //*PROCESS statements.

`//*FORMAT PR,option,option...`

Specifies options for SYSOUT data. See topic 4, figure 6-37.

`//*MAIN option,option...`

Specifies job processing options. See topic 2, figure 6-6.

`//*NET option,option...`

Specifies dependencies between jobs.

`//*NETACCT option,option...`

Specifies job accounting information. The statement must immediatly follow the JOB statement.

`//*OPERATOR message`

Sends a message to the operator. This statement may be placed anywhere after the JOB card.

`//**PAUSE`

Pauses the input reader until the operator issues a *START operator command. This statement must be placed *before* the JOB statement.

`//*PROCESS option`

Controls JES3 job processing. An //*ENDPROCESS statement must follow any //*PROCESS statements.

`//*ROUTE XEQ node`

Routes the job to another JES3 node.

`/*SIGNOFF`

Ends a remote job session. This statement may be placed anywhere in the job stream.

`/*SIGNON          workn AR passwd-1    passwd-2    new-passwd`

Begins a remote job entry session. *Workn* begins in column 16; *passwd-1* begins in column 25; *passwd-2* begins in column 35; *new-passwd* begins in column 44. An A in column 22 indicates an automatic reader, and an R in column 23 indicates that print output will be rescheduled if the device is not ready. If coded, this statement must be the first statement in the job stream.

Figure 6-1   JES2 and JES3 control statements (part 2 of 2)

Basic format of JES2/JES3 control statements

```
identifier operation [parameters]
```

Explanation

identifier	For JES2 control statements, a slash in column 1 and an asterisk in column 2 (/*).
	For JES3 control statements, slashes in columns 1 and 2 and an asterisk in column 3 (//*). Exceptions: the JES3 SIGNON and SIGNOFF statements use the same identifier format as JES2 control statements (/*), and the identifier for the PAUSE statement is two slashes followed by two asterisks (//**).
operation	The name of the JES2/JES3 control statement. It should immediately follow the identifier with no intervening spaces. It should be followed by at least one space.
parameters	One or more parameters, depending on the operation. Individual parameters are usually separated from one another by commas, with no intervening spaces. In some cases, parameters are separated from one another by one or more spaces.

Figure 6-2   JES2/JES3 control statement fields

Just as in a JCL statement, the operation field of a JES2/JES3 control statement indicates the statement's function. However, it immediately follows the identifier field without any space, like this:

```
/*JOBPARM
```

or like this:

```
//*MAIN
```

If you mistakenly leave a space between the identifier field and the operation field, MVS can't tell if the statement is a JES control statement or a JCL comment or delimiter statement.

You code parameters for JES control statements much as you code them for JCL statements. Many of the parameters are positional parameters that are separated by commas. A few statements have positional parameters that are separated by spaces. And a couple of statements have keyword parameters that can be coded in any order you wish, separated by commas.

There's only one JES2 control statement that you can continue to more than one line (/*OUTPUT), and it has an unusual continuation rule that I'll explain in topic 4. It's easy to continue a JES3 control statement: Just end the line with a comma, code //* on the next line in columns 1 through 3, and continue the parameters field in column 4. Do not code a space in column 4 or MVS won't be able to tell the JES3 continuation statement from a JCL comment statement.

JES2

```
//SYDOEX     JOB   USER=SYDOE,PASSWORD=XXXXXXXX
/*JOBPARM    SYSAFF=MVSA
//STEP1      EXEC  PGM=SORT
//SYSOUT     DD    SYSOUT=*
 .
 .
 .
```

JES3

```
//SYDOEX     JOB   USER=SYDOE,PASSWORD=XXXXXXXX
//*MAIN      SYSTEM=MVSA
//STEP1      EXEC  PGM=SORT
//SYSOUT     DD    SYSOUT=*
 .
 .
 .
```

Figure 6-3   Examples of JES2 and JES3 control statements in a job stream

Where to place JES2/JES3 control statements in the job stream

Normally, you code JES2 and JES3 control statements between the job's JOB statement and its first EXEC statement. Figure 6-3 shows examples of JES2 and JES3 control statements coded in this position. These statements follow the JOB statement so that JES2/JES3 can associate them with a particular job. The descriptions of the JES2/JES3 commands in figure 6-1 point out the exceptions to this standard position.

Discussion

Because JES2 and JES3 statements are coded along with a job's JCL statements, and because they follow a similar format, the distinction between JES control statements and JCL statements isn't really very important. So, if you wish, you can think of JES2/JES3 control statements as additional JCL statements that have slightly different coding rules than the basic JCL statements.

Objective

Describe the rules you must follow when coding JES2/JES3 control statements.

Topic 2

JCL and JES2/JES3 facilities to manage job and program execution

In chapter 5, you learned how to code basic forms of the JOB and EXEC statements to identify jobs and job steps. Now, I'll explain additional parameters you can code on the JOB and EXEC statements to exercise greater control over how your jobs and programs are scheduled and executed. Figures 6-4 and 6-5 show the formats of the EXEC and JOB statements, including all of the parameters I'll cover in this topic. These formats are nearly complete; although there are a few other JOB and EXEC statement parameters documented in IBM literature, they're rarely used.

Besides the JOB and EXEC JCL statements, both JES2 and JES3 provide statements that affect job processing. Under JES3, the //*MAIN statement, shown in figure 6-6, includes parameters that affect job processing. Under JES2, the /*JOBPARM statement, shown in figure 6-7, has a similar function. (The /*PRIORITY statement, which I'll show you later in this topic, affects job processing too.) The //*MAIN and /*JOBPARM formats in figures 6-6 and 6-7 show just the parameters I'll describe in this topic; there are others, but they're either too advanced to cover here or they don't relate to job processing. Whenever you use the //*MAIN and the /*JOBPARM statements, they should be placed after the JOB statement and before the first EXEC statement in your job stream.

The JCL and JES2/JES3 facilities I'll describe in this topic fall into six broad categories that let you: (1) influence the way your job is scheduled, (2) specify a job's or program's storage requirements, (3) control a job's or program's performance, (4) establish job or program processing limits, (5) execute job steps conditionally, and (6) specify special data sets that affect job processing.

How to influence the way your job is scheduled

When you submit a job, JES2 or JES3 reads the job from a reader (usually an internal reader) and places it on a spool volume. Then, the job waits to be selected for execution by an active initiator. By coding certain JCL and JES2/JES3 parameters, you can influence the scheduling process.

The EXEC statement

```
//stepname EXEC   PGM=program-name
```

$$[,ADDRSPC= \left\{ \begin{array}{l} \underline{VIRT} \\ REAL \end{array} \right\}]$$

$$[,COND=([(value,op,step)...][, \left\{ \begin{array}{l} EVEN \\ ONLY \end{array} \right\}])]$$

```
[ ,DPRTY=([value1][,value2]) ]
[ ,PARM=information ]
[ ,PERFORM=group ]
```

$$[,REGION= \left\{ \begin{array}{l} valueK \\ valueM \end{array} \right\}]$$

$$[,TIME= \left\{ \begin{array}{l} ([min][,sec]) \\ NOLIMIT \\ MAXIMUM \end{array} \right\}]$$

Positional parameter

PGM   Specifies the name of the program to be executed for this job step.

Keyword parameters

ADDRSPC   Optional; specifies whether the step requires virtual or real storage. The default is
               VIRT.

COND   Optional; specifies one or more conditions which, if true, cause MVS to bypass the
               step. EVEN means the step should execute even if a previous step has abended;
               ONLY means the step should execute only if a previous step has abended.

DPRTY   Optional; specifies a dispatching priority, which determines the job step's impor-
               tance relative to other job steps that are currently executing. The dispatching
               priority is calculated by multiplying *value1* by 16 and adding *value2*.

PARM   Optional; specifies information that's passed to the program.

PERFORM   Optional; associates the step with a performance group.

REGION   Optional; sets a limit for the largest amount of virtual or real storage the step may
               use.

TIME   Optional; limits the amount of time the step can use the processor in minutes and
               seconds. For MVS/ESA only, you can specify NOLIMIT to allow the step to run
               indefinitely, or MAXIMUM to limit the step to 357,912 minutes.

Figure 6-4   The EXEC statement

The JOB statement

```
//jobname  JOB   [ accounting information ] [ ,programmer name ]

                 [ ,ADDRSPC= {VIRT } ]
                             {REAL }

                 [ ,BYTES= {value                  } ]
                           {([value][,action])     }

                 [ ,CARDS= {value                  } ]
                           {([value][,action])     }

                 [ ,CLASS=class ]

                 [ ,COND=((value,op)...) ]

                 [ ,LINES= {value                  } ]
                           {([value][,action])     }

                 [ ,MSGCLASS=class ]

                 [ ,MSGLEVEL=(stmt,msg) ]

                 [ ,NOTIFY=user-id ]

                 [ ,PAGES= {value                  } ]
                           {([value][,action])     }

                 [ ,PASSWORD=password ]

                 [ ,PERFORM=group ]

                 [ ,PRTY=priority ]

                 [ ,REGION= {valueK } ]
                            {valueM }

                 [ ,TIME=  {([min][,sec])  } ]
                           {NOLIMIT        }
                           {MAXIMUM        }

                            {COPY    }
                 [ ,TYPRUN= {HOLD    } ]
                            {JCLHOLD }
                            {SCAN    }

                 [ ,USER=user-id ]
```

Positional parameters

accounting information	May or may not be required, depending on the installation. For JES2 installation, see figure 5-7 for format.
programmer name	May or may not be required, depending on the installation. If required, the installation may dictate a specialized format.

Figure 6-5   The JOB statement (part 1 of 3)

Keyword parameters

ADDRSPC	Optional; specifies whether the job requires virtual or real storage. The default is VIRT.
BYTES	Optional; MVS/ESA only. Specifies the maximum number of bytes (in thousands) of SYSOUT data the job can produce. *Value* is a one- to six-digit number. If *value* is omitted, an installation-defined default is assumed. *Action* specifies what the system should do if the limit is exceeded. Specify WARNING to issue an operator message, CANCEL to cancel the job, or DUMP to cancel the job and produce a storage dump. If *action* is omitted, an installation-defined default is assumed.
CARDS	Optional; MVS/ESA only. Specifies the maximum number of cards of SYSOUT data the job can produce. *Value* is a one- to eight-digit number. If *value* is omitted, an installation-defined default is assumed. *Action* specifies what the system should do if the limit is exceeded. Specify WARNING to issue an operator message, CANCEL to cancel the job, or DUMP to cancel the job and produce a storage dump. If *action* is omitted, an installation-defined default is assumed.
CLASS	Optional; specifies a single-character job class used to schedule the job.
COND	Optional; specifies a condition which, if true, causes MVS to terminate the job.
LINES	Optional; MVS/ESA only. Specifies the maximum number of lines (in thousands) of SYSOUT data the job can produce. *Value* is a one- to six-digit number. If *value* is omitted, an installation-defined default is assumed. *Action* specifies what the system should do if the limit is exceeded. Specify WARNING to issue an operator message, CANCEL to cancel the job, or DUMP to cancel the job and produce a storage dump. If *action* is omitted, an installation-defined default is assumed.
MSGCLASS	Optional; specifies a single-character output class to be used for the job's message output.
MSGLEVEL	Optional; controls the amount of system messages produced for the job. See figure 5-9 for details.
NOTIFY	Optional; specifies a TSO user to be notified when the job completes.
PAGES	Optional; MVS/ESA only. Specifies the maximum number of pages of SYSOUT data the job can produce. *Value* is a one- to eight-digit number. If *value* is omitted, an installation-defined default is assumed. *Action* specifies what the system should do if the limit is exceeded. Specify WARNING to issue an operator message, CANCEL to cancel the job, or DUMP to cancel the job and produce a storage dump. If *action* is omitted, an installation-defined default is assumed.
PASSWORD	May be required to supply a password that authorizes access to the system.
PERFORM	Optional; associates the job with a performance group.
PRTY	Optional; specifies a number from 0 through 14 (JES3) or 15 (JES2) that indicates a job's scheduling priority within its job class.
REGION	Optional; sets a limit for the largest amount of virtual or real storage any of the job's steps may use.

Figure 6-5   The JOB statement (part 2 of 3)

Keyword parameters

TIME   Optional; limits the amount of time the job can use the processor in minutes and seconds. For MVS/ESA only, you can specify NOLIMIT to allow the job to run indefinitely, or MAXIMUM to limit the job to 357,912 minutes.

TYPRUN   Optional; indicates special JES processing. COPY (JES2 only) means that the job stream is printed as a SYSOUT data set but not processed; HOLD means that the job must be released by the operator before it will be processed; JCLHOLD (JES2 only) is similar to HOLD, but the job is held before its JCL is scanned rather than after; SCAN means the job isn't executed but its JCL is scanned for syntax errors.

USER   May be required to specify the user-id of the user who submitted the job.

Figure 6-5   The JOB statement (part 3 of 3)

How to specify a job class

You learned in chapter 3 that initiators select jobs for execution based on job classes. For example, an initiator that can process class A, B, and C jobs selects only jobs with class A, B, or C. An installation can control the level of multiprogramming by carefully specifying which classes each initiator can process.

Normally, when you submit a job, JES2/JES3 assigns a default job class that's determined by the reader that processes the job. As a result, jobs submitted from TSO might have a different default job class than jobs submitted from a particular RJE station. It's a simple matter to specify a job class that's different from the default, however. All you do is code the CLASS parameter on your job's JOB statement, as in example 1 in figure 6-8. Here, the job SYDOEA will be scheduled as a class F job.

Under JES3, you can also specify the job class in a //*MAIN statement, as in example 2 in figure 6-8. Unless there's some compelling reason to specify the job class this way, I suggest you specify it on the JOB statement instead. There's no JES2 control statement parameter that lets you specify a job class.

How to specify a job's scheduling priority

If there's more than one job of the same class in the JES spool, the initiator uses the jobs' priorities to determine which job to execute first. As a result, job priority lets you specify a job's importance relative to other jobs with the same class. If there's more than one job with the same class and priority, the jobs are processed in the order in which they were submitted.

The JES3 //*MAIN statement

```
//*MAIN     [ BYTES=(value[,action]) ]

            [ ,CARDS=(value[,action]) ]

            [ ,CLASS=job-class ]

            [ ,HOLD= { YES } ]
                     { NO  }

                        { LOW  }
            [ ,IORATE= { MED  } ]
                        { HIGH }

            [ ,LINES=(value[,action]) ]

            [ ,LREGION=valueK ]

            [ ,PAGES=(value[,action]) ]

            [ ,SYSTEM=system ]
```

Figure 6-6   The JES3 //*MAIN statement (part 1 of 2)

Figure 6-9 shows two ways to specify a job's priority. In example 1, I coded the PRTY parameter of the JOB statement to assign a priority of 12 to the job. Example 2 is for JES2 only; it includes a JES2 /*PRIORITY statement to assign the job priority. Since the JOB PRTY parameter and the /*PRIORITY statement are equivalent, I recommend you use the JOB PRTY parameter. (Notice in example 2 that the /*PRIORITY statement is placed *before* the JOB statement to which it applies. The /*PRIORITY statement is one of the few JES2/JES3 statements that's placed before rather than after the JOB statement.)

There's a slight difference in the priority values you can specify for JES2 and JES3 systems. Under JES2, you can specify a one- or two-digit number ranging from 0 to 15; 15 is the highest priority, 0 is the lowest. Under JES3, the upper priority limit is 14. For both systems, an installation default applies if you don't specify a priority value.

Explanation

BYTES

Optional; specifies the maximum number of bytes (in thousands) of SYSOUT data the job may produce. *Value* is a one- to six-digit number. *Action* specifies what JES3 action should be taken if the maximum is exceeded. Specify WARNING or W to issue an operator message, CANCEL or C to cancel the job, or DUMP or D to cancel the job and produce a storage dump.

CARDS

Optional; specifies the maximum number of SYSOUT card records (in hundreds) the job may produce. *Value* is a one- to four-digit number. *Action* specifies what JES3 action should be taken if the maximum is exceeded. Specify WARNING or W to issue an operator message, CANCEL or C to cancel the job, or DUMP or D to cancel the job and produce a storage dump.

CLASS

Optional; specifies a single-character job class for the job.

HOLD

Optional; specifies whether the job is to be held. A held job must be released by the operator before it will execute. The default is NO.

IORATE

Optional; estimates the I/O rate for the job.

LINES

Optional; specifies the maximum number (in thousands) of SYSOUT print records the job may produce. *Value* is a one- to four-digit number. *Action* specifies what JES3 action should be taken if the maximum is exceeded. Specify WARNING or W to issue an operator message, CANCEL or C to cancel the job, or DUMP or D to cancel the job and produce a storage dump.

LREGION

Optional; estimates the size of the largest region required by the job in kilobytes. *Value* is a one- to four-digit number.

PAGES

Optional; specifies the maximum number of SYSOUT pages the job may produce. *Value* is a one- to eight-digit number. *Action* specifies what JES3 action should be taken if the maximum is exceeded. Specify WARNING or W to issue an operator message, CANCEL or C to cancel the job, or DUMP or D to cancel the job and produce a storage dump.

SYSTEM

Optional; indicates which system or systems may process the job. *System* may be coded in one of several ways. ANY means that any system can run the job, JGLOBAL means that the global processor must run the job, and JLOCAL means that any local processor can run the job. Or, you may specify one or more one- to eight-character main-names, which identify individual processors. If you code more than one main-name, the list must be enclosed in parentheses. Code a slash (/) in front of the list to indicate that the job can run on any processors other than the ones listed.

Figure 6-6   The JES3 //*MAIN statement (part 2 of 2)

The JES2 / *JOBPARM statement

```
/*JOBPARM    [ BYTES=value ]
             [ ,CARDS=value ]
             [ ,LINES=value ]
             [ ,PAGES=value ]
             [ ,SYSAFF=(system) ]
             [ ,TIME=value ]
```

Explanation

BYTES	Optional; specifies the maximum number of bytes (in thousands) of SYSOUT data the job may produce. *Value* is a one- to six-digit number.
CARDS	Optional; specifies the maximum number of SYSOUT card records the job may produce. *Value* is a one- to seven-digit number.
LINES	Optional; specifies the maximum number (in thousands) of SYSOUT print records the job may produce. *Value* is a one- to four-digit number.
PAGES	Optional; specifies the maximum number of SYSOUT pages the job may produce. *Value* is a one- to five-digit number.
SYSAFF	Optional; indicates which system or systems may process the job. *System* may be coded in one of three ways: ANY, meaning that any available JES2 system may be used; an asterisk (*), meaning that the system that reads the job will also process it; or a four-character system-id of the system you want to process the job.
TIME	Optional; specifies an estimate of the job's elapsed execution time in minutes. *Value* is a one- to four-digit number.

Figure 6-7   The JES2 / *JOBPARM statement

How to hold a job

Sometimes, you want a job to be placed in a hold status so it won't be scheduled for execution until an operator issues a command that releases the job. For example, you might want a tape processing job to remain in the job queue until the system operator is ready to mount the tape. Or, you might want a job to wait until another job has completed.

Figure 6-10 shows three ways you can specify that your job be held. In example 1, I specified TYPRUN=HOLD on the JOB statement. That works for both JES2 and JES3. In example 2, I used the CLASS parameter of the JOB statement to specify a *held job class* (in this case, class H). Simply put, all jobs submitted for a held job class are held whether or not TYPRUN=HOLD is specified on their job cards. The use of held job classes is installation dependent, so be sure to find out if your installation has any.

Example 1

```
//SYDOEA    JOB   USER=SYDOE,PASSWORD=XXXXXXXX,CLASS=F
```

Example 2 (JES3 only)

```
//SYDOEA    JOB   USER=SYDOE,PASSWORD=XXXXXXXX
//*MAIN CLASS=F
```

Figure 6-8   Two ways to assign a job class

Example 1

```
//SYDOEA    JOB   USER=SYDOE,PASSWORD=XXXXXXXX,CLASS=F,PRTY=12
```

Example 2 (JES2 only)

```
/*PRIORITY  12
//SYDOEA    JOB   USER=SYDOE,PASSWORD=XXXXXXXX,CLASS=F
```

Figure 6-9   Two ways to assign a scheduling priority

Example 1

```
//SYDOEA    JOB   USER=SYDOE,PASSWORD=XXXXXXXX,TYPRUN=HOLD
```

Example 2

```
//SYDOEA    JOB   USER=SYDOE,PASSWORD=XXXXXXXX,CLASS=H
```

Example 3 (JES3 only)

```
//SYDOEA    JOB   USER=SYDOE,PASSWORD=XXXXXXXX
//*MAIN      HOLD=YES
```

Figure 6-10   Three ways to hold a job

Example 3 in figure 6-10 shows how to use the HOLD parameter of the JES3 //*MAIN statement. This has the same effect as coding TYPRUN=HOLD on the JOB statement.

How to scan a job for syntax errors without scheduling it for execution

The TYPRUN option of the JOB statement has another function besides specifying that a job be held: You can use it to cause JES2/JES3 to scan a job stream for syntax errors without scheduling the job for execution. To scan a job, just code TYPRUN=SCAN on the JOB statement.

A job that specifies TYPRUN=SCAN is processed by the JES2/JES3 converter, which converts the JCL and JES2/JES3 statements in your job into an internal form. In the process, the converter retrieves JCL procedures, lists the JCL and JES2/JES3 statements in the job stream, and detects most coding errors. It can't catch every error, though. For example, the converter can't detect an incorrect data set name or incorrect DCB information. But it will catch things like misspelled parameters or incorrectly coded continuation lines. If you have a complicated job that you want to be sure isn't terminated because of a simple syntax error, it's a good idea to submit the job with TYPRUN=SCAN before you submit it for execution.

How to schedule a job for a specific system

As you know, both JES2 and JES3 can be used to manage a *multiprocessor network* that consists of more than one system. In a multiprocessor network, each system operates under the control of its own copy of MVS. However, the JES components of each processor's operating system are connected in various ways to the JES components of the other processors. And a common spool is used to service all of the processors. As a result, JES2 and JES3 can control how the systems within the multiprocessor network process jobs.

When you log on under TSO, you're connected to one of the systems in the network. By default, that system is used to process any batch jobs you submit. Standard JCL doesn't provide any way to change that default, but both JES2 and JES3 do. Figure 6-11 shows several examples of specifying which system within a multiprocessor network should process a job. The first two examples are for JES2; the others are for JES3. In both JES2 and JES3, the term *system affinity* is used to describe the relationship between a job and the system on which it executes.

How to specify system affinity under JES2   Examples 1 and 2 of figure 6-11 are for JES2 systems. Here, I coded the SYSAFF parameter of the /*JOBPARM statement to specify which system should

---

Example 1 (JES2 only)

```
//SYDOEA    JOB    USER=SYDOE,PASSWORD=XXXXXXXX
/*JOBPARM   SYSAFF=MVSA
```

Example 2 (JES2 only)

```
//SYDOEA    JOB    USER=SYDOE,PASSWORD=XXXXXXXX
/*JOBPARM   SYSAFF=(MVSA,MVSB)
```

Example 3 (JES3 only)

```
//SYDOEA    JOB    USER=SYDOE,PASSWORD=XXXXXXXX
//*MAIN     SYSTEM=MVSA
```

Example 4 (JES3 only)

```
//SYDOEA    JOB    USER=SYDOEA,PASSWORD=XXXXXXXX
//*MAIN     SYSTEM=(MVSA,MVSC,MVSD)
```

Example 5 (JES3 only)

```
//SYDOEA    JOB    USER=SYDOEA,PASSWORD=XXXXXXXX
//*MAIN     SYSTEM=/MVSB
```

Figure 6-11   Specifying system affinity

execute the job. Under JES2, each system within a network is given a unique four-character name. So, the easiest way to cause a job to execute on a particular system is to specify that system's name in the SYSAFF parameter. That's just what example 1 does.

Example 2 shows how to specify that any of several systems can execute the job. Here, I specified two processors, enclosed in parentheses. When the job is ready to be scheduled, JES2 will use one of the two processors I listed to execute the job.

There are two other ways you can code the SYSAFF parameter under JES2. First, you can specify that the job should run on the system from which it is submitted by coding SYSAFF=*. There's little reason to code this, though, since it's the default. Second, you can tell JES2 to decide which system to use for the job by coding SYSAFF=ANY. Then, JES2 selects any available processor to execute the job.

How to specify system affinity under JES3   Under JES3, you use the SYSTEM parameter of the //*MAIN statement to indicate which processor or processors are eligible to process a job. Examples 3 and 4 in figure 6-11 show that you can code the //*MAIN SYSTEM parameter much like you code the /*JOBPARM SYSAFF parameter under JES2. In addition, you can code SYSTEM=ANY, SYSTEM=JGLOBAL, or SYSTEM=JLOCAL. ANY means that any available processor can be used to process the job. JGLOBAL means that the JES3 global processor must process the job. (The global processor is the one that's in charge of the entire network.) JLOCAL means that any JES3 local processor can be used for the job. (A local processor is a processor that's controlled by the global processor.)

If you code a slash after the equal sign in the SYSTEM parameter, JES3 will use a processor other than the ones you list to process the job. This might be useful if, for example, a job can be processed by any processor in the network except one. Example 5 illustrates this. Here, the job can be processed by any processor except the one named MVSB.

How to specify a job's storage requirements

As you know, each job on an MVS system executes within its own private address space. Within the address space, a region is allocated to provide storage for job steps. MVS JCL provides two parameters, ADDRSPC and REGION, that let you specify how that storage is allocated. ADDRSPC specifies whether the region is pageable or non-pageable, and REGION limits the size of the region.

Both of these parameters can be coded on an EXEC statement or on the JOB statement. If you specify ADDRSPC or REGION on a JOB statement, your specification applies to each step in the job. In that case, any ADDRSPC or REGION parameters you code on EXEC statements for the job are ignored.

A related parameter, the LREGION parameter of the JES3 //*MAIN statement, lets you specify an estimate of a job's storage requirements. I'll describe it after I describe the ADDRSPC and REGION parameters.

How to request real storage: the ADDRSPC parameter

You use the ADDRSPC parameter to specify that one or all of your job steps require real rather than virtual storage. If you specify ADDRSPC=REAL, the entire region allocated for the job step is not subject to the paging process. In other words, the storage pages are fixed in real storage and not paged out.

Frankly, you may never find a need to specify ADDRSPC=REAL. Only specialized programs need non-pageable storage. And, unless your program absolutely requires non-pageable storage, you shouldn't request it because it can severely degrade the performance of other jobs on the system.

How to limit a region size: the REGION parameter

When a job step begins, MVS allocates a region of storage that's large enough to hold the program and any required control blocks. As the program executes, it can enlarge its region by acquiring additional storage. For example, programs that process VSAM files often need to acquire additional storage for buffer space as they execute. As a result, the amount of storage required and used by a program can vary as the program executes.

You can use the REGION parameter on a JOB or EXEC statement to limit the amount of storage that can be acquired for a job step's region. You specify that limit in terms of kilobytes or megabytes; REGION=512K limits the region to about 512 thousand bytes, and REGION=4M limits the region to about four million bytes. If you specify the region limit in terms of kilobytes, you should specify an even number. For megabytes, you can specify an even or odd number.

If you omit the REGION parameter, an installation dependent default applies. Typically, the default is 256K. If you specify REGION=0K or REGION=0M, no limit is set; your program can acquire as much storage as is available in its private address space.

How to specify a storage estimate:
the LREGION parameter (JES3 only)

Under JES3, you can provide an estimate of the storage requirements of the largest step in your job by coding the LREGION parameter on the //*MAIN statement. For example, the statement

```
//*MAIN LREGION=120K
```

gives 120K as the job's storage estimate. The value you code in the LREGION parameter doesn't limit the amount of storage your job can acquire. Instead, it's used by JES3 to improve job scheduling.

If you specify an accurate value for the LREGION parameter, JES3 can utilize the processors under its control as efficiently as possible. It's not always easy to determine an accurate LREGION value, however. That's because LREGION doesn't indicate the total amount of virtual storage a job step needs. Instead, it estimates the job step's *working set*, which indicates the amount of real storage required to support the job step's virtual storage requirements.

How to control a job's performance

Several of the parameters you've learned how to use in this topic, such as CLASS and LREGION, affect your job's performance by controlling how the job is scheduled. Two other JOB and EXEC statement parameters, PERFORM and DPRTY, affect a job's or step's performance in a more direct way. The PERFORM parameter associates a job or step with a performance group, which an installation uses for performance control. And the DPRTY parameter controls a step's performance during program execution.

How to assign a job to a performance group: the PERFORM parameter

For each MVS installation, systems programmers create several *performance groups*. Each performance group has performance characteristics associated with it, so an installation can control the performance of various types of jobs. For example, a performance group for TSO users would emphasize fast response time for a relatively short duration. One of the main functions of performance groups is to control how frequently a job's address space can be swapped in and out.

Each job class is associated with a default performance group. You can, however, specify the PERFORM parameter on a JOB or EXEC statement to override the performance group associated with the job class. For example, PERFORM=100 specifies that performance group 100 rather than the default performance group should be used. The value you specify should be one of the installation's defined performance groups, which is always in the range of 1 through 999.

How to specify a job step's dispatching priority: the DPRTY parameter

A job step's *dispatching priority* determines its importance relative to other job steps that are currently swapped in and competing for processor resources. As a result, once a job step is swapped in, its dispatching priority can have a dramatic effect on performance.

To specify a dispatching priority, you code one or two values in the DPRTY parameter on an EXEC statement. The first value you specify is multiplied by 16. The second value, if specified, is then added to the result to determine the dispatching priority. For example, if you specify DPRTY=2, the dispatching priority is 32

(2 x 16 = 32). If you specify DPRTY=(1,5), the dispatching priority is 21 (1 x 16 + 5 = 21). Both values must be between 0 and 15. Job steps with higher dispatching priority values are given preference over those with lower values.

Just as each job class has a default performance group, each job class also has a default dispatching priority that applies to each step in the job. So you should specify the DPRTY parameter only when you want to override a job step's default dispatching priority.

How to establish processing limits

MVS provides several ways an installation can limit a job's processing. By specifying a default time limit, an installation can limit how long a job can execute. By specifying default SYSOUT limits, the installation can limit the amount of SYSOUT data a job can produce. The default limits are usually large enough that most jobs won't exceed them. However, some jobs might take an unusually long time to execute or produce unusually large amounts of output. For jobs like that, you may need to increase the job class defaults for processing limits to prevent the job from being canceled.

How to specify a job's execution time limit

To override the default execution time limit, you specify the TIME parameter on a JOB or EXEC statement. In the TIME parameter, you specify a value for minutes and an optional value for seconds. For example,

```
TIME=30
```

specifies a time limit of thirty minutes. And,

```
TIME=(2,30)
```

specifies a time limit of two minutes and thirty seconds. If you omit the minutes value, you must use parentheses and a comma to indicate the missing value. For example,

```
TIME=(,30)
```

specifies a time limit of 30 seconds.

If you specify a time limit of 1440 minutes, no time checking is done at all. As a result, you should specify TIME=1440 for a job that you want to allow to execute indefinitely. (1440 corresponds to the number of minutes in 24 hours.)

MVS/ESA has two additional options for the TIME parameter. To allow a job to run indefinitely with no time limit at all, specify the NOLIMIT option:

```
TIME=NOLIMIT
```

This has the same effect as coding TIME=1440. To specify the maximum time limit, code the TIME parameter like this:

```
TIME=MAXIMUM
```

The maximum time limit is 357,912 minutes, which allows your job to run uninterrupted for more than 248 days.

If you specify a TIME parameter on a JOB statement, the time limit applies to the entire job. As each step is executed, its execution time is added to the total execution time for the job; if the job's time limit is exceeded, the job is canceled. In contrast, when you specify a time limit on an EXEC statement, it applies only to that job step.

A potential conflict occurs when an EXEC statement specifies a time limit that's more than the limit remaining for the entire job. In that case, the job time limit takes precedence over the step time limit. To illustrate, suppose a three step job specifies TIME=60 on the JOB statement and TIME=50 on the EXEC statement for the third step. If the first and second steps each execute for 10 minutes, there's just 40 minutes left on the job time limit for the third step. Thus, the third step is effectively limited to 40 minutes, not 50 minutes as the EXEC statement's TIME parameter specifies.

Because the job time limit has precedence over a step time limit, you should always specify a TIME parameter on a JOB statement if you specify one on an EXEC statement. Otherwise, the default job time limit may nullify the TIME parameter you specify on the EXEC statement. For example, if one of your job steps needs to run indefinitely, you should specify TIME=1400 or TIME=NOLIMIT (MVS/ESA only) on both the JOB and EXEC statements.

How to specify SYSOUT limits

Both JES2 and JES3 provide control statement parameters that let you limit the amount of SYSOUT data a job produces. For JES2, you code a /*JOBPARM statement; for JES3, you code a //*MAIN statement. Under both subsystems, you can limit (1) the total number of bytes of SYSOUT data produced, (2) the number of SYSOUT card records produced, (3) the number of SYSOUT print lines produced, or (4) the number of SYSOUT print pages produced. As

I've already mentioned, the default values for these limits are usually large. So you need to override them only for jobs that produce unusually large amounts of output.

Under JES2, you specify the BYTES, CARDS, LINES, and PAGES parameters to specify output processing limits. For example, if you specify LINES=20000 on a /*JOBPARM statement, your job is terminated if it produces more than 20,000 lines of print output. The range of values you can specify depends on the parameter; see figure 6-7 for details.

Under JES3, you specify the BYTES, CARDS, LINES, and PAGES parameters much as you do under JES2. However, JES3 allows an additional subparameter that specifies what action to take if the limit is exceeded. For example, if you specify PAGES=(1000,C) on a //*MAIN statement, the job is canceled if more than 1,000 output pages are produced. If you specify PAGES=(1000,W), however, a warning message is produced. If you specify PAGES= (1000,D), the job is canceled when 1,000 pages are produced. In addition, a storage dump is printed.

Under MVS/ESA, you can set SYSOUT limits by using the new BYTES, CARDS, LINES, and PAGES parameters on the JOB statement. Like JES3, the new ESA JOB parameters let you specify an action to take if the limit is exceeded. For example, if you code PAGE=(1000,CANCEL) on a JOB statement, the job is canceled if more than 1,000 pages of SYSOUT data are produced. If you don't specify an action, your installation's default is used.

How to specify processing limits using the JES2 accounting information parameter

At a JES2 installation, you may be able to specify processing limits in the accounting information parameter of the JOB statement. Figure 6-12 shows the format of the accounting information parameter and an example of coding it with processing limits. The three subparameters that specify processing limits are *time*, which specifies an execution time limit for the job, *lines*, which limits the amount of SYSOUT printed output the job can produce, and *cards*, which limits the amount of SYSOUT punched output the job can produce. For a more complete discussion of the accounting information parameter, refer back to chapter 5.

JES2 accounting information parameter

`(pano,room,`*`time,lines,cards,`*`forms,copies,log,linect)`

(See figure 5-7 for details of the JES2 accounting information subparameters)

Example

`//SYDOEA    JOB    (1234,,30,2500,1000)...`

Figure 6-12   Using the JES2 accounting information parameter to supply processing limits

How to execute job steps conditionally

When a program completes execution normally (that is, it does not abend), it passes a value called a *return code* back to MVS. In some cases, the value of a job step's return code may affect subsequent processing. So, JCL provides facilities that let you test return codes to determine whether certain processing steps should be bypassed.

Return codes can be generated by a system utility program, such as a compiler. Or, user-written programs can generate a return code. In either case, return codes usually follow the conventions described in figure 6-13. Here, 0 means the job step executed normally with no unusual conditions encountered; 4 means that something unusual but not too serious happened; 8 or 12 means that more serious conditions were encountered; and 16 means that the program terminated itself because of an error from which it could not recover. Other return codes, especially for user-written programs, might indicate specific conditions that were encountered. Although a return code can range in value from 0 to 4096, most return codes are multiples of four between 0 and 16, according to the conventions described in figure 6-13.

There are three ways to code JCL to test for condition codes. First, you can code a COND parameter on the job's JOB statement. In this case, the job is terminated if the specified conditions occur. Second, you can code a COND parameter on an EXEC statement. In this case, the job step is bypassed if the specified conditions occur. Third, if you're using MVS/ESA, you can use the //IF, //ELSE, and //ENDIF JCL statements to control job step execution.

Return code	Meaning
0	Program ran to successful completion.
4	Program encountered a minor error but was able to recover.
8	The program encountered a problem that inhibited successful execution.
12	The program encountered a problem that inhibited successful execution; normally, this indicates a more serious error than return code 8.
16	The program encountered a serious error and was not able to continue.

Figure 6-13   Typical return codes issued by MVS programs

How to use the COND parameter in a JOB statement

When you specify the COND parameter in a JOB statement, you specify the conditions that cause the job to stop processing. For example, suppose you have a job with several steps, each of which issues a return code. If any of the steps issues a return code of 4 or more, the job should stop processing; in other words, all of the remaining steps in the job should be bypassed. To do this, you could code the JOB statement like this:

```
//SYDOEA    JOB   USER=SYDOE,PASSWORD=XXXXXXXX,
//                COND=(4,LE)
```

Here, COND=(4,LE) means that if 4 is less than or equal to the return code issued by any job step, the remaining job steps are to be bypassed.

Figure 6-14 shows the relational operators you can code in the COND parameter. Frankly, the way you use these relational operators in the COND parameter can be confusing. Remember that the value you code in the COND parameter is compared with the actual return code using the relational operator you specify. If the relationship is true, all remaining job steps are bypassed. So the COND parameter specifies not the conditions under which processing is to continue, but the conditions under which processing is to be terminated.

Figure 6-15 shows three examples of the COND parameter on a JOB statement. In example 1, processing is stopped if any job step issues a return code of 8. Examples 2 and 3 show how you can combine conditions in a single COND parameter; you can combine up to eight conditions in this way. When you combine conditions, job processing stops if any of the conditions you specify are true. So,

Relational operator	Meaning
GT	Greater than
GE	Greater than or equal to
LT	Less than
LE	Less than or equal to
EQ	Equal to
NE	Not equal to

Figure 6-14   Relational operators for the COND parameter

Example 1

```
COND=(8,EQ)
```

Example 2

```
COND=((8,EQ),(16,LE))
```

Example 3

```
COND=((8,EQ),(12,EQ),(16,EQ))
```

Figure 6-15   Examples of the COND parameter on a JOB statement

in example 2, remaining job steps will be bypassed if a job step issues a return code that's greater than or equal to 16 or equal to 8. And, in example 3, job steps are bypassed if a return code of 8, 12, or 16 is issued. Note how the parentheses are coded in examples 2 and 3: Each condition is enclosed in a set of parentheses, and the entire list of conditions is enclosed in parentheses too.

How to use the COND parameter in an EXEC statement

The COND parameter of the EXEC statement is more flexible than the COND parameter of the JOB statement. It lets you specify a return code and a relational operator to determine whether to skip a particular job step. In addition, it lets you specify a step name in order to test the return code for a specific job step. And, it provides two additional subparameters, EVEN and ONLY, that let you specify how an abend affects job step execution. The complete format of the EXEC statement COND parameter was shown in figure 6-4, and figure 6-16 shows five examples of how you code it.

Example 1

```
COND=(7,LT)
```

Example 2

```
COND=(8,EQ,EDSTEP)
```

Example 3

```
COND=((8,EQ,STEP1),(12,LE,STEP2))
```

Example 4

```
COND=EVEN
```

Example 5

```
COND=ONLY
```

Figure 6-16   Examples of the COND parameter on an EXEC statement

The COND parameter in example 1 says to bypass this job step if 7 is less than the return code issued by any previous step. In other words, a return code of 8 or more causes the step to be bypassed. In example 2, the return code from the step named EDSTEP is tested; if it's equal to 8, the current job step is bypassed. Example 3 shows how you can specify multiple conditions; the current job step will be bypassed if 8 is equal to the return code from step STEP1 or if 12 is less than or equal to the return code from STEP2. You can specify up to eight conditions in this way. Notice that each condition is enclosed in parentheses, and the entire list of conditions is enclosed as well.

Example 4 shows the EVEN subparameter. When you specify COND=EVEN, you tell MVS to execute the job step whether or not a previous step has abended (that is, ended abnormally due to a program failure). The ONLY subparameter, shown in example 5, tells MVS to execute the job step only if a previous step has abended; if an abend has not occurred, the step is not executed. EVEN is useful for steps that don't depend on the successful completion of previous steps. ONLY is useful for steps that perform recovery processing that should be invoked only in the event of an abend. If you don't specify EVEN or ONLY, the step is bypassed if an abend has occurred. In other words, unless a job contains a step that specifies EVEN or ONLY, an abend in any job step causes the rest of the job steps to be bypassed.

EVEN and ONLY are mutually exclusive; you can't specify then together in the same COND parameter. In addition, when you specify multiple conditions in a COND parameter, EVEN or ONLY counts as one of the eight allowable conditions. So you can specify eight conditions without EVEN or ONLY, or you specify seven conditions plus EVEN or ONLY.

How to use the IF, ELSE, and ENDIF JCL statements

With Version 4 of MVS/ESA, IBM introduced three new JCL statements designed to replace the awkward COND parameter for conditional testing: IF, ELSE, and ENDIF. These statements let you code conditions in much the same way as you would in COBOL, C, or any other high-level programming language.

Figure 6-17 shows the format of these new commands. To begin conditional execution, you code an IF statement that includes the condition you want to test. You follow the IF statement with whatever JCL statements you want executed if the condition is true. Then, you code an ELSE statement followed by whatever JCL statements you want executed if the condition is false. Finally, you code an ENDIF statement to end the conditional structure. The IF and ENDIF statements are always required to set up conditional processing, but you can omit the ELSE statement if you don't need its function.

You specify the condition you want to test in an IF statement by coding a relational expression. A relational expression can contain the operators and keywords shown in figure 6-17. In addition, an expression can contain specific values that you want to test.

Figure 6-18 shows seven examples of IF statements. Notice in the first three examples that a space is included both before and after each operator in the relational expressions. Although this isn't necessary, it can help make the statements more readable. If you use the letter equivalents of the operators (GT, LT, EQ, etc.), you must type a space before and after the operator.

The first example in figure 6-18 includes a simple condition that tests to see if the highest return code issued by any prior job step is greater than 0. The condition in example 2 is true if the return code issued by job step STEP1 is equal to 6. Example 3 shows how you can use AND to test two conditions at once. This statement evaluates to true if STEP1 issues a return code equal to 6 and STEP2 issues a return code less than 16. Examples 4 and 5 show how you can test to see if a specific job step has abended. Example 6 shows how you can test to see if a specific job step abended with a specific

---

The IF, ELSE, and ENDIF statements

```
//[name] IF (relational-expression) THEN
.
.
.
   statements-executed-if-true
.
.
.
//[name] ELSE
.
.
.
   statements-executed-if-not-true
.
.
.
//[name] ENDIF
```

Operators

NOT	¬	Logical not
GT	>	Greater than
LT	<	Less than
NG	¬>	Not greater than
NL	¬<	Not less than
EQ	=	Equal to
NE	¬=	Not equal to
GE	>=	Greater than or equal to
LE	<=	Less than or equal to
AND	&	And
OR			Or

Keywords

RC	The highest return code issued by any job step previously executed.
stepname.RC	The return code issued by the specified job step.
ABEND	True if an abend has occurred.
stepname.ABEND	True if the specified job step has abended.
¬ABEND	True if an abend has not occurred.
stepname.¬ABEND	True if the specified job step has not abended.
ABENDCC=Sxxx	True if the most recent system abend code equals the abend code specified.
ABENDCC=Uxxxx	True if the most recent user abend code equals the abend code specified.
stepname.RUN	True if the specified job step started execution.
stepname.¬RUN	True if the specified job step did not start execution.

Note: You can also code a procedure step name following stepname *to test a step within a cataloged proce-*
dure. See chapter 7 for details on cataloged procedures.

Figure 6-17   The IF, ELSE, and ENDIF statements

Example 1

```
IF  RC  >  0  THEN
```
        Evaluates to true if any previous job step has issued a return code greater than 0.

Example 2

```
IF  STEP1.RC  =  6  THEN
```
        Evaluates to true if the return code for job step STEP1 is 6.

Example 3

```
IF  STEP1.RC  =  6  AND  STEP2.RC  <  16  THEN
```
        Evaluates to true if the return code for job step STEP1 is 6 and the return code for STEP2 is less than 16.

Example 4

```
IF  STEP1.ABEND
```
        Evaluates to true if STEP1 ended abnormally.

Example 5

```
IF  STEP1.¬ABEND
```
        Evaluates to true if STEP1 ended normally.

Example 6

```
IF  STEP1.ABENDCC=S0C4
```
        Evaluates to true if STEP1 ended abnormally with a system abend code of S0C4.

Example 7

```
IF  STEP1.ORD2000A.RUN
```
        Evaluates to true if the procedure step named ORD2000A in STEP1 started execution.

Figure 6-18   Examples of the IF statement

system abend code. And example 7 shows how you can test to see if a specific step in a cataloged procedure started execution.

Figure 6-19 shows how you can use the IF, ELSE, and ENDIF statements together in a job stream. Here, the job step TRERR is executed if any previous job step has issued a return code greater than or equal to 8. Otherwise, the step named TRSUM is executed. Notice that I didn't code the name parameter on any of these statements. If you omit this parameter, you must leave column 3 blank. Then, you can start the operation field (IF, ELSE, or ENDIF) anywhere after column 3. In this example, I started them in column 4.

```
// IF RC >= 8 THEN
//TRERR    EXEC PGM=AR5340
//SYSOUT   DD   SYSOUT=*
//ERRLOG   DD   DSNAME=MMA2.ERRLOG,DISP=MOD
// ELSE
//TRSUM    EXEC PGM=AR5350
//SYSOUT   DD   SYSOUT=*
//TRANFILE DD   DSNAME=MMA2.TRANFILE,DISP=SHR
// ENDIF
```

Figure 6-19   Using the IF, ELSE, and ENDIF statements in a job stream

You can nest IF statements up to 15 levels, but be aware that the structure of your job will be nearly impossible to sort out if you nest IF statements more than a few levels deep. If you do nest IF statements, be sure that each IF statement has a corresponding ENDIF statement.

How to specify execution-related data sets

So far, all of the JCL and JES2/JES3 features I've presented have been either JOB or EXEC statement parameters or JES2/JES3 statement parameters that provide equivalent functions. Now, I'll show you how to code DD statements for two special types of data sets related to job processing. First, I'll show you how to specify a private program library from which programs can be retrieved for execution. Then, I'll show you how to specify SYSOUT data sets MVS uses to print storage dumps if a job step abends.

How to specify a private program library

When an EXEC statement with the PGM parameter is executed, MVS searches a series of system libraries to find the program you specify. The libraries that are included in that search are specified by systems programmers when MVS is initialized. Normally, the search is limited to libraries that contain programs of system-wide usage. The search always includes the system program library, SYS1.LINKLIB, and it usually includes other libraries as well.

Sometimes you need to execute a program that doesn't reside in one of those system libraries. To do that, you code a DD statement in your job stream to identify a *private library* that's searched before the system libraries are searched. You can specify your private library as a *job library* or as a *step library*. A job library applies

throughout the job; a step library is searched only for the step to
which it applies.

To specify a job library, you code a DD statement using JOBLIB
as the ddname, as in the first example in figure 6-20. The JOBLIB
DD statement must be the first JCL statement following the JOB
statement for the job; JES2/JES3 control statements can be placed
between the JOB and the JOBLIB DD statement, but other JCL
statements can't. When a job library is in effect, MVS searches it first
to locate any programs specified in EXEC statements. If a program
isn't found in the job library, the standard system libraries are then
searched.

To specify a step library, you code a DD statement named
STEPLIB *after* the EXEC statement for the step in which you want
the step library to apply. The second example in figure 6-20 shows
the proper location for a STEPLIB DD statement. If you include both
a JOBLIB and a STEPLIB DD statement, the step library is searched
before the system libraries; the job library is ignored for the job step.

How to specify a dump data set

If a job step abends, MVS tries to print the contents of the virtual
storage areas used by the program before it terminates the job step.
This listing is called a *storage dump*, and it is often the only way to
determine what caused the program to fail. To obtain a storage
dump for a job step, you must provide a DD statement named
SYSUDUMP, SYSABEND, or SYSMDUMP. Which ddname you
specify depends on the type of information you want in the dump.

If you specify a SYSUDUMP DD statement, you'll receive a
listing of all of the virtual storage allocated to your program. In
other words, SYSUDUMP provides a dump of the user region of
your job's private address space. If you specify SYSABEND, the
dump will include the user region as well as system areas outside
the user region that are associated with your job step. SYSMDUMP
provides a dump of system areas and the entire private address
space. SYSMDUMP isn't as commonly used as SYSUDUMP or
SYSABEND because it's unformatted; you have to run a special
program to interpret and print the dump.

Unlike SYSMDUMP, both SYSUDUMP and SYSABEND pro-
duce dumps that can be printed directly. As a result, you'll usually
specify these data sets as standard SYSOUT data sets, like this:

```
//SYSUDUMP DD SYSOUT=*
```

Here, the SYSUDUMP data set will be printed using the same output
class as the job's message output. If you want a storage dump for each

Establishing a job library

```
//SYDOEA    JOB   USER=SYDOE,PASSWORD=XXXXXXXX
//JOBLIB    DD    DSNAME=SYDOE.LOADLIB,DISP=SHR
//STEP1     EXEC  PGM=IEBGENER
 .
 .
 .
//STEP2     EXEC  PGM=ORD2200A
 .
 .
 .
```

Establishing a step library

```
//SYDOEA    JOB   USER=SYDOE,PASSWORD=XXXXXXXX
//STEP1     EXEC  PGM=IEBGENER
 .
 .
 .
//STEP2     EXEC  PGM=ORD2200A
//STEPLIB   DD    DSNAME=SYDOE.LOADLIB,DISP=SHR
 .
 .
 .
```

Figure 6-20   Using a job and step library

job step that abends, be sure to specify a SYSUDUMP or SYSABEND DD statement for each step in the job. If a job step ends normally (that is, doesn't abend), the SYSUDUMP or SYSABEND DD statement is ignored.

Discussion

This topic has presented a lot of JCL and JES2/JES3 parameters that are at best loosely related. Obviously, you won't use all of these parameters in every job you code. However, you should be familiar with all of them so that when the need for one arises, you'll know which parameter to use. So, although I don't recommend you memorize every detail this topic has presented, I do hope you'll spend enough time on this topic to have a general understanding of each parameter's function.

Terminology

held job class

multiprocessor network

system affinity

working set

performance group

dispatching priority

return code

private library

job library

step library

storage dump

Objectives

1. Code JCL or JES2/JES3 statements to influence job scheduling in the following ways:
   a. specify the job's class
   b. specify the job's scheduling priority
   c. hold the job
   d. scan the job for syntax errors
   e. specify the job's system affinity

2. Code the JOB and EXEC parameters necessary to specify a job's real and virtual storage requirements.

3. Code the JOB and EXEC parameters necessary to specify a job's or job step's performance group or dispatching priority.

4. Code JCL or JES2/JES3 statements to set the following processing limits:
   a. execution time
   b. SYSOUT print data
   c. SYSOUT punch data

5. Code the COND parameter on a JOB or EXEC statement to conditionally execute job steps based on the return codes issued by previous job steps.

6. Code IF, ELSE, and ENDIF statements to control job step execution based on return codes issued by previous job steps.

7. Code DD statements to allocate the following execution-related data sets:
   a. job library
   b. step library
   c. dump data set

Exercises

1. Code a JOB statement that specifies job execution class Q and scheduling priority 8, such that the job will be held in the job queue until the operator releases it for execution.

2. Code an EXEC statement that executes a program named KZB0100 and limits the region to 6MB.

3. Code an EXEC statement that executes a program named KZB0200 and specifies that the step should execute with performance group 50 and dispatching priority 8.

4. Code an MVS/ESA JOB statement that limits the job's total execution time to 4 hours and the number of pages of SYSOUT data to 5000.

5. Code an EXEC statement with a COND parameter that executes a program named PPZ0050 if the condition code from the job step named STEP1 is 4 or less.

6. Code a series of JCL statements that includes IF, ELSE, and ENDIF statements to execute a program named PPZ0100 if the return code from the step named STEP1 is 4 or less; otherwise, execute the program named PPZ0200.

7. Code a DD statement that allocates USER.LOADLIB as a job library, then indicate the position in the following job stream where you would insert the DD statement.

```
 1 →
    //SYDOEJ    JOB   USER=SYDOE,PASSWORD=XXXXXXXX
 2 →
    //STEP1     EXEC  PGM=EGAX401
 3 →
    //SYSOUT    DD    SYSOUT=A
```

Topic 3

JCL facilities to manage data set allocation

In chapter 5, you learned how to code DD statements to allocate the data sets processed by a job step. In this topic, I'll build on the basic DD statement format you learned in chapter 5 by presenting additional DD statement parameters that let you control how data sets are allocated. For your reference, figure 6-21 shows the format of the DD statement as it's used to allocate DASD data sets. It shows not only the parameters you learned in chapter 5, but the parameters you'll learn in this topic as well.

How to allocate a dummy data set

A *dummy data set* is a data set that doesn't really exist; MVS simulates the data set. By using a dummy data set, you can execute a program that processes a file without actually having the file present. When you use a dummy file, MVS simulates all of the housekeeping tasks associated with file processing, but no data is transferred to or from the file. When a program tries to read a record from a dummy file, MVS indicates an end-of-file condition. And when a program writes a record to a dummy file, the data is discarded.

To understand the value of dummy data sets, consider a report-preparation program that reads the records of a master file and produces five reports, each written to a different SYSOUT data set. Sometimes, you may need to run that program to get just one of the five reports. To do that, you just specify DUMMY for the four SYSOUT data sets you don't need.

There are two ways you can specify a dummy file on a DD statement: you can code the DUMMY parameter, or you can specify DSNAME=NULLFILE (or DSN=NULLFILE). Both have the same effect: The data set allocated by the DD statement is a dummy data set. DUMMY is a positional parameter; if you code it, it must be the first parameter on the DD statement.

Although you don't normally need to code additional parameters on a DD statement for a dummy data set, there are two cases in which you should: (1) if a COBOL program specifies BLOCK CONTAINS 0 RECORDS for the file, you should specify the block size in the DCB parameter (DCB=BLKSIZE=n); and (2) if the program expects a VSAM file, you should specify AMP=AMORG.

The DD statement for DASD data sets

```
//ddname  DD  [ DUMMY ]
              [ ,DSNAME=data-set-name ]
              [ ,DISP=(status,normal-disp,abnormal-disp) ]
              [ ,UNIT=unit ]
              [ ,VOL=SER=vol-ser ]
                                                            ⎧CONTIG⎫
              [ ,SPACE=(unit,(prim[,sec][,dir])[,RLSE][,⎨MXIG  ⎬ ]
                                                            ⎩ALX   ⎭
                [,ROUND]) ]
                              ⎧U⎫
              [ ,AVGREC= ⎨K⎬ ]
                              ⎩M⎭
              [ ,DCB=(option,option...) ]
              [ ,LIKE=data-set-name ]
              [ ,STORCLAS=storage-class ]
              [ ,DATACLAS=data-class ]
              [ ,MGMTCLAS=management-class ]
```

Explanation

DUMMY	Specifies that the file is a DUMMY data set; no DASD I/O operations are performed.
DSNAME	Specifies the file's data set name.
DISP	Specifies the file's status and normal and abnormal dispositions. See figure 5-15 for valid subparameters.
UNIT	Specifies a unit address, generic name, or group name that identifies the device where the file resides. Not required for cataloged data sets.
VOL=SER	Specifies the six-character vol-ser of the volume that contains the file. Not required for cataloged data sets.
SPACE	Specifies the DASD space to be allocated for the file. For a complete explanation of the subparameters, see figure 6-27.
AVGREC	SMS only; indicates that the allocation unit specified in the SPACE parameter is records and whether the values specified for primary and secondary space allocation represent units (U), thousands of records (K), or millions of records (M).
DCB	Specifies options to be used for the file's data control block. See figure 5-18 for valid options.
LIKE	SMS only; copies data set characteristics from the specified data set.
STORCLAS	SMS only; specifies the storage class for the data set.
DATACLAS	SMS only; specifies the data class for the data set.
MGMTCLAS	SMS only; specifies the management class for the data set.

Figure 6-21   The DD statement for DASD data sets

(You'll learn more about the AMP parameter in chapter 9.) If you code other parameters, such as UNIT, VOLUME, and SPACE, they are checked for proper syntax but otherwise ignored.

Figure 6-22 shows four examples of allocating dummy data sets. Example 1 shows the simplest way to allocate a dummy data set and illustrates a common use for them. Here, the standard ddname, SYSIN, provides control statement input to a system utility program. For some system utilities (like IEBGENER, which copies sequential files), you can specify a dummy data set for SYSIN if there aren't any unusual processing requirements.

Example 2 in figure 6-22 shows you how to allocate a dummy data set when the program anticipates a VSAM file. Because I specified AMP=AMORG, MVS simulates a VSAM file. Example 3 shows a DD statement that specifies the full range of DD statement parameters for a dummy file. Most of the parameters coded here are checked for syntax but ignored. To actually process the file, you can remove just the DUMMY parameter. Example 4 is similar to example 3, except that I used DSNAME=NULLFILE rather than the DUMMY parameter to indicate a dummy file. To process an actual file, you would just change the DSNAME specification so it supplies the data set name.

How to allocate a temporary data set

Many jobs require data sets that exist only for the duration of the job or a job step. To illustrate, consider a report-preparation job that requires two steps. The first step sorts a file into the sequence required for the report, storing the sorted records in a new file. Then, the second step reads the sorted records, produces the report, and deletes the sorted file. In addition to the sorted file that's created at the beginning of the job and deleted at the end, additional data sets are required for the sort job step. These data sets are often called *work files*.

You can implement the processing I just described without using any special MVS facilities. For the data set that's processed by one or more job steps and then deleted, you could create the data set and specify KEEP or CATLG as the disposition. Then, each subsequent job step that processes the data set would specify DISP=OLD or DISP=SHR except the last, which would specify DELETE as the final disposition. For the data sets that are required only for a single job step, you could just specify DISP=(NEW,DELETE) or omit the DISP parameter altogether since (NEW,DELETE) is the default. However, MVS provides a special kind of data set, called a *temporary data set*, that simplifies the coding requirements for this kind of processing.

Example 1

```
//SYSIN     DD    DUMMY
```

Allocate a dummy data set; MVS simulates input and output processing, but no I/O operations are actually performed.

Example 2

```
//CUSTMAST DD    DUMMY,AMP=AMORG
```

Allocate a dummy VSAM data set.

Example 3

```
//TRANFILE DD    DUMMY,DSNAME=AR.TRANS.FILE,DISP=(NEW,KEEP),
//               UNIT=SYSDA,VOL=SER=MPS800,
//               SPACE=(CYL,(5,1)),
//               DCB=(DSORG=PS,RECFM=FB,LRECL=80,BLKSIZE=3200)
```

Allocate a dummy data set using the specified file characteristics. When the DUMMY parameter is removed, this DD statement will allocate an actual data set.

Example 4

```
//TRANFILE DD    DSNAME=NULLFILE,DISP=(NEW,KEEP),
//               UNIT=SYSDA,VOL=SER=MPS800,
//               SPACE=(CYL,(5,1)),
//               DCB=(DSORG=PS,RECFM=FB,LRECL=80,BLKSIZE=3200)
```

Allocate a dummy data set using the specified file characteristics. When DSNAME=NULLFILE is changed to specify a data set name, this DD statement will allocate an actual data set.

Figure 6-22   Allocating dummy data sets

Temporary data sets are always deleted at the end of a job, unless you explicitly delete them sooner by specifying DELETE in the DISP parameter. And, a temporary data set can take advantage of another MVS facility: *Virtual Input/Output*, or just *VIO*. Simply put, a VIO data set looks just like a standard DASD data set to a program, but it doesn't reside on DASD. Instead, it resides in virtual storage. As a result, VIO data sets can be processed more efficiently than standard DASD data sets. VIO is used only for temporary data sets.

How to use a single-step temporary data set

To allocate a work file—that is, a temporary data set that's created and deleted in a single job step—you can code just a bare minimum of information on the DD statement. In fact, only two DD statement parameters are absolutely required for a work file: UNIT, which should

Example 1

```
//WORK1     DD    UNIT=SYSDA,SPACE=(CYL,(10,5))
```

Allocate a temporary data set on a SYSDA volume using 10 cylinders of primary and 5 cylinders of secondary space. DISP=(NEW,DELETE) is assumed.

Example 2

```
//WORK2     DD    UNIT=SYSDA,DISP=(NEW,DELETE),
//                SPACE=(3200,(500,500)),
//                DCB=BLKSIZE=3200
```

Allocate a temporary data set on a SYSDA volume using 500 blocks of primary and secondary space. DISP=(NEW,DELETE) is specified, but could be omitted since it's the default. The block size is 3200 bytes.

Figure 6-23   Allocating a one-step temporary data set

specify a DASD device type like SYSDA, and SPACE. You can code DISP=(NEW,DELETE) to indicate that the data set is created and deleted in the same job step, but that's the default. And the DSNAME parameter isn't required since no other DD statement will have to refer to the data set. (MVS creates a unique data set name when you omit the DSNAME parameter, but it's not important for this kind of file.) Besides these parameters, you may also need to include a DCB parameter to supply file characteristics such as block and record size if those characteristics aren't supplied by your program.

Figure 6-23 shows two examples of DD statements for work files. The first includes just the minimum DD statement parameters: UNIT and SPACE. It allocates 10 cylinders of primary and 5 cylinders of secondary DASD space for the work file. Example 2 specifies the DISP parameter, which simply duplicates the default value, and it includes a DCB parameter to supply a block size.

How to use a multi-step temporary data set

If your temporary data set is to be processed by more than one job step, there are a few other coding details you need to know. Before I present those coding details, I want you to know about two MVS terms that describe how temporary data sets are typically processed by multiple job steps: pass and receive. To *pass* a data set means to retain it so that a subsequent job step can process it. In other words, when a passed temporary data set is deallocated, it is not deleted.

To *receive* a temporary data set means to allocate a temporary data set that was previously passed.

In a way, passing a data set is like temporarily cataloging it. MVS retains the unit and volume information for passed data sets in virtual storage, so subsequent DD statements that receive the passed data set don't have to repeat that information. In fact, whenever you allocate a data set without specifying unit and volume information, MVS first checks to see if the data set has been passed. MVS goes to the catalog only after it determines that the data set wasn't passed.

To pass and receive a temporary data set, you must assign it a data set name that follows a specific format. In particular, the name can be no longer than eight characters; compound names joined by periods are not allowed for temporary data sets. In addition, the name must be preceded by two ampersands. (The ampersands aren't included in the eight-character limit.) As a result, &&TEMP and &&ACCOUNT are valid temporary data set names.

MVS creates the actual data set name for a temporary data set using the data set name you supply, the job name, and a time value. MVS uses the same time value for each temporary data set you create in a job. So don't try to create two temporary data sets using the same name; the time values won't make them unique.

A common mistake to avoid is coding only one ampersand in a temporary data set name rather than two. JCL procedures, which you'll learn about in the next chapter, use one ampersand to mark symbolic parameters. If you code a data set name that starts with one ampersand, MVS assumes you're specifying a symbolic parameter. If the symbolic parameter isn't assigned a value, MVS treats the name as a temporary data set name. However, this can lead to confusion and unintended results, so be sure to use two ampersands in a temporary data set name.

The DISP parameter controls whether a temporary data set is passed so that it can be received by a subsequent job step or deleted when the current step completes. In the job step that creates the temporary data set, the DD statement should specify DISP=(NEW,PASS). Then, in subsequent job steps that process the data set, the DD statement should specify DISP=(OLD,PASS). That way, the data set will be received and passed on to additional job steps that need the data set.

In the last job step that processes the temporary data set, you should explicitly delete the file by specifying DISP=(OLD,DELETE). Alternatively, you can specify DISP=(OLD,PASS) again. Then, when the job ends, the temporary data set will be deleted automatically. It's a good idea to delete temporary data sets when you're done with them, however. That way, the DASD space they occupy

```
//SYDOEA    JOB   USER=SYDOE,PASSWORD=XXXXXXXX,MSGCLASS=A
//SORT      EXEC  PGM=SORT
//SYSOUT    DD    SYSOUT=*
//SORTIN    DD    DSNAME=MMA2.AR.CUSTOMER.MASTER,DISP=SHR
//SORTWK01  DD    UNIT=SYSDA,SPACE=(TRK,(1,1))
//SORTWK02  DD    UNIT=SYSDA,SPACE=(TRK,(1,1))
//SORTWK03  DD    UNIT=SYSDA,SPACE=(TRK,(1,1))
//SORTOUT   DD    DSNAME=&&SORTCUST,DISP=(NEW,PASS),
//                UNIT=SYSDA,SPACE=(TRK,(1,1))
//SYSIN     DD    *
 SORT FIELDS=(2,13,A,20,1,A),FORMAT=CH
/*
//REPORT    EXEC  PGM=IEFBR14
//SYSOUT    DD    SYSOUT=*
//CUSTMAST  DD    DSNAME=&&SORTCUST,DISP=(OLD,DELETE)
//ATB       DD    SYSOUT=*
//SYSUDUMP  DD    SYSOUT=*
```

Figure 6-24   A two-step job that uses temporary data sets

is released as soon as possible. And, if you don't delete the temporary data set in the last job step that uses it, additional processing time is required because, to delete the file, MVS must allocate the data set again when the job ends.

Figure 6-24 shows a two-step sort and report job that uses temporary data sets. The first job step sorts a data set, producing a temporary data set that's passed to the next job step. In addition, the sort step allocates sort work files, which are temporary data sets required by the sort program to do a large sort. Because the work files are only needed during the sort step, I didn't give them data set names.

How to use a VIO temporary data set

The MVS Virtual Input/Output facility lets you process temporary data sets that reside entirely in virtual storage rather than on DASD. To your program, a VIO data set looks like a standard DASD data set. But because MVS can access data in virtual storage faster than it can access data in a standard DASD file, a VIO temporary data set can be processed more efficiently than an equivalent DASD temporary data set. You can use VIO temporary data sets that are created and deleted by a single job step, or you can use them for temporary data sets that are passed from step to step. However, you can't use VIO for data sets that are retained at the end of the job.

To use VIO, you must specify a device type in the UNIT parameter that's eligible for VIO. Sometimes, VIO is defined as a group name used just for VIO data sets. So, if you specify UNIT=VIO, the data set will use the VIO facility. In addition, an installation can specify that other groups are eligible for VIO, provided that certain conditions are met. SYSDA is usually defined in this way, so that if you specify UNIT=SYSDA, the file will automatically use VIO if possible.

Besides specifying a VIO-eligible unit, there are two other requirements a file must meet before it can use VIO. First, as I've already pointed out, the file must be a temporary data set. That means the DISP parameter must specify PASS or DELETE (not KEEP or CATLG), and the DSNAME parameter must either be omitted or specify a name that follows the temporary data set naming convention. Second, the file's allocation must specify a non-specific volume request; in other words, don't code the VOLUME parameter.

Interestingly, the SPACE parameter is optional for a VIO data set. If you omit it, a default value is assumed: SPACE=(1000,(10,50)). In other words, the primary space allocation is 10 1,000-byte blocks, and the secondary space allocation is 50 1,000-byte blocks. In many cases, you'll want to override this default. But if the default is sufficient, the DD statement for a VIO data set that's created and deleted in a single job step in this:

```
//TEMP1     DD    UNIT=VIO
```

Here, the default space allocation applies and the default disposition is DISP=(NEW,DELETE). Bear in mind, however, that the default SPACE value works only for VIO data sets; for a temporary data set on DASD, you must specify a SPACE value. And don't forget to specify the DCB parameter if your program doesn't provide complete DCB information.

How to concatenate data sets

Sometimes, you want to treat two or more input data sets as if they were a single data set. To do that, you concatenate them. (The word *concatenate* means to link or chain together.) Then, if the data sets are sequential input files, MVS processes the records in the concatenated data sets in the order in which you concatenate them. (You can't concatenate data sets opened for output processing.) If the data sets you concatenate are partitioned data sets, MVS searches them in the order in which you concatenate them for a member you specify.

Example 1

```
//TRANS     DD    DSNAME=MMA2.TRANS.WEEK1,DISP=SHR
//          DD    DSNAME=MMA2.TRANS.WEEK2,DISP=SHR
//          DD    DSNAME=MMA2.TRANS.WEEK3,DISP=SHR
```

Allocate three transaction files, processing them one after the other in the sequence in which they're listed.

Example 2

```
//SYSLIB    DD    DSNAME=MMA2.COBOL.OBJLIB,DISP=SHR
//          DD    DSNAME=SYS1.COBLIB,DISP=SHR
```

Allocate the two partitioned data sets, searching their directories in the order in which they're listed.

Example 3

```
//SYSUT1    DD    DSNAME=SYDOE.TEXT,DISP=OLD,
//                UNIT=TAPE,VOL=SER=M00023
//          DD    DSNAME=SYDOE.SOURCE.COBOL(ARMAST),DISP=SHR
//          DD    *
  (input data records)
/*
```

Allocate the three files, processing them in the sequence in which they're listed: first the tape file, then the partitioned data set member, and, finally, the in-stream data set.

Figure 6-25   Concatenating data sets

To concatenate files, you code the first DD statement just as you normally would. Then, you code the next DD statement directly after it, but you don't code a ddname for it. To understand this, consider example 1 in figure 6-25. Here, three sequential data sets are concatenated. The program will first read all of the records from MMA2.TRANS.WEEK1. When the end-of-file condition is detected for that file, MVS switches to the next file in the concatenation, so records are read from MMA2.TRANS.WEEK2. Similarly, when all of the records from the second file have been read, records are retrieved from the third file in the concatenation, MMA2.TRANS.WEEK3. You can concatenate up to 255 sequential files in this way.

When you concatenate partitioned data sets, as in example 2 in figure 6-25, the effect is a little different. When a member is requested from a series of concatenated partitioned data sets, all of the concatenated libraries are searched. In other words, the PDS directories are concatenated. The libraries are searched in the order in which you concatenate them, so if more than one concatenated library has a member with the same name, the member from the library that's earlier in the concatenation will be used. You can concatenate up to 16 partitioned data sets.

As a general rule, the characteristics of data sets you concatenate should be similar. For example, you can't mix sequential and partitioned data sets in a concatenation. But as long as the data sets are of the same type, certain data set attributes can vary. For example, you can concatenate sequential data sets on tape or DASD, partitioned data set members (which are treated as sequential files), and SYSIN data sets in any combination you wish. You can also concatenate data sets with different block sizes. However, if you're using an older version of MVS prior to Data Facility Product 2.3, you must make sure that the data set with the largest block size is first in the series of concatenated data sets. Example 3 in figure 6-25 shows how different types of data sets can be concatenated. Here, three separate files are concatenated: a tape file, a PDS member (treated as a sequential file), and in-stream data.

How to allocate multi-volume DASD data sets

In chapter 5, you learned how to code simple forms of the UNIT and VOLUME parameters to allocate data sets that reside on a single DASD or tape volume. Although most data sets fall into that category, some data sets are so large that more than one DASD or tape volume is required to store them. Data sets like that are called *multi-volume data sets* because they require multiple volumes.

Both the UNIT and the VOLUME parameters provide options that let you specify how multi-volume non-VSAM data sets should be allocated. (There are no JCL considerations for multi-volume VSAM files.) In this topic, I'll show you how to use the VOLUME parameter to allocate more than one volume for a multi-volume data set that resides on permanently resident DASD. (Removable DASD units aren't commonly used for multi-volume data sets.) No special coding is required in the UNIT parameter for that kind of data set. In chapter 11, when I describe tape processing, I'll explain the UNIT parameter and additional parameters of the VOLUME parameter that apply specifically to multi-volume tape data sets.

To allocate a new or existing, but uncataloged, multi-volume DASD data set, you list all of the DASD volumes in the VOLUME parameter as in figure 6-26. Here, three DASD volumes are allocated: MVS300, MVS301, and MVS302. The list of volume serial numbers must be enclosed in parentheses. You can list up to 255 volume serial numbers in a VOLUME parameter. For an existing

```
//CUSTMAST DD    DSNAME=MMA2.CUSTOMER.MASTER,DISP=(NEW,CATLG),
//               UNIT=SYSDA,VOL=SER=(MVS300,MVS301,MVS302),
//               SPACE=(CYL,(400,200))
```

Figure 6-26   Allocating a multi-volume data set

data set, be sure you list the volume serial numbers in the same order as you listed them when you created the data set.

When you create a multi-volume data set, the primary space you specify in the SPACE parameter is allocated on the first volume listed in the VOLUME parameter. Then, up to 15 secondary extents are allocated on the first volume. When a total of 16 extents have been allocated on the first volume, or when the first volume is full, a secondary extent is allocated on the next volume. When 16 secondary extents have been allocated on that volume, or the volume is full, a secondary extent is allocated on the next volume. This process can continue until all of the volumes you specify in the VOLUME parameter are used.

To allocate a cataloged multi-volume data set, you don't have to specify the VOLUME parameter. Instead, MVS obtains the volume information from the catalog. If your program adds records to a multi-volume non-VSAM data set, however, it's essential that you specify CATLG as the data set's disposition. That way, if the data set is extended onto a new volume, the updated volume information will be stored in the catalog.

How to use advanced space allocation subparameters

Figure 6-27 shows the complete format of the DD statement's SPACE parameter. It includes several subparameters that let you control the way MVS allocates DASD space to your data set. The RLSE subparameter lets you specify that unused space should be released so it can be allocated to other data sets; CONTIG, MXIG, and ALX indicate that space should be allocated in groups of adjacent cylinders; and ROUND indicates that space should be allocated in terms of whole cylinders even though you specify the amount of space in terms of blocks. Figure 6-28 shows five examples of these advanced SPACE subparameters. Now, I'll describe each subparameter in more detail.

The SPACE parameter

```
                                            ⎧CONTIG⎫
SPACE=(unit,(primary[,second][,dir])[,RLSE][,⎨MXIG  ⎬][,ROUND])
                                            ⎩ALX   ⎭
```

Explanation

unit	Specifies the unit of measure for the primary and secondary allocation. Specify CYL for cylinders, TRK for tracks, or a decimal value representing a block size. With SMS, you can also specify a record size. In that case, you must code the AVGREC parameter.
primary	Specifies the number of units to allocate for the file's primary space allocation.
secondary	Specifies the number of units to allocate for the file's secondary space allocations.
dir	Specifies the number of directory blocks to allocate for a partitioned data set. See chapter 13 for this subparameter's function under ISAM.
RLSE	Specifies that space that's allocated but not used should be freed when the data set is closed.
CONTIG	Specifies that the primary allocation must be satisfied in a single extent.
MXIG	Specifies that the primary allocation should be the largest available extent on the volume; the minimum size of the allocation is specified in the *primary* subparameter.
ALX	Specifies that up to five extents should be allocated; the minimum size of each extent is specified in the *primary* subparameter.
ROUND	Specifies that the primary allocation should be made in terms of cylinders, even though the *unit* subparameter specifies a block size.

Figure 6-27   The SPACE parameter

How to release unused space: the RLSE subparameter

Sometimes, you don't know exactly how much space a DASD file will require; the best you can do is estimate. In a case like this, it's often a good idea to specify a primary allocation that's relatively large (at least large enough to accommodate your estimate) and specify the RLSE subparameter so that DASD space that's not actually used by the file will be released for use by other data sets. That way, you can be sure that the amount of DASD space dedicated to your file is just right.

Example 1 in figure 6-28 shows how the RLSE subparameter is coded. Here, a primary allocation of 100 cylinders and a secondary allocation of 20 cylinders is specified. If the file uses less than that amount, however, the excess space will be released.

Example 1

```
SPACE=(CYL,(100,20),RLSE)
```

The initial space allocation is 100 cylinders of primary space and 20 cylinders of secondary space; any unused space is released when the job step ends.

Example 2

```
SPACE=(CYL,(100,20),,CONTIG)
```

The primary allocation (100 cylinders) must be obtained from contiguous cylinders.

Example 3

```
SPACE=(CYL,(100,20),,MXIG)
```

Obtain the largest available extent for the file's primary allocation; it must be at least 100 cylinders.

Example 4

```
SPACE=(CYL,(100,20),,ALX)
```

Obtain up to five extents, each of which must be at least 100 cylinders, as the file's primary allocation.

Example 5

```
SPACE=(3200,(5000,1000),,,ROUND)
```

Allocate the space, which is specified in terms of 3200-byte blocks, in units of whole cylinders.

Figure 6-28   Examples of the SPACE parameter

The effect of the RLSE subparameter occurs when your program closes the file. During CLOSE processing, MVS compares the space allocated to the file with the actual space occupied by the file's records. If the file's last extent (whether it's the primary or a secondary extent) includes space that's not used by the file, that extent is trimmed back and the unused space is returned to the VTOC as a free extent. Because RLSE happens during CLOSE processing, the unused space won't be released if the data set isn't properly closed (for example, if your program abends).

The obvious advantage of using the RLSE subparameter is that your files use only the amount of DASD space they need; unused space isn't wasted. That's especially important if your installation charges for DASD use based on the exact amount of DASD space occupied by your files. There are, however, two disadvantages to using RLSE. First, if you expect your file to grow, RLSE releases space that would have otherwise been available for expansion without the need for allocating a secondary extent. As the file approaches its 16-extent limit, that becomes important. Second, using RLSE may contribute to *volume fragmentation,* a situation where the available free space on a volume is spread out in a large number of small extents. If that happens, the amount of space released when your file is closed might be too small to be used by other files. Despite these disadvantages, however, I recommend you use the RLSE parameter whenever possible.

How to request contiguous space: the CONTIG, MXIG, and ALX subparameters

If MVS can't locate an extent large enough to accommodate a file's primary space allocation, up to five extents will be combined. The resulting allocation will be the proper size, but two problems result. First, the space consists of two or more areas of DASD space that aren't adjacent; that is, they aren't *contiguous.* Second, each extent counts toward the 16-extent limit. So, your primary allocation might use 5 of the file's 16 available extents. That could prove to be a problem if you expect the file to grow.

The CONTIG, MXIG, and ALX subparameters each address those problems by specifying that the primary space should be allocated using contiguous (adjacent) cylinders. You'll probably use CONTIG most frequently; MXIG and ALX provide additional functions that you don't normally want. Examples 2, 3, and 4 in figure 6-28 show how to code CONTIG, MXIG, and ALX. Notice that an extra comma is coded to indicate that the positional RLSE subparameter is omitted.

When you specify CONTIG, you tell MVS that the primary allocation must be made with a single extent of contiguous cylinders. If the volume doesn't contain a free extent large enough to hold the primary allocation, the job step abends. CONTIG applies only to the primary allocation amount; secondary allocations can still use up to five extents each.

MXIG is similar to CONTIG, except that it tells MVS to allocate the largest available free extent on the volume to your file. When you use MXIG, the primary allocation amount you specify indicates the minimum size of the file; MVS won't allocate an extent that's smaller than the primary allocation amount. You won't use MXIG often; its most common use is to allocate all of an empty volume to a single file.

ALX takes the function of MXIG one step further; it says to allocate up to five extents, each of which is at least as large as the primary allocation amount. ALX is designed to allocate all of the remaining space on a DASD volume to your file. But it accomplishes that only if there are five or fewer free extents on the volume. Like MXIG, I don't expect you to use ALX often.

How to force allocation on a cylinder boundary: the ROUND subparameter

When you specify a primary and secondary allocation amount in terms of blocks rather than tracks or cylinders, MVS converts the block allocation into tracks and allocates the required number of tracks. If you code the ROUND subparameter, however, MVS converts the block allocation you specify into cylinders. The advantage is that the data set will begin and end at a cylinder boundary. In some cases, that might give you a slight performance benefit.

Example 5 in figure 6-28 shows how you code the ROUND subparameter. Notice that three commas are required to mark the omission of two positional subparameters (RLSE and CONTIG/MXIG/ALX). Also notice that the primary and secondary space is specified in terms of 3200-byte blocks. ROUND is ignored if you allocate space in terms of tracks or cylinders.

How to obtain information from a previous DD statement

A JCL facility called *backwards reference* or *referback* can sometimes simplify your JCL by letting you obtain information from a previous DD statement (in the same job) rather than code the information again. For example, if you want to allocate several data sets with the same DCB information, you can specify the DCB information on just the first DD statement. Then, subsequent DD statements needing the same DCB information don't have to duplicate the DCB subparameters; instead, they can use a referback.

The referback facility applies to three DD statement parameters: DSNAME, VOLUME, and DCB. The general form of a referback is this:

```
parameter=*.stepname.ddname
```

If the ddname is from a DD statement in the same job step, you can omit the step name. To illustrate, suppose you want to copy DCB information from a DD statement named TRAN1 in the same job step. In this case, you would code the DCB parameter like this:

```
DCB=*.TRAN1
```

If the DD statement were in a previous job step named STEP3, you would code this parameter:

```
DCB=*.STEP3.TRAN1
```

The format of a referback for the DSNAME parameter is the same, but for a VOLUME parameter, it's different. Instead of coding VOL=SER as you usually do, you must code VOL=REF, like this:

```
VOL=REF=*.STEP3.TRAN1
```

Here, volume information is obtained from the TRAN1 DD statement in the STEP3 job step.

You can also use a referback in the PGM parameter of an EXEC statement. That might seem odd, but remember that the PGM parameter names a member of a partitioned data set. So, if you code the statement

```
//STEP3      EXEC PGM=*.STEP1.LOADMOD
```

the PDS member defined by the LOADMOD DD statement in the STEP1 job step is invoked as the program for the STEP3 job step.

Quite frankly, I don't think you'll use the referback facility often. In general, coding a referback is more error prone than just duplicating the parameter you're referring to. Referbacks are best used in situations where you want to be sure several DD statements use the same parameters, and you expect those parameter values to change frequently. Then, you can set up your job so you have to change the parameter value only once; all other DD statements that require the same parameter value obtain the information through referbacks. However, JCL procedures, which you'll learn about in the next chapter, have better facilities to deal with situations like that.

How to use a job or step catalog

As you know, all VSAM data sets on an MVS system must be cataloged in a user catalog or the master catalog. In addition, most permanent non-VSAM data sets should be cataloged, too. MVS uses the high-level qualifier of a data set name to indicate the catalog that owns the file. For example, a file named MMA2.CUSTOMER.MASTER.FILE is cataloged in the catalog indicated by MMA2. Since the file name indicates the catalog that owns the file, no additional JCL coding is required to identify the catalog. (With MVS/ESA, more than one level of qualification may be used to identify the user catalog that owns a file.)

You can, however, override the catalog indicated by the high-level qualifier by coding one or both of two special DD statements to indicate the catalog you want MVS to use. You can code a JOBCAT DD statement before the first job step to identify a *job catalog* used throughout the job to locate data sets. Or, within a job step, you can code a STEPCAT DD statement to identify a *step catalog* used for a single job step. If you code a STEPCAT DD statement for a job step, the job catalog (if specified) is ignored for that job step. If MVS doesn't find a data set in the job or step catalog, it uses the data set's high-level qualifier as usual.

Under MVS, job and step catalogs are rarely used. However, if you're working with an older version of OS, such as OS/VS1, you may have to use job and step catalogs. That's because OS/VS1 doesn't use the high-level qualifier of a data set name to identify the catalog that owns the file. In that case, you'll have to use a job or step catalog unless your files are cataloged in the master catalog.

To allocate a job catalog, you code a JOBCAT DD statement like this:

```
//JOBCAT   DD   DSNAME=ACCT.USER.CATALOG,DISP=SHR
```

Be sure to place the JOBCAT DD statement before the job's first EXEC statement. And if you also code a JOBLIB DD statement, the JOBCAT DD statement should follow it; the JOBLIB DD statement must always immediately follow the JOB statement. (I described the JOBLIB DD statement in topic 2 of this chapter.)

The DD statement for a step catalog is the same as for a job catalog, except that the ddname is STEPCAT. It should follow the EXEC statement for the step to which it applies. And it should be coded after any STEPLIB DD statement, which must immediately follow the EXEC statement. (Like the JOBLIB DD statement, I described the STEPLIB DD statement in the previous topic.)

If your job or job step uses data sets from more than one catalog, you can concatenate the catalogs on the JOBCAT or STEPCAT DD statement, like this:

```
//JOBCAT   DD DSNAME=ACCT.USER.CATALOG,DISP=SHR
//           DD DSNAME=GROUP2.USER.CATALOG,DISP=SHR
```

Here, the two user catalogs ACCT.USER.CATALOG and GROUP2.USER.CATALOG are searched in that order to locate the cataloged data sets used by the job.

How to create a data set using SMS

If your installation uses the *Storage Management Subsystem* (*SMS*), five additional DD statement parameters are available: LIKE, AVGREC, STORCLAS, DATACLAS, and MGMTCLAS. As long as

Example 1

```
//TRANX      DD    DSNAME=SYDOE.TRANS.NEW,DISP=(NEW,CATLG),
//                 UNIT=SYSDA,VOL=SER=MPS8BV,
//                 LIKE=SYDOE.AR.TRANS
```

The new data set is created using attributes from the file SYDOE.AR.TRANS.

Example 2

```
//TRANX      DD    DSNAME=SYDOE.TRANS.NEW,DISP=(NEW,CATLG),
//                 UNIT=SYSDA,VOL=SER=MPS8BV,
//                 LIKE=SYDOE.AR.TRANS,
//                 SPACE=(TRK,(5,3))
```

The new data set is created using attributes from the file SYDOE.AR.TRANS.
However, the space allocation for SYDOE.AR.TRANS is overridden by the SPACE
parameter.

Figure 6-29   Examples of the LIKE parameter

SMS is installed and active on your system, you can use the LIKE
parameter to model any data set after another data set whether or
not the data sets are managed by SMS. You can use the AVGREC
parameter to allocate space for a file in terms of records rather than
blocks, tracks, or cylinders. And you can use the STORCLAS,
DATACLAS, and MGMTCLAS parameters to create data sets that
are placed under SMS management. (You can also use the
DATACLAS parameter to create data sets that aren't managed by
SMS as long as SMS is active.)

How to model a data set after an existing data set: the LIKE parameter

You use the LIKE parameter to model a new data set after an existing data set. The existing data set must be cataloged and must
reside on DASD, but it does not have to be managed by SMS. The
data set attributes copied from the existing data set include the
record format (RECFM), record length (LRECL), and space allocation (SPACE and AVGREC). Key length and offset (KEYLEN and
KEYOFF) are also copied for VSAM key-sequenced data sets. (You'll
learn more about these parameters in chapter 9.)

Figure 6-29 shows two examples of DD statements that use the
LIKE parameter. In the first example, all data set characteristics are
copied from the existing data set. You can also copy just some of a file's

characteristics by coding parameters that override the characteristics you don't want to copy. For example, the second example in figure 6-29 shows how you can code a SPACE parameter along with the LIKE parameter to override the existing data set's space allocation.

How to allocate space by records: the AVGREC parameter

When you code the SPACE parameter, you normally specify the units in terms of blocks, tracks, or cylinders. With SMS, however, you can also allocate space in terms of records. To do that, you specify the record size for the unit subparameter of the SPACE parameter, and you code the AVGREC parameter. This parameter tells MVS that you're coding a record size rather than a block size. In addition, it supplies a multiplier that affects how the primary and secondary allocation amounts are interpreted. If you code AVGREC=K, the primary and secondary values are multiplied by 1024 (1K). If you code AVGREC=M, they're multiplied by 1,048,576 (1M). Coding AVGREC=U doesn't affect the primary and secondary allocation amounts. In other words, the multiplier is 1.

To illustrate, consider these parameters:

```
SPACE=(312(5,2)),
AVGREC=K
```

Here, the AVGREC parameter tells MVS that 312 is the average length of a record and that the primary and secondary allocation amounts are to be multiplied by 1024. So the primary allocation will be enough to store 5120 (5K) 312-byte records, and the secondary allocation will be enough to store 2048 (2K) 312-byte records.

How to create a new SMS-managed data set

An *SMS-managed data set* is a data set that's managed by the Storage Management Subsystem. As you'll see in a moment, SMS makes it easier to define new data sets. Keep in mind, however, that even if your installation uses SMS, not all data sets have to be managed by SMS.

When a data set is managed by SMS, it is given three *class values* that govern the data set's characteristics. The *storage class* helps SMS select the volume that will be used to store the data set; the *data class* provides default data set characteristics, including the amount of space allocated to the data set; and the *management class* governs how often the data set is backed up. Each of these three classes has a corresponding DD statement parameter: STORCLAS, DATACLAS, and MGMTCLAS. The meanings of the class values you specify in a STORCLAS, DATACLAS, or MGMTCLAS parameter depend entirely

Example 1

```
//TRANX     DD    DSNAME=SYDOE.TRANS.NEW,DISP=(NEW,CATLG),
//                STORCLAS=MVPS100,
//                DATACLAS=MVPD050,
//                MGMTCLAS=MVPM010
```

The new data set is created using storage class MVPS100, data class MVPD050, and management class MVPM010.

Example 2

```
//TRANX     DD    DSNAME=SYDOE.TRANS.NEW,DISP=(NEW,CATLG),
//                DATACLAS=MVPD050
```

The new data set is created using data class MVPD050. Storage class and management class are allowed to default to values selected by the installation's ACS routines.

Example 3

```
//TRANX     DD    DSNAME=SYDOE.TRANS.NEW,DISP=(NEW,CATLG),
//                DATACLAS=MVPD050,
//                LRECL=1000
```

The new data set is created using data class MVPD050. Storage class and management class are allowed to default to values selected by the installation's ACS routines. The logical record length specified in the MVPD050 data class is overridden by the LRECL parameter.

Figure 6-30   Examples of the STORCLAS, DATACLAS, and MGMTCLAS parameters

on how your SMS administrator has configured SMS. As a result, you'll have to find out what values are acceptable for these parameters.

When an installation configures SMS, the administrator defines *automatic class selection*, or *ACS*, *routines*. These routines determine what happens if you omit the STORCLAS, DATACLAS, or MGMTCLAS parameter from a DD statement for a new data set. If you omit DATACLAS or MGMTCLAS, SMS is usually set up to assign a default class. If you omit STORCLAS, however, the ACS routine must determine whether or not the data set is to be managed by SMS. If it is, the routine must then assign a storage class to the data set. SMS can also be set up to override the classes you specify on the STORCLAS, DATACLAS, or MGMTCLAS parameters. So you'll want to be sure to find out how SMS is configured at your installation.

Figure 6-30 shows three examples of how you can use the STORCLAS, DATACLAS, and MGMTCLAS parameters. You can refer to this figure as I describe each of these parameters.

Storage class: the STORCLAS parameter   It's the presence of a storage class that identifies a data set as SMS-managed. Thus, to create an SMS-managed data set, you can simply associate the data set with a storage class by coding the STORCLAS parameter on the DD statement that defines the data set, as in the first example in figure 6-30. Or, if SMS is set up to assign a storage class automatically, you can omit the STORCLAS parameter.

The storage class specified for an SMS-managed data set supplies the information that's normally supplied by the UNIT and VOLUME parameters. As a result, you can omit the UNIT and VOLUME parameters when you create an SMS-managed data set. If you code the UNIT parameter, it's ignored. In most cases, the VOLUME parameter is ignored as well. However, SMS may be set up so that volume serial numbers you specify on the VOLUME parameter override the volumes specified by SMS. Usually, though, you should let the storage class specify the unit as well as the volume information.

Data class: the DATACLAS parameter   The data class for an SMS-managed data set governs the individual characteristics of the data set. These characteristics include:

- The record format (RECFM)
- The logical record length (LRECL)
- The space allocation (SPACE and AVGREC)
- The volume count (VOLUME parameter volume-count field)
- The retention period or expiration date (RETPD or EXPDT)
- The key length for direct data sets (KEYLEN, covered in chapter 14)
- VSAM options (RECORG, KEYLEN, KEYOFF, IMBED, REPLICATE, CISIZE, FREESPACE, and SHAREOPTIONS, covered in chapters 9 and 10)

All three examples in figure 6-30 include the DATACLAS parameter. Notice in the third example, however, that I specified the LRECL parameter. The value of this parameter will override any value that's assigned by SMS.

You can override any or all of the data set characteristics specified by the data class with DD statement parameters. For example, suppose the SMS administrator creates a data class named PLIB for cataloged procedure libraries with these attributes:

```
RECFM=VB
LRECL=255
SPACE=(80,(5,1,20))
AVGREC=K
```

These attributes specify a primary allocation large enough to hold 5,000 records averaging 80-characters each. Suppose you want to create a library but need room for only 1,000 records. Then, you could use a DD statement like this to override the data class:

```
//LIB1       DD  DSNAME=SYDOE.PROCLIB,DISP=(NEW,CATLG),
//               DATACLAS=PLIB,SPACE=(80,(1,1,20))
```

In this example, all of the parameters from the PLIB data class will be used to define the data set except for SPACE, which will be obtained from the DD statement itself.

Management class: the MGMTCLAS parameter   Unlike STORCLAS and DATACLAS, MGMTCLAS doesn't provide options that would otherwise be specified by other DD statement parameters. Instead, it associates the data set with a management class that the installation uses to manage disk storage space. The management class usually governs how often a data set is backed up, how many backup versions are maintained and for how long, and whether or not the data set is subject to being archived to off-line storage (that is, tape) or even deleted should its retention period expire. If you omit MGMTCLAS as in the second and third examples in figure 6-30, SMS is usually set up to assign a management class for you.

How to use the IEFBR14 program

Up to now, this topic has presented DD statement parameters and subparameters. But there's one final MVS facility that affects data set allocation I want you to know about. It's not a DD statement parameter or subparameter; instead, it's a special IBM-supplied program called IEFBR14 that you invoke with an EXEC statement.

IEFBR14 is unusual in that it doesn't do anything. In fact, its name is derived from an assembler language instruction that causes a return to the program that called it: a branch (BR) to register 14, which contains the address to return to after a call. In the case of IEFBR14, the BR 14 instruction returns control directly to MVS. That's all IEFBR14 does; it doesn't open or close data sets or do any other processing. When it's invoked, it returns immediately to MVS.

IEFBR14 is useful, however, because it forces MVS to perform step allocation and deallocation. In other words, even though the program itself doesn't do anything, it forces MVS to process any DD statements you include in the IEFBR14 program's job step. As a result, any data sets you create by specifying DISP=(NEW,KEEP) or DISP=(NEW,CATLG) are allocated and kept or cataloged. And you can delete or uncatalog a data set by specifying

```
//           EXEC  PGM=IEFBR14
//DD1        DD    DSNAME=MMA2.COPYLIB.COBOL,DISP=(NEW,CATLG),
//                 UNIT=SYSDA,VOL=SER=MPS8BV,
//                 SPACE=(3200,(1000,250,5),,,ROUND),
//                 DCB=(DSORG=PO,RECFM=FB,LRECL=80,BLKSIZE=3200)
//DD2        DD    DSNAME=SYDOE.TEST.DATA,DISP=(OLD,DELETE)
```

Figure 6-31   An IEFBR14 job step

DISP=(OLD,DELETE) or DISP=(OLD, UNCATLG). Figure 6-31 shows a simple IEFBR14 job step that creates one data set and deletes another.

In the past, IEFBR14 was the standard way of creating empty data sets or deleting data sets that were no longer needed. With TSO and ISPF, however, those functions can be done interactively. So if you have access to TSO and/or ISPF, you probably won't use IEFBR14 as much.

Terminology

dummy data set
work file
temporary data set
Virtual Input/Output
VIO
pass a data set
receive a data set
concatenate
multi-volume data set
volume fragmentation
contiguous
backwards reference

referback
job catalog
step catalog
Storage Management Subsystem
SMS
SMS-managed data set
storage class
data class
management class
automatic class selection routine
ACS routine

Objectives

1. Code the JCL necessary to allocate a dummy data set.

2. Code the JCL necessary to (1) create a temporary data set and (2) allocate a passed temporary data set.

3. Code the JCL necessary to allocate concatenated data sets.

4. Code the JCL necessary to allocate more than one DASD volume to a single data set.

5. Code the SPACE parameter to:
   a. release unused space
   b. request a contiguous space allocation
   c. allocate the largest extent available on a volume
   d. allocate the five largest extents available on a volume

6. Use the referback facility to obtain DSNAME, VOLUME, or DCB information from a previous DD statement.

7. Code the JCL necessary to allocate a job or step catalog.

8. Use the LIKE parameter to model a new data set after an existing data set.

9. Use the AVGREC parameter to allocate the space for a new data set by records.

10. Use the STORCLAS, DATACLAS, and MGMTCLAS parameters to assign SMS classes to a new data set.

11. Code an IEFBR14 job step to allocate and deallocate data sets.

Exercises

1. Code a DD statement for a dummy data set using the ddname X401PARM.

2. Code two DD statements to process a temporary data set. The first DD statement should use the name X401EXTR and should allocate 20 cylinders of primary space and 10 cylinders of secondary space on a SYSDA unit named TSO001. The second DD statement, which would appear in a subsequent job step, should use the same ddname. It should allocate the passed temporary data set and delete it when the step completes.

3. Code the DD statements required to concatenate three partitioned data sets named SYDOE.COBLIB.PRIVATE, EGAX.COBLIB, and SYS1.COBLIB using the ddname SYSLIB.

4. Code a DD statement that allocates three SYSDA-class DASD volumes named TSO001, TSO002, and TSO003 for a new data set named EGAX.SAMPLE. Provide for up to 250 cylinders of primary space and 100 cylinders for secondary allocations.

5. Examine the following SPACE parameters:

```
SPACE=(CYL,(20,5),,CONTIG)
SPACE=(CYL,(20,5),RLSE)
SPACE=(CYL,(20,5),,ALX)
SPACE=(CYL,(20,5),,MXIG)
```

   a. Which of the parameters above releases any unused space so other data sets can use it?
   b. Which requests a contiguous space allocation?
   c. Which allocates the largest extent available on a volume?
   d. Which allocates the five largest extents available on a volume?

6. Code a DCB parameter to refer back to a previous DD statement defined in a previous job step named UP1. The previous ddname is UPFILE.

7. Code a DD statement that allocates SYDOE.PRIVATE.UCAT as a job catalog, then indicate the position in the following job stream where you would insert the DD statement.

```
1 →
    //SYDOEJ    JOB   USER=SYDOE,PASSWORD=XXXXXXXX
2 →
    //STEP1     EXEC  PGM=EGAX401
3 →
    //SYSOUT    DD    SYSOUT=A
```

8. Code a DD statement that creates a new cataloged data set named X401.PROJ.EXTR that has a primary allocation of 5000 records, a secondary allocation of 2000 records, resides on a SYSDA volume named TSO001, and specifies that all other data set attributes are to be copied from a data set named X401.MODEL.EXTR. Each record in the file is 500 bytes.

9. Code a DD statement that creates a new cataloged data set named X401.PROJ.MASTER. The data set should be assigned to storage class X400S1, data class X400D3, and management class X400M1.

10. Code an IEFBR14 job step that deletes a cataloged data set named X401.TEMP.SAMPLE.

Topic 4

JCL and JES2/JES3 facilities to manage SYSOUT data

In chapter 5, you learned how to code a simple form of the DD statement for output data sets that are processed by the Job Entry Subsystem as SYSOUT data. This topic builds on that basic format by showing you additional JCL elements that apply to SYSOUT data. First, I'll introduce a new JCL statement, the OUTPUT statement, that's available with later releases of MVS. Then, I'll describe the DD and OUTPUT statement parameters you use to manage SYSOUT data sets. (Many of the DD and OUTPUT statement parameters are the same.) Finally, I'll briefly describe two JES2/JES3 statements, /*OUTPUT and //*FORMAT, that duplicate the facilities provided by the DD and OUTPUT statement.

The OUTPUT JCL statement

You code many of the JCL parameters to manage SYSOUT data directly on the DD statement that allocates the SYSOUT data set. There's another JCL statement, however, that lets you specify options for SYSOUT processing: the OUTPUT statement shown in figure 6-32. Many of the OUTPUT statement's parameters are the same as DD statement parameters. You need to know about the OUTPUT statement, though, for two reasons. First, it lets you supply default SYSOUT processing options, so you don't have to code the same parameters on each DD statement in a job. And second, some of the OUTPUT statement parameters have no DD statement equivalents.

Before I go on, you should know that if your installation is using an older version of MVS, the OUTPUT statement may not be available. If that's the case, you'll have to rely on DD statement parameters and the JES2/JES3 control statements I'll present later in this topic.

The OUTPUT statement can be used in two ways. First, you can code a default OUTPUT statement to specify processing options that apply to all SYSOUT data sets produced by your job. Second, you can code a specific OUTPUT statement that must be referenced directly by a DD statement.

The OUTPUT JCL statement

```
//name     OUTPUT     [ ADDRESS= { addr                        } ]
                                 { (addr[,addr...])            }

           [ ,BUILDING=building ]

           [ ,BURST= { YES } ]
                     { NO  }

           [ ,CHARS=character-set ]

           [ ,CLASS=class ]

                          { PROGRAM }
           [ ,CONTROL=   { SINGLE  } ]
                          { DOUBLE  }
                          { TRIPLE  }

           [ ,COPIES = { nnn                                      } ]
                       { (,(group-value[,group-value...]))       }

           [ ,DEFAULT= { YES } ]
                       { NO  }

           [ ,DEPT=dept ]

           [ ,DEST=destination ]

           [ ,FCB=fcb ]

           [ ,FLASH=overlay ]

           [ ,FORMDEF=form-def ]

           [ ,FORMS=form ]

                        { ALL }
           [ ,JESDS=   { JCL } ]
                        { LOG }
                        { MSG }

           [ ,LINECT=count ]

           [ ,MODIFY=module ]

           [ ,NAME=name ]

           [ ,OUTDISP=(normal-disp[,abnormal-disp]) ]

           [ ,PAGEDEF=page-def ]

           [ ,PRTY=priority ]

           [ ,ROOM=room ]

           [ ,TITLE=title ]

           [ ,UCS=character-set ]
```

Figure 6-32   The OUTPUT JCL statement (part 1 of 3)

Explanation

ADDRESS	MVS/ESA only; specifies an address to be printed on the job's separator pages. *Addr* can be up to 60 characters. It must be enclosed in apostrophes if it includes spaces or other special characters. You can specify up to four addresses.
BUILDING	MVS/ESA only; specifies a building identification that is printed on the job's separator pages. *Building* can be up to 60 characters. It must be enclosed in apostrophes if it includes spaces or other special characters.
BURST	Specifies whether or not the burster-trimmer-stacker feature of the 3800 should be used.
CHARS	Specifies a one- to four-character character set name for a 3800. Specify DUMP for a compressed-format dump (SYSUDUMP or SYSABEND only).
CLASS	Specifies an output class. Code * to obtain the output class from the MSGCLASS parameter on the JOB statement.
CONTROL	Specifies line spacing; code PROGRAM to use program-generated control characters; code SINGLE, DOUBLE, or TRIPLE to force single, double, or triple line spacing. The default is PROGRAM.
COPIES	Specifies how many copies of the data set should be printed. Code *nnn* to print the indicated number of copies of the entire data set; code group values to print multiple copies of each page of the data set.
DEFAULT	Specifies whether or not this OUTPUT statement supplies default SYSOUT processing values. The default is NO.
DEPT	MVS/ESA only; specifies a department identification that is printed on the job's separator pages. *Dept* can be up to 60 characters. It must be enclosed in apostrophes if it includes spaces or other special characters.
DEST	Specifies a destination for the SYSOUT data set.
FCB	Specifies the one- to four-character name of the forms control buffer to be downloaded to the printer.
FLASH	Specifies the one- to four-character name of the overlay the operator should mount in the 3800 printer's flash unit.
FORMDEF	Specifies the one- to six-character name of a form definition for a 3800.
FORMS	Specifies the one- to four-character name of the form the operator should mount on the printer.
JESDS	Specifies the JES data sets to which this OUTPUT statement applies.
LINECT	Specifies a value (0 to 255) that indicates how many lines JES should print on each page. Ignored under JES3.
MODIFY	Specifies the one- to four-character name of a copy modification module for a 3800.
NAME	MVS/ESA only; specifies a name that is printed on the job's separator pages. *Name* can be up to 60 characters. It must be enclosed in apostrophes if it includes spaces or other special characters.

Figure 6-32 The OUTPUT JCL statement (part 2 of 3)

Explanation

OUTDISP

MVS/ESA only; specifies the disposition for a SYSOUT data set under JES2. *Normal-disp* specifies the disposition if the job terminates normally; *abnormal-disp* specifies the disposition if the job terminates abnormally. Valid dispositions are:

WRITE	The SYSOUT data set is to be printed, then deleted.
HOLD	The SYSOUT data set is to be held in the output queue until released by the operator or user. When released, the data set is printed and deleted.
KEEP	The SYSOUT data set is to be printed, then retained in the output queue.
LEAVE	The SYSOUT data set is to be held in the output queue until released by the operator or user. When released, the data set is printed, then retained in the queue.
PURGE	The SYSOUT data set is deleted without being printed.

PAGEDEF   Specifies the one- to six-character name of a page definition for a 3800.

PRTY   Specifies a priority for the output data set (1 to 255).

ROOM   MVS/ESA only; specifies a room identification that is printed on the job's separator pages. *Room* can be up to 60 characters. It must be enclosed in apostrophes if it includes spaces or other special characters.

TITLE   MVS/ESA only; specifies a title that is printed on the job's separator pages. *Title* can be up to 60 characters. It must be enclosed in apostrophes if it includes spaces or other special characters.

UCS   Specifies the one- to four-character name of the print band or train (impact) or character set (3800) to be used to print the data set.

Figure 6-32   The OUTPUT JCL statement (part 3 of 3)

Now, I'll show you how to code an OUTPUT statement and how to relate a DD statement to it. Because the individual parameters of the OUTPUT statement are the same as many DD statement parameters, I'll describe the DD and OUTPUT parameters together in the next section.

How to code a default OUTPUT JCL statement

If you specify DEFAULT=YES or DEFAULT=Y on an OUTPUT JCL statement, the OUTPUT statement specifies default SYSOUT processing options that are applied to all subsequent SYSOUT data sets that don't explicitly refer to a specific OUTPUT statement. For example, consider this OUTPUT statement:

```
//OUT1     OUTPUT DEFAULT=YES,CLASS=H
```

Here, a default OUTPUT statement specifies that SYSOUT data sets should have output class H. The name field—OUT1 in this example—is always required in an OUTPUT statement; it must be unique for all OUTPUT statements in the job.

If you place a default OUTPUT statement before the first EXEC statement of the job, the OUTPUT statement applies to all SYSOUT data sets in the job that don't specify a particular OUTPUT statement. If you place a default OUTPUT statement within a job step, the default applies only to SYSOUT data sets within the step. If a step includes a step-level default OUTPUT statement, any job-level OUTPUT statements are ignored for that step.

To refer to a default SYSOUT statement from a DD statement, you code the DD statement like this:

```
//REPORT    DD    SYSOUT=(,)
```

Here, the SYSOUT parameter associates a null output class with the SYSOUT data set. That way, the output class specified on the OUTPUT statement will be used. If you code a class in the SYSOUT parameter, it overrides a class specification on the OUTPUT statement.

You can code more than one job-level or step-level default OUTPUT statement for a job or job step. Then, one copy of each SYSOUT data set is produced for each OUTPUT statement, and each can be handled in a different way. For example, you might code two job-level default OUTPUT statements: one specifying normal class A printing, the other specifying that SYSOUT data should be routed to a remote destination. Then, each SYSOUT data set produced by the job will be printed twice: once using normal class A output processing, and again after being routed to the remote destination.

How to code an explicitly referenced OUTPUT JCL statement

To code an OUTPUT statement that must be explicitly referenced by a DD statement, you omit the DEFAULT parameter or code DEFAULT=NO or DEFAULT=N on the OUTPUT statement. Then, you code an OUTPUT parameter on the DD statement for a SYSOUT data set. In the OUTPUT parameter, you specify the name of the related OUTPUT statement.

For example, consider this DD statement:

```
//REPORT    DD    SYSOUT=(,),OUTPUT=*.OUT1
```

Here, OUT1 is the name of an OUTPUT statement that appears at the job level or in the same job step as the DD statement. Notice that the OUTPUT parameter is similar in format to a referback. Also notice that the SYSOUT parameter is coded without an output class just as it is when you code a DD statement that refers to a default OUTPUT statement.

To refer to an OUTPUT statement that's not at the job level or in the same step as the DD statement, you must supply the step name in the OUTPUT parameter like this:

```
//REPORT    DD    SYSOUT=(,),OUTPUT=*.STEP1.OUT1
```

Here, the OUTPUT statement named OUT1 in step STEP1 is used. There's one important restriction: The job step you refer to must be a prior job step; you can't refer to a later job step in an OUTPUT parameter.

If you wish, you can specify more than one OUTPUT statement in an OUTPUT parameter. To do that, just list the OUTPUT statement names in parentheses, like this:

```
//REPORT    DD    SYSOUT=(,),
//                 OUTPUT=(*.STEP1.OUT1,*STEP1.OUT2)
```

Here, two OUTPUT statements are referenced, so two versions of the REPORT SYSOUT data set will be produced. You can specify up to 128 OUTPUT statements like this.

How to code an OUTPUT JCL statement for JES data sets

As you know, JES produces three SYSOUT data sets that contain information relating to your job's execution. The JES message log lists messages produced by JES2/JES3 as it processes your job. The JCL listing simply lists the JCL statements for your job. And the MVS message log contains allocation and other messages produced as your job executes. Two JOB statement parameters let you control how these data sets are handled: The MSGLEVEL parameter lets you suppress some or all of this output, and the MSGCLASS parameter lets you associate an output class with the JES data sets.

Another OUTPUT statement parameter, JESDS, lets you associate an OUTPUT statement with one or more of the JES data sets to provide greater control over how they are handled. If you specify JESDS=LOG on an OUTPUT statement, the OUTPUT statement is used for the JES message log; if you specify JESDS=JCL, it's used for the JCL listing; if you specify JESDS=MSG, it's used for the MVS message log. If you specify JESDS=ALL, the OUTPUT statement applies to all three SYSOUT data sets.

```
//SYDOEA    JOB   USER=SYDOE,PASSWORD=XXXXXXXX
//DEFAULT   OUTPUT DEFAULT=YES,COPIES=4,CLASS=A
//OUT1      OUTPUT COPIES=2,FORMDEF=INV1,PAGEDEF=INV1,BURST=YES,CLASS=C
//STEP1     EXEC PGM=AR4320
//SYSOUT    DD    SYSOUT=(,)
//INVLIST   DD    SYSOUT=(,)
//INVRPT    DD    SYSOUT=(,)
//INVOICE   DD    SYSOUT=(,),OUTPUT=*.OUT1
```

Figure 6-33   A job that uses OUTPUT statements

An OUTPUT JCL statement example

Figure 6-33 shows an example of a single-step job that uses two job-level OUTPUT statements. The first, named DEFAULT, provides default SYSOUT options (in this case, COPIES =4 and CLASS=A) that apply to three SYSOUT data sets: SYSOUT, INVLIST, and INVRPT. The second, OUT1, provides options that apply to the INVOICE data set, which names OUT1 in an OUTPUT parameter. (Don't worry about the options used in these example; they'll be presented in the next section.) I didn't include an OUTPUT statement for JES data sets, but it would be coded in the same location as the default OUTPUT statement.

DD and OUTPUT statement parameters for SYSOUT processing

As you've seen, the OUTPUT statement has lots of parameters, each of which lets you control SYSOUT processing in various ways. Many of the OUTPUT statement's parameters have parallels on the DD statement. As a result, to invoke a particular SYSOUT processing function, you might code an OUTPUT statement parameter, a DD statement parameter, or both. Figure 6-34 shows the format of the DD statement as it's used for SYSOUT data sets; if you'll compare it with figure 6-32, you'll see the similarities between the two statements.

Before I describe how you use OUTPUT and DD statement parameters to control SYSOUT processing, there are two other factors you need to know about: whether a parameter applies only to an impact printer, a 3800 Printing Subsystem, or both and whether a parameter applies to JES2, JES3, or both. In this section, unless I say otherwise, each parameter works for both types of printers and both Job Entry Subsystems.

The DD statement for SYSOUT data

```
//ddname       DD  [ SYSOUT=(class[,writer][, {form-name ])} ]
                                              {code-name
```

```
               [ ,BURST= {YES} ]
                         {NO }
```

```
               [ ,CHARS=character-set ]
```

```
               [ ,COPIES=nnn(,(group-value[,group-value...])) ]
```

```
               [ ,DEST=destination ]
```

```
               [ ,FCB=fcb ]
```

```
               [ ,FLASH=overlay ]
```

```
               [ ,HOLD= {YES} ]
                        {NO }
```

```
               [ ,MODIFY=module ]
```

```
               [ ,OUTLIM=number ]
```

```
               [ ,OUTPUT=name ]
```

```
               [ ,SPIN= {UNALLOC} ]
                        {NO     }
```

```
               [ ,UCS=character-set ]
```

Explanation

SYSOUT   Specifies the SYSOUT class, the name of an output writer used to process the file, and the name of special forms used to print the file. See figure 6-35 for details of each subparameter.

BURST   Specifies whether or not the burster-trimmer-stacker feature of the 3800 should be used.

CHARS   Specifies a one- to four-character character set name for a 3800. Specify DUMP for a compressed-format dump (SYSUDUMP or SYSABEND only).

COPIES   Specifies how many copies of the data set should be printed. Code *nnn* to print the indicated number of copies of the entire data set; code group values to print multiple copies of each page of the data set.

DEST   Specifies a destination for the SYSOUT data set.

FCB   Specifies the one- to four-character name of the forms control buffer to be downloaded to the printer.

FLASH   Specifies the one- to four-character name of the overlay the operator should mount in the 3800 printer's flash unit.

HOLD   Specifies whether or not the data set should be held. The default is NO.

MODIFY   Specifies the one- to four-character name of a copy modification module for a 3800.

OUTLIM   Specifies a limit for the number of records written to the data set.

Figure 6-34   The DD statement for SYSOUT data sets (part 1 of 2)

Explanation

OUTPUT	Associates the SYSOUT data set with the named OUTPUT statement.
SPIN	MVS/ESA only; specifies when the data set should be released for printing. UNALLOC releases the data set when the job step ends; NO retains the data set until the end of the job. The default is NO.
UCS	Specifies the one- to four-character name of the print band or train (impact) or character set (3800) to be used to print the data set.

Figure 6-34   The DD statement for SYSOUT data sets (part 2 of 2)

How to specify an output class

As you know, a SYSOUT data set's output class can affect the way the data set is printed by indicating which printer or printers may print the data set, whether the data set should be held, and the data set's importance relative to data sets with other output classes. Normally, you specify a SYSOUT data set's class in the SYSOUT parameter of the DD statement.

I've shown you two ways to code the SYSOUT parameter to tell JES2/JES3 to obtain the output class from another source. If you specify SYSOUT=*, the job's message class, specified in the MSGCLASS parameter on the JOB statement, is used. And, if you specify SYSOUT=(,), the output class in an OUTPUT statement is used.

To specify an output class in an OUTPUT statement, you code the CLASS parameter, like this:

```
//OUT1      OUTPUT DEFAULT=YES,CLASS=C
```

Here, class C becomes the default output class for all SYSOUT data sets. That class is overridden when a DD statement specifies a class in the SYSOUT parameter or specifies SYSOUT=*.

If you code SYSOUT=(,) on a DD statement and then don't provide a CLASS parameter on an OUTPUT JCL statement, the job's message class is used. If you don't code a MSGCLASS parameter on the JOB statement, an installation-dependent default message class is used. Throughout most of this book, I code SYSOUT=* so that the output class of my SYSOUT data sets defaults to the job's message class. Whether or not you use OUTPUT statements, you could code SYSOUT=(,) to achieve the same result.

How to specify an output priority

Normally, SYSOUT data sets are printed on a first-come, first-serve basis, as soon as a printer that's eligible for the output class becomes available. In some cases, a SYSOUT data set contains important information and must be printed sooner than other SYSOUT data sets waiting in the output spool. To alter the first-come, first-serve printing sequence, you can code the PRTY parameter on an OUTPUT JCL statement to specify an output priority. There's no PRTY parameter on the DD statement, so you must use the OUTPUT statement to specify an output priority.

In the PRTY parameter, you specify a one- to three-digit number ranging from 0 to 255, like this:

```
//OUT1        OUTPUT PRTY=175
```

The higher the number, the higher the SYSOUT data set's priority. For example, a data set with a priority of 200 will be printed before a data set with a priority of 100, even if the lower priority data set has been in the output queue longer. If you omit the PRTY parameter, an installation-dependent default value is used.

How to control line spacing and the number of lines printed on each page

Two OUTPUT statement parameters, CONTROL and LINECT, let you control the line spacing and the number of lines on each page of SYSOUT output. These parameters can be coded only on an OUTPUT statement; they aren't provided for by the DD statement.

The CONTROL parameter lets you vary the line spacing of a SYSOUT data set. If you omit CONTROL or specify CONTROL=PROGRAM, JES assumes that the first position of each line in the SYSOUT data set contains a carriage control character that affects line spacing. That's normally the case. However, you can override the line spacing specified by carriage control characters by specifying CONTROL=SINGLE, CONTROL=DOUBLE, or CONTROL=TRIPLE to achieve single, double, or triple spacing. Although double or triple spacing might come in handy for some output data sets, it obviously requires more paper. So use it sparingly.

The LINECT parameter changes the JES2 default for the maximum number of lines printed on each page of a SYSOUT data set; LINECT is ignored under JES3. Usually, the default LINECT value is 66 lines per page, which is the physical maximum that can be printed using normal line spacing on standard 11 X 14 paper. If you want fewer lines per page or if you're using smaller paper, you should reduce the line count accordingly.

How to use special forms

Although most SYSOUT data sets are printed on standard computer paper, some must be printed on special forms. For example, payroll checks are usually printed on blank check forms, and invoices are printed on blank invoice forms. When you use special forms for SYSOUT data sets, you need to know how to code several DD and OUTPUT statement parameters. The parameters you code depend on whether you're using an impact printer or a 3800 Printing Subsystem.

To print on special forms using a standard impact printer, you need to specify two things: the form name and the FCB name. The form name is a one- to four-character name that identifies the form you want to use. It's used in a message to the operator that indicates which form to mount on the printer. The FCB name is a one- to four-character name that identifies a *forms control buffer* that corresponds to the form. A forms control buffer is a series of coded instructions that's loaded into the printer's memory; it provides information the printer needs to print on the form, such as the length of the form. Usually, the FCB name and the form name are the same.

You specify the FCB name in an FCB parameter on a DD or OUTPUT statement. And, you specify the form name in the SYSOUT parameter of a DD statement or in the FORMS parameter of an OUTPUT statement. Figure 6-35 shows the complete format of the DD statement SYSOUT parameter. It has three positional subparameters. You already know about the first; it specifies the SYSOUT data set's output class. The second is rarely used; it lets you bypass the Job Entry Subsystem. The third positional subparameter has two functions: it can provide a form name, or it can identify a JES2 control statement (/*OUTPUT) that applies to the SYSOUT data set. I'll describe the JES2 /*OUTPUT statement function later.

To illustrate how to provide a form name, suppose you want to print a SYSOUT data set on pre-printed invoices. The form name and the FCB name are both INV1, so you code the DD statement like this:

```
//INVOICE  DD    SYSOUT=(C,,INV1),FCB=INV1
```

Alternatively, you could code an OUTPUT statement like this:

```
//OUT1      OUTPUT CLASS=C,FORM=INV1,FCB=INV1
```

Then, if the DD statement refers to this OUTPUT statement, the effect is the same.

The SYSOUT parameter

$$SYSOUT=(class[,writer][, \begin{Bmatrix} form-name \\ code-name \end{Bmatrix}])$$

Explanation

class	Specifies a one-character output class to be associated with the SYSOUT data set.
writer	Specifies the name of an output writer that's to process the SYSOUT data set rather than JES2/JES3.
form-name	Specifies the one- to four-character name of the form that the operator is to mount in the printer.
code-name	Specifies a one- to four-character code name that associates a JES2 /*OUTPUT statement with this SYSOUT data set.

Figure 6-35   The SYSOUT parameter

On a 3800 Printing Subsystem, pre-printed forms aren't generally used. Instead, one of two techniques is used to print the form along with the data on blank paper. If you use the *forms-flash technique*, where the operator loads a photographic negative image of the form into the printer, you code the FLASH parameter on a DD or OUTPUT statement. In the FLASH parameter, you code a one- to four-character overlay name, like this:

```
//OUT1        OUTPUT FLASH=INV1
```

Here, the operator is instructed to mount the INV1 negative into the printer before the data set is printed.

On newer models of the 3800 Printing Subsystem, you can generate forms using an *electronic overlay*. Creating an overlay is a complicated process that's beyond the scope of this book. But coding the JCL to use an overlay is simple. You just name the overlay components you need in two OUTPUT statement parameters: FORMDEF and PAGEDEF. The FORMDEF parameter names a form definition, which contains the specifications for the actual form the 3800 is to generate. The PAGEDEF parameter names a page definition, which contains formatting instructions that control how data is printed on the page. Both parameters name a one- to six-character name, and you can code them only on an OUTPUT statement; the DD statement doesn't support them.

How to use an alternate character set

In some cases, you might want a data set printed using other than the standard character set for a printer. How you specify that depends on whether you're using an impact printer or a 3800. For an impact printer, you code the UCS parameter on a DD or OUTPUT statement. For a 3800, you code the UCS or CHARS parameter on a DD or OUTPUT statement.

For an impact printer, the UCS parameter supplies a one- to four-character name of a print band or train that the operator is to mount on the printer before the data set is printed. (UCS stands for *Universal Character Set*.) Because of the operator overhead involved, you should avoid specifying UCS for impact printers.

For the 3800 Printing Subsystem, operator intervention isn't required to load an alternate character set. Instead, character sets are defined in much the same way as electronic forms overlays. To use a 3800 character set, you provide the one- to four-character name of the character set in a UCS or CHARS parameter; the two parameters serve the same function.

On the 3800 Printing Subsystem, you can also specify CHARS=DUMP to print a dump using a compressed character set that prints 204 characters per print line. When you do that, the dump is printed faster and it uses less paper. You can specify CHARS=DUMP only for dump data sets (SYSUDUMP or SYSABEND).

How to produce multiple copies of a SYSOUT data set

There are two ways to produce multiple copies of SYSOUT data on an impact printer. One way is to use multi-part paper. When you do that, the data set is printed only once, but several copies result from that single printing. The other way is to print the SYSOUT data set several times. There are many cases where it's clearly better to print the data set several times. For example, if the data set is short, it's probably faster to print it several times rather than have the operator change the paper in the printer. Or, if each copy must have the quality of an original, you'll have to print it several times. And, if you're using a 3800, you'll have to print copies separately because multi-part paper won't work in a 3800.

To print a SYSOUT data set more than once, you code the COPIES parameter on a DD statement or an OUTPUT statement. In its simplest form, you code the COPIES parameter like this:

```
//REPORT    DD    SYSOUT=A,COPIES=4
```

Here, four copies of the REPORT data set will be produced.

When you print multiple copies of a data set this way, the data set is sent to the printer twice; when the first copy has finished printing, JES2/JES3 sends the second copy. If the two copies are to be sent to different users, this is efficient for the operator, who can just separate the copies and deliver them. However, it's inefficient because the data set must be processed twice.

For efficiency, then, the 3800 Printing Subsystem provides an alternative method for printing multiple copies of a data set. This alternative is to print multiple copies of each page as the data set is processed. For example, if you request two copies of a data set, the copies are printed in this order: two copies of page 1, two copies of page 2, and so on. Of course, this may make it more difficult for the operator to separate the copies. But it's a more efficient use of the machine, because JES processes the data set just once. It's the 3800 itself that produces the additional copies.

To request this form of printing, you code a group value in the COPIES parameter, like this:

```
COPIES=(,(4))
```

Here, I omitted the first subparameter but left the comma because it's positional. And I enclosed the second subparameter, a group value, in parentheses. The result of this COPIES parameter is that each page in the output listing is printed four times.

Before I go on, I want to remind you that you can also cause multiple copies of a data set to be printed by associating a SYSOUT data set with more than one OUTPUT statement. You do that by providing more than one default OUTPUT statement or by naming more than one OUTPUT statement in the DD statement's OUTPUT parameter. As a result, if two OUTPUT statements apply to a data set and they each say to print four copies, a total of eight copies of that data set are produced.

How to use the burster-trimmer-stacker feature

For data sets printed on a 3800 Printing Subsystem, you can code the BURST parameter on a DD or OUTPUT statement to specify whether or not the *burster-trimmer-stacker feature* should be used. (The burster-trimmer-stacker-feature automatically separates pages, trims the 1/2-inch strip of perforations, and stacks the output.) If you specify BURST=YES or BURST=Y, the pages of the SYSOUT data set are separated, trimmed, and stacked automatically. If you specify BURST=NO or BURST=N, the pages are not separated. If you omit the BURST parameter, an installation-defined default is used. Most likely, the default is BURST=NO.

How to route a data set to a specific destination

Normally, JES2/JES3 determines which printer prints a particular data set depending on the output class, the source of the job, and which printers are available. Sometimes, you want JES2/JES3 to route a SYSOUT data set to a particular printer, terminal, or user. The DEST parameter on a DD or OUTPUT statement lets you do that. For example, if you code the DD statement

```
//REPORT     DD     SYSOUT=A,DEST=R100
```

the output data set is routed to the remote terminal named R100. The rules for specifying a destination depend on how your installation's configuration is defined and whether you're using JES2 or JES3, so you'll have to find out what destinations are valid at your installation.

How to specify the disposition of a SYSOUT data set

Sometimes, you don't want a SYSOUT data set to be printed immediately. For example, when you submit a job from TSO, you usually want to display the job's output at your terminal before you actually print it. To keep a SYSOUT data set in an output queue until you're ready to print it, you can use the HOLD parameter on a DD statement. If you specify HOLD=YES or HOLD=Y, the SYSOUT data set is held; if you omit HOLD or code HOLD=NO or HOLD=N, the data set isn't held. Another way to hold a SYSOUT data set is to specify a held output class in the SYSOUT parameter.

Under MVS/ESA, a new parameter is available on the OUTPUT statement that lets you specify the disposition of a SYSOUT data set under JES2: OUTDISP. The options that are available for this parameter are WRITE, HOLD, KEEP, LEAVE, and PURGE. WRITE causes the data set to be printed, then deleted. HOLD causes the data set to be held in the output queue. This is the same as coding HOLD=YES on a DD statement. KEEP causes the data set to be printed but kept in the output queue. LEAVE causes the data set to be held in the output queue. The difference between HOLD and LEAVE is that after you print a data set with HOLD disposition, the data set is deleted. With LEAVE, the data set is kept in the output queue. The last OUTDISP parameter, PURGE, causes the data set to be deleted without being printed.

When you code the OUTDISP parameter, you can specify two dispositions. The first one tells JES2 what to do if the job terminates normally, and the second one tells it what to do if the jobs terminates abnormally. For example, if you code the OUTDISP parameter

```
OUTDISP=(PURGE,HOLD)
```

the SYSOUT data set is deleted without being printed if the job terminates normally. If the job terminates abnormally, however, the SYSOUT data set is held in the output queue.

If you code an OUTDISP parameter without specifying an abnormal disposition, JES2 uses the normal disposition if the job terminates abnormally. If you specify an abnormal disposition without a normal disposition, the normal disposition defaults to WRITE. And if you omit the OUTDISP parameter, JES2 uses the normal and abnormal dispositions for the SYSOUT class for the data set.

How to set an output limit

You already know how to limit the amount of spooled output a job can produce by coding output limits on the JOB statement or a JES2/JES3 control statement. You can also use the OUTLIM parameter on a DD statement to limit the number of print or punch records written to a particular SYSOUT data set. For example, if you want to limit a report to 2,000 lines, you code this DD statement:

```
//REPORT     DD    SYSOUT=A,OUTLIM=2000
```

If you omit the OUTLIM parameter or specify OUTLIM=0, any limits you specify in JES control statements are used.

How to release a SYSOUT data set for immediate processing

Normally, all of a job's SYSOUT data sets are held in the JES output queue until the job completes. Then, the SYSOUT data sets are printed together. In some cases, you might not want to wait until a job finishes to begin printing a SYSOUT data set. For example, suppose a job has two steps: the first produces a long report, and the second sorts a huge file. If the sort step takes several hours to complete, the user must wait unnecessarily for the report to begin printing. In that case, you can use the SPIN parameter on the DD statement to force the SYSOUT data set to begin printing before the job finishes, like this:

```
//REPORT     DD    SYSOUT=A,SPIN=UNALLOC
```

This releases the REPORT data set for printing as soon as the job step ends. The SPIN parameter is available only with MVS/ESA.

JES2/JES3 control statements to manage SYSOUT data

Both JES2 and JES3 provide control statements that let you manage how SYSOUT data is handled. I don't expect you'll use them, however, because most of the functions they provide duplicate functions provided by the standard DD and OUTPUT JCL statements. The only case where I recommend you use the JES2/JES3 control systems I'll present here is when you need to use an advanced feature of the 3800 Printing Subsystem and your version of MVS doesn't support the OUTPUT statement. I'm not going to describe the individual parameters of the JES2/JES3 statements here. Instead, I'll focus on how you code the JES2/JES3 statements and how you relate them to particular SYSOUT data sets.

The /*OUTPUT statement (JES2)

The JES2 /*OUTPUT statement lets you specify output processing parameters for SYSOUT data sets under JES2. Figure 6-36 gives a partial format of the JES2 /*OUTPUT statement. As you can see, most of the parameters duplicate the DD and OUTPUT statement parameters you just learned about. As a result, I'll concentrate here on how you relate a specific SYSOUT data set to an /*OUTPUT statement.

The first parameter of the /*OUTPUT statement is a one- to four-character code that can be any value you wish. To relate a SYSOUT data set to a particular /*OUTPUT statement, you just specify the /*OUTPUT statement's code in the form-name position of the SYSOUT parameter. To illustrate, suppose you specify this /*OUTPUT statement:

```
/*OUTPUT OUT1 COPIES=4
```

Then, to relate a SYSOUT data set to this /*OUTPUT statement, you would code the DD statement like this:

```
//REPORT     DD     SYSOUT=(A,,OUT1)
```

Here, OUT1 in the SYSOUT parameter corresponds to the OUT1 code specified in the /*OUTPUT statement.

The /*OUTPUT statement itself should be placed after the JOB statement and before the first EXEC statement. If you want the options specified in the /*OUTPUT statement to apply to more than one SYSOUT data set, just list the /*OUTPUT statement's code in the SYSOUT parameter of each DD statement. You can code more

The /*OUTPUT statement (JES2)

```
/*OUTPUT    code
        [ ,BURST= {YES}  ]
                 {NO }
        [ ,CHARS=character-set ]
        [ ,COPIES= {nnn                                            }  ]
                   {(nnn[,(group-value[,group-value...])])}
        [ ,COPYG=(group-value[,group-value...]) ]
        [ ,DEST=destination ]
        [ ,FCB=fcb-name ]
        [ ,FLASH=overlay ]
        [ ,FORMS=form ]
        [ ,LINECT=count ]
        [ ,MODIFY=module ]
        [ ,UCS=character-set ]
```

Explanation

code	A one- to four-character value that's coded in a DD statement SYSOUT parameter to refer to the /*OUTPUT statement. Code * to continue a previous /*OUTPUT statement.
BURST	Specifies whether or not the burster-trimmer-stacker feature of the 3800 should be used. BURST may be abbreviated B.
CHARS	Specifies a one- to four-character character set name for a 3800. CHARS may be abbreviated X.
COPIES	Specifies how many copies of the data set should be printed. Code *nnn* to print the indicated number of copies of the entire data set; code group values to print multiple copies of each page of the data set. Note that *nnn* is required but ignored if you code group values. COPIES may be abbreviated N.
COPYG	Specifies group values as in a COPIES parameter, but doesn't include the *nnn* subparameter. This is a simpler way to specify group values. COPYG may be abbreviated G.
DEST	Specifies a destination for the SYSOUT data set. DEST may be abbreviated D.
FCB	Specifies the one- to four-character name of the forms control buffer to be downloaded to the printer. FCB may be abbreviated C.
FLASH	Specifies the one- to four-character name of the overlay the operator should mount in the 3800 printer's flash unit. FLASH may be abbreviated O.
FORMS	Specifies the one- to four-character name of the form the operator should mount on the printer. FORMS may be abbreviated F.

Figure 6-36   The /*OUTPUT statement (part 1 of 2)

Explanation

LINECT	Specifies a value (0 to 255) that indicates how many lines JES2 should print on each page. LINECT may be abbreviated K.
MODIFY	Specifies the one- to four-character name of a copy modification module for a 3800. MODIFY may be abbreviated Y.
UCS	Specifies the one- to four-character name of the print band or train to be used to print the data set. UCS may be abbreviated T.

Figure 6-36   The /*OUTPUT statement (part 2 of 2)

than one /*OUTPUT statement, if you wish. Just be sure each has a different code. Unlike the OUTPUT JCL statement, there's no way to specify a default /*OUTPUT statement.

The /*OUTPUT statement has a lot of parameters. If you need to specify more parameters than you can code on a single statement, you can continue the /*OUTPUT statement by coding two or more /*OUTPUT statements in a row. On the second and each subsequent /*OUTPUT statement, specify an asterisk (*) as the code name. Then, the parameters you specify are added to the parameters you specified on the previous /*OUTPUT statement.

The //*FORMAT PR statement (JES3)

Under JES3, the //*FORMAT PR statement lets you specify options for handling SYSOUT data sets. Figure 6-37 shows the format of the JES3 //*FORMAT PR statement. Most of the //*FORMAT parameters in figure 6-37 duplicate DD and OUTPUT statement parameters. So I'll focus on how you code the //*FORMAT PR statement and relate it to a particular SYSOUT data set rather than on the meaning of each parameter. (Incidentally, a related JES3 statement, //*FORMAT PU, lets you specify output processing for SYSOUT punch data. I don't think you'll use it, though, so I won't cover it here.)

The DDNAME parameter specifies the SYSOUT data set or data sets to which the //*FORMAT PR statement applies. For example, the //*FORMAT PR statement

```
//*FORMAT PR DDNAME=GO.REPORT,FCB=FCB1
```

applies only to the REPORT DD statement in the GO step.

You can specify a //*FORMAT PR statement for system-produced SYSOUT data by specifying SYSMSG, JESJCL, or JESMSG in the DDNAME parameter. SYSMSG refers to the output messages

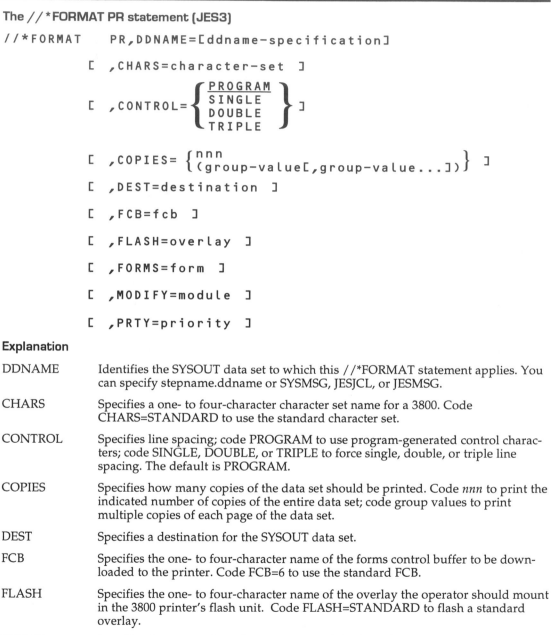

The //*FORMAT PR statement (JES3)

```
//*FORMAT    PR,DDNAME=[ddname-specification]

        [  ,CHARS=character-set  ]

        [  ,CONTROL= { PROGRAM
                       SINGLE
                       DOUBLE
                       TRIPLE  }  ]

        [  ,COPIES= { nnn
                      (group-value[,group-value...]) }  ]

        [  ,DEST=destination  ]

        [  ,FCB=fcb  ]

        [  ,FLASH=overlay  ]

        [  ,FORMS=form  ]

        [  ,MODIFY=module  ]

        [  ,PRTY=priority  ]
```

Explanation

DDNAME	Identifies the SYSOUT data set to which this //*FORMAT statement applies. You can specify stepname.ddname or SYSMSG, JESJCL, or JESMSG.
CHARS	Specifies a one- to four-character character set name for a 3800. Code CHARS=STANDARD to use the standard character set.
CONTROL	Specifies line spacing; code PROGRAM to use program-generated control characters; code SINGLE, DOUBLE, or TRIPLE to force single, double, or triple line spacing. The default is PROGRAM.
COPIES	Specifies how many copies of the data set should be printed. Code *nnn* to print the indicated number of copies of the entire data set; code group values to print multiple copies of each page of the data set.
DEST	Specifies a destination for the SYSOUT data set.
FCB	Specifies the one- to four-character name of the forms control buffer to be downloaded to the printer. Code FCB=6 to use the standard FCB.
FLASH	Specifies the one- to four-character name of the overlay the operator should mount in the 3800 printer's flash unit. Code FLASH=STANDARD to flash a standard overlay.
FORMS	Specifies the one- to four-character name of the form the operator should mount on the printer. Code FORMS=STANDARD to use a standard form.
MODIFY	Specifies the one- to four-character name of a copy modification module for a 3800.
PRTY	Specifies a priority for the output data set (1 to 255).

Figure 6-37   The //*FORMAT PR statement

produced by MVS during your job's execution. JESJCL refers to the JCL listing produced by JES3. And JESMSG refers to JES3 messages.

You can create a default format by coding the DDNAME parameter like this:

```
//*FORMAT PR DDNAME=,FCB=FCB1
```

Because I omitted the ddname in the DDNAME parameter, this //*FORMAT statement applies to each SYSOUT data set the job produces other than SYSOUT data sets referred to explicitly by other //*FORMAT PR statements.

To produce multiple copies of SYSOUT data with each copy handled in a different way, you code two or more //*FORMAT PR statements, each specifying the same ddname in the DDNAME parameter. That's similar to providing more than one OUTPUT JCL statement for a single SYSOUT data set.

Discussion

This topic has covered a lot of ground. If you're a bit confused, it's probably because SYSOUT data sets can be processed in many different ways depending on an installation's environment, and because there are often three or four ways to request the same function.

If there's any consolation, it's that most of the material in this topic is necessary only in limited situations. In fact, for the majority of SYSOUT data sets you process, you won't use any of the parameters this topic presents. Instead, you'll just code SYSOUT=* on the DD statement, as you learned in chapter 5. So keep the information this topic presented in that perspective. It's here to refer to when you need it. But you probably won't need it for most of the jobs you develop.

Terminology

forms control buffer
forms-flash technique
electronic overlay
Universal Character Set
burster-trimmer-stacker feature

Objectives

1. Code a job stream that uses default and explicitly referenced OUTPUT statements.

2. Code OUTPUT and DD statement parameters to perform advanced SYSOUT handling functions.

3. Identify the JES2 or JES3 control statements that duplicate the functions of the OUTPUT and DD statements.

Exercises

1. Modify the following job stream so that all of its SYSOUT data sets except PRDETL use a default OUTPUT statement that prints 2 copies of each data set using SYSOUT class B. The PRDETL data set should refer to an OUTPUT DD statement named OUT1 that prints 4 copies using SYSOUT class B.

```
//SYDOEA      JOB    USER=SYDOE,PASSWORD=XXXXXXXX
//STEP1       EXEC   PGM=PR3310
//SYSOUT      DD     SYSOUT=A
//PRLIST      DD     SYSOUT=A
//PRSUM       DD     SYSOUT=A
//PRDETL      DD     SYSOUT=A
```

2. Code a DD statement that creates SYSOUT output using SYSOUT class D, that is limited to 2000 lines, and that is held in the output queue until released by the operator. Use the ddname HOLDOUT.

3. Modify the job stream shown in exercise 1 so that it uses JES2 or JES3 control statements to print 2 copies of the PRLIST and PRSUM data sets and 4 copies of the PRTDETL data set.

**Chapter
7**

JCL procedures

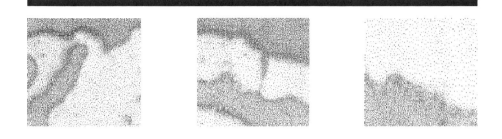

In this chapter, you'll learn about an important JCL feature: procedures. Simply put, a *JCL procedure* is a pre-written segment of code that you can include in a job stream. By using procedures, the amount of JCL coding you have to do is reduced. And, as a result, you're less likely to make a coding error. Because of the importance of JCL procedures, I hope you'll spend the time it takes to master the information in this chapter.

To illustrate the benefits of using JCL procedures, consider the IBM-supplied procedure COBUCG. If you've compiled and executed a COBOL program under MVS, you're probably already familiar with this procedure. It contains the JCL statements necessary to execute two job steps. The first step invokes the COBOL compiler to compile a COBOL source program; the second step invokes the loader to load and execute the compiled program. If it weren't for this procedure, you'd have to search the COBOL documentation to determine the JCL necessary to execute the COBOL compiler. Then, you'd have to read the linkage-editor/loader documentation to find out how to invoke those programs. And you'd have to figure out a way to execute both programs in the same job so that the resulting job would both compile and execute your program. That's not a simple task, so the COBUCG procedure clearly saves you much time and effort. In addition, the COBUCG procedure lets an installation standardize such things as the options used by the compiler and the loader, the location and size of the compiler's work files, and so on.

Procedures are often used for jobs that perform application processing, too. For example, consider the JCL statements in figure

```
//INV3010   EXEC  PGM=INV3010
//SYSOUT    DD    SYSOUT=*
//INVMAST   DD    DSNAME=MMA2.INVENTRY.MASTER,DISP=SHR
//INVSEL    DD    DSNAME=&&INVSEL,DISP=(NEW,PASS),
//                UNIT=SYSDA,SPACE=(CYL,(20,10))
//SELCTL    DD    DUMMY
//INV3020   EXEC  PGM=INV3020
//SYSOUT    DD    SYSOUT=*
//INVMAST   DD    DSNAME=&&INVSEL,DISP=(OLD,DELETE)
//INVSLST   DD    SYSOUT=*
```

Figure 7-1   JCL statements to invoke two application programs

7-1. Here, two programs are invoked: INV3010 and INV3020. Suppose that these two programs are required by many jobs throughout an application. Rather than duplicate this code in each job, you could place the code in a procedure that's invoked by each job that needs to execute the programs. That way, you reduce coding and the chance for errors.

How to invoke a procedure

You invoke a procedure by specifying its name in an EXEC statement. In that respect, invoking a procedure is much like invoking a program. Rather than invoke a program directly, however, a procedure-invoking EXEC statement causes previously stored JCL statements to be read into your job stream. The JCL statements of the procedure, in turn, invoke programs and allocate data sets.

To invoke a procedure, you code an EXEC statement, like this:

```
//STEP1     EXEC INV3000
```

or like this:

```
//STEP1     EXEC PROC=INV3000
```

In both examples, the procedure name is INV3000. (STEP1 is the name of the job step that invokes the procedure.) The word PROC is optional and is usually omitted. Whether or not you include the keyword PROC, though, the PROC parameter is positional; if you code it, it must be the first parameter on the EXEC statement.

An important point to realize here is that the JCL statements contained in a procedure are processed by the reader/interpreter component of the Job Entry Subsystem. As a result, the procedure statements are processed *before* the job actually begins to execute. If there's an error in your JCL or in the procedure's JCL, or if the procedure you specify can't be located, the job won't be scheduled for execution.

Another important point to realize is that even though you invoke a procedure with a single EXEC statement, the invoked procedure may contain more than one EXEC statement. In other words, by invoking a procedure, you can indirectly invoke more than one job step with a single EXEC statement. The EXEC statements within a procedure, however, must all invoke programs. You can't invoke a procedure from another procedure.

Cataloged and in-stream procedures   When you invoke a procedure by specifying its name in an EXEC statement, the procedure's JCL statements are retrieved from one of two places, depending on whether you're invoking a cataloged procedure or an in-stream procedure. A *cataloged procedure* is stored in a partitioned data set and may be invoked by any job on the system. (Don't let the term "cataloged procedure" confuse you; it has nothing to do with data set cataloging.) In contrast, the statements of an *in-stream procedure* appear in the job that invokes the procedure. An in-stream procedure is available only to the job that contains it; other jobs on the system can't invoke it.

Most JCL procedures are cataloged so that they can be invoked by any job that needs them. In-stream procedures are used mostly for testing procedures that will eventually be cataloged. Sometimes, though, you may need to create a job stream that has many job steps, each requiring the same JCL statements. In that case, you might use an in-stream procedure to avoid coding the same JCL statements repeatedly.

How to code a job that uses an in-stream procedure

Suppose I want to place the JCL statements in figure 7-1 in a procedure so that they can be retrieved by several jobs. Before I catalog the procedure in a procedure library, I want to be sure it works properly. So, to test the procedure, I'll create an in-stream procedure. An in-stream procedure consists of a PROC statement, followed by the JCL for the procedure, followed by a PEND statement.

You place the in-stream procedure definition (that is, the PROC statement, the procedure's JCL statements, and the PEND statement) near the beginning of your job stream, before any EXEC statement that refers to it. When the reader/interpreter encounters a PROC statement, it treats the statements that follow as procedure statements; they are not executed, but instead, are scanned for syntax errors and retained as a temporary procedure. When the PEND statement is encountered, the reader/interpreter returns to its normal processing, and the JCL statements that follow the in-stream procedure definition are interpreted as normal JCL.

To understand, look at figure 7-2. Here, the top part of the figure lists a job stream I submitted for execution. The first statement after the JOB statement is a PROC statement that marks the beginning of an in-stream procedure named INV3000. A name is always required on a PROC statement. After the PROC statement are the JCL statements that make up the procedure; they're identical to the JCL statements in figure 7-1. Then, to mark the end of the procedure, I coded a PEND statement. Following the PEND statement, I coded two EXEC statements, each of which invokes the INV3000 procedure.

The bottom part of figure 7-2 shows the JCL listing that appears in the job output for this job. This listing appears normal up to the first EXEC statement that invokes the INV3000 procedure. Then, following that EXEC statement, you can see the statements that were retrieved from the in-stream procedure; they're identified by plus signs rather than slashes in columns 1 and 2. These procedure statements are executed as they appear in the listing, as if they were included in this location in the original job stream. Similarly, the procedure statements appear again following the second EXEC statement that invokes the procedure.

I want to be sure you understand how this works, so let's review the sequence of program execution in the bottom part of figure 7-2. The EXEC statements between the PROC and PEND statements are not executed when they're first encountered in the job stream. Instead, those statements are saved as a procedure so they can be processed later. Then, when the STEPA1 EXEC statement is processed, the two job steps in the in-stream procedure are executed: first INV3010, then INV3020. Next, the STEPA2 EXEC statement is processed; it too invokes the in-stream procedure, so the INV3010 and INV3020 steps are executed a second time.

The plus sign in columns 1 and 2 of the JCL listing indicate that the JCL statements were obtained from an in-stream procedure. Figure 7-3 shows other identifying values that can appear at the beginning of each line in the JCL listing, both for in-stream and cataloged procedures.

Job stream

```
//SYDOEA      JOB   USER=SYDOE,PASSWORD=XXXXXXXX
//INV3000     PROC
//INV3010     EXEC  PGM=INV3010
//SYSOUT      DD    SYSOUT=*
//INVMAST     DD    DSNAME=MMA2.INVENTRY.MASTER,DISP=SHR
//INVSEL      DD    DSNAME=&&INVSEL,DISP=(NEW,PASS),
//                  UNIT=SYSDA,SPACE=(CYL,(20,10))
//SELCTL      DD    DUMMY
//INV3020     EXEC  PGM=INV3020
//SYSOUT      DD    SYSOUT=*
//INVMAST     DD    DSNAME=&&INVSEL,DISP=(OLD,DELETE)
//INVSLST     DD    SYSOUT=*
//            PEND
//STEPA1      EXEC  INV3000
//STEPA2      EXEC  INV3000
```

JCL listing in job output

```
//SYDOEA      JOB   USER=SYDOE,PASSWORD=XXXXXXXX
//INV3000     PROC
//INV3010     EXEC  PGM=INV3010
//SYSOUT      DD    SYSOUT=*
//INVMAST     DD    DSNAME=MMA2.INVENTRY.MASTER,DISP=SHR
//INVSEL      DD    DSNAME=&&INVSEL,DISP=(NEW,PASS),
//                  UNIT=SYSDA,SPACE=(CYL,(20,10))
//SELCTL      DD    DUMMY
//INV3020     EXEC  PGM=INV3020
//SYSOUT      DD    SYSOUT=*
//INVMAST     DD    DSNAME=&&INVSEL,DISP=(OLD,DELETE)
//INVSLST     DD    SYSOUT=*
//            PEND
//STEPA1      EXEC  INV3000
++INV3000     PROC
++INV3010     EXEC  PGM=INV3010
++SYSOUT      DD    SYSOUT=*
++INVMAST     DD    DSNAME=MMA2.INVENTRY.MASTER,DISP=SHR
++INVSEL      DD    DSNAME=&&INVSEL,DISP=(NEW,PASS),
++                  UNIT=SYSDA,SPACE=(CYL,(20,10))
++SELCTL      DD    DUMMY
++INV3020     EXEC  PGM=INV3020
++SYSOUT      DD    SYSOUT=*
++INVMAST     DD    DSNAME=&&INVSEL,DISP=(OLD,DELETE)
++INVSLST     DD    SYSOUT=*
//STEPA2      EXEC  INV3000
++INV3000     PROC
++INV3010     EXEC  PGM=INV3010
++SYSOUT      DD    SYSOUT=*
++INVMAST     DD    DSNAME=MMA2.INVENTRY.MASTER,DISP=SHR
++INVSEL      DD    DSNAME=&&INVSEL,DISP=(NEW,PASS)),
++                  UNIT=SYSDA,SPACE=(CYL,(20,10))
++SELECTL     DD    DUMMY
++INV3020     EXEC  PGM=INV3020
++SYSOUT      DD    SYSOUT=*
++INVMAST     DD    DSNAME=&&INVSEL,DISP=(OLD,DELETE))
++INVSLST     DD    SYSOUT=*
```

Figure 7-2   Invoking the INV3000 procedure

Identifier for in-stream procedure	Identifier for cataloged procedure	Meaning
//	//	Statement from input JCL
++	XX	Statement from procedure
+/	X/	Procedure statement that you modified
++*	XX*	Procedure statements, other than comment statements, that were converted to comments (probably because of an error)
***	***	Comments and JES2/JES3 control statements

Figure 7-3   Identifying in-stream and cataloged procedure statements in a job's JCL listing

How procedure libraries are searched for cataloged procedures

Once an in-stream procedure has been thoroughly tested, you'll probably want to catalog it so that you don't have to include the procedure definition in each job stream that invokes the procedure. There are several ways to actually place a procedure in a procedure library, the easiest of which is to use ISPF facilities. I won't show you how to do that, however, because that function is usually done by systems programmers so they can maintain control over what goes into procedure libraries. But I do want you to know how procedure libraries are searched to locate a cataloged procedure.

When JES2 or JES3 is initialized, the system procedure library (a partitioned data set named SYS1.PROCLIB) is allocated to the JES address space. SYS1.PROCLIB contains mostly system-oriented procedures, like COBUCG and the other language-translation procedures. Each installation also concatenates various libraries to SYS1.PROCLIB, so that if a procedure isn't found in one library, another is searched. Before MVS/ESA Version 4, the procedure library allocations were fixed once JES was initialized. Unlike program libraries or catalogs, there was no way to allocate a private procedure library for use by a single job or job step. With MVS/ESA Version 4, however, you can use the JCLLIB statement to do that. I'll present that statement later in this chapter.

Even if you're not using MVS/ESA Version 4, that doesn't mean that all cataloged procedures must be stored in SYS1.PROCLIB or one of the procedure libraries that are concatenated to it. Both JES2 and JES3 let you establish *alternate procedure libraries*, which you can use instead of the SYS1.PROCLIB concatenation. But the procedure for establishing these libraries is awkward. First, the alternate procedure libraries must be allocated to the JES address space by the JCL that starts JES. Second, you must code a /*JOBPARM (JES2) or //*MAIN (JES3) statement that specifies which procedure library concatenation to use for a job. I won't describe the details of doing that here. Instead, I refer you to IBM's JCL manual for an explanation of how to code the appropriate JES2/JES3 control statement and to your systems programming group to see which procedure library concatenations are available.

One important point about cataloged procedures before I go on: A cataloged procedure should never contain a PEND statement. The PEND statement is used only in an in-stream procedure to mark the end of the procedure statements. Also, the PROC statement is optional in a cataloged procedure, but I usually code it.

How to modify a procedure's statements

Frankly, procedures wouldn't be very useful if they provided the same JCL statements every time you invoked them. The biggest benefit of procedures is that you can make minor adjustments to the JCL they contain to meet varying processing needs. There are several ways to do that. Right now, I'll show you how to code JCL statements that change or supplement the JCL statements contained in a procedure. Later in this chapter, I'll show you how to code more generalized procedures that use symbolic parameters.

There are three ways you can modify the statements of a procedure you're invoking. First, you can modify parameters coded on EXEC statements within the procedure. Second, you can modify parameters coded on DD statements within the procedure. And third, you can add entirely new DD statements to the procedure. After I describe these three ways to modify procedure statements, I'll show you how you can provide for optional data sets in a procedure. Then, I'll show you a job that modifies procedure statements.

How to modify EXEC statement parameters   To change a parameter that's coded on an EXEC statement within a procedure or to add a parameter to one of the procedure's EXEC statements, you code a *parameter override* on the EXEC statement that invokes the procedure. The format of a parameter override is this:

```
parameter.procstepname=value
```

Here, you identify not just the parameter that you're overriding, but also the step name coded on an EXEC statement within the procedure; that indicates which EXEC statement in the procedure the parameter override applies to. To use overrides effectively, each step in a procedure should be given a unique name.

To illustrate, consider the standard IBM-supplied procedure COBUCG, which has two job steps: COB and GO. Suppose you invoke the procedure like this:

```
//       EXEC COBUCG,PARM.COB='XREF,CLIST'
```

In this case, if the EXEC statement for the COB step doesn't have a PARM parameter, the parameter is added to it. If the EXEC statement in the procedure already has a PARM parameter, however, that parameter is replaced.

If you code a parameter without specifying a step name, it usually overrides or is added to each EXEC statement in the procedure. The only exceptions are the PARM and TIME parameters. If you code a PARM parameter without a step name, it applies just to the first step of the invoked procedure. If you code a TIME parameter without a step name, the entire procedure is timed as if it was a single job step.

When you override a parameter that has more than one subparameter, be sure to repeat *all* of the subparameters in the override parameter, even if you only change one of the subparameter values. That's because an override parameter completely replaces the parameter specified in the procedure, without regard for subparameters. For example, suppose a procedure contains this statement:

```
//STEP2    EXEC PGM=INV3200,COND((4,LT,STEP1),EVEN)
```

If you wanted to change this EXEC statement's COND parameter so that the return code from STEP1 must be zero for the INV3200 program to execute, you would code the parameter override like this:

```
COND((0,EQ,STEP1),EVEN)
```

Notice that I repeated the EVEN subparameter on the parameter override even though I didn't change its specification. If I omitted EVEN, the specification would be lost because the COND parameter override completely replaces the COND parameter specified in the procedure.

To nullify the effect of a parameter coded on an EXEC statement within a procedure, you code the parameter and procedure step name on the invoking EXEC statement, but omit the value after the equals sign. For example, the statement

```
//       EXEC AR3600,TIME.PSTEP1=
```

nullifies the TIME parameter that was coded on the procedure step named PSTEP1.

How to modify DD statement parameters You can also change DD statement parameters that are coded in a procedure or add parameters to a DD statement. To do that, you code a DD statement following the invoking EXEC statement in this format:

```
//procstepname.ddname DD parameter=value
```

Then, the parameter values you specify are used on the DD statement in the procedure. For example, if you code the statements

```
//          EXEC AR3000
//AR3010.SYSOUT  DD  SYSOUT=C
```

the output class for the SYSOUT DD statement in the AR3010 step is changed to C.

When you code an override DD statement, you don't have to override every parameter that's specified in the procedure DD statement. For example, if you code the override DD statement

```
//AR3010.INVSEL  DD  SPACE=(CYL,(30,10))
```

only the SPACE parameter of the INVSEL data set is changed. The other parameters are used as they're coded in the procedure.

Actually, you have to code the procedure step name only for the first DD statement you override in each procedure step. When you omit the procedure step name, the most recently specified step name is assumed. So, assuming the STEP1 step has three DD statements (DD1, DD2, and DD3), the JCL

```
//STEP1.DD1  DD  ...
//STEP1.DD2  DD  ...
//STEP1.DD3  DD  ...
```

is equivalent to this:

```
//STEP1.DD1  DD  ...
//DD2        DD  ...
//DD3        DD  ...
```

To avoid mistakes, however, I usually code the procedure step name on each DD statement override.

If you omit the step name from each override DD statement, you must be sure to code the overriding DD statements in the same sequence as the original DD statements appear in the procedure. For example, suppose a procedure step named STEP1 has three DD statements in this order: DD1, DD2, and DD3. To change a parameter value on all three, you must code the overriding DD statements in this order: STEP1.DD1, DD2, and DD3. If you code the step name on each override DD statement, you don't have to worry about the order.

Most DD statement parameter overrides work like EXEC statement overrides: parameters are replaced completely, without regard for subparameters coded on the procedure DD statement. However, when you override a DCB parameter, only the subparameters you code on the override DD statement are changed; other DCB subparameters coded on the original DD statement remain unchanged. Thus, if the procedure contains the DCB parameter

```
DCB=(DSORG=PS,LRECL=200,BLKSIZE=800,RECFM=FB)
```

and you want to change the block size to 3200, you can code just

```
DCB=BLKSIZE=3200
```

on the overriding DD statement. The other DCB subparameters coded in the procedure aren't changed.

How to add a DD statement   Sometimes, you'll need to add a DD statement to a procedure you're invoking. There are two cases where that's likely. The first is when a procedure is invoked repeatedly using a different input or output file each time. In a case like this, the file may just be omitted from the procedure, so you have to code a DD statement for it each time you invoke the procedure. The second case is when a procedure requires in-stream data. In-stream data sets aren't allowed within procedures, so you have to provide them in the invoking JCL.

To add a DD statement to a procedure, all you do is code the DD statement following the EXEC statement that invokes the procedure and any override DD statements. For example, suppose a procedure step has two DD statements, DD1 and DD2, and you want to change a parameter on DD1 and DD2 and add a third DD statement, DD3. To do that, you must code the DD statements in this order: DD1, DD2, and DD3. In other words, the added DD statement must follow the DD statement overrides.

How to use the DDNAME parameter in a procedure DD statement
A DD statement parameter you might find useful when you develop procedures is the DDNAME parameter, which lets you relate a DD statement coded in the procedure to an overriding DD statement that has a different ddname. In the DDNAME parameter, you specify the ddname that should be specified in the override DD statement. For example, suppose you code this statement in a procedure:

```
//SYSIN    DD    DDNAME=CNTLDD
```

Then, when MVS attempts to allocate the SYSIN DD statement, it obtains its allocation information from the CNTLDD DD statement.

What makes the DDNAME parameter particularly useful in procedures is that the DD statement referred to in the DDNAME parameter

Invoking JCL

```
//STEPB1    EXEC  INV3000,PARM.INV3010='0050000'
//INV3010.SYSOUT DD DUMMY
//INVSEL    DD    SPACE=(CYL,(5,5))
```

JCL listing in job output

```
//STEPB1    EXEC  INV3000,PARM.INV3010='0050000'
++INV3000   PROC
++INV3010   EXEC  PGM=INV3010
//INV3010.SYSOUT DD DUMMY
+/SYSOUT    DD    SYSOUT=*
++INVMAST   DD    DSNAME=MMA2.INVENTRY.MASTER,DISP=SHR
//INVSEL    DD    SPACE=(CYL,(5,5))
+/INVSEL    DD    DSNAME=&&INVSEL,DISP=(NEW,PASS),
++                UNIT=SYSDA,SPACE=(CYL,(20,10))
++SELCTL    DD    DUMMY
++INV3020   EXEC  PGM=INV3020
++SYSOUT    DD    SYSOUT=*
++INVMAST   DD    DSNAME=&&INVSEL,DISP=(OLD,DELETE)
++INVSLST   DD    SYSOUT=*
```

Figure 7-4   Modifying statements in the INV3000 procedure

is optional. If the specified DD statement is present, it's used. But if it isn't, the data set is treated as if DUMMY were specified; I/O operations for the data set are ignored. As a result, the DDNAME parameter is a good way to provide for data sets that are optional.

You might be wondering at this point why you wouldn't just code DUMMY on the DD statement in the procedure and provide an override DD statement if the data set is needed. The reason is that the only way to override a DUMMY parameter is to code a DSNAME parameter on the overriding DD statement. And when you do that, you can't use in-stream data. So if you want to allow an in-stream data set to override a DUMMY data set (and you often will), you'll have to use DDNAME instead of DUMMY.

One restriction when you code the DDNAME parameter is that you can code only two parameters along with it: AMP (for VSAM files) or DCB (for non-VSAM files). And if you code DCB, you can code only three subparameters: BLKSIZE, BUFNO, and DIAGNS. Of the three, BLKSIZE is the only one you're likely to use.

An example of modifying procedure statements   To illustrate the techniques I've just presented, figure 7-4 shows how you can modify the statements of the INV3000 procedure I presented in figure 7-2. The top part of figure 7-4 lists the JCL I coded to invoke the INV3000 procedure. On the EXEC statement, I coded a PARM parameter that applies to the INV3010 step. (The value specified in the PARM parameter is simply passed to the INV3010 program; what the program does with it doesn't matter.) I also coded two DD statements: the first overrides the SYSOUT DD statement in the INV3010 step by changing it to a dummy data set; the second changes the space parameter of the INVSEL data set in the same job step.

The bottom part of figure 7-4 shows the JCL as it appears in the job's JCL listing. The two overridden DD statements are highlighted. As you can see, the override DD statement is listed before the DD statement it overrides, and the DD statement that's affected by the override is marked by a + / in columns 1 and 2. (If INV3000 was a cataloged procedure, X/ would appear instead of + /.) Notice that the JCL listing doesn't show the final effect of the JCL; you have to figure that out for yourself. For example, to determine which parameters are used in the INVSEL data set, you have to combine the parameters coded in the override DD statement with those coded on the procedure's original DD statement.

How to use symbolic parameters to generalize a procedure

Although the facilities for modifying procedures that I've presented so far are flexible, they can be awkward to use. A better way to create procedures for generalized use is to provide *symbolic parameters*. When you use symbolic parameters, you don't code actual parameter values in the procedure's JCL statements. Instead, you code symbolic parameters which, much like program variables, can take on specific values when you invoke the procedures.

How to code symbolic parameters   To code a symbolic parameter in a procedure, you code an ampersand (&) followed by a one- to seven-character name. For example, &SPACE is a valid symbolic parameter. You can use any name you wish except a name that's a keyword parameter for the EXEC statement. Thus, you can't use &PARM or &TIME as symbolic parameters because PARM and TIME are EXEC statement parameters.

In the procedure, you code the symbolic parameter anywhere you would code a JCL statement parameter or subparameter value. For example, you could code the DD statement SYSOUT parameter like this:

```
SYSOUT=&CLASS
```

Here, the value assigned to the &CLASS symbolic parameter when the procedure is executed will be used in the SYSOUT parameter to specify an output class.

You can use the same symbolic parameter in a procedure as many times as you wish. So, you could use the &CLASS symbolic parameter in the SYSOUT parameter of all DD statements that define SYSOUT data sets in the procedure. That way, you can be sure that all SYSOUT data sets are processed using the same output class. If you need to assign different classes to the SYSOUT data sets, however, you have to use more than one symbolic parameter.

How to specify symbolic parameter values   When you invoke a procedure that uses symbolic parameters, you supply values for its symbolic parameters by coding them on the EXEC statement, like this:

```
EXEC INV3000,CLASS=A
```

Here, the &CLASS symbolic parameter is given a value of A. So, any SYSOUT parameter in the procedure that specifies the symbolic parameter &CLASS will be interpreted like this:

```
SYSOUT=A
```

In other words, &CLASS in the procedure statement is replaced by A, the value supplied for the &CLASS symbolic parameter. Notice that you do not include the ampersand in the symbolic parameter when you code the EXEC statement that invokes the procedure.

If the value you're giving the symbolic parameter contains any special characters (like commas, asterisks, and so on), you enclose the entire value in apostrophes, like this:

```
EXEC INV3000,CLASS='(,)'
```

Here, (,) becomes the value of the &CLASS symbolic parameter.

To illustrate how symbolic parameters are used, figure 7-5 shows another version of the INV3000 procedure. Here, I've used three symbolic parameters to make the procedure more generalized. In the DD statements for the SYSOUT data sets, I've specified &CLASS as the output class so I can easily change the output class when I invoke the procedure. Similarly, I've specified &DEPT as a part of the data set name for the INVMAST data set. Notice that I coded two periods following &DEPT; I'll explain why when I discuss how symbolic parameter values are used. Finally, I used a symbolic parameter named &SPACE as a subparameter in the SPACE parameter of the INVSEL DD statement. That way, I can allocate a different amount of space to this data set each time I invoke the procedure.

The middle section of figure 7-5 shows the EXEC statement I used to invoke the procedure:

```
//          EXEC INV3000,CLASS=M,DEPT=MMA2,SPACE='5,1'
```

Procedure

```
//INV3000   PROC
//INV3010   EXEC  PGM=INV3010
//SYSOUT    DD    SYSOUT=&CLASS
//INVMAST   DD    DSNAME=&DEPT..INVENTRY.MASTER,DISP=SHR
//INVSEL    DD    DSNAME=&&INVSEL,DISP=(NEW,PASS)),
//                UNIT=SYSDA,SPACE=(CYL,(&SPACE))
//SELCTL    DD    DUMMY
//INV3020   EXEC  PGM=INV3020
//SYSOUT    DD    SYSOUT=&CLASS
//INVMAST   DD    DSNAME=&&INVSEL,DISP=(OLD,DELETE)
//INVSLST   DD    SYSOUT=&CLASS
```

Invoking EXEC statement

```
//STEPA1    EXEC  INV3000,CLASS=M,DEPT=MMA2,SPACE='5,1'
```

Effective JCL

```
//INV3010   EXEC  PGM=INV3000
//SYSOUT    DD    SYSOUT=M
//INVMAST   DD    DSNAME=MMA2.INVENTRY.MASTER,DISP=SHR
//INVSEL    DD    DSNAME=&&INVSEL,DISP=(NEW,PASS),
//                UNIT=SYSDA,SPACE=(CYL,(5,1))
//SELCTL    DD    DUMMY
//INV3020   EXEC  PGM=INV3020
//SYSOUT    DD    SYSOUT=M
//INVMAST   DD    DSNAME=&&INVSEL,DISP=(OLD,DELETE)
//INVSLST   DD    SYSOUT=M
```

Figure 7-5   The INV3000 procedure with symbolic parameters

Notice that the value for the &SPACE symbolic parameter is enclosed in apostrophes because it includes a special character (a
comma). As a result, 5,1 is the value that's associated with &SPACE.

The bottom part of figure 7-5 shows the JCL as it's interpreted
using the symbolic parameter values supplied by the EXEC statement. Each SYSOUT data set specifies SYSOUT=M, the class indicated by the &CLASS symbolic parameter. The name of the inventory master file is MMA2.INVENTRY.MASTER. And the SPACE
parameter is SPACE=(CYL,(5,1)). (This isn't the way the listing
appears in your job output, but it helps you see the JCL statements
as they're actually processed.)

You can nullify the value of a symbolic parameter by coding the symbolic parameter's name followed by an equal sign without a value. For example, if you coded the EXEC statement

```
//           EXEC INV3000,SPACE=
```

the value of the &SPACE symbolic parameter would be null. When you do this, however, you have to be sure that the JCL statement has a valid syntax after the symbolic parameter's value is applied. In this case, the SPACE parameter for the INVMAST DD statement would look like this:

```
SPACE=(CYL,())
```

That would cause a JCL error.

To use symbolic parameters effectively, you need to understand the rules MVS follows when it substitutes symbolic parameter values. In some situations, those rules can be confusing.

How symbolic parameter values are used   To illustrate how symbolic parameter values are used in a procedure's JCL statements, figure 7-6 presents seven examples. In each example, assume that the procedure was invoked with this EXEC statement:

```
//           EXEC proc-name,VAR1=TEST,VAR2=LIST
```

So the value of &VAR1 is TEST and the value of &VAR2 is LIST.

Example 1 shows a simple case; here, the value of the &VAR1 symbolic parameter is used as the value for the DSNAME parameter. So, TEST is used as the data set name.

Example 2 illustrates that a symbolic parameter can be mixed with other text to form the final parameter value. Here, the letter A is combined with the symbolic parameter's value to form the data set name ATEST. In this example, no special coding is required to combine the text with the symbolic parameter value. That's because the ampersand acts as punctuation to separate the text from the symbolic parameter.

Adding text to the end of a symbolic parameter isn't a problem either as long as the text starts with a special character, as in example 3. Here, DSNAME=&VAR1(&VAR2) becomes DSNAME=TEST(LIST). Because the left parenthesis is a special character, no special coding is needed to distinguish it from the &VAR1 symbolic parameter name.

Adding text after a symbolic parameter when the text begins
with a letter or digit, however, is another matter. That's because
MVS can't separate the start of the text from the end of the symbolic parameter name. For example, suppose you want to add the
letter A to the end of a symbolic parameter value. If you coded this:

```
DSNAME=&VAR1A
```

MVS would look for a symbolic parameter named &VAR1A.

To solve this problem, you must use a period as a *delimiter*
between the symbolic parameter and the text, as in example 4.
When the period is encountered in a symbolic parameter name, it
marks the end of the parameter name and any text that follows it is
added after the symbolic parameter's value. The period itself is
dropped out, so it doesn't become a part of the final JCL text. In
example 4, &VAR1.A becomes TESTA.

A period is often required as a delimiter when you want to
nullify a symbolic parameter. For example, consider this procedure
statement:

```
//INVSLST   DD    &DUMMY.SYSOUT=A
```

Here, I coded the &DUMMY symbolic parameter before the
SYSOUT parameter, using the period as a delimiter. If I nullify the
&DUMMY symbolic parameter, it and the period are dropped, so
the statement is processed like this:

```
//INVSLST   DD    SYSOUT=A
```

If you assign a value to a symbolic parameter coded this way, you
should include a trailing comma. For example, if I specify
&DUMMY='DUMMY,' when I invoke the procedure, the INVLST
DD statement is processed like this:

```
//INVSLST   DD    DUMMY,SYSOUT=A
```

As a result, INVSLST becomes a dummy data set. If I used a comma
rather than a period to separate the positional symbolic parameter
from the keyword SYSOUT parameter, a syntax error would result
if I nullified &DUMMY.

Unfortunately, the use of a period as a delimiter creates the need
for another rule: If you want the period to appear in the final JCL
statement, you have to code two periods as in example 5 in figure 7-6.
The first period is a delimiter that marks the end of the symbolic
parameter name. The second period becomes a part of the data set
name. So, &VAR1..A becomes TEST.A. As you might guess, this type
of coding is common when forming data set names. That's how I used
the &DEPT symbolic parameter for the high-level qualifier of the
inventory file's data set name in figure 7-5.

Example	As coded in procedure	As interpreted by JES
1	DSNAME=&VAR1	DSNAME=TEST
2	DSNAME=A&VAR1	DSNAME=ATEST
3	DSNAME=&VAR1(&VAR2)	DSNAME=TEST(LIST)
4	DSNAME=&VAR1.A	DSNAME=TESTA
5	DSNAME=&VAR1..A	DSNAME=TEST.A
6	DSNAME=&VAR1&VAR2	DSNAME=TESTLIST
7	DSNAME=&VAR1..&VAR2	DSNAME=TEST.LIST

Note: *In each example, the procedure is invoked with this EXEC statement:*

```
//        EXEC proc-name,VAR1=TEST,VAR2=LIST
```

Figure 7-6   Examples of using symbolic parameters

Example 6 shows that you don't need to use a period to place two symbolic parameters back to back. That's because the ampersand itself separates the two symbolic parameters. So DSNAME=&VAR1&VAR2 becomes DSNAME=TESTLIST. You can use a period if you wish, but it's not necessary. So DSNAME=&VAR1.&VAR2 has the same result as example 6 in figure 7-6. If you want the period to remain between the two symbolic parameters, however, you must again code two periods, as in example 7. Here, &VAR1..&VAR2 becomes TEST.LIST.

How to assign default values to symbolic parameters   So far, I've shown you how to assign values to symbolic parameters when you invoke a procedure. For most procedures you'll code, many of the symbolic parameters will have certain values that are used most of the time. For example, it's safe to assume that the &CLASS symbolic parameter in figure 7-5 will be set to * most of the time, so that the SYSOUT data sets will have the same output class as the job's message output. Rather than force the programmer to specify CLASS='*' each time the procedure is invoked, you can provide a default symbolic parameter value by coding CLASS='*' on the procedure's PROC statement. Then, if the programmer doesn't code CLASS on the EXEC statement, the default value (*) will be used.

Figure 7-7 shows a version of the INV3000 procedure that supplies default values for the &CLASS and &SPACE parameters. I didn't supply a default value for &DEPT, so DEPT must always be coded on the EXEC statement that invokes this procedure. Figure 7-7 also shows the effect of invoking the procedure with an EXEC statement that provides a value for &DEPT, overrides the default for &SPACE, and relies on the default value for &CLASS.

Procedure

```
//INV3000    PROC  CLASS='*',SPACE='1,1'
//INV3010    EXEC  PGM=INV3010
//SYSOUT     DD    SYSOUT=&CLASS
//INVMAST    DD    DSNAME=&DEPT..INVENTRY.MASTER,DISP=SHR
//INVSEL     DD    DSNAME=&&INVSEL,DISP=(NEW,PASS),
//                 UNIT=SYSDA,SPACE=(CYL,(&SPACE))
//SELCTL     DD    DUMMY
//INV3020    EXEC  PGM=INV3020
//SYSOUT     DD    SYSOUT=&CLASS
//INVMAST    DD    DSNAME=&&INVSEL,DISP=(OLD,DELETE)
//INVSLST    DD    SYSOUT=&CLASS
```

Invoking EXEC statement

```
//STEPA1     EXEC  INV3000,DEPT=MMA2,SPACE='10,5'
```

Effective JCL

```
//INV3010    EXEC  PGM=INV3010
//SYSOUT     DD    SYSOUT=*
//INVMAST    DD    DSNAME=MMA2.INVENTRY.MASTER,DISP=SHR
//INVSEL     DD    DSNAME=&&INVSEL,DISP=(NEW,PASS),
//                 UNIT=SYSDA,SPACE=(CYL,(10,5))
//SELCTL     DD    DUMMY
//INV3020    EXEC  PGM=INV3020
//SYSOUT     DD    SYSOUT=*
//INVMAST    DD    DSNAME=&&INVSEL,DISP=(OLD,DELETE)
//INVSLST    DD    SYSOUT=*
```

Figure 7-7   The INV3000 procedure with default symbolic parameters

How to use MVS/ESA Version 4 features for cataloged procedures

With MVS/ESA Version 4, IBM introduced several new features that make cataloged procedures easier to use. To begin, you can now use the JCLLIB statement to establish a *private procedure library* without having to set up a special SYS1.PROCLIB concatenation or alternate procedure library. In addition, MVS/ESA Version 4 lets you modify symbolic parameter values by using the new SET statement, and it lets you copy JCL statements directly into your job stream using the new INCLUDE statement.

How to set up and use a private procedure library   Cataloged procedures have been a mainstay feature of MVS since its earliest

The JCLLIB statement

```
//name        JCLLIB ORDER=(library[,library...])
```

Explanation

library   The complete data set name for a procedure library you want JES to search for cataloged procedures. If only one library is specified, you can omit the parentheses.

Figure 7-8   The JCLLIB statement

versions, but it wasn't until MVS/ESA Version 4 was released that individual programmers could create their own libraries of cataloged procedures without special assistance from systems programmers. With ESA Version 4, however, you can easily set up your own procedure library. Just create a partitioned data set and use the new JCLLIB statement to identify it as a procedure library.

Figure 7-8 shows the format of the JCLLIB statement. You code this statement after the JOB statement and before the first EXEC statement in the job. On it, you list the data set name of your private procedure library. If you want, you can list more than one procedure library; when you do, MVS searches the libraries in the order in which you list them. MVS always searches the system procedure library (SYS1.PROCLIB) after it has searched all of the libraries you specify in the JCLLIB statement, so using JCLLIB doesn't affect your ability to use standard procedures like COBUCG.

Figure 7-9 shows an example of how the JCLLIB statement is used. Here, you can see that I specified the library named MMA2.PROCLIB as my private procedure library. When the EXEC statement invokes the INV3000 procedure, MVS will search for the INV3000 member first in MMA2.PROCLIB. If it doesn't find it there, it will search SYS1.PROCLIB.

Figure 7-10 shows three examples of the JCLLIB statement. Example 1 is identical to the JCLLIB statement I used in Figure 7-9. It specifies a single procedure library. Example 2 shows how you can code two or more libraries on a single JCLLIB statement; notice that the libraries are enclosed in parentheses. In this example, MVS will search for cataloged procedures first in MMA2.PROCLIB, then in TEST.PROCLIB. If it doesn't find the procedure in either of these libraries, it will search SYS1.PROCLIB.

Example 3 shows how you can force MVS to search its system procedure libraries before it searches any private libraries: Just list

```
//SYDOEA    JOB   USER=SYDOE,PASSWORD=XXXXXXXX
//          JCLLIB ORDER=MMA2.PROCLIB
//STEPB1    EXEC INV3000,PARM.INV3010='0050000'
//INV3010.SYSOUT DD DUMMY
//INVSEL    DD    SPACE=(CYL,(5,5))
```

Figure 7-9   Using the JCLLIB statement

Example 1

```
//          JCLLIB ORDER=MMA2.PROCLIB
```

MMA2.PROCLIB is searched, followed by SYS1.PROCLIB.

Example 2

```
//          JCLLIB ORDER=(MMA2.PROCLIB,TEST.PROCLIB)
```

MMA2.PROCLIB is searched, followed by TEST.PROCLIB, followed by SYS1.PROCLIB.

Example 3

```
//          JCLLIB ORDER=(SYS1.PROCLIB,SYDOE.PROCLIB)
```

SYS1.PROCLIB is searched, followed by SYDOE.PROCLIB. Then, SYS1.PROCLIB is searched again.

Figure 7-10   Examples of the JCLLIB statement

SYS1.PROCLIB as the first library in the JCLLIB statement. If MVS doesn't find a procedure in SYS1.PROCLIB, it then searches the private library. Interestingly, if the procedure can't be found in the private library, MVS is forced to search SYS1.PROCLIB again. That's because MVS *always* searches SYS1.PROCLIB after searching all of the libraries listed in the JCLLIB statement, even if SYS1.PROCLIB is one of the libraries listed.

How to use the SET statement   Before MVS/ESA Version 4, the only way to set the value of a symbolic parameter was by naming it in an EXEC or PROC statement. Version 4 introduces a new command—SET—that lets you set the value of a symbolic variable at any time. Figure 7-11 presents its format. You can code the SET statement anywhere in a job following the JOB statement.

The SET statement

```
//            SET parameter=value[,parameter=value...]
```

Explanation

parameter   The name of a symbolic parameter you want to assign a value to.

value   The value you want assigned.

Figure 7-11   The SET statement

Figure 7-12 shows how you might use SET statements to set parameter values before invoking a cataloged procedure. The cataloged procedure shown here is identical to the one previously shown in figure 7-7. But here, instead of specifying parameter values on the invoking EXEC statement, I used two SET statements to set the values of the symbolic parameters SPACE and DEPT before invoking the procedure. If you'll study the effective JCL, you'll see that the parameter values established by the SET statements are reflected in the procedure.

The advantage of the SET statement is that you don't have to use it in conjunction with procedures at all. For example, suppose you have a job that you frequently use with only minor variations. If you use a SET statement at the beginning of the job to set a symbolic parameter that's used throughout the job, you can use a text editor to change the SET statement each time you submit the job. Often, this type of coding can eliminate the need for a cataloged procedure altogether.

There's one peculiarity of the SET statement you need to be aware of: It's not subject to the conditional processing imposed by IF, ELSE, or ENDIF statements. If you enclose a SET statement within an IF/ELSE/ENDIF construct, the SET statement will be executed regardless of the results of the IF statement's condition tests.

How to use the INCLUDE statement   MVS/ESA Version 4 also lets you use the INCLUDE statement to copy text directly into your job stream. The INCLUDE statement works much like a cataloged procedure, except that the JCL copied into the job stream doesn't have to consist of entire job steps. You can use INCLUDE to copy just portions of a step, such as a single DD statement or a group of commonly used DD statements. The included JCL statements can include symbolic parameters.

Procedure

```
//INV3000   PROC  CLASS='*',SPACE='1,1'
//INV3010   EXEC  PGM=INV3010
//SYSOUT    DD    SYSOUT=&CLASS
//INVMAST   DD    DSNAME=&DEPT..INVENTRY.MASTER,DISP=SHR
//INVSEL    DD    DSNAME=&&INVSEL,DISP=(NEW,PASS),
//                UNIT=SYSDA,SPACE=(CYL,(&SPACE))
//SELCTL    DD    DUMMY
//INV3020   EXEC  PGM=INV3020
//SYSOUT    DD    SYSOUT=&CLASS
//INVMAST   DD    DSNAME=&&INVSEL,DISP=(OLD,DELETE)
//INVSLST   DD    SYSOUT=&CLASS
```

Invoking JCL

```
//SYDOEA    JOB   USER=SYDOE,PASSWORD=XXXXXXXX
//          SET   SPACE='10,5'
//          SET   DEPT=MMA2
//STEPA1    EXEC  INV3000
```

Effective JCL

```
//INV3010   EXEC  PGM=INV3010
//SYSOUT    DD    SYSOUT=*
//INVMAST   DD    DSNAME=MMA2.INVENTRY.MASTER,DISP=SHR
//INVSEL    DD    DSNAME=&&INVSEL,DISP=(NEW,PASS),
//                UNIT=SYSDA,SPACE=(CYL,(10,5))
//SELCTL    DD    DUMMY
//INV3020   EXEC  PGM=INV3020
//SYSOUT    DD    SYSOUT=*
//INVMAST   DD    DSNAME=&&INVSEL,DISP=(OLD,DELETE)
//INVSLST   DD    SYSOUT=*
```

Figure 7-12   Using the SET statement to set symbolic parameter values

Figure 7-13 shows the format of the INCLUDE statement, and figure 7-14 shows an example of how it might be used. In this example, I created a private procedure library member named INVMAST, which contains the DD statement used to allocate the INVMAST data set. Then, instead of coding a DD statement for INVMAST in the job stream, I coded an INCLUDE statement to copy the INVMAST member into the job. MVS retrieved the INVMAST member and processed the INVMAST DD statement as if I had coded it directly in the job stream.

The INCLUDE statement

```
//              INCLUDE MEMBER=name
```

Explanation

name   The name of the member you want to include. The member must exist in a private
                procedure library specified in a JCLLIB statement or in SYS1.PROCLIB.

Figure 7-13   The INCLUDE statement

JCL submitted for processing

```
//SYDOEA    JOB   USER=SYDOE,PASSWORD=XXXXXXXX
//                JCLLIB ORDER=MMA2.PROCLIB
//                SET   CLASS=*
//                SET   SPACE='10,5'
//                SET   DEPT=MMA2
//INV3010   EXEC  PGM=INV3010
//SYSOUT    DD    SYSOUT=&CLASS
//                INCLUDE INVMAST
//INVSEL    DD    DSNAME=&&INVSEL,DISP=(NEW,PASS),
//                UNIT=SYSDA,SPACE=(CYL,(&SPACE))
//SELCTL    DD    DUMMY
//INV3020   EXEC  PGM=INV3020
//SYSOUT    DD    SYSOUT=&CLASS
//INVMAST   DD    DSNAME=&&INVSEL,DISP=(OLD,DELETE)
//INVSLST   DD    SYSOUT=&CLASS
```

INVMAST JCL library member

```
//INVMAST   DD    DSNAME=&DEPT..INVENTRY.MASTER,DISP=SHR
```

Effective JCL

```
//INV3010   EXEC PGM=INV3010
//SYSOUT    DD    SYSOUT=*
//INVMAST   DD    DSNAME=MMA2.INVENTRY.MASTER,DISP=SHR
//INVSEL    DD    DSNAME=&&INVSEL,DISP=(NEW,PASS),
//                UNIT=SYSDA,SPACE=(CYL,(10,5))
//SELCTL    DD    DUMMY
//INV3020   EXEC PGM=INV3020
//SYSOUT    DD    SYSOUT=*
//INVMAST   DD    DSNAME=&&INVSEL,DISP=(OLD,DELETE)
//INVSLST   DD    SYSOUT=*
```

Figure 7-14   Using the INCLUDE statement

You can nest INCLUDE statements if you wish. In other words, a member copied into a job by an INCLUDE statement can itself contain an INCLUDE statement. Although you can nest INCLUDE statements up to 15 levels deep, you'll probably never need to nest more than two or three levels at the most.

Discussion

As I said at the start of this chapter, learning how to use JCL procedures is an important component of your JCL education. Whether or not you use procedures heavily for application processing depends on your shop's standards and practices. But procedures form a major part of the interface to many IBM-supplied software products, like the COBOL compiler, CICS, and IMS. As a result, to use those products effectively, you need a solid understanding of the JCL procedure facilities this chapter presents.

Terminology

JCL procedure
cataloged procedure
in-stream procedure
alternate procedure library
parameter override
symbolic parameter
delimiter
private procedure library

Objectives

1. Code a job stream that invokes a procedure, adding or overriding EXEC and DD statement parameters if necessary.

2. Given specifications, code a JCL procedure (cataloged or in-stream) using any or all of the facilities presented in this chapter, including symbolic parameters.

3. Code a JCLLIB statement to establish a private procedure library for a job.

4. Use the INCLUDE statement to copy JCL statements into a job stream.

Exercises

1. Assume the following procedure is cataloged under the name
    DUMP:

    ```
    //STEP1      EXEC PGM=IEBGENER
    //SYSPRINT  DD   SYSOUT=*
    //SYSUT1    DD   DUMMY
    //SYSUT2    DD   DUMMY
    ```

    Code a job stream that invokes the procedure, overriding the
    SYSUT1 DD statement so that it refers to a cataloged data set
    named SYDOE.ENGR.SAMPLE.

2. Code a procedure named PRINT that invokes the IEBGENER
    utility to print a cataloged data set. Allow the user to specify the
    name of the data set to be printed by coding the parameter
    DSN=name on the EXEC statement that invokes the procedure,
    like this:

    ```
    //          EXEC PRINT,DSN=SYDOE.ENGR.SAMPLE
    ```

3. Code a JCLLIB statement that allocates SYDOE.PROCLIB as a
    private procedure library, then indicate the position in the follow-
    ing job stream where you would insert the JCLLIB statement.

    ```
    1→
        //SYDOEJ    JOB  USER=SYDOE,PASSWORD=XXXXXXXX
    2→
        //STEP1     EXEC PRINT
    3→
    ```

4. Suppose that the DD statement for a data set named
    EGA.CUSTOMER.EXTRACT resides in the member named
    X401EXTR in a private procedure library. Code an INCLUDE
    statement that includes this DD statement in a job stream.

Section 3

VSAM data management

VSAM, which stands for Virtual Storage Access Method, is by far the most commonly used access method on MVS systems. Because it's so widely used, you need to understand it to code production job streams for most MVS systems. VSAM does more than just replace the non-VSAM access methods (QSAM, ISAM, and BDAM) with its entry-sequenced data sets (ESDS), key-sequenced data sets (KSDS), and relative-record data sets (RRDS). It also provides efficiency improvements and a comprehensive catalog management facility that centralizes information about all VSAM data sets. In addition, VSAM includes a multi-function utility program called Access Method Services (AMS) that lets you perform a variety of file-related functions for VSAM as well as non-VSAM files. (AMS is also called IDCAMS; IDC is an IBM prefix associated with VSAM.)

Because VSAM has a broad scope, the three chapters of this section present a lot of information. Chapter 8 introduces you to the important VSAM concepts and terms you need to know. Chapter 9 shows you how to code JCL for VSAM files. And chapter 10 shows you how to use AMS.

Chapter 8

VSAM concepts and terminology

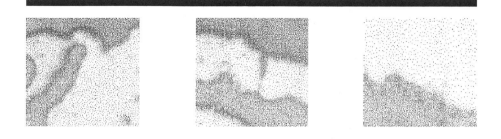

This chapter presents the concepts and terms you need to know to understand VSAM. First, it describes VSAM catalogs and explains how they are used to manage space for VSAM files. Second, it presents VSAM record management concepts, which form the underlying structure of all types of VSAM files. And finally, it explains the various types of files VSAM supports.

VSAM catalogs and space management

As you already know, VSAM includes a comprehensive catalog facility that stores information about VSAM data sets and other files. There are two types of catalogs: *master catalogs* and *user catalogs*. Although each MVS system has just one active master catalog, it can have an unlimited number of user catalogs. All VSAM data sets must be cataloged in the master catalog or in a user catalog, and all user catalogs must be cataloged in the master catalog. By convention, the first qualifier of a cataloged data set's name indicates the catalog that owns the file, either directly or through a catalog alias.

The original intention of VSAM catalogs was to replace the DASD volume's VTOC as the main source of information for DASD files. With data sets maintained by non-VSAM access methods (like ISAM and BDAM), descriptive information is stored in the file labels in the VTOC. Basically, the VTOC labels provide two types of information: file characteristics and DASD allocation information.

To replace the VTOC's function, VSAM catalogs contain descriptive file information as well as detailed allocation information. Out of necessity, VSAM had to be designed to coexist with conventional data management, which uses the VTOC for space allocation. To do that, the concept of data space was introduced. Simply put, a *data space*, or just *space*, is an area of a DASD volume that's under the control of VSAM. To indicate that control, VSAM makes an entry in the volume's VTOC for the space. Thus, to MVS data management, a VSAM space looks just like another file. However, VSAM has complete control over subsequent space allocations *within* the data space.

Within the space, VSAM can create *suballocated files*. Whenever a suballocated file needs to be created, extended, or deleted, VSAM uses its own space management facilities. Alternatively, an entire space can be allocated to a single VSAM file. In that case, allocation for the file, called a *unique file*, is managed by MVS rather than by VSAM. Allocation information for unique files is maintained in two places: the VSAM catalog entry for the file and the VTOC entry for the space that contains the unique file.

To illustrate the difference between suballocated and unique files, figure 8-1 shows two DASD volumes. The first volume has a VSAM data space that contains two suballocated files. Notice that there's unused space within the data space too. That space isn't available to non-VSAM files because it's already under VSAM's control. The second DASD volume contains two unique VSAM data sets. All of the unused space on the volume is available to both VSAM and non-VSAM data sets.

Because of problems associated with duplicating allocation information, IBM made substantial changes to the VSAM catalog structure in the early 1980s, announcing a new catalog structure called the *Integrated Catalog Facility*, or just *ICF*. Under ICF, VSAM space management has been integrated with MVS space management, and all space allocation information for VSAM and non-VSAM files is stored in the VTOC.

Most installations have already converted to ICF. However, because VSAM and ICF catalogs can coexist, you may find yourself working with one or both. Fortunately, although the differences between VSAM and ICF catalogs are significant, they are largely internal. They don't have much effect on the way you code JCL for VSAM files.

VSAM record management

A major component of VSAM, called *record management*, is responsible for maintaining the logical records of a VSAM file. (A *logical record* is a record as it's processed by an application program.)

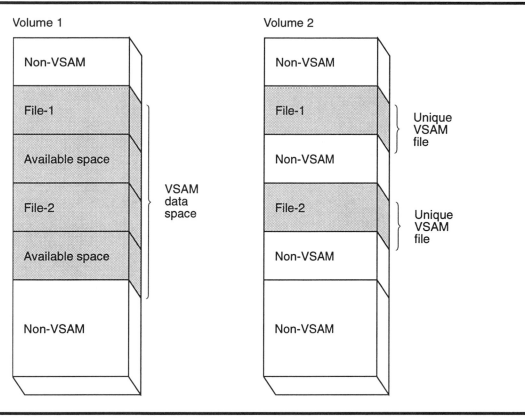

Figure 8-1   Suballocated and unique data sets

Record management provides a common ground for all types of VSAM files; it's used to store and retrieve records for all VSAM files, regardless of organization.

Record management groups logical records into blocks called *control intervals*. Control intervals, in turn, are grouped together into *control areas*. Figure 8-2 illustrates this structure. Here, logical record 29, which is shaded, is stored in control interval 10, which is part of control area 2.

Control intervals and control areas

The control interval is the unit of data VSAM transfers between virtual and disk storage. The control interval concept is similar to the concept of blocking for non-VSAM files; a control interval

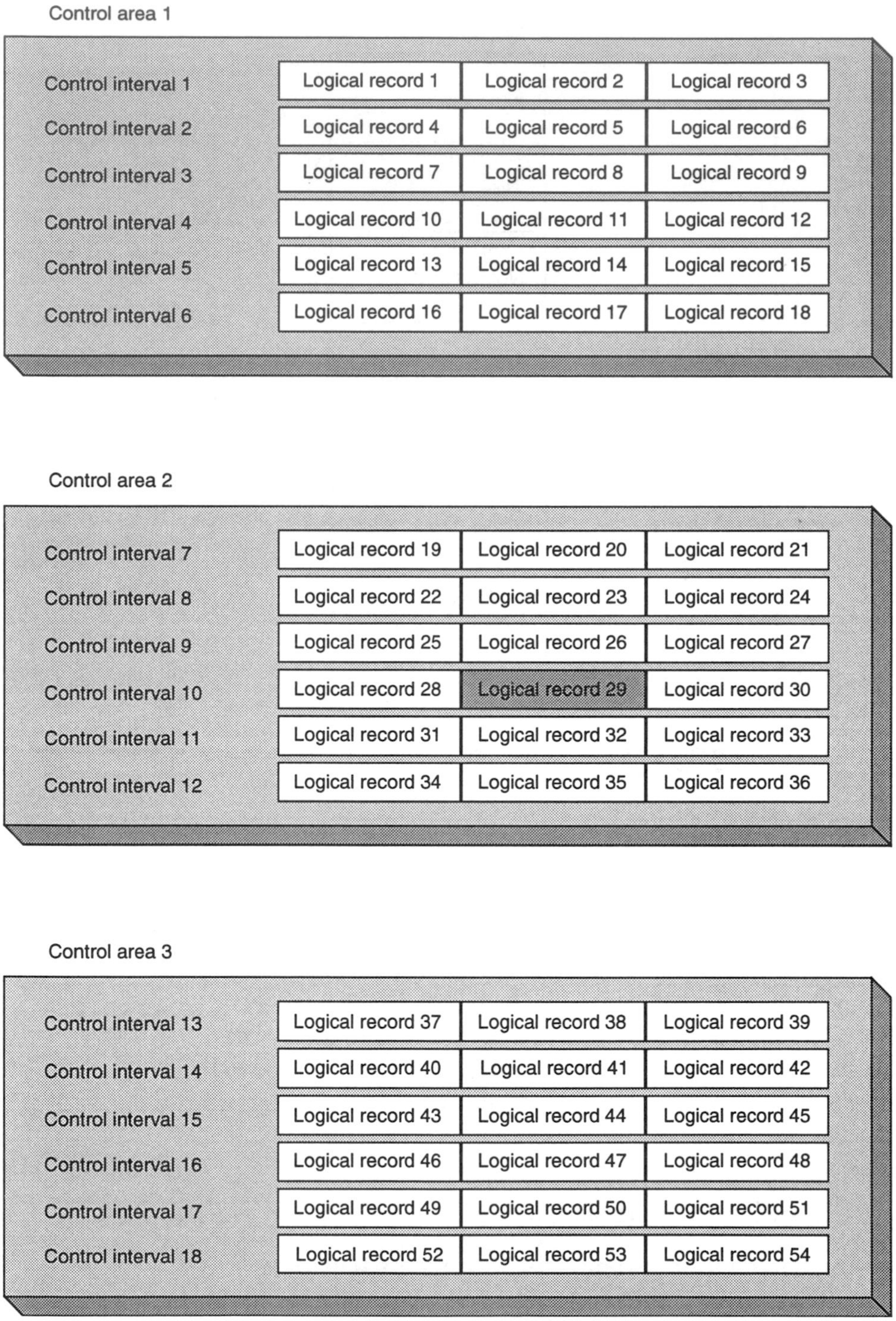

Figure 8-2   How records are grouped together in control intervals, and control intervals are grouped together in control areas

Increments of 512 (Up to 8192 bytes)		Increments of 2048 (Over 8192 bytes)	
512	4608	10240	26624
1024	5120	12288	28672
1536	5632	14336	30720
2048	6144	16384	32768
2560	6656	18432	
3072	7168	20480	
3584	7680	22528	
4096	8192	24576	

Figure 8-3   Valid sizes for control intervals

usually contains more than one record. And just as the block size for a non-VSAM file affects performance, the size of a control interval affects performance for a VSAM file.

The size of a control interval must be between 512 and 32,768 bytes (32K). Up to 8192 bytes (8K), the control interval size must be a multiple of 512; beyond that, it must be a multiple of 2048 (2K). For most VSAM files, control intervals are 2K or 4K. For your reference, figure 8-3 lists the valid control interval sizes.

Although control intervals are similar to non-VSAM file blocks, they have a different structure, shown in figure 8-4. As you can see, a control interval consists of three basic parts: one or more logical records, control information, and (optionally) unused space. The logical records are grouped together at the beginning of the control interval, and the control information is at the end of the control interval. That leaves the free space in the middle. If one or more of the records in the control interval is expanded or deleted or if another record is added, the unused space in the middle of the control interval is adjusted as needed.

VSAM determines the size of a control area based on the amount of space you allocate to the file and the characteristics of the device on which the file is stored. As additional extents are allocated to a VSAM file, they're added in units of adjacent control areas, if possible.

Just as a control interval may contain unused space, so may a control area. The available space in a control area is used to add additional control intervals as they're needed. You'll learn about how free space within control areas is managed for the various data set types in just a moment.

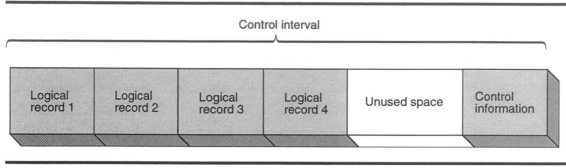

Figure 8-4   The structure of a control interval

Characteristics of VSAM data sets

Now that you know how VSAM stores logical records on disk, you're ready to learn the characteristics of VSAM entry-sequenced, key-sequenced, and relative-record data sets, as well as linear data sets, alternate indexes, and reusable data sets. Before I describe the characteristics of these data sets though, I want you to know that VSAM files are often called *clusters*. Simply put, a cluster is the set of catalog entries that represents a file. A cluster consists of one or two *components*: a *data component*, which contains the actual records of a file; and, for a key-sequenced data set only, an *index component*, which contains the indexes used to access records in the data component.

Entry-sequenced data sets

An entry-sequenced data set is a sequential file, much like a conventional QSAM file. Records are typically retrieved in the order in which they are written to the data set. And additions are always made at the end of the file.

Figure 8-5 shows how the records of an ESDS are stored in control intervals. For clarity, I've omitted the control information that would be stored in each control interval. As you can see, the records are stored in order within the control intervals. There's available free space in control interval 3 after record 10 (the last record in the file). And all of control interval 4 is available, since no records have been written to it. Notice the small amount of free space in control interval 2. That space—left over because the records of that control interval don't completely fill it—cannot be used. You can't write a new record to it, nor can you expand one of the records in control interval 2 to use it.

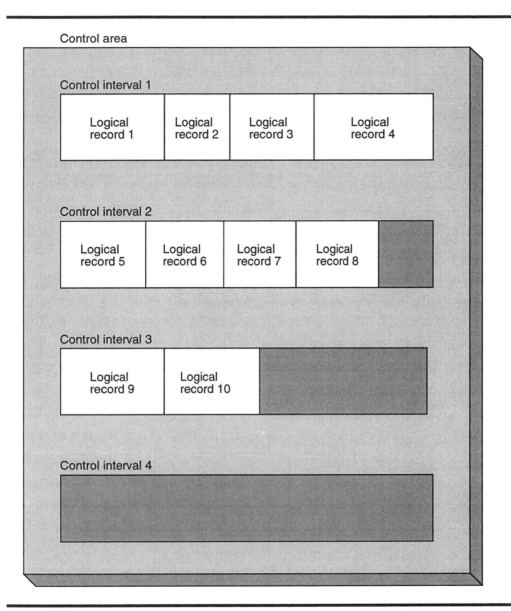

Figure 8-5   Record organization in an ESDS

Although it's uncommon, you can process the records of an ESDS directly rather than sequentially. That's because each record can be identified by a *relative byte address*, or *RBA*. The RBA is an indication of how far in bytes each record is displaced from the beginning of the file. For example, if all of the records in an ESDS are 256 bytes in length, the RBA for the first record is 0, the RBA for the second record is 256, the RBA for the third record is 512, and so on to the end of the control interval. Beyond the first control interval, however, records do *not* have RBAs that are multiples of 256. That's because the control information at the end of each control internal is included as part of the RBA value.

Key-sequenced data sets

A key-sequenced data set is similar in many ways to an ISAM file. In fact, one of the reasons IBM developed VSAM was to replace ISAM. Because VSAM has a better index structure and improved overflow handling, most ISAM users have long since converted their applications to VSAM. As a result, the VSAM KSDS is the most common file organization in use today.

Like as ISAM file, you can process a KSDS sequentially or randomly. When you use sequential processing, records are processed one at a time in the order of the key values stored in the file's index. When you use random processing, you supply the value of the key in the record you want to process.

As I already mentioned, a KSDS consists of two components: a data component and an index component. The data component contains the records, and the index component contains the indexes used to access them. Figure 8-6 shows the structure of these two KSDS components.

The index component   As you can see in figure 8-6, the index component of a KSDS has two parts: a *sequence set* and a *index set*. The sequence set is the lowest level of the index. It's searched to determine which control interval in the data component contains a particular record. The index set is used to locate sequence set records.

Index set records are arranged in one or more levels. The index set in figure 8-6 has two levels. In an index set with more than one level, each higher level index set record contains pointers to records at the next level down; the records of the lowest level of the index set contain pointers to sequence set records. The highest level of an index set always has just one record.

To understand how the KSDS index structure works, consider the simple file in figure 8-7. In this example, the KSDS data component consists of three control areas, each with four control intervals. The numbers in the control intervals are the key values for the logical records. For example, the first control interval in control area 1 contains the three logical records whose key values are 012, 049, and 187.

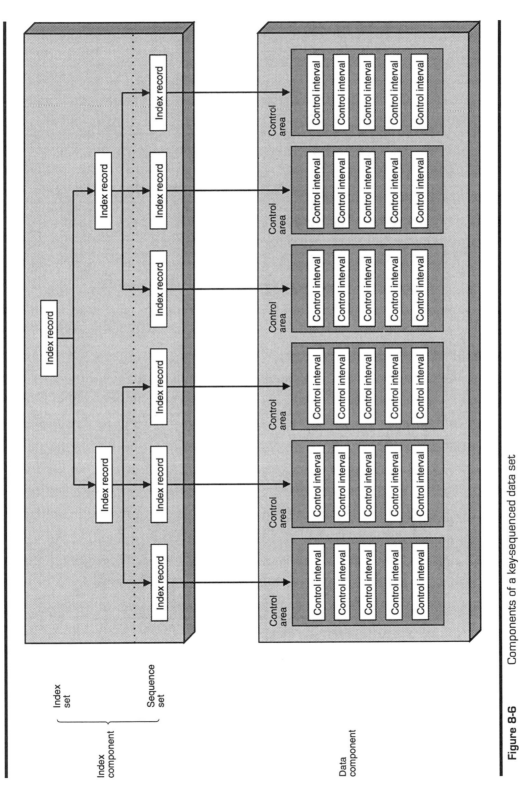

Figure 8-6   Components of a key-sequenced data set

For each control area in the data component of a KSDS, there is one record in the sequence set. As a result, the sequence set in figure 8-7 contains three records. Each sequence set record contains an *index entry* for each control interval in the corresponding control area. That index entry contains the highest key value stored in the corresponding control interval. Notice that within the sequence set records, index entries are stored in sequence from right to left. (The sequence set records also contain free pointers, which I'll explain in a moment.)

The entries in the index set record in figure 8-7 contain the highest values stored in each of the sequence set records. Many key-sequenced files use just one index set record; that's enough for 58 sequence set records, assuming an index control interval size of 512 bytes. Since each sequence set record indexes a control area, which is typically a full cylinder, a single index set record provides for up to 58 cylinders of data. On a 3350, that's about 32 million bytes. If the file is larger than that, VSAM automatically creates additional index set records as needed, arranging them in levels as you saw in figure 8-6.

The solid arrows and the highlighting in figure 8-7 show the processing necessary to locate the record whose key value is 501. First, the index set record is read and searched to determine which sequence set record to use. Then, the correct sequence set record is read and searched to determine which control interval to use. Finally, the control interval is read and searched to locate the correct record.

The data component and free space   When you define a KSDS cluster using AMS, you can reserve free space to accommodate new records within the data component. You can reserve this space in two ways: (1) you can leave space within each control interval, and (2) you can leave entire control intervals empty.

Figure 8-8 shows a control area that consists of four control intervals. Three of the four control intervals contain four logical records and enough space for one more. For clarity, I omitted the control information in each control interval. It's that control infor-mation that tells VSAM about the free space within each control interval. The fourth control interval is empty. VSAM knows about it because each sequence set record in the index component contains a pointer to each free control interval in its associated control area. If you'll look back to figure 8-7, you'll see those pointers.

Notice that within the control intervals, logical records are stored in key sequence. When a record is added to a KSDS, it's inserted in its correct sequential location in the proper control

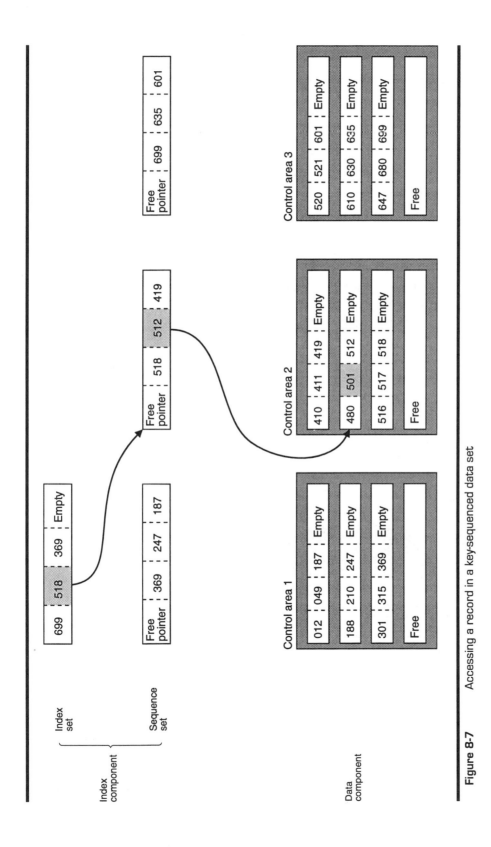

Figure 8-7   Accessing a record in a key-sequenced data set

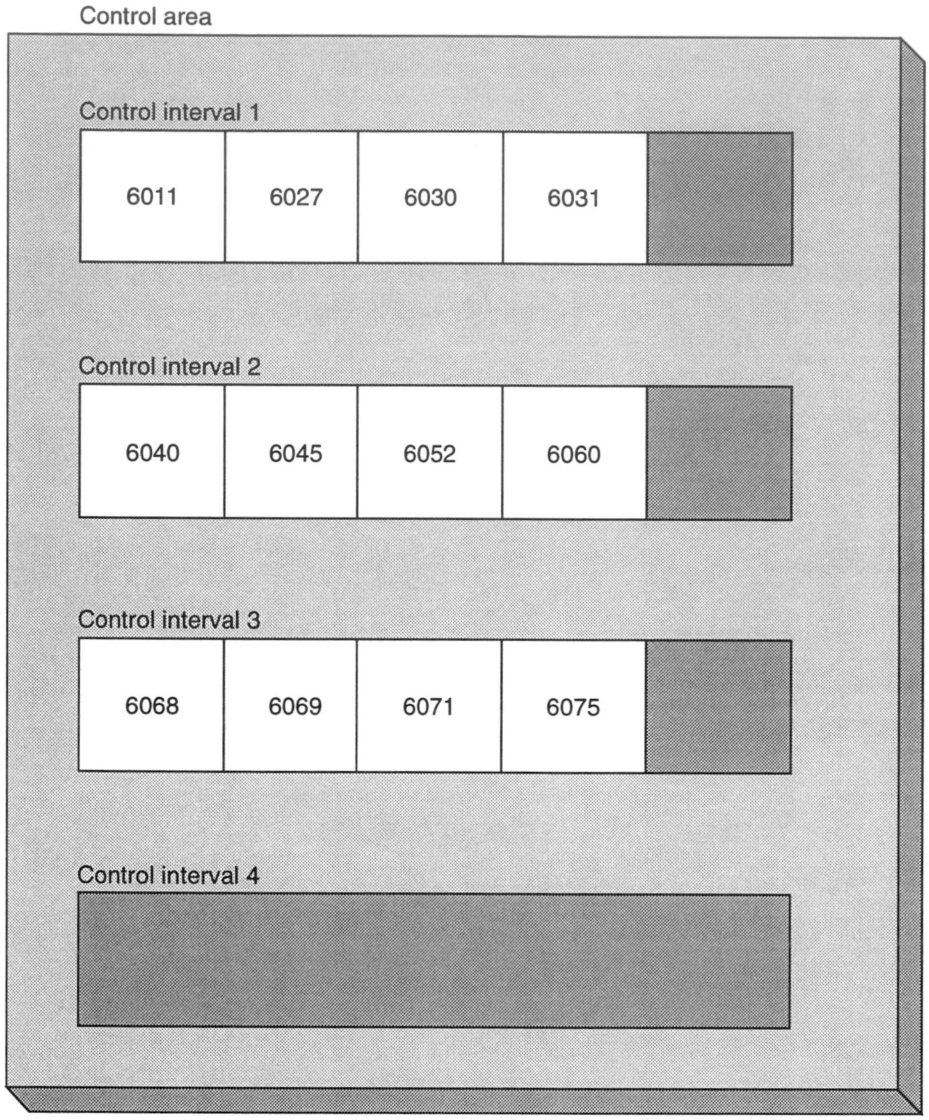

Control area

Control interval 1

| 6011 | 6027 | 6030 | 6031 | |

Control interval 2

| 6040 | 6045 | 6052 | 6060 | |

Control interval 3

| 6068 | 6069 | 6071 | 6075 | |

Control interval 4

Figure 8-8   Free space distribution in the data component of a KSDS

interval, and the records that follow it in the control interval are shifted. If there isn't enough space in the control interval to hold the inserted record, some of the records in the control interval are moved to one of the free control intervals; that's called a *control interval split*. If there isn't a free control interval in the control area, a *control area split* occurs. In a control area split, VSAM allocates a new control area, moves about half the control intervals from the original control area to the new one, and then performs a control interval split using one of the newly freed control intervals.

Relative-record data sets

Figure 8-9 shows a VSAM relative-record data set. An RRDS consists of fixed-length *slots* that are numbered. It's those numbers—called *relative record numbers* (or *RRNs*)— that let you access the records of an RRDS directly. This is similar to the way blocks in a BDAM data set can be accessed using relative block addresses, as you'll learn in chapter 14. Each slot in an RRDS contains a record or is empty.

Records in an RRDS can be accessed sequentially or randomly. When sequential processing is used, VSAM automatically skips over empty slots. So sequential processing for an RRDS is similar to sequential processing for an ESDS or KSDS.

Random processing is based on each record's relative position in the file. Because an RRDS doesn't have an index component to search, it can be processed more efficiently than a KSDS. So, if an application lends itself to the RRN addressing scheme, an RRDS can be a practical alternative to a KSDS.

Additions to an RRDS can be done in two ways. First, records can be added to the end of the file. Second, new records can be inserted in empty slots in the file. To do so, however, the application program must be able to identify the empty slots. And that's not always easy to do.

Although less common, VSAM also supports *variable-length relative record data sets*. In a variable-length RRDS, the records do not all have to be the same length. Variable-length RRDSs do not use slots to store records; instead, each record in the file is assigned a unique RRN, and the records are written to the file in ascending RRN sequence.

Linear data sets

A *linear data set* is a VSAM data set that has no record organization. Data stored in a linear data set is written or read one control interval at a time; VSAM does not add any control information to the data to distinguish records from one another. Because linear data sets aren't typically used for user-written application programs, I won't show you how to create or use them in this book.

Control area

Control interval 1

| Slot 1 | Slot 2 | Slot 3 | Slot 4 | Slot 5 |

Control interval 2

| Slot 6 | Slot 7 | Slot 8 (empty) | Slot 9 | Slot 10 |

Control interval 3

| Slot 11 | Slot 12 (empty) | Slot 13 | Slot 14 (empty) | Slot 15 |

Control interval 4

| Slot 16 (empty) | Slot 17 | Slot 18 | Slot 19 | Slot 20 (empty) |

Figure 8-9   Record organization in an RRDS

Alternate indexes

An *alternate index* lets you access the records of a VSAM key-sequenced data set in an order other than the file's *primary key* (or *base key*). The data set over which an alternate index exists is called a *base cluster*. Although you can also use an entry-sequenced data set as the base cluster for an alternate index, most alternate indexes are built over KSDS clusters.

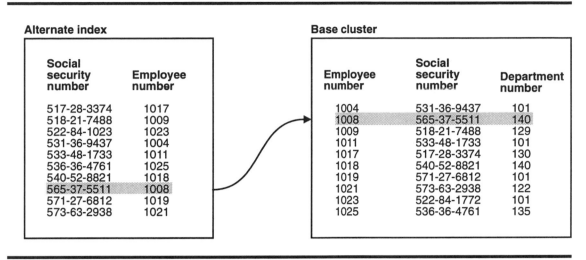

Figure 8-10   An alternate index with unique keys

To understand the concept of an alternate index, consider figure 8-10. Here, an alternate index exists for a base cluster KSDS that contains three fields: employee number, social security number, and department number. The primary key for the base cluster is employee number. As a result, you can access the base cluster sequentially or randomly based on each record's employee number.

The alternate index in figure 8-10 lets you process the base cluster in social security number sequence by relating each *alternate key* value to a primary key value. So, as the shading indicates, when you tell VSAM to retrieve the record for the employee whose social security number is 565-37-5511, VSAM searches the alternate index, retrieves the primary key (1008), and uses that value to locate the correct record in the base cluster.

In figure 8-10, each alternate key is associated with one primary key. This type of alternate key is called a *unique key*. In contrast, figure 8-11 shows an alternate index with *non-unique*, or *duplicate*, *keys*. Here, the alternate key is department number.

To understand non-unique keys, consider the alternate index for department number 101. Here, four employee numbers are specified: 1004, 1011, 1019, and 1023. When you process this file sequentially, all four employee records can be retrieved in turn. However, when you process an alternate index file with duplicate keys directly, only the first base cluster record for each alternate key value is available.

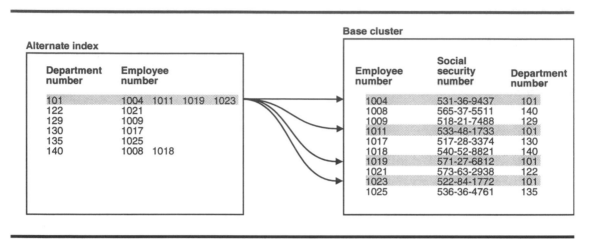

Figure 8-11   An alternate index with non-unique keys

An alternate index is itself a key-sequenced data set. If the base cluster is a KSDS, each record in the alternate index's data component contains an alternate key value and one or more primary key values for the corresponding base cluster records. If the base cluster is an ESDS, each record in the alternate index's data component contains an alternate key value and one or more RBAs for the corresponding base cluster records.

The index component of the alternate index contains the alternate keys that index the records in the data component, just as in a standard KSDS. To simplify the example in figures 8-10 and 8-11, I didn't show the index and data components or the control areas and control intervals of the alternate index or the base cluster.

You might be surprised to learn that VSAM doesn't require that an alternate index be *upgraded* every time its base cluster is changed. An alternate index is an *upgradable index* only if you specify (via AMS) that VSAM should update it automatically whenever changes are made to the base cluster. Because upgradable indexes add considerable overhead to alternate index processing, alternate indexes are often not upgradable. Instead, the alternate indexes are rebuilt nightly, and users have to realize that additions or changes to their data sets won't be reflected in the alternate indexes until the next day.

Reusable data sets

Some applications call for temporary data sets or work files that must be created, used, and deleted each time the application is run. For non-VSAM files, MVS provides a temporary data set facility that you already know about. VSAM provides a similar facility by letting you create *reusable files*. A reusable file is a standard ESDS, KSDS, or RRDS. The only difference is that if you open an existing reusable file for output processing, VSAM treats the file as if it was empty. Any records in the file are ignored. It's as if the file was just defined but no data has been loaded yet. So, if you use a reusable file, you don't have to define it and then delete it each time you use it. Instead, you define it just once.

To understand how a reusable data set works, you need to know about a field that's stored in the catalog entry for each VSAM file: the *high-used RBA field*. This field indicates the RBA of the last byte of the last record in the data set. When you open a reusable data set for output processing, VSAM resets the high-used RBA field to zero. The file's records aren't actually erased. But because the high-used RBA field is zero, it's as if they weren't there.

Discussion

If you look at the terminology list that follows this chapter, you'll see right away that there's a lot to learn about VSAM, especially considering that this chapter has presented only a superficial overview. That's because, frankly, VSAM is complicated. To me, the most complicated aspect of VSAM is that it frequently changes, and it exists alongside conventional MVS data management, which frequently changes too. As a result, it's important that you find out how VSAM is used at your installation. For example, you need to find out whether your installation uses VSAM catalogs, ICF catalogs, or both.

Terminology

master catalog	ICF
user catalog	record management
data space	logical record
space	control interval
suballocated file	control area
unique file	cluster
Integrated Catalog Facility	component

data component
index component
relative byte address
RBA
sequence set
index set
index entry
control interval split
control area split
slot
relative record number
RRN
variable-length relative-record data set
linear data set
alternate index
primary key
base key
base cluster
alternate key
unique key
non-unique key
duplicate key
upgrade
upgradable index
reusable file
high-used RBA field

Objectives

1. Describe how VSAM catalogs, ICF catalogs, and the VTOC participate in DASD space management for VSAM files.

2. Explain the function of control intervals and control areas.

3. Name and describe three types of VSAM files. Then, compare them to the native MVS access methods.

4. Explain the function of an alternate index and a reusable data set.

**Chapter
9**

JCL requirements for VSAM data sets

How to allocate existing VSAM files
The DSNAME parameter
The DUMMY parameter
The DISP parameter
The AMP parameter
How to create VSAM files

Among other things, one of the design objectives of VSAM was to reduce and, someday, perhaps completely eliminate the need for JCL statements to allocate data sets. Although you still have to code a DD statement for a VSAM file, the only crucial piece of information it supplies is the actual data set name. You don't have to specify any of the characteristics of the file on the DD statement.

VSAM accomplishes this JCL simplification by centralizing functions such as defining, deleting, and altering file characteristics in the AMS utility program. In contrast, for an ISAM file, you specify file characteristics in the JCL statements of the job that creates the file. The same is true for QSAM, BDAM, and partitioned data sets. As a result, VSAM has much simpler JCL requirements than files of other access methods. In this chapter, you'll learn those requirements.

Don't misunderstand; the use of VSAM doesn't eliminate complexity, it just transfers it from JCL to the AMS utility program. In the next chapter, you'll see just how complicated AMS jobs can be. But in terms of JCL, VSAM is simple.

Interestingly, IBM reversed its efforts towards JCL simplification when it introduced the Storage Management Subsystem (SMS). When SMS is installed and activated, VSAM data sets can be created entirely through JCL. So, after I show you the JCL for allocating existing VSAM files, I'll show you how to create VSAM files using JCL.

The DD statement for allocating existing VSAM files

```
//ddname    DD  { DSNAME=data-set-name }
                { DUMMY                 }

                [ ,DISP=({ OLD },normal-disp,abnormal-disp) ]
                        ({ SHR }

                [ ,AMP=(option,option...) ]
```

Explanation

DSNAME	Specifies the name of the VSAM data set. Normally, the high-level qualifier of the name identifies the owning catalog.
DUMMY	Specifies that a VSAM file should not be allocated; instead, MVS should simulate a VSAM file.
DISP	Specifies the file's status and, under SMS, the file's normal and abnormal disposition. The valid status options are OLD for exclusive access and SHR for shared access. All of the disposition options except UNCATLG are valid for VSAM files.
AMP	Specifies one or more processing options for VSAM files. See figure 9-3 for details.

Figure 9-1   The DD statement for allocating existing VSAM files

How to allocate existing VSAM files

Figure 9-1 shows the format of the DD statement as you code it to allocate existing VSAM files. As you can see, I've included just four parameters: DSNAME, DUMMY, DISP, and AMP. As I describe each of these parameters, you can refer to the DD statement examples shown in figure 9-2.

The DSNAME parameter

As you already know, the DSNAME parameter supplies the data set name for a VSAM file. Usually, the data set name also identifies the catalog that owns the file. For example, each data set name in figure 9-2 begins with the four-character prefix SYDOE. On my system, SYDOE is the alias of a user catalog where I'm authorized to define data sets.

The only other thing you need to know about the DSNAME parameter is that you can't code a temporary data set name for a VSAM file as you can for a non-VSAM file. In other words, you can't code a name like &&TEST. That's because VSAM doesn't support temporary data sets in the same way as MVS data manage-

Example 1

```
//CUSTMAST DD    DSNAME=SYDOE.CUSTOMER.MASTER,DISP=SHR
```

Allocate a VSAM file for shared access.

Example 2

```
//CUSTMAST DD    DSNAME=SYDOE.CUSTOMER.MASTER,DISP=OLD
```

Allocate a VSAM file for exclusive access.

Example 3

```
//PAYTRAN  DD    DSNAME=SYDOE.PAYMENT.TRANS,DISP=(OLD,DELETE)
```

Allocate a VSAM file for exclusive access and delete it when the job step completes.

Example 4

```
//PAYTRAN  DD    DUMMY,AMP=AMORG
```

Allocate a dummy VSAM file.

Example 5

```
//CUSTMAST DD    DSNAME=SYDOE.CUSTOMER.MASTER,DISP=SHR,
//              AMP=(BUFND=2,BUFNI=6)
```

Allocate a VSAM file for shared access, specifying that 2 data buffers and 6 index buffers should be used.

Example 6

```
//CUSTISAM DD    DSNAME=SYDOE.CUSTOMER.MASTER,DISP=SHR,
//              AMP=(AMORG,OPTCD=IL,RECFM=FB)
```

Allocate a VSAM file using the ISAM interface program: AMORG identifies the file as VSAM; OPTCD specifies how logically deleted records should be handled; and RECFM specifies that the program expects fixed-length blocked records.

Figure 9-2   Examples of DD statements for allocating existing VSAM files

ment does. To use a VSAM temporary data set, you invoke AMS and define a cluster that specifies the REUSE option. You'll see how to do that in the next chapter. Then, whenever you open the data set for output processing, any records in the file are ignored.

The DUMMY parameter

The DUMMY parameter lets you simulate the presence of a VSAM file without actually processing a file. When a program tries to read data from a dummy file, VSAM returns an end-of-file indication. And when a program tries to write data to the file, the data is simply discarded. As you'll see in a moment, you must also specify AMP=AMORG to process a dummy VSAM file.

The DISP parameter

For most VSAM files, the DISP parameter has just one function: It indicates whether or not the file can be processed simultaneously by more than one job. If you specify DISP=SHR as in example 1 in figure 9-2, the file can be shared by several jobs executing at the same time. If you specify DISP=OLD as in example 2, the file can not be shared; the job that's processing it has exclusive access to it. If you define the cluster using AMS, you can control the type of sharing that's allowed when you specify DISP=SHR by coding the SHAREOPTIONS parameter. I'll have more to say about that in the next chapter.

If your installation is using SMS, you can also code a normal and abnormal termination disposition in the DISP parameter. That means that you can delete a VSAM file by coding the DISP parameter as in example 3. Without SMS, VSAM files are always retained after they are processed. Then, to delete the file, you use the AMS utility program.

The AMP parameter

The AMP parameter is for VSAM files what the DCB parameter is for non-VSAM files. It specifies execution-time information that affects how the file is processed. Figure 9-3 lists the subparameters you can specify on the AMP parameter. As I describe each one, remember that you normally don't need to code AMP at all. It's required only in the special cases I'll point out.

The AMORG subparameter   AMORG indicates that the file being accessed is a VSAM file. Normally, MVS realizes that a VSAM file is being processed when it retrieves the catalog information for the file. So you only need to specify AMP=AMORG when MVS doesn't search the catalog. That's the case when you specify DUMMY, so always code AMP=AMORG for a dummy VSAM file. Example 4 in figure 9-2 illustrates this case.

You should also specify AMP=AMORG if you code the UNIT and VOLUME parameters on the DD statement for a VSAM file. I didn't show UNIT and VOLUME on the DD statement format in figure 9-1 because they're only valid for older removable DASD units like 3330s.

The AMP parameter

```
AMP=[ AMORG ]
    [ ,BUFND=n ]
    [ ,BUFNI=n ]
    [ ,BUFSP=n ]
    [ ,OPTCD=options ]
    [ ,RECFM=format ]
    [ ,STRNO=N ]
```

Explanation

AMORG	Specifies that the data set is a VSAM file. Normally not required.
BUFND	Specifies the number of buffers to allocate for the data component.
BUFNI	Specifies the number of buffers to allocate for the index component.
BUFSP	Specifies the total amount of space in bytes to allocate for data and index buffers.
OPTCD	Specifies options for the ISAM interface. Code I, L, or IL. I means that if OPTCD=L is specified for the file in the processing program, records marked for deletion by hex FF in the first byte should be physically deleted from the file. If OPTCD=L is not specified in the program, specify OPTCD=IL in the DD statement for the same effect. If you specify OPTCD=L in the DD statement, records marked for deletion remain in the data set but are ignored when read sequentially.
RECFM	Specifies the format in which the ISAM program expects to process records. Specify F, FB, V, or VB.
STRNO	Specifies the number of concurrent requests the program may issue against the file.

Figure 9-3   The AMP parameter for VSAM files

AMP performance subparameters   Four of the AMP subparameters in figure 9-3, BUFND, BUFNI, BUFSP, and STRNO, let you specify performance options when you execute your program. BUFND, BUFNI, and BUFSP let you specify in various ways how much buffer space VSAM should use. STRNO specifies how many separate requests the program may make against the file at one time. Although these subparameters are easy enough to code, determining an optimum value to specify is another matter that's beyond the scope of this book. Example 5 in figure 9-2 shows a DD statement that specifies performance options. Here, I specified that the program should use two data buffers and six index buffers.

AMP subparameters for the ISAM interface program   Two of the AMP subparameters, OPTCD and RECFM, let you specify processing options for the *ISAM interface program*, or *IIP*. The ISAM interface program lets you use VSAM files with programs that were designed to process ISAM files. To do that, you just change the DD statement in the job stream so that it refers to a VSAM file that was created from the data in the old ISAM file.

The OPTCD subparameter lets you specify how records marked for deletion are to be handled. (Under ISAM, records with hex FF in the first byte are considered to be deleted records.) If you specify OPTCD=L, deleted records are processed just as they are under ISAM: They remain in the data set, but are ignored during a sequential read. So, if you copy the file by reading each record sequentially and writing it to a new file, records marked for deletion will be deleted because they won't be read.

If, on the other hand, you specify OPTCD=IL, VSAM actually deletes the records when they're written to the file. In other words, if the ISAM program writes a record that has hex FF in the first byte, VSAM doesn't put the record in the file. And if the ISAM program rewrites a record placing hex FF in the first byte, VSAM deletes the existing record.

If you specify just OPTCD=I, delete processing depends on how the application program defines the file. If the program specifies OPTCD=L when it defines the file, records with the delete byte are deleted as if you specified OPTCD=IL. If the program doesn't specify OPTCD, the delete byte has no significance.

The RECFM subparameter lets you specify how the ISAM program expects the file's records to be formatted: variable or fixed length, blocked or unblocked. You can specify F, FB, V, or VB depending on your program's requirements.

Example 6 in figure 9-2 shows a DD statement for a VSAM file that's processed by the ISAM interface program. I specified AMORG in the AMP parameter just for clarity; it's not required. I specified OPTCD=IL so that records marked for deletion will be physically deleted from the file. And I specified RECFM=FB to indicate that the ISAM program expects the records in fixed blocked format.

How to create VSAM files

If SMS is installed and activated at your installation, you can create VSAM files directly in JCL without using the AMS program. This doesn't mean you'll never use AMS. AMS lets you set several important data set options that can't be set through JCL, such as the control interval size and index performance options. Still, there are many cases where creating a VSAM file directly through JCL is expedient.

The DD statement for creating new VSAM files (SMS only)

```
//ddname     DD   DSNAME=data-set-name
                 ,DISP=(NEW,normal-disp,abnormal-disp)
             [ ,UNIT=unit ]
             [ ,VOL=SER=vol-ser ]
             [ ,SPACE=(unit,(primary,secondary)) ]

                       ⎧ U ⎫
             [ ,AVGREC={ K } ]
                       ⎩ M ⎭

                       ⎧ KS ⎫
             [ ,RECORG={ ES } ]
                       ⎩ RR ⎭

             [ ,LRECL=length ]
             [ ,KEYLEN=length ]
             [ ,KEYOFF=offset ]
             [ ,LIKE=data-set-name ]
             [ ,STORCLAS=storage-class ]
             [ ,DATACLAS=data-class ]
             [ ,MGMTCLAS=management-class ]
```

Figure 9-4   The DD statement for creating VSAM files (part 1 of 2)

Figure 9-4 shows the format of the DD statement you use to create VSAM files. As you can see, it combines parameters you already know (like DSNAME and DISP) with a few new parameters that are used to supply information VSAM requires to create the file. In particular, the RECORG parameter supplies the file organization (KSDS, ESDS, or RRDS), and the KEYOFF parameter provides the key offset for key-sequenced files. (The KEYLEN parameter supplies the key length, but it is not a new parameter.)

Figure 9-5 shows three examples of DD statements that create VSAM files. Example 1 creates a VSAM KSDS with 120-byte records and a 7-byte key that begins in byte 5. The file is given 200 cylinders of primary space on volume MPS800.

Example 2 shows how you can code a non-specific volume request for a VSAM file by specifying the UNIT parameter but omitting the VOL=SER parameter. In this example, MVS will determine which volume to place the file on. This example illustrates one of the advantages of creating VSAM files in JCL rather than with AMS: AMS doesn't allow non-specific requests.

Example 3 shows how you can create a VSAM file using SMS storage, management, and data classes. Interestingly enough, you

Explanation

DSNAME	Specifies the file's data set name.
DISP	Specifies the file's status and normal and abnormal dispositions. Usually coded as (NEW,CATLG) to create and catalog a new file.
UNIT	Specifies the type of device where the file will reside. Usually coded as SYSDA.
VOL=SER	Specifies the six-character vol-ser of the volume where the file is to be created. If omitted, SMS will select a volume.
SPACE	Specifies the space to be allocated for the file. Unit indicates the unit of measure: CYL for cylinders, TRK for tracks, or record size for records. If the unit is records, you must include the AVGREC parameter.
AVGREC	Indicates that the allocation unit specified in the SPACE parameter is records and whether the values specified for primary and secondary space allocation represent units (U), thousands of records (K), or millions of records (M).
RECORG	Specifies the type of file organization: KSDS (KS), ESDS (ES), or RRDS (RR).
LRECL	Specifies the record length.
KEYLEN	Specifies the length of the key for a KSDS.
KEYOFF	Specifies the position of the first byte of the key for a KSDS.
LIKE	Copies data set characteristics from the specified data set.
STORCLAS	Establishes the storage class for the data set.
DATACLAS	Establishes the data class for the data set.
MGMTCLAS	Establishes the management class for the data set.

Figure 9-4   The DD statement for creating VSAM files (part 2 of 2)

can't tell that the DD statement creates a VSAM file simply by looking at it. You'd have to examine the MVPD050 data class to determine the attributes of the data set being created.

Discussion

As I said at the start of this chapter, VSAM achieves its JCL simplification by centralizing the critical functions of defining, deleting, and maintaining its files in a single utility program, AMS. That's why this chapter is trivial and the next chapter, which shows you how to use AMS, is more complex. Even if your installation uses SMS, you should study the next chapter carefully. As I mentioned, AMS lets you set several important VSAM data set options that aren't accessible via JCL parameters.

Terminology

ISAM interface program   IIP

Example 1

```
//DUNNING   DD    DSNAME=SYDOE.DUNNING.FILE,DISP=(NEW,CATLG),
//                UNIT=SYSDA,VOL=SER=MPS800,
//                SPACE=(CYL,(200,50)),
//                RECORG=KS,LRECL=120,KEYLEN=7,KEYOFF=5
```

Create and catalog a new key-sequenced data set.

Example 2

```
//DUNNING   DD    DSNAME=SYDOE.DUNNING.FILE,DISP=(NEW,CATLG),
//                UNIT=SYSDA,
//                SPACE=(CYL,(200,50)),
//                RECORG=KS,LRECL=120,KEYLEN=7,KEYOFF=5
```

Create and catalog a new key-sequenced data set without specifying a particular volume.

Example 3

```
//DUNNING   DD    DSNAME=SYDOE.DUNNING.FILE,DISP=(NEW,CATLG),
//                STORCLAS=MVPS100,
//                DATACLAS=MVPD050,
//                MGMTCLAS=MVPM010
```

Create and catalog a new data set using storage class MVPS100, data class MVPD050, and management class MVPM010.

Figure 9-5   Examples of DD statements for creating VSAM files

Objective

Given the requirements for a job that processes VSAM files, code the required DD statements.

Exercises

1. Code a JCL statement that allocates an existing VSAM data set named X401.PROJ.EXTR for shared access.

2. Code a JCL statement for a system on which SMS is installed to create a new VSAM data set named X401.PROJ.MASTER on a SYSDA volume named TSO001. The file is a key-sequenced data set with 240-byte records and keys in the first 9 bytes of each record. The file will require 30 cylinders of primary space and 15 cylinders of secondary space.

Chapter 10

How to use Access Method Services

In the last chapter, you learned that if your installation uses SMS, you can create VSAM data sets using JCL. Because Access Method Services lets you set options that you can't set using JCL, however, you'll still want to use AMS to create many of your VSAM data sets. And if your installation doesn't use SMS, you'll have to use AMS to create all of your VSAM data sets. You can also use AMS to perform routine catalog maintenance functions and to copy and print VSAM files. That's what you'll learn in this chapter. But first, you need to know how to code AMS job streams.

How to code AMS job streams

To properly code a job that invokes AMS, you need to know how to do two things. First, you must know how to code the JCL statements to invoke AMS. And second, you must know the rules to follow when you code AMS commands.

JCL requirements for AMS

Figure 10-1 shows a simple job that invokes AMS and tells it to list the entries in a catalog. Although this job is simple, it illustrates the basic JCL requirements for AMS jobs. In the EXEC statement, you specify the program IDCAMS. That invokes AMS. Then, you must code two DD statements. The first, SYSPRINT, is used for printed output produced by AMS; you code it like any other SYSOUT data set. The second DD statement, SYSIN, defines the data set that contains the AMS commands; usually, this is an in-stream data set as in figure 10-1.

```
//SYDOEJ    JOB   USER=SYDOE,PASSWORD=XXXXXXXX
//          EXEC  PGM=IDCAMS
//SYSPRINT DD     SYSOUT=*
//SYSIN     DD    *
  LISTCAT ENTRIES(SYDOE.CUSTOMER.MASTER) -
          VOLUME
/*
```

Figure 10-1   An AMS job

If you include an AMS command that causes the records in a data set to be processed, you may also have to include an additional DD statement to allocate that data set. When you code the DD statement, you can use any ddname you wish; AMS lets you specify the ddname for the file in the command that processes it.

AMS commands

As I mentioned, you use the SYSIN data set to supply the commands that tell AMS what you want it to do. The complexity in coding AMS jobs is in coding the commands; some of them have complicated formats, and the rules you must follow when coding them are sometimes obscure.

Figure 10-2 is an overview of the AMS commands you're most likely to use. As you can see, they are divided into two categories. The *functional commands* instruct AMS to actually do something, while the *modal commands* control the execution of the functional commands. In this chapter, I'll introduce you to the following functional commands: DEFINE CLUSTER, LISTCAT, DELETE, ALTER, PRINT, and REPRO. The other functional commands and the modal commands are beyond the scope of this book.

AMS command format   Before I present the individual AMS commands, you need to become familiar with their basic format. You can code AMS commands anywhere in columns 2 through 72. It's easy to code your commands in column 1, so be sure to avoid that common mistake.

Each AMS command follows the general format

```
verb parameters...
```

where *verb* is one of the commands listed in figure 10-2. (In figure 10-1, the verb is LISTCAT.) The *parameters* supply additional information that tells AMS how you want the command processed. The

AMS command	Function
Functional commands	
ALTER	Changes information specified for a catalog, cluster, alternate index, or path at define time.
BLDINDEX	Builds an alternate index.
DEFINE ALTERNATEINDEX	Defines an alternate index.
DEFINE CLUSTER	Defines a VSAM file, whether it's key-sequenced, entry-sequenced, or relative-record.
DEFINE MASTERCATALOG	Defines a master catalog.
DEFINE PATH	Defines the path that relates an alternate index to its base cluster.
DEFINE USERCATALOG	Defines a user catalog.
DELETE	Removes a catalog entry for a catalog, cluster, alternate index, or path.
EXPORT	Produces a transportable file.
IMPORT	Copies a previously exported file.
LISTCAT	Lists information about data sets.
PRINT	Prints the contents of a VSAM or non-VSAM file.
REPRO	Copies records from one file to another. The input and output files can be VSAM or non-VSAM.
Modal commands	
IF	Controls the flow of command execution by testing condition codes returned by functional commands.
SET	Controls the flow of command execution by altering condition codes returned by functional commands.
PARM	Sets option values that affect the way AMS executes.

Figure 10-2   Commonly used AMS commands

LISTCAT command in figure 10-1 has two parameters:
ENTRIES(SYDOE.CUSTOMER.MASTER) and VOLUME.

Most AMS commands require more than one parameter. To make your AMS commands easy to read, I suggest you code one parameter per line. To do that, you need to know how to code continuation lines. To continue an AMS command, you code one or more spaces followed by a hyphen immediately after the last parameter in the line. In figure 10-1, you can see how I coded a hyphen on the first line of the LISTCAT command to continue it on the next line.

Most AMS parameters require that you code a value enclosed in parentheses, like this:

```
RECORDS(500)
```

If a parameter requires more than one value, you code a list of subparameters separated by spaces or commas:

```
KEYS(5 0)
```

or

```
ENTRIES(FILE1,FILE2,FILE3,FILE4)
```

In the examples in this book, I use spaces rather than commas to separate subparameters.

AMS has strict rules about how you must use parentheses, so pay attention to the command formats as I present them. If you omit a required parenthesis, your command won't be executed.

How to define a cluster: the DEFINE CLUSTER command

To create a VSAM file from AMS, you must issue a DEFINE CLUSTER command. DEFINE CLUSTER is the most complicated of the AMS commands; it has dozens of parameters, many of which can be coded once, twice, or three times on the command. How you code these parameters depends on the characteristics of the file you're creating: whether it's a KSDS, ESDS, or RRDS, how much space it requires, and so on.

Figure 10-3 is a partial format of the DEFINE CLUSTER command. As you can see, the command consists of three sets of parameters, labeled CLUSTER, DATA, and INDEX; the CATALOG parameter stands by itself. Parameters you code at the CLUSTER level apply to the entire cluster. Parameters you code at the DATA or INDEX level apply only to the cluster's data or index component. Although you can code many of the DEFINE CLUSTER command's parameters at the CLUSTER, DATA, or INDEX level, I recommend you code most of the parameters I describe in this topic at the CLUSTER level. As I describe the parameters, I'll point out which ones you should code at the DATA and INDEX levels.

Quite frankly, the syntax of the DEFINE CLUSTER command is confusing. To help you understand it, figure 10-4 presents four examples. The first example defines a key-sequenced data set. Here, I coded parameters at the CLUSTER, DATA, and INDEX levels. The second and third examples define an entry-sequenced and a relative-record data set. Because those data sets don't have an index

The DEFINE CLUSTER command

```
DEFINE CLUSTER (     NAME(entry-name)
                     [ OWNER(owner-id) ]
                     [ FOR(days) | TO(date) ]
                     [ INDEXED | NONINDEXED | NUMBERED ]
                     [ RECORDSIZE(avg max) ]
                     [ CISZ(size) ]
                     [ SPANNED | NONSPANNED ]
                     [ KEYS(length offset) ]
                     [ FREESPACE(ci ca) ]
                     [ VOLUMES(vol-ser...) ]
                     [ FILE(ddname) ]
                        ⎧ CYLINDERS ⎫
                        ⎪ KILOBYTES ⎪
                     [ ⎨ MEGABYTES ⎬ (primary secondary) ]
                        ⎪ TRACKS    ⎪
                        ⎩ RECORDS   ⎭
                     [ UNIQUE | SUBALLOCATION ]
                     [ REUSE | NOREUSE ]
                     [ SHAREOPTIONS(a b) ]
                     [ IMBED | NOIMBED ]         )
                     [ STORAGECLASS(storage-class) ]
                     [ DATACLASS(data-class) ]
                     [ MANAGEMENTCLASS(management-class) ]
      [ DATA      ( [ NAME(entry-name) ]
                     [ VOLUMES(vol-ser...) ]
                     [ FILE(ddname) ]
                        ⎧ CYLINDERS ⎫
                        ⎪ KILOBYTES ⎪
                     [ ⎨ MEGABYTES ⎬ (primary secondary) ] ) ]
                        ⎪ TRACKS    ⎪
                        ⎩ RECORDS   ⎭
      [ INDEX     ( [ NAME(entry-name) ]
                     [ VOLUMES(vol-ser...) ]
                        ⎧ CYLINDERS ⎫
                        ⎪ KILOBYTES ⎪
                     [ ⎨ MEGABYTES ⎬ (primary secondary) ] ) ]
                        ⎪ TRACKS    ⎪
                        ⎩ RECORDS   ⎭

      [CATALOG(name[/password]) ]
```

Figure 10-3   The DEFINE CLUSTER command (part 1 of 2)

Explanation

NAME(entry-name)	Specifies the name of the cluster or component.
OWNER(owner-id)	Specifies a one- to eight-character owner-id.
FOR(days) TO(date)	Specifies a retention period (in the format dddd) or an expiration date (in the format yyddd).
INDEXED NONINDEXED NUMBERED	Specifies the file organization: KSDS (INDEXED), ESDS (NONINDEXED), or RRDS (NUMBERED). The default is INDEXED.
RECORDSIZE(avg max)	Specifies the average and maximum record size.
CISZ(size)	Specifies the size of the control intervals.
SPANNED NONSPANNED	Specifies whether records can cross control interval boundaries. The default is NONSPANNED.
KEYS(length offset)	Specifies the length and offset of the primary key.
FREESPACE(ci ca)	Specifies the percentage of free space to reserve in the control intervals and control areas.
VOLUMES(vol-ser)	Specifies one or more volumes that will contain the cluster or component.
FILE(ddname)	Specifies a ddname that identifies a DD statement that allocates the volume or volumes. Required only for mountable DASD volumes.
primary	Specifies the amount of space to initially allocate, expressed in terms of cylinders, kilobytes, megabytes, tracks, or records.
secondary	Specifies the secondary space allocation.
UNIQUE SUBALLOCATION	Specifies whether the file is unique or suballocated. The default is SUBALLOCATION. Ignored under ICF.
REUSE NOREUSE	Specifies whether a file is reusable. The default is NOREUSE.
SHAREOPTIONS(a b)	Specifies the level of the file sharing permitted. See figure 10-5.
IMBED NOIMBED	Specifies whether sequence set records should be imbedded in the data component of a KSDS. The default is NOIMBED.
STORAGECLASS	SMS only; specifies the storage class for the file.
DATACLASS	SMS only; specifies the data class for the file.
MANAGEMENTCLASS	SMS only; specifies the management class for the file.
CATALOG (name[/password])	Specifies the name and password of the catalog that will own the cluster. If omitted, the high-level qualifier of the cluster name or the stepcat, jobcat, or master catalog identifies the catalog.

Figure 10-3   The DEFINE CLUSTER command (part 2 of 2)

Example 1: Define a key-sequenced data set

```
DEFINE CLUSTER    ( NAME(SYDOE.CUSTOMER.MASTER)        -
                    OWNER(SYDOE)                        -
                    INDEXED                             -
                    RECORDSIZE(200 200)                 -
                    KEYS(6 0)                           -
                    VOLUMES(TS0001)                     -
                    UNIQUE                              -
                    TO(94365)                           -
                    SHAREOPTIONS(2 3)                   -
                    IMBED )                             -
        DATA      ( NAME(SYDOE.CUSTOMER.MASTER.DATA)    -
                    CYLINDERS(50 5)                     -
                    CISZ(4096) )                        -
        INDEX     ( NAME(SYDOE.CUSTOMER.MASTER.INDEX) )
```

Example 2: Define an entry-sequenced data set

```
DEFINE CLUSTER    ( NAME(SYDOE.AR.TRAN)                 -
                    OWNER(SYDOE)                        -
                    NONINDEXED                          -
                    RECORDSIZE(190 280)                 -
                    VOLUMES(TS0001)                     -
                    FOR(365)                            -
                    REUSE )                             -
        DATA      ( NAME(SYDOE.AR.TRAN.DATA)            -
                    CYLINDERS(10 1) )
```

Example 3: Define a relative-record data set

```
DEFINE CLUSTER    ( NAME(SYDOE.GL.ACCOUNT.MASTER)       -
                    OWNER(ACCT1)                        -
                    NUMBERED                            -
                    RECORDSIZE(502 502)                 -
                    VOLUMES(TS0001)                     -
                    UNIQUE                              -
                    TO(94365)                           -
                    SHAREOPTIONS(1 3) )                 -
        DATA      ( NAME(SYDOE.GL.ACCOUNT.MASTER.DATA)  -
                    CYLINDERS(10 1) )
```

Example 4: Define an SMS-managed key-sequenced data set

```
DEFINE CLUSTER    ( NAME(SYDOE.CUSTOMER.MASTER)        -
                    STORAGECLASS(MVPS100)               -
                    DATACLASS(MVPD050)                  -
                    MANAGEMENTCLASS(MVPM010) )          -
        DATA      ( NAME(SYDOE.CUSTOMER.MASTER.DATA)    -
                    CYLINDERS(50 5) )                   -
        INDEX     ( NAME(SYDOE.CUSTOMER.MASTER.INDEX) )
```

Figure 10-4　　　Three examples of the DEFINE CLUSTER command

component, these commands have parameters only at the CLUSTER and DATA levels. The fourth example defines a key-sequenced data set that's managed by SMS. As you can see, SMS makes it easier to define a data set using AMS just as it does when you use JCL. As I describe the individual parameters of the DEFINE CLUSTER command, I'll refer to both the syntax diagram in figure 10-3 and the three examples in figure 10-4.

Parameters that identify the file

Three of the DEFINE CLUSTER parameters listed in figure 10-3 simply identify the file you're defining by supplying its name (NAME), who's responsible for it (OWNER), and what catalog will own it (CATALOG).

The NAME parameter   The NAME parameter lets you supply a name for your file. The name you specify must follow the standard MVS data set naming rules. When you code a value for the NAME parameter at the CLUSTER level, that name applies only to the cluster entry. Then, if you don't specify otherwise, VSAM creates a name for the data component (and, for a KSDS, for the index component) that's long and cryptic. As a result, I suggest you code the NAME parameter at all levels of your DEFINE CLUSTER command. That way, you'll be able to identify individual components in LISTCAT output listings. And, for unique files, the names you code at the DATA and INDEX levels will appear in the volume's VTOC entries for the file. In figure 10-4, you can see that I coded a NAME parameter at each level of all three DEFINE CLUSTER commands. To form the data and index component names, I suggest you add DATA and INDEX to the cluster names as I did in figure 10-4.

The OWNER parameter   The OWNER parameter supplies an eight-character value that indicates who's responsible for the file. The owner-id you supply is used for documentation only; it doesn't affect the way VSAM processes the file. If you issue the DEFINE CLUSTER command from a TSO terminal, VSAM uses your TSO user-id for the owner-id if you omit the OWNER parameter. The first two examples in figure 10-4 specify SYDOE as the owner-id; the third specifies ACCT1.

The CATALOG parameter   The last parameter in figure 10-3, CATALOG, lets you specify the catalog that will own the cluster you're defining. As I've already mentioned, the CATALOG parameter is the only DEFINE CLUSTER parameter that's not coded at the CLUSTER, DATA, or INDEX level. As a result, when you use the

CATALOG parameter, you'll always code it as the last parameter on the DEFINE CLUSTER command.

If you omit the CATALOG parameter, as I did in each example in figure 10-4, the high-level qualifier of the cluster name is used to identify the catalog that owns it. If the high-level qualifier isn't defined as a user catalog or alias, a step catalog, job catalog, or the master catalog is used.

Parameters that describe the file's characteristics

The next group of DEFINE CLUSTER parameters I'll explain describe the characteristics of the file: its organization, record size, and so on.

The file-type parameter   To indicate what type of cluster you're defining, you code INDEXED, NONINDEXED, or NUMBERED. As the examples in figure 10-4 indicate, you code INDEXED to define a KSDS, NONINDEXED to define an ESDS, and NUMBERED to define an RRDS. If you omit this parameter, AMS defaults to INDEXED.

The RECORDSIZE parameter   The RECORDSIZE parameter specifies the length of the logical records in your file. On it, you code two values: the average record length and the maximum record length. The average length indicates the length of most of the records in the file. The maximum length indicates the length of the largest record.

In most cases, the value you code for the average record length doesn't matter. The only case where it does is when you allocate space to the file based on how many records the file will contain rather than on how many tracks or cylinders it will require. But, as you'll learn in a few moments, I recommend you don't do that.

It's easy to get the idea from the IBM manuals that coding the same value for average and maximum record length will restrict the file to fixed-length records. But that's not the case. Whether you code the same or different values for average and maximum record size, the file can contain records that vary in length up to the maximum you specify. In other words, VSAM doesn't require that the records all have the same length, even if you specify the same value for average and maximum length. (To define a fixed-length relative-record file, however, you should code the same value for the average and maximum length.)

If you omit the RECORDSIZE parameter, VSAM's default depends on whether or not you specify the SPANNED parameter, which I'll describe in a moment. If you omit SPANNED and RECORDSIZE, VSAM assumes 4089 for both the average and the maximum record length. If you specify SPANNED and omit RECORDSIZE, VSAM assumes 4086 average and 32600 maximum. The examples in figure 10-4 show a variety of average and maximum record lengths.

The CISZ parameter   The CISZ parameter lets you specify the size of your file's control intervals. Determining the best size for a particular file's control intervals is a complicated subject that's beyond the scope of this book. Fortunately, it's safe to say that for most files, you can specify 4096 as the control interval size, unless the records are large (say, over 1,000 bytes). Then, you might want to consider a larger control interval size, like 6144 or 8192. If you omit the CISZ parameter, VSAM is likely to pick an inappropriate control interval size. Therefore, I recommend you always code the CISZ parameter.

The SPANNED parameter   If your file will contain records that are longer than one control interval, you need to code the SPANNED parameter. Otherwise, you can let the parameter default to NONSPANNED. Since spanned records are uncommon, I don't think you'll use the SPANNED parameter often.

The KEYS parameter   You code the KEYS parameter at the CLUS-TER or DATA level to identify a key-sequenced data set's primary key. On the KEYS parameter, you supply the key's length and displacement, like this:

```
KEYS(6 0)
```

Here, the primary key occupies the first six positions of each record.

The FREESPACE parameter   The FREESPACE parameter lets you control the amount of free space within the data component of a KSDS. You can specify free space at one or two levels by coding one or two values on the parameter. To specify the amount of space within each control interval that's to be reserved for insertions, you code a percentage as the first value for the parameter. The second parameter value specifies the percentage of control intervals in each control area to be left empty. For example, you code

```
FREESPACE(30 20)
```

to specify that 30 percent of each control interval and 20 percent of each control area should be left empty.

Since VSAM's default is to leave no free space, it's a good idea to provide some if file additions are likely. You should be aware that the free space you request is taken from, not added to, the amount of space you allocate for the file. So if you provide for free space, be sure to include an additional amount of space in the space allocation.

Parameters that specify the file's space allocation

The next group of parameters I'll describe specifies how space is allocated to the file. The VOLUMES and FILE parameters specify the DASD volume or volumes where the file will be allocated. The UNIQUE/SUBALLOCATION parameter specifies whether a file will be allocated to a unique space or will be suballocated out of existing VSAM space. Finally, the space allocation parameter specifies the amount of space that should be allocated to the file.

The VOLUMES parameter   When you code the VOLUMES parameter at the CLUSTER level, you name the volume or volumes (up to 123) where the cluster will reside. In each of the examples in figure 10-4, the file resides on a single volume named TSO001.

If you code more than one volume name in the VOLUMES parameter, the additional volumes can be used if the file requires more space than is available on a single volume. For example, suppose you code the VOLUMES parameter like this:

```
VOLUMES(TSO001 TSO002 TSO003)
```

Here, the file can reside on one, two, or all three of the volumes named TSO001, TSO002, and TSO003. Normally, you'll code just one vol-ser in the VOLUMES parameter.

If you code two VOLUMES parameters, one at the DATA level and one at the INDEX level, VSAM puts the file's data and index components on the volumes you name. In some cases, that might improve performance for the file. However, unless you want to split the data and index components like that, I recommend you code just one VOLUMES parameter at the CLUSTER level.

The FILE parameter   Older releases of VSAM required a DD statement to define a file. Now, there's only one case where you must supply a DD statement: when you define a file that resides on a removable DASD volume. Since most DASD volumes in use today are permanently resident, you don't need the DD statement. However, to create a VSAM file on a Mass Storage System volume or another similar removable device, you must use the FILE parameter and a DD statement to allocate the volume.

The FILE parameter specifies the ddname of the required DD statement. So, if you code FILE(MSSDD), the DD statement named MSSDD allocates the Mass Storage System volume. On the DD statement, you should specify UNIT, VOL=SER, and DISP, like this:

```
//MSSDD     DD    UNIT=3330V,VOL=SER=MPS8BV,
//                DISP=OLD
```

Here, 3330V identifies the unit as a Mass Storage System volume, and VOL=SER specifies MPS8BV as the vol-ser. No data set name is required.

The UNIQUE/SUBALLOCATION parameter   This parameter lets you specify whether a file should be suballocated out of existing VSAM space or created in its own space. If you specify SUB-ALLOCATION (or let it default as in example 2 of figure 10-4), the file is suballocated out of VSAM space. As a result, the volume must contain enough VSAM space to hold your file. If you specify UNIQUE as in examples 1 and 3 of figure 10-4, the file is created in its own space. So there must be enough non-VSAM space on the volume to contain your file.

The space allocation parameter   You use the space allocation parameter to specify how much space to allocate to your file. The space allocation parameter has the general format

```
allocation-unit (primary secondary)
```

where the allocation unit can be CYLINDERS, KILOBYTES, MEGA-BYTES, TRACKS, or RECORDS. The primary value specifies the number of units initially allocated to your file. The secondary value specifies the size of any secondary extents that may be required. In each of the examples in figure 10-4, I coded the allocation parameter at the DATA level. I'll explain what happens when you code it at other levels in a moment.

In example 1 of figure 10-4, I coded the allocation parameter like this:

```
CYLINDERS(50 5)
```

Here, the initial space allocation for the file will be 50 cylinders. If the data set grows beyond that initial allocation, secondary extents of 5 cylinders each are allocated. Up to 122 secondary extents can be allocated to the file before it must be reorganized.

For most files, you should allocate space in terms of cylinders. That's because if you specify CYLINDERS as the allocation unit, the file's control areas will be one cylinder each. For key-sequenced data sets, that allows the index component to be structured most efficiently.

For suballocated files that require less than one cylinder of disk space, I suggest you allocate space in terms of records or tracks rather than cylinders. However, if a unique file requires less than one cylinder, you may as well allocate a whole cylinder to it. A unique file can't be smaller than one cylinder anyway.

If you don't know what type of device a file will be placed on, you should specify the space allocation in terms of kilobytes or megabytes. When you do that, the minimum number of tracks or cylinders that are needed to contain the specified number of kilobytes or megabytes are allocated. That way, the number of tracks or cylinders that are allocated will depend on the device.

As you can see in figure 10-3, you can code an allocation parameter at the CLUSTER, DATA, and INDEX level of a DEFINE CLUSTER command. When you define an entry-sequenced or relative-record data set, it doesn't matter whether you specify the allocation parameter at the CLUSTER or DATA level. Either way, the amount of space you specify is allocated to your file's data component. For a key-sequenced data set, however, you can code the allocation parameter in three ways: at the CLUSTER level only, at the DATA level only, or at both the DATA and INDEX levels.

If you specify an allocation parameter at the cluster level when you define a KSDS, VSAM uses that space for both the data component and the index component. VSAM determines how much space to allocate to the index component and gives the rest to the data component. If the space remaining for the data component isn't a multiple of a control area (usually a cylinder), VSAM rounds the amount up.

For example, suppose you specify CYLINDERS(5 1) at the CLUSTER level. For this file, VSAM will probably allocate just one track to the index component. Because the amount of space left for the file's data component is four cylinders plus several tracks, VSAM rounds the data component space allocation up to five cylinders. As a result, the total space initially allocated to this new KSDS is five cylinders plus one track; that's more than the requested five cylinders.

If you code an allocation parameter only at the DATA level when you define a KSDS, VSAM allocates the amount you specify to the file's data component and calculates an additional amount to allocate to the index component. For example, if you specify CYLINDERS(5 1) at the DATA level, VSAM allocates five cylinders to the data component. Then, it allocates an additional amount of space (again, probably just one track) for the index component.

In most cases, the end result is the same whether you code the allocation parameter at the CLUSTER or DATA level. Either way, the full amount of space you specify is allocated to your file's data component, and an additional amount of less than one cylinder is allocated to the index component. Only in rare cases does the index component require more than one cylinder.

Whether you code the allocation parameter at the CLUSTER or DATA level, VSAM calculates how much space to allocate to the index component. If you wish, you can code an allocation parameter at the INDEX level to override VSAM's calculation. However, because VSAM's index space calculation is almost always correct, I suggest you don't code an allocation parameter at the INDEX level.

Parameters for SMS-managed files

In chapter 6, you learned about three parameters you can code on a DD statement that assign class values to an SMS-managed file: STORCLAS, DATACLAS, and MGMTCLAS. AMS provides similar parameters for defining an SMS-managed file. The STORAGE-CLASS parameter identifies a data set as SMS-managed and assigns a storage class to the file. The DATACLASS parameter assigns a data class to the file that provides characteristics such as record size, key length and offset, and space allocation. And the MANAGE-MENTCLASS parameter assigns a management class that provides storage management information. As you can see in figure 10-3, you code all three of these parameters at the CLUSTER level. Note that the STORAGECLASS and MANAGEMENTCLASS parameters can be coded only for SMS-managed files. However, you can code the DATACLASS parameter for any file as long as SMS is installed and active.

Example 4 in figure 10-4 shows how you can use the STORAGE-CLASS, DATACLASS, and MANAGEMENTCLASS parameters to define a key-sequenced file. If I had omitted any of these parameters, the automatic class selection routines would have been used to determine the classes assigned to the file. This works the same way it does when you define an SMS-managed file using JCL. Also notice that I coded the CYLINDERS parameter at the DATA level. This parameter overrides the space allocation specified by the data class.

Other DEFINE CLUSTER parameters

The parameters you've learned so far make up a basic subset of the DEFINE CLUSTER command. Using them, you can define any of the three types of VSAM files. However, there are other parameters you can, and often should, code on a DEFINE CLUSTER command. For example, you can use the FOR or TO parameter to specify a retention period or an expiration date for your file. Now, I'll describe the REUSE, FOR and TO, SHAREOPTIONS, and IMBED parameters in detail.

The REUSE parameter   In chapter 8, you learned that reusable files can be used for applications that require temporary work files. For example, a data-collection application might collect transactions in a reusable file. Then, when the transactions are posted to a master file, the reusable file is reset, deleting any records it contains.

To define a reusable work file, you specify REUSE on the DE-FINE CLUSTER command at the CLUSTER or DATA level. If you omit REUSE, or if you code NOREUSE, the file will not be reusable. Whenever you open a reusable file for output, any records in the file are logically deleted. But you can process the file as usual by opening it for input or I/O.

The FOR and TO parameters   You can code FOR or TO to specify how long the file you're defining should remain current. If you omit both of these parameters, a DELETE command can delete the cluster at any time. If you code one of these parameters, you can still delete the file at any time. But you have to code a special parameter on the DELETE command to delete a file while it's still current.

If you code FOR, the value you code is the number of days (0 to 9999) that the file should be retained. If you code TO, the value you include is an expiration date in the format *yyddd*, where *yy* is the year (00 to 99) and *ddd* is the day (001 to 366).

In figure 10-4, examples 1 and 3 specify TO(94365). That way, the files will be current until the last day of 1994. In example 2, I specified FOR(365) to indicate that the file should remain current for one year.

The SHAREOPTIONS parameter   The SHAREOPTIONS parameter tells VSAM whether you want to let two or more jobs process your file at the same time. You code two values in the SHARE-OPTIONS parameter. The first specifies the *cross-region share option*. This option lets you control how two or more jobs on a single system can share a file. The second value specifies the *cross-system share option*, which controls how jobs on different systems of a multi-processor complex can share a file. Examples 1 and 3 in figure 10-4 use the SHAREOPTIONS parameter.

Figure 10-5 summarizes the meaning of each type of share option. Usually, you'll specify 1, 2, or 3 for the cross-region share option. Share option 4 isn't very useful because it overly restricts the type of processing you can do for the file. For the cross-system share option, you'll usually specify 3 for the same reason. Options 1 and 2 aren't available for cross-system sharing.

The IMBED parameter   In chapter 8, I pointed out that the index component of a KSDS consists of two types of records: sequence set

---

Cross-region share options (a)

1   The file can be processed simultaneously by multiple jobs as long as all jobs open the file for input only. If a job opens the file for output, no other job can open the file.

2   The file can be processed simultaneously by multiple jobs as long as only one job opens the file for output; all other jobs must open the file for input only.

3   Any number of jobs can process the file simultaneously for input or output; VSAM does nothing to insure the integrity of the file.

4   Any number of jobs can process the file simultaneously for input or output; VSAM imposes these restrictions:

   •   direct retrieval always reads data from disk even if the desired index or data records are already in a VSAM buffer

   •   data may not be added to the end of the file

   •   a control area split is not allowed

Cross-system share options (b)

3   Any number of jobs on any system can process the file simultaneously for input or output; VSAM does nothing to insure the integrity of the file.

4   Any number of jobs on any system can process the file simultaneously for input or output; VSAM imposes the same restrictions as for cross-region share option 4.

Figure 10-5   Cross-region and cross-system share options

records, which directly index data component control intervals, and index set records, which provide an index to the sequence set. For most key-sequenced data sets, you can improve processing performance by specifying the IMBED parameter, which causes sequence set records to be stored in the space allocated to the data component rather than in the space allocated to the index component.

When you specify IMBED, the first track of each control area is used to store the sequence set record that indexes the data component control intervals in that control area. Because each control area usually occupies one cylinder of DASD space, that means VSAM can access a sequence set record and all of the data component control intervals it indexes without moving the DASD access mechanism. And that's a performance improvement; without the IMBED option, the access mechanism must move between the index and data components to access records.

Because the performance benefit of IMBED is usually substantial, I recommend you specify IMBED for all your key-sequenced data sets, as in example 1 in figure 10-4. Be aware when you do, however, that you must allow for the space taken up by the sequence set records when you calculate the amount of space for your file. In other words, remember that the first track of each data component cylinder isn't available for data component records.

How to use AMS to maintain catalogs

Now that you know how to define a VSAM file, you're ready to learn how to use three AMS commands for maintaining catalogs: LISTCAT, ALTER, and DELETE. The LISTCAT command lets you list the contents of a catalog. The ALTER command lets you change the characteristics of an existing VSAM file. And the DELETE command lets you delete a VSAM file by removing its catalog entry.

The LISTCAT command

Often, you need to know what VSAM files are defined in a particular user catalog. Or, you need to know the characteristics of a particular file. To get that information, you use the LISTCAT command, whose format is given in figure 10-6. The parameters you code on the LISTCAT command identify the catalog, the names of the entries to be listed, the types of entries to be listed, and the amount of information about each entry to be listed.

The CATALOG parameter   The first LISTCAT parameter, CATALOG, names the catalog whose contents you want to list. If you omit the catalog parameter, VSAM uses its standard search order to determine which catalog to use. The high-level qualifier of a file name is used if one is supplied in a subsequent ENTRIES or LEVEL parameter; otherwise, a step catalog or job catalog is used. If no job or step catalog is in effect, the master catalog is used.

The ENTRIES and LEVEL parameters   The next two parameters, ENTRIES and LEVEL, identify the catalog entries you want to list. If you omit the ENTRIES and LEVEL parameters, VSAM lists *all* of the entries in the catalog. Do that with caution, however; user catalogs can contain hundreds of entries.

The ENTRIES parameter lets you specify one or more names for the catalog entries you want listed. For example, if you want to list the catalog entry for a VSAM file named SYDOE.CUSTOMER.MASTER,

The LISTCAT command

```
LISTCAT   [ CATALOG(name[/password]) ]

          [ { ENTRIES(entry-name[/password]...) }  ]
            { LEVEL(level)                        }

          [ entry-type ]

            ⎧ NAME       ⎫
            ⎪ HISTORY    ⎪
          [ ⎨ VOLUME     ⎬ ]
            ⎪ ALLOCATION ⎪
            ⎩ ALL        ⎭
```

Parameters

CATALOG(name[/password])	Specifies the name and, if required, password of the catalog from which entries are to be listed.
ENTRIES(entry-name[/password]...)	Specifies the names of the entries you want to list. If omitted, all entries in the specified catalog are listed.
LEVEL(level)	Specifies one or more levels of qualification. Any data sets whose names match those levels are listed.
entry-type	Specifies the type of entries you want listed. If both ENTRIES/LEVEL and entry-type are omitted, all entries of all types in the specified catalog are listed. Code one of these values:
	ALIAS
	ALTERNATEINDEX or AIX
	CLUSTER
	DATA
	GENERATIONDATAGROUP or GDG
	INDEX
	NONVSAM
	PAGESPACE
	PATH
	USERCATALOG
NAME	Specifies that only the names and types of the specified entries are to be listed. NAME is the default.
HISTORY	Specifies that the information listed by NAME, plus the history information (such as creation and expiration dates), is to be listed.
VOLUME	Specifies that the information listed by HISTORY, plus the volume locations of the specified entries, is to be listed.
ALLOCATION	Specifies that the information listed by VOLUME, plus detailed extent information, is to be listed.
ALL	Specifies that all available catalog information for the specified entries is to be listed.

Figure 10-6   The LISTCAT command

you would code this:

```
ENTRIES(SYDOE.CUSTOMER.MASTER)
```

To list information for more than one file, just code several file names in a single ENTRIES parameter, like this:

```
ENTRIES(SYDOE.CUSTOMER.MASTER    -
        SYDOE.EMPLOYEE.MASTER    -
        SYDOE.DAILY.TRANS)
```

Here, three catalog entries will be listed.

You can specify a *generic entry name* by replacing one or more levels of the file name with an asterisk. For example, if you code

```
ENTRIES(SYDOE.*.MASTER)
```

all files whose names consist of three levels, with SYDOE as the first level and MASTER as the third level, are listed. SYDOE.CUS-TOMER.MASTER and SYDOE.EMPLOYEE.MASTER meet these criteria, so they would be listed.

The LEVEL parameter is similar to generic entry names in an ENTRIES parameter. In the LEVEL parameter, you code a partial name consisting of one or more levels. VSAM then lists all the catalog entries whose names begin with the partial name. For example, if you code

```
LEVEL(SYDOE)
```

all catalog entries whose first level is SYDOE are listed. In this example, it doesn't matter how many levels are actually present in the entry name, as long as the *first* level is SYDOE. Similarly, if you code

```
LEVEL(SYDOE.EMPLOYEE)
```

any entry whose name begins with SYDOE.EMPLOYEE is listed, regardless of how many additional levels are in its name.

To understand how the ENTRIES and LEVEL parameters work, look at figure 10-7. Here, I've listed five LISTCAT commands that use the ENTRIES or LEVEL parameter, and I've shown which of five VSAM file names would be selected by each of the five commands. If you study this figure for a moment, I think you'll understand the difference between the ENTRIES and LEVEL parameters.

The entry-type parameter The third LISTCAT parameter, entry-type, lets you specify that only certain types of catalog entries are to be listed (such as clusters, alternate indexes, and so on). If you omit the entry-type parameter, all entries that match the ENTRIES or LEVEL parameter will be listed.

Component name	Example				
	1	2	3	4	5
SYDOE.CUSTOMER	X				X
SYDOE.CUSTOMER.MASTER			X		X
SYDOE.EMPLOYEE				X	X
SYDOE.EMPLOYEE.MASTER		X	X	X	X
SYDOE.EMPLOYEE.FILE		X		X	X

Example 1

```
LISTCAT ENTRIES(SYDOE.CUSTOMER)
```

Example 2

```
LISTCAT ENTRIES(SYDOE.EMPLOYEE.*)
```

Example 3

```
LISTCAT ENTRIES(SYDOE.*.MASTER)
```

Example 4

```
LISTCAT LEVEL(SYDOE.EMPLOYEE)
```

Example 5

```
LISTCAT LEVEL(SYDOE)
```

Figure 10-7   Examples of the ENTRIES and LEVEL parameters of the LISTCAT command

You can specify more than one entry-type value on a LISTCAT command. For example, if you want to list clusters and alternate indexes, you could code both CLUSTER and ALTERNATEINDEX (or AIX) on the LISTCAT command.

How to limit the amount of catalog information listed   The next LISTCAT parameter lets you limit the amount of catalog information that's listed for each entry. If you specify NAME, or let it default, VSAM lists just the entry's name, type, and owning catalog. To illustrate, figure 10-8 shows the output from this command:

```
LISTCAT LEVEL(SYDOE) -
        NAME
```

As you can see, several files whose names begin with SYDOE are listed as a result of this command.

```
IDCAMS   SYSTEM SERVICES

LISTCAT LEVEL(SYDOE) -
        NAME

CLUSTER ------- SYDOE.CUSTOMER.MASTER
       IN-CAT --- ICFCAT.VSTORO2

DATA ---------- SYDOE.CUSTOMER.MASTER.DATA
       IN-CAT --- ICFCAT.VSTORO2

INDEX --------- SYDOE.CUSTOMER.MASTER.INDEX
       IN-CAT --- ICFCAT.VSTORO2

GDG BASE ------ SYDOE.DAILYEMS
       IN-CAT --- ICFCAT.VSTORO2

NONVSAM ------- SYDOE.DAILYEMS.G0930V93
       IN-CAT --- ICFCAT.VSTORO2

CLUSTER ------- SYDOE.IPCS.DUMPDIR
       IN-CAT --- ICFCAT.VSTORO2

DATA ---------- SYDOE.IPCS.DUMPDIR.DATA
       IN-CAT --- ICFCAT.VSTORO2

INDEX --------- SYDOE.IPCS.DUMPDIR.INDEX
       IN-CAT --- ICFCAT.VSTORO2

NONVSAM ------- SYDOE.ISFSRC
       IN-CAT --- ICFCAT.VSTORO2

NONVSAM ------- SYDOE.ISPEDA
       IN-CAT --- ICFCAT.VSTORO2

NONVSAM ------- SYDOE.ISPEDB
       IN-CAT --- ICFCAT.VSTORO2

NONVSAM ------- SYDOE.ISPPLIB
       IN-CAT --- ICFCAT.VSTORO2

NONVSAM ------- SYDOE.ISPPROF
       IN-CAT --- ICFCAT.VSTORO2

NONVSAM ------- SYDOE.ISPTLIB
       IN-CAT --- ICFCAT.VSTORO2

NONVSAM ------- SYDOE.JMROUT.SCAN
       IN-CAT --- ICFCAT.VSTORO2
```

Figure 10-8   Output from a LISTCAT command with the NAME parameter

```
IDCAMS  SYSTEM SERVICES

LISTCAT ENTRIES(SYDOE.CUSTOMER.MASTER) -
        HISTORY

CLUSTER ------- SYDOE.CUSTOMER.MASTER
     IN-CAT --- ICFCAT.VSTOR02
     HISTORY
        OWNER-IDENT--------SYDOE        CREATION--------1994.129
        RELEASE----------------2        EXPIRATION------1994.365

   DATA ------- SYDOE.CUSTOMER.MASTER.DATA
     IN-CAT --- ICFCAT.VSTOR02
     HISTORY
        OWNER-IDENT-------(NULL)        CREATION--------1994.129
        RELEASE----------------2        EXPIRATION------1994.365

  INDEX ------ SYDOE.CUSTOMER.MASTER.INDEX
     IN-CAT --- ICFCAT.VSTOR02
     HISTORY
        OWNER-IDENT-------(NULL)        CREATION--------1994.129
        RELEASE----------------2        EXPIRATION------1994.365
```

Figure 10-9   Output from a LISTCAT command with the HISTORY parameter

Figure 10-9 shows what happens if you list an entry for a specific file (SYDOE.CUSTOMER.MASTER) and specify the HISTORY
parameter. Here, the entry's name and type are listed along with its
history information: owner-id, creation and expiration dates, and
the VSAM release under which the entry was created. In addition,
the HISTORY parameter causes VSAM to list any entries that are
associated with the entry you specify. In this example, the cluster is
a key-sequenced data set. So VSAM lists the DATA and INDEX
component entries too. If the cluster had any associated paths or
alternate indexes, they would have been listed as well.

In figure 10-10, I specified the VOLUME parameter rather than
the HISTORY parameter. As a result, VSAM listed the same information listed for HISTORY, plus the names of the DASD volumes
that contain the data and index components. In this case, both are
contained on a volume named TSO001.

If you specify ALLOCATION instead of VOLUME, the output
looks like figure 10-11. Here, detailed information about the file's
disk extents is shown. For example, you can see that the data component occupies one extent that fills 15 tracks, or one cylinder.

If you want to know all of the characteristics of a VSAM file,
specify the ALL parameter. Then, the output looks like figure 10-12.

```
IDCAMS   SYSTEM SERVICES


LISTCAT ENTRIES(SYDOE.CUSTOMER.MASTER) -
        VOLUMES

CLUSTER ------- SYDOE.CUSTOMER.MASTER
     IN-CAT --- ICFCAT.VSTORO2
     HISTORY
         OWNER-IDENT--------SYDOE        CREATION--------1994.129
         RELEASE---------------2         EXPIRATION------1994.365

   DATA ------- SYDOE.CUSTOMER.MASTER.DATA
     IN-CAT -- ICFCAT.VSTORO2
     HISTORY
         OWNER-IDENT-------(NULL)        CREATION--------1994.129
         RELEASE---------------2         EXPIRATION------1994.365
     VOLUMES
         VOLSER-----------TS0001         DEVTYPE------X'3010200F'

   INDEX ------ SYDOE.CUSTOMER.MASTER.INDEX
     IN-CAT --- ICFCAT.VSTORO2
     HISTORY
         OWNER-IDENT-------(NULL)        CREATION--------1994.129
         RELEASE---------------2         EXPIRATION------1994.365
     VOLUMES
         VOLSER-----------TS0001         DEVTYPE------X'3010200F'
```

Figure 10-10   Output from a LISTCAT command with the VOLUMES parameter

Here, several new categories of information are listed. In the
ATTRIBUTES group, you can see which attributes were specified
for the file when it was defined. For example, in figure 10-12, you
can see that SHAREOPTIONS(2 3) was specified for the file.

As figure 10-12 illustrates, LISTCAT output can be lengthy. If
you run a job to print all the entries in a typical user catalog and you
specify ALL, the output can easily fill hundreds of pages. So be as
specific as you can about the information you need when you run
an AMS LISTCAT job. The less output you request, the simpler it
will be for you to read and the less system time it will take to create
and print it.

How to list information about data spaces   To list information about
data spaces rather than data sets (VSAM catalogs only), you code
SPACE as the entry type on the LISTCAT command. When you do,
there are a few things I want you to realize. First, data spaces don't
have names, so you can't specify them by name with ENTRIES or
LEVEL parameters. However, you can code the ENTRIES parameter to
print information about spaces that reside on specific volumes. Just

```
IDCAMS  SYSTEM  SERVICES

LISTCAT ENTRIES(SYDOE.CUSTOMER.MASTER) -
        ALLOCATION

CLUSTER ------ SYDOE.CUSTOMER.MASTER
    IN-CAT --- ICFCAT.VSTOR02
    HISTORY
        OWNER-IDENT------SYDOE          CREATION------------1994.129
        RELEASE-------------2           EXPIRATION----------1994.365

DATA ------ SYDOE.CUSTOMER.MASTER.DATA
    IN-CAT --- ICFCAT.VSTOR02
    HISTORY
        OWNER-IDENT------(NULL)         CREATION------------1994.129
        RELEASE-------------2           EXPIRATION----------1994.365
    ALLOCATION
        SPACE-TYPE------CYLINDER        HI-ALLOC-RBA------688128      HI-ALLOC-RBA------688128
        SPACE-PRI-----------1           HI-USED-RBA-------688128      HI-USED-RBA-------688128
        SPACE-SEC-----------1
    VOLUME
        VOLSER---------TS0001           PHYREC-SIZE--------4096
        DEVTYPE-----X'3010200F'         PHYRECS/TRK----------12
        VOLFLAG--------PRIME            TRACKS/CA------------15
        EXTENTS:
        LOW-CCHH----X'016A0000'         LOW-RBA-------------0          TRACKS--------------15
        HIGH-CCHH---X'016A000E'         HIGH-RBA--------688127                                    EXTENT-NUMBER--------1
                                                                                                 EXTENT-TYPE------X'00'

INDEX ------ SYDOE.CUSTOMER.MASTER.INDEX
    IN-CAT --- ICFCAT.VSTOR02
    HISTORY
        OWNER-IDENT------(NULL)         CREATION------------1994.129
        RELEASE-------------2           EXPIRATION----------1994.365
    ALLOCATION
        SPACE-TYPE------TRACK           HI-ALLOC-RBA-------41472      HI-ALLOC-RBA-------39936
        SPACE-PRI-----------1           HI-USED-RBA--------41472      HI-USED-RBA-----------0
        SPACE-SEC-----------1
    VOLUME
        VOLSER---------TS0001           PHYREC-SIZE--------1536
        DEVTYPE-----X'3010200F'         PHYRECS/TRK----------26
        VOLFLAG--------PRIME            TRACKS/CA------------1
        EXTENTS:
        LOW-CCHH----X'0138000B'         LOW-RBA-------------0          TRACKS---------------1
        HIGH-CCHH---X'0138000B'         HIGH-RBA---------39935
    VOLUME
        VOLSER---------TS0001           PHYREC-SIZE--------1536        HI-ALLOC-RBA-------41472
        DEVTYPE-----X'3010200F'         PHYRECS/TRK----------26        HI-USED-RBA--------41472
        VOLFLAG--------PRIME            TRACKS/CA------------15
        EXTENTS:
        LOW-CCHH----X'016A0000'         LOW-RBA---------39936          TRACKS--------------15         EXTENT-NUMBER--------1
        HIGH-CCHH---X'016A000E'         HIGH-RBA---------41471                                        EXTENT-TYPE------X'80'
```

Figure 10-11 Output from a LISTCAT command with the ALLOCATION parameter

```
IDCAMS  SYSTEM  SERVICES                          TIME: 20:48:59      05/09/94      PAGE   8

 LISTCAT ENTRIES(SYDOE.CUSTOMER.MASTER) -
       ALL
CLUSTER ------- SYDOE.CUSTOMER.MASTER
    IN-CAT --- ICFCAT.VSTOR02
    HISTORY
        OWNER-IDENT------SYDOE            CREATION-------1994.129
        RELEASE----------2                EXPIRATION-----1994.365
        PROTECTION-PSWD----(NULL)          RACF----------(NO)
    ASSOCIATIONS
        DATA-----SYDOE.CUSTOMER.MASTER.DATA
        INDEX----SYDOE.CUSTOMER.MASTER.INDEX

DATA ------- SYDOE.CUSTOMER.MASTER.DATA
    IN-CAT --- ICFCAT.VSTOR02
    HISTORY
        OWNER-IDENT------(NULL)            CREATION-------1994.129
        RELEASE----------2                EXPIRATION-----1994.365
        PROTECTION-PSWD----(NULL)          RACF----------(NO)
    ASSOCIATIONS
        CLUSTER-SYDOE.CUSTOMER.MASTER
    ATTRIBUTES
        KEYLEN----------6     AVGLRECL-------100     BUFSPACE-------9728     CISIZE-------4096
        RKP-------------0     MAXLRECL-------200     EXCPEXIT------(NULL)     CI/CA---------168
        SHROPTNS(2,3)  RECOVERY  UNIQUE    NOERASE   INDEXED   NOWRITECHK    IMBED   NOREPLICAT
        UNORDERED      NOREUSE  NONSPANNED
    STATISTICS
        REC-TOTAL-------3     SPLITS-CI--------0     EXCPS-----------15
        REC-DELETED-----0     SPLITS-CA--------0     EXTENTS----------1
        REC-INSERTED----0     FREESPACE-%CI----0     SYSTEM-TIMESTAMP:
        REC-UPDATED-----0     FREESPACE-%CA----0         X'A940C5A06C47E734'
        REC-RETRIEVED---0     FREESPC-BYTES--684032
    ALLOCATION
        SPACE-TYPE----CYLINDER  HI-ALLOC-RBA----688128   HI-ALLOC-RBA----688128
        SPACE-PRI--------1      HI-USED-RBA-----688128   HI-USED-RBA-----688128
        SPACE-SEC--------1
    VOLUME
        VOLSER-------TSO001     PHYREC-SIZE----4096
        DEVTYPE------X'3010200F'  PHYRECS/TRK----12
        VOLFLAG------PRIME     TRACKS/CA-------15        TRACKS----------15
        EXTENTS:
        LOW-CCHH----X'016A0000'   LOW-RBA---------0       EXTENT-NUMBER----1
        HIGH-CCHH---X'016A000E'   HIGH-RBA---688127       EXTENT-TYPE----X'00'
```

Figure 10-12 Output from a LISTCAT command with the ALL parameter (part 1 of 2)

```
IDCAMS  SYSTEM  SERVICES                                   TIME: 20:48:59      05/09/94      PAGE    9

INDEX ------ SYDOE.CUSTOMER.MASTER.INDEX
   IN-CAT -- ICFCAT.VSTOR02
   HISTORY
      OWNER-IDENT-----(NULL)        CREATION------1994.129
      RELEASE----------2           EXPIRATION----1994.365
      PROTECTION-PSWD--(NULL)       RACF----------(NO)
   ASSOCIATIONS
      CLUSTER--SYDOE.CUSTOMER.MASTER
   ATTRIBUTES
      KEYLEN-----------6           AVGLRECL--------0         BUFSPACE--------0          CISIZE-------1536
      RKP--------------0           MAXLRECL-----1529         EXCPEXIT----(NULL)         CI/CA----------26
      SHROPTNS(2,3)  RECOVERY  UNIQUE        NOERASE         NOWRITECHK  IMBED          NOREPLICAT  UNORDERED
      NOREUSE
   STATISTICS
      REC-TOTAL--------1           SPLITS-CI-------0         EXCPS----------4           INDEX:
      REC-DELETED------0           SPLITS-CA-------0         EXTENTS--------2             LEVELS----------1
      REC-INSERTED-----0           FREESPACE-%CI---0         SYSTEM-TIMESTAMP:            ENTRIES/SECT---12
      REC-UPDATED------0           FREESPACE-%CA---0              X'A94OC5A06C47E734'     SEQ-SET-RBA--39936
      REC-RETRIEVED----0           FREESPC-BYTES-39936                                   HI-LEVEL-RBA-39936
   ALLOCATION
      SPACE-TYPE----TRACK          HI-ALLOC-RBA-41472
      SPACE-PRI--------1           HI-USED-RBA--41472
      SPACE-SEC--------1
   VOLUME
      VOLSER------TS0001           PHYREC-SIZE--1536         HI-ALLOC-RBA-39936         EXTENT-NUMBER----1
      DEVTYPE--X'3010200F'         PHYRECS/TRK----26         HI-USED-RBA-----0          EXTENT-TYPE--X'00'
      VOLFLAG----PRIME             TRACKS/CA-------1
      EXTENTS:
         LOW-CCHH---X'0138000B'    LOW-RBA---------0
         HIGH-CCHH--X'0138000B'    HIGH-RBA----39935
   VOLUME
      VOLSER------TS0001           PHYREC-SIZE--1536         HI-ALLOC-RBA-41472         EXTENT-NUMBER----1
      DEVTYPE--X'3010200F'         PHYRECS/TRK----26         HI-USED-RBA--41472         EXTENT-TYPE--X'80'
      VOLFLAG----PRIME             TRACKS/CA------15
      EXTENTS:
         LOW-CCHH---X'016A0000'    LOW-RBA-----39936         TRACKS---------15
         HIGH-CCHH--X'016A000E'    HIGH-RBA----41471
```

Figure 10-12 Output from a LISTCAT command with the ALL parameter (part 2 of 2)

code one or more vol-sers in the ENTRIES parameter. For example, suppose you code this command:

```
LISTCAT ENTRIES(TSO001) -
        SPACE
```

Here, AMS lists information about all the spaces on the volume named TSO001.

Second, you'll probably need to use the CATALOG parameter or a job or step catalog to identify the catalog that owns the space. If you don't, AMS uses the master catalog. You can't rely on the high-level qualifier of the name you code in the ENTRIES parameter, because vol-sers don't follow that naming convention.

Finally, the LISTCAT output for a space includes a listing of the names of the data sets contained in the space. That information can be useful if you want to delete a space.

The ALTER command

With the ALTER command, shown in figure 10-13, you can change a VSAM file's name, volume allocation, and other characteristics assigned to the file when you defined it. Besides the parameters shown in figure 10-13, you can also code many DEFINE parameters on the ALTER command. For example, you can use an ALTER command to change the FREESPACE specification for a key-sequenced data set. Or, you can change a file's SHAREOPTIONS settings. Unfortunately, there are many restrictions on how you can code those parameters. As a result, I won't describe them in detail here. Instead, I suggest you consult the appropriate AMS reference manual to see how to use those parameters on your system when you need to.

Figure 10-14 gives three examples of the ALTER command. As I describe how to use ALTER to change a file's name, volume allocation, and DEFINE parameters, you should refer to the examples in this figure.

How to change a file's name   Example 1 in figure 10-14 shows how to change a VSAM file's name. To do that, you code two parameters on the ALTER command: the name of the existing VSAM file and, in the NEWNAME parameter, the new name for the file. The file you're renaming can be a cluster, component, alternate index, path, or catalog.

How to change a file's volume allocation   When you define a VSAM file, you specify at least one volume where space for the file can be allocated. If you specify more volumes than are necessary to

The ALTER command

```
ALTER   entry-name[/password]
    [ CATALOG(name[/password]) ]
    [ NEWNAME(entry-name) ]
    [ ADDVOLUMES(vol-ser...) ]
    [ REMOVEVOLUMES(vol-ser...) ]
```

Explanation

entry-name[/password]	Specifies the name and, if required, password of the object whose catalog entry is to be altered.
CATALOG(name[/password])	Identifies the catalog that contains the object to be altered. Required only if the catalog can't be located by the standard search sequence.
NEWNAME(entry-name)	Specifies a new entry name for the entry.
ADDVOLUMES(vol-ser...)	Adds the specified volumes to the list of volumes where space may be allocated to the object.
REMOVEVOLUMES(vol-ser...)	Removes the specified volumes from the list of volumes where space may be allocated to the object. Ignored if space has already been allocated on the specified volumes.

Figure 10-13   The ALTER command

hold the file, the extra volumes are available for future expansion of the file. With the ADDVOLUMES and REMOVEVOLUMES parameters of the ALTER command, you can add or remove volumes from the list of volumes.

To illustrate, consider example 2 in figure 10-14. Here, I've decided to change the volumes for a data component named SYDOE.CUSTOMER.MASTER.DATA. Rather than using VOL281 and VOL282, I want the file to use VOL291 and VOL292, if necessary. So, I listed the volumes I want dropped in the REMOVE-VOLUMES parameter. Notice that I specified the data component as the entry to be altered; you can't code ADDVOLUMES or REMOVEVOLUMES for the cluster itself.

One restriction of the REMOVEVOLUMES parameter is that you can not remove a volume if the file already has space allocated for it on that volume. To see the volumes where a file has space allocated, issue a LISTCAT command with the ALLOCATION or ALL parameter.

How to change other DEFINE attributes   Example 3 in figure 10-14 shows how to change other DEFINE attributes for VSAM files. Here, I changed the free space allocation for a KSDS cluster. Notice that the

Example 1

```
ALTER SYDOE.CUSTOMER.MASTER      -
      NEWNAME(SYDOE.CUSTMAST)
```

Change the file name of SYDOE.CUSTOMER.MASTER to SYDOE.CUSTMAST.

Example 2

```
ALTER SYDOE.CUSTOMER.MASTER.DATA   -
      ADDVOLUMES(VOL291 VOL292)    -
      REMOVEVOLUMES(VOL281 VOL282)
```

Add VOL291 and VOL292 to the list of eligible volumes for
SYDOE.CUSTOMER.MASTER.DATA and remove VOL281 and VOL282.

Example 3

```
ALTER SYDOE.CUSTOMER.MASTER.DATA   -
      FREESPACE(10 10)
```

Change the free space specification for SYDOE.CUSTOMER.MASTER.DATA to
(10 10).

Figure 10-14   Examples of the ALTER command

entry name I coded on the ALTER command is the name of the file's
data component, not the cluster itself. That's because the FREESPACE
parameter applies to a file's data component only, even though you can
code it at the CLUSTER or DATA level of the DEFINE CLUSTER
command. In any event, there are many other DEFINE parameters you
can change with the ALTER command. As I've already mentioned, you
can find out about them in your AMS reference manual.

The DELETE command

You use the DELETE command to remove entries from a VSAM
catalog. Its format, shown in figure 10-15, is simple. To delete a
VSAM file, all you normally need to include on the DELETE command is the name of the file. To delete more than one file, list the
names in parentheses. If you want to delete the file regardless of
whether its retention period has expired, code PURGE as well. The
CATALOG parameter lets you specify the catalog that owns the file
to be deleted. If you omit it, AMS uses the high-level qualifier of the
file name or the step, job, or master catalog.

   You can use a generic name in a DELETE command by replacing
one level of the entry name with an asterisk, like this:

```
DELETE SYDOE.CUSTOMER.*
```

The DELETE command

```
DELETE { entry-name[/password]          }
        { (entry-name[/password]...)     }
        [ CATALOG(name[/password]) ]
        [ entry-type ]
        [ PURGE | NOPURGE ]
        [ ERASE | NOERASE ]
```

Explanation

entry-name[/password] (entry-name[/password]...)	Specifies the name and password of the entry or entries to be deleted. If you specify more than one entry name, you must enclose the list in parentheses. To delete a space, specify a vol-ser as the entry name.
CATALOG(name[/password])	Specifies the name and password of the catalog that owns the entries to be deleted. Required only if the correct catalog can't be found using the standard search sequence.
entry-type	Specifies that only entries of the listed types should be deleted. The valid entry types are the same as for the LISTCAT command.
PURGE NOPURGE	PURGE means that an object should be deleted even if its retention period has not expired. NOPURGE means to delete entries only if their retention periods have expired. NOPURGE is the default.
ERASE NOERASE	ERASE means that the data component of a cluster or alternate index should be erased (overwritten with binary zeros). NOERASE means that the data component should not be erased. NOERASE is the default.

Figure 10-15   The DELETE command

Here, all entries whose names consist of three levels, with the first two levels being SYDOE.CUSTOMER, will be deleted. That includes names like SYDOE. CUSTOMER.MASTER and SYDOE.CUS-TOMER.HISTORY.

Although DELETE removes catalog records for an entry, it leaves the file itself on the disk until it's overwritten by another file. You can cause AMS to overwrite the data in a file you delete by coding the ERASE option on the DELETE command. Then, AMS writes binary zeros over the entire file. That way, once the file is deleted, it can't be accessed under any circumstances. Bear in mind, however, that erasing a file can take a lot of time. So use ERASE only when the file contains sensitive data that actually should be erased when deleted.

Example 1

```
DELETE SYDOE.CUSTOMER.MASTER -
       PURGE
```

Delete SYDOE.CUSTOMER.MASTER, whether or not it is expired.

Example 2

```
DELETE (SYDOE.CUSTOMER.MASTER        -
        SYDOE.CUSTMAST.DISTRICT AIX  -
        SYDOE.CUSTMAST.DISTRICT.PATH)
```

Delete the three named files.

Example 3

```
DELETE SYDOE.CUSTMAST.*.AIX  -
       ALTERNATEINDEX
```

Delete all alternate indexes whose names match the generic specification SYDOE.CUSTMAST.*.AIX.

Figure 10-16   Examples of the DELETE command

The entry-type parameter lets you limit the delete operation to certain types of entries. The values you can code here are the same as the entry types you can code in a LISTCAT command. Normally, you don't need to specify an entry type since the names you specify indicate which entries you want deleted. But if you use a generic name, you might want to specify that just entries of certain types should be deleted.

Figure 10-16 shows three examples of the DELETE command. In example 1, I deleted a single file named SYDOE.CUSTOMER.MASTER. Because I specified the PURGE parameter, this file will be deleted whether or not its expiration date has arrived.

Examples 2 and 3 show how to delete several files with a single DELETE command. In example 2, I listed three names on the command. In example 3, I used a generic file name to delete all alternate indexes whose names follow the form SYDOE.CUSTOMER.*.AIX.

How to use AMS to copy and print files

Besides defining files and performing catalog maintenance functions, you'll often use AMS to print and copy files. To do that, you use the PRINT and REPRO commands. The format of both commands is similar. I'll cover PRINT first because it's a bit simpler than REPRO.

The PRINT command

Figure 10-17 gives the format of the PRINT command. You must always code at least one parameter, INFILE or INDATASET, to identify the file you want to print. If you code INFILE, you specify the ddname of a file identified in the JCL with a DD statement. If you code INDATASET, you supply the VSAM file name, and you don't have to provide a DD statement for the file; VSAM uses dynamic allocation to allocate the data set.

The CHARACTER, HEX, and DUMP parameters let you specify the format of the printed output. If you specify CHARACTER, AMS prints the actual characters contained in each file record. Many files, however, contain unprintable characters like packed-decimal fields. For those files, you should specify HEX or DUMP. HEX prints the hexadecimal value of each byte in the file's records, and DUMP prints both the character and the hex values. If you omit CHARAC-TER, HEX, and DUMP, the default format is DUMP.

The next two sets of parameters let you select specific records to be printed. If you don't specify otherwise, AMS starts printing with the first record in the data set. If you don't want to start printing at the beginning of the data set, you can code SKIP, FROMKEY, FROMNUMBER, or FROMADDRESS. The SKIP parameter lets you bypass a specified number of records. So to begin printing with the 50th record, code SKIP(49). You can use SKIP with any type of file organization. For a KSDS, you can code FROMKEY with the key value of the first record you want to process. (If the key contains commas, semicolons, blanks, parentheses, or slashes, you must code the key between apostrophes.) For an RRDS, you can use the FROMNUMBER parameter to specify the relative record number of the first record you want printed. And, for an ESDS or a KSDS, you can specify a relative byte address in the FROMADDRESS parameter.

Printing continues until AMS reaches the end of the data set unless you code COUNT, TOKEY, TONUMBER, or TOADDRESS to specify where printing should end. COUNT indicates how many

The PRINT command

```
PRINT    { INDATASET(entry-name[/password]) }
         { INFILE(ddname[/password])         }

         [{ CHARACTER }]
         [{ HEX       }]
         [{ DUMP      }]

          { SKIP(count)          }
         [{ FROMKEY(key)         }]
         [{ FROMNUMBER(number)   }]
          { FROMADDRESS(address) }

          { COUNT(count)      }
         [{ TOKEY(key)        }]
         [{ TONUMBER(number)  }]
          { TOADDRESS(address) }
```

Explanation

INDATASET(entry-name[/password])
INFILE(ddname[/password])

INDATASET specifies the file name of the VSAM file to be printed. INFILE specifies the name of a DD statement that identifies the file.

CHARACTER
HEX
DUMP

Specifies the format of the output. CHARACTER and HEX print the data in character or hex format. DUMP prints data in both character and hex format. DUMP is the default.

SKIP(count)
FROMKEY(key)
FROMNUMBER(number)
FROMADDRESS(address)

Specifies the first record of the file to be printed. For *count*, specify a number of records to be skipped before the print operation begins. Valid for all file types. For *key*, specify the value of the key where the print operation should begin. Valid only when printing a KSDS or an ISAM file. For *number*, specify the relative record number where the print operation should begin. Valid only when printing an RRDS. For *address*, specify the RBA of the first record to be printed. Valid only when printing a KSDS or ESDS.

COUNT(count)
TOKEY(key)
TONUMBER(number)
TOADDRESS(address)

Specifies the last record of the file to be printed. For *count*, specify a numeric value to indicate the number of records to be printed. Valid for all file types. For *key*, specify the value of the key where the print operation should end. Valid only when printing a KSDS or an ISAM file. For *number*, specify the relative record number where the print operation should end. Valid only when printing an RRDS. For *address*, specify an RBA that lies within the last record to be printed. Valid only when printing a KSDS or ESDS.

Figure 10-17   The PRINT command

Example 1

```
PRINT INDATASET(SYDOE.CUSTOMER.MASTER)    -
      CHARACTER                           -
      SKIP(28)                            -
      COUNT(3)
```

Print records 29, 30, and 31 in character format.

Example 2

```
PRINT INDATASET(SYDOE.CUSTOMER.MASTER)    -
      HEX                                 -
      SKIP(28)                            -
      COUNT(3)
```

Print records 29, 30, and 31 in hex format.

Example 3

```
PRINT INDATASET(SYDOE.CUSTOMER.MASTER)    -
      DUMP                                -
      SKIP(28)                            -
      COUNT(3)
```

Print records 29, 30, and 31 in dump format.

Figure 10-18   Examples of the PRINT command

records should be processed; it's valid for any type of file. For a KSDS, you can use TOKEY to indicate where in the file to stop printing. For an RRDS, you can use TONUMBER. And for an ESDS or KSDS, you can use TOADDRESS.

Figure 10-18 presents three PRINT commands that print a customer master file. In each case, I coded SKIP(28) to bypass the first 28 records and COUNT(3) to print only three records. As a result, these jobs print the 29th, 30th, and 31st records in the file. Each PRINT command in figure 10-18 specifies a different print format: CHARACTER, HEX, and DUMP. Figures 10-19, 10-20, and 10-21 show the output produced by each PRINT command.

```
IDCAMS   SYSTEM  SERVICES

LISTING  OF  DATA  SET  -SYDOE.CUSTOMER.MASTER

KEY  OF  RECORD  -  287760
287760JOHN WARDS AND ASSOC5600 N CLARKE          CHICAGO     IL603002027   010200

KEY  OF  RECORD  -  295562
295562NATIONAL INDUSTRIES 3879 NE FOOTE     WASHINGTON DC200190003   010210

KEY  OF  RECORD  -  295732
295732UNIVERSAL SERVICES   2115  FULTON RD     POMONA     CA917680223   010220

IDC0005I NUMBER  OF  RECORDS  PROCESSED  WAS  3

IDC0001I FUNCTION COMPLETED, HIGHEST CONDITION CODE WAS 0
```

Figure 10-19   Output produced by the PRINT command in example 1 of figure 10-18 (CHARACTER format)

```
IDCAMS  SYSTEM  SERVICES

LISTING OF DATA SET -SYDOE.CUSTOMER.MASTER

KEY OF RECORD - F2F8F7F7F6F0
F2F8F7F7F6F0D1D6C8D540E6C1D9C4E240C1E2E2D6C3F5F6F0F0D540C3D3C1D9D2C540404040404040C3C8C9C3C1C7D6404040C9
D3F6F0F3F0F2F0F74040F0F1F0F2F0F04040

KEY OF RECORD - F2F9F5F5F6F2
F2F9F5F5F6F2D5C1E3C9D6D5C1D340C9D5C4E4E2E3D9C9C5E240F3F8F7F940D5C540C6D6D6E3C540404040404040404040E6C1E2C8C9D5C7E3D6D540C4
C3F2F0F0F1F9F0F0F3F04040F0F1F0F2F1F04040

KEY OF RECORD - F2F9F5F7F3F2
F2F9F5F7F3F2E4D5C9E5C5D9E2C1D340E2C5D9E5C9C3C5E24040F2F1F1F540C6E4D3E3D6D540D9C44040404040404040407D6D4D6D5C14040404040C3
C1F9F1F7F6F8F0F2F2F34040F0F1F0F2F2F04040

IDC0005I NUMBER OF RECORDS PROCESSED WAS 3

IDC0001I FUNCTION COMPLETED, HIGHEST CONDITION CODE WAS 0
```

Figure 10-20 Output produced by the PRINT command in example 2 of figure 10-18 (HEX format)

```
IDCAMS  SYSTEM  SERVICES


LISTING OF DATA SET -SYDOE.CUSTOMER.MASTER

KEY OF RECORD - F2F8F7F7F6F0
000000  F2F8F7F7 F6F0D1D6 C8D540E6 C1D9C4E2  40C1D5C4 40C1E2E2 D6C3F5F6 F0F040D5  *287760JOHN WARDS AND ASSOC5600 N*
000020  40C3D3C1 D9D2C540 40404040 40404040  C3C8C9C3 C1C7D640 40404040 D3F6F0F3  * CLARKE      CHICAGO    IL603*
000040  F0F0F2F0 F2F74040 F0F1F0F2 F0F04040                                      *002027 010200              *

KEY OF RECORD - F2F9F5F5F6F2
000000  F2F9F5F5 F6F2D5C1 E3C9D6D5 C1D340C9  D5C4E4E2 E3D9C9C5 E240F3F8 F7F940D5  *295562NATIONAL INDUSTRIES 3879 N*
000020  C540C6D6 D6E3C540 40404040 40404040  E6C1E2C8 C9D5C7E3 D6D540C4 C3F2F0F0  *E FOOTE      WASHINGTON DC200*
000040  F1F9F0F0 F0F34040 F0F1F0F2 F1F04040                                      *190003 010210              *

KEY OF RECORD - F2F9F5F7F3F2
000000  F2F9F5F7 F3F2E4D5 C9E5C5D9 E2C1D340  E2C5D9E5 C9C3C5E2 4040F2F1 F1F540C6  *295732UNIVERSAL SERVICES 2115 F*
000020  E4D3E3D6 D540D9C4 40404040 40404040  D7D6D4D6 D5C14040 40404040 C1F9F1F7  *ULTON RD     POMONA     CA917*
000040  F6F8F0F2 F2F34040 F0F1F0F2 F2F04040                                      *680223 010220              *


IDC0005I NUMBER OF RECORDS PROCESSED WAS 3

IDC0001I FUNCTION COMPLETED, HIGHEST CONDITION CODE WAS 0
```

Figure 10-21 Output produced by the PRINT command in example 3 of figure 10-18 (DUMP format)

The REPRO command

```
REPRO       { INDATASET(entry-name[/password]) }
            { INFILE(ddname[/password])        }

            { OUTDATASET(entry-name[/password]) }
            { OUTFILE(ddname[/password])        }

              ┌ SKIP(count)            ┐
            [ { FROMKEY(key)           } ]
              { FROMNUMBER(number)     }
              └ FROMADDRESS(address)   ┘

              ┌ COUNT(count)           ┐
            [ { TOKEY(key)             } ]
              { TONUMBER(number)       }
              └ TOADDRESS(address)     ┘

            [ REUSE  |  NOREUSE ]

            [ REPLACE  |  NOREPLACE ]
```

Figure 10-22   The REPRO command (part 1 of 2)

The REPRO command

You use the REPRO command to copy the contents of a data set into
another data set. Figure 10-22 gives the format of the REPRO command. Its format is similar to the PRINT command, with two important differences. First, you must specify an output file as well as an
input file. You do that by coding the OUTFILE or OUTDATASET
parameter. If you code OUTFILE, you must specify the name of a
DD statement that identifies the file. If you code OUTDATASET,
you provide the VSAM file name. Second, the REPRO command
doesn't support the CHARACTER/HEX/DUMP parameters.

The output file you specify in a REPRO command must exist. In
other words, you must define the output file before you can copy
records to it. If the output file is empty, VSAM processes the file in
load mode, and records are copied one by one from the input file to
the output file. If the output file contains records when the REPRO
command starts, records from the input file are merged with the
records in the output file depending on the file's organization. For
an ESDS, records are added at the end of the output file. For an

Explanation

INDATASET(entry-name[/password]) INFILE(ddname[/password])	INDATASET specifies the name of the data set to be copied. INFILE specifies the name of a DD statement that identifies the file to be copied.
OUTDATASET(entry-name[/password]) OUTFILE(ddname[/password])	OUTDATASET specifies the name of the data set where the input file is to be copied. OUTFILE specifies the name of a DD statement that identifies the file where the input file is to be copied.
SKIP(count) FROMKEY(key) FROMNUMBER(number) FROMADDRESS(address)	Specifies the first record of the file to be copied. For *count*, specify a numeric value to indicate the number of records to be skipped before the copy operation begins. Valid for all file types. For *key*, specify the value of the key where the copy operation should begin. Valid only when copying a KSDS or an ISAM file. For *number*, specify the relative record number where the copy operation should begin. Valid only when copying an RRDS. For *address*, specify the RBA of the first record to be copied. Valid only when copying a KSDS or ESDS.
COUNT(count) TOKEY(key) TONUMBER(number) TOADDRESS(address)	Specifies the last record of the file to be copied. For *count*, specify a numeric value to indicate the number of records to be copied. Valid for all file types. For *key*, specify the value of the key where the copy operation should end. Valid only when copying a KSDS or an ISAM file. For *number*, specify the relative record number where the copy operation should end. Valid only when copying an RRDS. For *address*, specify an RBA that lies within the last record to be copied. Valid only when copying a KSDS or ESDS.
REUSE <u>NOREUSE</u>	REUSE specifies that the output file should be reset if it is reusable. NOREUSE specifies that a reusable output file should not be reused. NOREUSE is the default.
REPLACE <u>NOREPLACE</u>	Specifies how duplicate records should be handled. If you specify REPLACE, duplicate records are replaced; if you specify NOREPLACE, duplicates are treated as errors. NOREPLACE is the default.

Figure 10-22   The REPRO command (part 2 of 2)

RRDS or KSDS, records are added at the correct positions based on relative record numbers or key values. Duplicates are handled according to how you code the REPLACE option. If you specify REPLACE, duplicates in the input file replace existing records in the output file; if you specify NOREPLACE, they do not.

Example 1

```
REPRO INDATASET(MMA2.CUSTOMER.MASTER) -
      OUTDATASET(MMA2.CUSTOMER.MASTER.COPY)
```

> Copy MMA2.CUSTOMER.MASTER to MMA2.CUSTOMER.MASTER.COPY.

Example 2

```
REPRO INFILE(CUSTMAST)   -
      OUTFILE(CUSTCOPY)
```

> Copy the data set identified by the CUSTMAST DD statement to the data set identified by the CUSTCOPY DD statement.

Example 3

```
REPRO INFILE(CUSTMAST)   -
      OUTFILE(CUSTCOPY)  -
      COUNT(1000)
```

> Copy the first 1000 records of the data set identified by the CUSTMAST DD statement to the data set identified by the CUSTCOPY DD statement.

Figure 10-23   Examples of the REPRO command

The REUSE parameter lets you specify that the file should be loaded even though it already contains records. When you specify REUSE, VSAM resets the file's high-used RBA field to zero, effectively deleting all records in the file. You can specify REUSE only for files you defined with the REUSE attribute.

You can use the SKIP, FROMKEY, FROMNUMBER, and FROMADDRESS parameters along with the COUNT, TOKEY, TONUMBER, and TOADDRESS parameters to limit the number of records copied. You code these parameters just as you do for a PRINT command.

If you wish, the input and output files can be different types of files. In other words, you can copy an ESDS input file to an RRDS output file. You can use non-VSAM files, too. So, you can copy an ISAM file to a KSDS. The only restriction on the combination of input and output file types is that you can't specify an ISAM file as the output file.

Figure 10-23 shows three examples of the REPRO command. In example 1, I used the INDATASET and OUTDATASET parameters to identify the input and output files; no DD statements are required because VSAM uses dynamic allocation to allocate the data sets. In example 2, I used the INFILE and OUTFILE parameters; DD statements are required to allocate the data sets. In example 3, I used the COUNT parameter to limit the copy operation to 1,000 records.

Discussion

In this chapter, I've presented a variety of AMS commands, some of which you'll use more often than others. Still, it's good to be familiar with all of the commands in this chapter so that you'll know which commands to use in many situations.

Terminology

functional commands	cross-region share option
modal commands	cross-system share option
verb	generic entry name
parameters	

Objectives

1. Code an AMS DEFINE CLUSTER job to define a VSAM file.

2. Code an AMS LISTCAT job to list catalog entries.

3. Code an AMS ALTER job to change file attributes.

4. Code an AMS DELETE job to delete a catalog entry.

5. Code an AMS PRINT job to print a file. The print operation may or may not require all of the file's records, and the output may be printed in character format, hex format, or both.

6. Code an AMS REPRO job to copy a file. The copy operation may or may not require all of the file's records.

Exercises

1. Code a DEFINE CLUSTER command to create a new VSAM data set named X401.PROJ.MASTER on a volume named TSO001. The file is a key-sequenced data set with 240-byte records and keys in the first 9 bytes of each record. The file will require 30 cylinders of primary space and 15 cylinders of secondary space. Assign the names X401.PROJ.MASTER.DATA and X401.PROJ.MASTER.INDEX to the data and index components.

2. Code an AMS LISTCAT job to list all VSAM data sets that begin with the high-level qualifier X401.

3. Code an AMS ALTER job to change the SHAREOPTIONS parameter for the file defined in exercise 1 to SHAREOPTIONS (2, 3).

4. Code an AMS PRINT job to print the file defined in exercise 1 in both character and hex format.

5. Code an AMS REPRO job to copy the first 50 records of the file defined in exercise 1 to a similarly defined file named X401.PROJ.TEST.

6. Code an AMS DELETE job to delete the file defined in exercise 1.

Section 4

Non-VSAM data management

In chapters 5 and 6, you learned how to use many MVS facilities that let you manage non-VSAM files. The four chapters in this section expand on what you've learned. Chapter 11 presents the special considerations you'll encounter when you process data sets that reside on tape rather than DASD volumes. Chapter 12 shows you how to use generation data groups, which let you maintain groups of chronologically related data sets. And chapters 13 and 14 show you how to use two access methods—ISAM and BDAM—that, although replaced by VSAM, are still sometimes used. The four chapters in this section are independent of one another, so you can study them in any order you wish.

Chapter 11

How to manage tape data sets

Today, more and more of the crucial data sets on a computer system are accessed directly by online applications such as CICS and IMS. Those data sets are most likely VSAM files stored in Key-Sequenced Data Set (KSDS) format. Despite the widespread use of directly-accessed files and online applications, however, there are still many applications for which data is best accessed sequentially. For example, many applications capture transactions as they enter the system, recording them in sequential data sets so they can be posted against master files later. And applications that post transactions against master files immediately as the transactions enter the system usually keep a record, or journal, of each transaction. Those journals are usually maintained in sequential data sets. Depending on the requirements of the application, these sequential data sets might be stored on DASD or tape.

In this chapter, you'll learn how to process sequential data sets that reside on tape. First, I'll explain how tape data sets are stored. Then, I'll describe the DD statement parameters that apply to tape processing. After that, I'll show you some examples of typical DD statements for tape files.

Tape file, volume, and label concepts

In chapter 3, you learned about the basic arrangement of labels on a tape volume. Each volume begins with a *volume label*, which identifies the volume by providing the volume's serial number. Following the volume label is a *file-header label*, which identifies a file by providing its file name and other characteristics. The actual records of the file follow the file's header label, and after the data records comes the *end-of-file label*, sometimes called a *file-trailer label*.

You'll often see the volume label referred to as the *VOL1 label*; that's because VOL1 is stored in the first four characters of a standard volume label. Similarly, header labels are often called *HDR1 labels*, and end-of-file labels are called *EOF1 labels*. (As you'll see later in this chapter, a tape can also have HDR2 and EOF2 labels. But that's not important at this point.)

Actually, the arrangement of labels on a particular tape volume can be more complicated than what I've just described. For example, although most tape volumes contain just one file, some tape volumes contain several files. Each file on these *multi-file volumes* is preceded by a header label and followed by a trailer label. And some files are too large to be contained on a single tape volume. For these *multi-volume files*, an *end-of-volume label* (or *EOV1 label*) replaces the trailer label for each volume except the last.

Figure 11-1 shows the arrangement of labels and data for single-file volumes, multi-volume files, and multi-file volumes. If you'll study this figure for a moment, I think the relationships among labels, files, and volumes, will be clear. (The shading in figure 11-1 highlights the labels.)

One other factor you need to know about is that the format used to record file labels can vary from one tape to another. On a single volume, or on all volumes of a multi-volume file, however, all labels must be recorded using the same format. In most cases, that format is the *IBM standard label* format. Some tapes, however, use a non-IBM label format called the *ISO/ANSI standard label* format. Some tapes have no labels at all; they're called *unlabelled tapes*. And, an installation can create its own *non-standard label* format. But that's rare.

DD statement parameters for tape files

Sequential files on tape are processed in much the same way as sequential files on DASD. In fact, the same access method (QSAM) is used. From the application program's viewpoint, it doesn't matter much if a sequential data set resides on tape or DASD; QSAM shelters the application program from that consideration. However, when you code a DD statement to allocate a tape file, you may have to make specifications that identify characteristics unique to tape files.

In chapter 5, you learned how to code the UNIT and VOLUME parameters for single-volume DASD files. The coding for single-volume tape files is almost identical. In the UNIT parameter, you

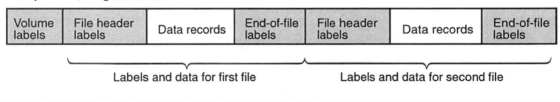

Single file, single volume

| Volume labels | File header labels | Data records | End-of-file labels | Unused |

Single file, multiple volumes

| Volume labels | File header labels | Data records | End-of-volume labels |

| Volume labels | File header labels | Data records | End-of-volume labels |

| Volume labels | File header labels | Data records | End-of-volume labels |

| Volume labels | File header labels | Data records | End-of-file labels | Unused |

Multiple files, single volume

| Volume labels | File header labels | Data records | End-of-file labels | File header labels | Data records | End-of-file labels |

Labels and data for first file   Labels and data for second file

Figure 11-1   Basic arrangements of labels and data on tape volumes

identify a tape unit using a generic name (like 3420) or group name (like TAPE), and in the VOLUME parameter, you name the tape's volume serial number. For a non-specific volume request, you can omit the VOLUME parameter; MVS will select a tape volume for you. And to retrieve a cataloged tape data set, you can omit both the UNIT and VOLUME parameters; MVS obtains the unit and volume information from the catalog.

The coding I've just described is for relatively simple tape processing. Now, I'll describe additional DD statement parameters and subparameters that let you take advantage of more advanced tape processing features. First, I'll describe a new JCL parameter,

LABEL, that lets you specify information related to a tape volume's labels. Next, I'll describe subparameters of the UNIT and VOLUME parameters that let you control how tape volumes are mounted and removed. Strictly speaking, the UNIT and VOLUME subparameters I'll present can apply to DASD data sets too, provided the DASD data sets reside on devices that have removable volumes. However, since most modern DASD units have fixed (permanently-resident) volumes, those subparameters of the UNIT and VOLUME parameters apply mostly to tape processing. Finally, I'll describe three DCB parameter options that relate directly to tape processing.

The LABEL parameter

When you code the DD statement for a data set that resides on tape, you may or may not need to include a LABEL parameter depending on the format of the tape and how you want to process it. Figure 11-2 shows the format of the DD statement LABEL parameter. It provides three basic functions: (1) it lets you specify which data set of a multi-file tape volume you want to process; (2) it indicates what format is used to record the tape volume's labels; and (3) it supplies a retention period that indicates how long the file should be considered current.

How to specify the data set sequence number   Although most tape volumes contain just one data set, some tapes contain two or more separate data sets. To access a file other than the first file on a tape, you have to supply the *data set sequence number* as the first positional subparameter in a LABEL parameter. The sequence number for the first data set on the volume is 1, the sequence number for the second data set is 2, and so on. If the data set is cataloged or passed from a previous job step (that is, if it's a temporary data set), you don't have to code the data set sequence number. That's because MVS can obtain the sequence number from the catalog entry or the passing DD statement. If you omit the data set sequence number for a data set that isn't cataloged or passed from a previous job step, the first data set on the volume is processed (assuming other label information like vol-ser and data set name are correct).

How to specify a label format   The second positional subparameter, label-type, provides the basic function of the LABEL parameter: It specifies the format of the tape's labels. As you know, most tapes use IBM standard labels. That's the assumed format if you specify SL as the label-type subparameter or if you omit the LABEL parameter altogether.

The **LABEL** parameter

```
LABEL=([data-set-sequence][,label-type][,{RETPD=nnnn
                                          EXPDT=yyddd}])
```

Explanation

data-set-sequence	A one- to four-digit number indicating the relative position of the file on the volume. If you omit this subparameter or code 0 or 1, the first data set is processed unless the data set is cataloged or is a passed temporary data set, in which case the data set sequence number is obtained from the catalog or the original DD statement.
label-type	Specifies the format of the tape's labels. Code one of the following:

SL	The tape has standard IBM labels
SUL	The tape has standard IBM labels and user labels
AL	The tape has ISO/ANSI labels
AUL	The tape has ISO/ANSI labels and user labels
NSL	The tape has non-standard labels
NL	The tape has no labels
BLP	The tape may or may not have labels; label processing is bypassed
LTM	This subparameter is the same as BLP, except that MVS skips the leading tape mark on the volume

RETPD=nnnn	Specifies a retention period for the data set; *nnnn* indicates how many days the data set should be retained. The data set can not be deleted by specifying DELETE in the DISP parameter before the retention period has expired.
EXPDT=yyddd	Specifies an expiration date for the data set; *yyddd* specifies the year and day before which the data set can not be deleted by specifying DELETE in the DISP parameter.

Figure 11-2   The LABEL parameter of the DD statement

When you use standard IBM tape labels, you can optionally include your own labels to supplement the information stored in the standard labels. If you do, you should specify SUL as the label-type subparameter to indicate that *user labels* are included along with the standard labels. That's uncommon, though, so you probably won't use SUL.

If you're creating or retrieving a tape that uses ISO/ANSI labels, you must specify AL as the label type. Like IBM labels, ISO/ANSI labels allow optional user labels; you specify AUL if user labels are to be included. Again, however, that's uncommon. So you probably won't use AUL.

To use non-standard labels, your installation must code special processing routines that create and analyze the labels to ensure they are correct. To invoke these label processing routines rather than the standard label processing routines supplied with MVS, you code NSL as the label-type subparameter.

Not all tapes have labels. To process an unlabelled tape, you code NL. Then, the operating system's label processing routines won't be invoked at all, except to make sure that the tape volume that's mounted does not have a standard volume (VOL1) label. If the operator mounts a labelled tape when you request an unlabelled tape by coding NL, MVS rejects the tape and asks the operator to mount another.

BLP, which stands for Bypass Label Processing, is similar to NL. The difference is that when you specify BLP, MVS doesn't check to see if the tape is labelled or unlabelled. BLP is commonly used when initializing blank tapes. If you code NL and the operator mounts a blank tape, MVS spins through the entire reel to make sure there's no VOL1 label. To avoid this, you can code BLP.

If you process a labelled tape and specify BLP in the LABEL parameter, you have to be careful about how you code the data-set-sequence subparameter. That's because each set of labels on the tape is treated as a separate data set. So, the volume header (VOL1) label along with the header labels for the first data set is data set sequence 1. The actual data records for that file are data set sequence 2. The trailer records are data set sequence 3. Header records for the next file are data set sequence 4. And so on. Fortunately, there's seldom reason to process a labelled tape in this way.

When you process an unlabelled tape or bypass label processing for a labelled tape, any data set name you code in a DSNAME parameter is insignificant. That's because MVS never reads the header label to make sure the correct data set is processed. Similarly, MVS never reads a volume label to make sure the correct tape volume is mounted. However, the vol-ser you code in the VOLUME parameter is important, because MVS uses it in the message that tells the operator which volume to mount. Because labels aren't read, you must also be sure to code complete DCB information (data set organization, record and block size, and so on). You can do that either in your program or in the DCB parameter on the DD statement.

The last label-type option, LTM, is the same as BLP except that a special mark called a *tape mark* is assumed to precede the first data set on the volume. Unlabelled and labelled tapes both use tape marks to separate data sets, but unlabelled tapes don't usually have leading tape marks. LTM lets you process tape volumes that do.

Figure 11-3 should help you understand the various label types. Here, I've indicated the expected arrangement of labels, data records, and tape marks for tapes processed using each label type option except NSL. (The arrangement of NSL tapes depends on the installation's routines for handling non-standard labels. It may be similar to SL and AL, or it may be radically different.) Notice that the examples for IBM (SL and SUL) and ISO/ANSI (AL and AUL) are the same. That's because although the detailed format of the labels are different, both label formats have the same basic arrangement of labels, data records, and tape marks.

By the way, if you need to code a label-type subparameter but not a data-set-sequence subparameter, you must code a comma to mark the place of the missing positional subparameter, like this:

```
LABEL=(,SUL)
```

Here, standard and user labels are specified.

How to specify an expiration date or retention period Because of the way tapes are handled under MVS, it's possible for an operator to mistakenly mount an incorrect tape. Usually, MVS catches the mistake. But it is possible that a tape can be mistakenly overwritten with a new data set. To reduce the chances of that happening, tape file header labels provide for *expiration date checking*. When expiration date checking is used, an expiration date is assigned to the file; the file can't be deleted or overwritten until that date has passed. (An unexpired file can be deleted, but special procedures are required to do so. It probably won't happen by accident.)

To assign an expiration date to a file, you specify the EXPDT or RETPD subparameter in the LABEL parameter. EXPDT lets you code a date in the form yyddd, where *yy* represents the year and *ddd* represents the day of the year (1 to 365). The file can't be deleted before that day arrives.

If you use EXPDT to specify an expiration date, you'll have to change the JCL to reflect a new expiration date each time you run your job. In contrast, RETPD lets you specify an expiration date that's relative to the current date. With RETPD, you just indicate the number of days you want the file retained. Then, MVS determines the expiration date by adding that number to the current date. For example, if you specify RETPD=30 on January 1, MVS calculates the expiration date as the 31st day of the current year.

Because RETPD and EXPDT parameters are keyword subparameters, you don't have to worry about leaving extra commas

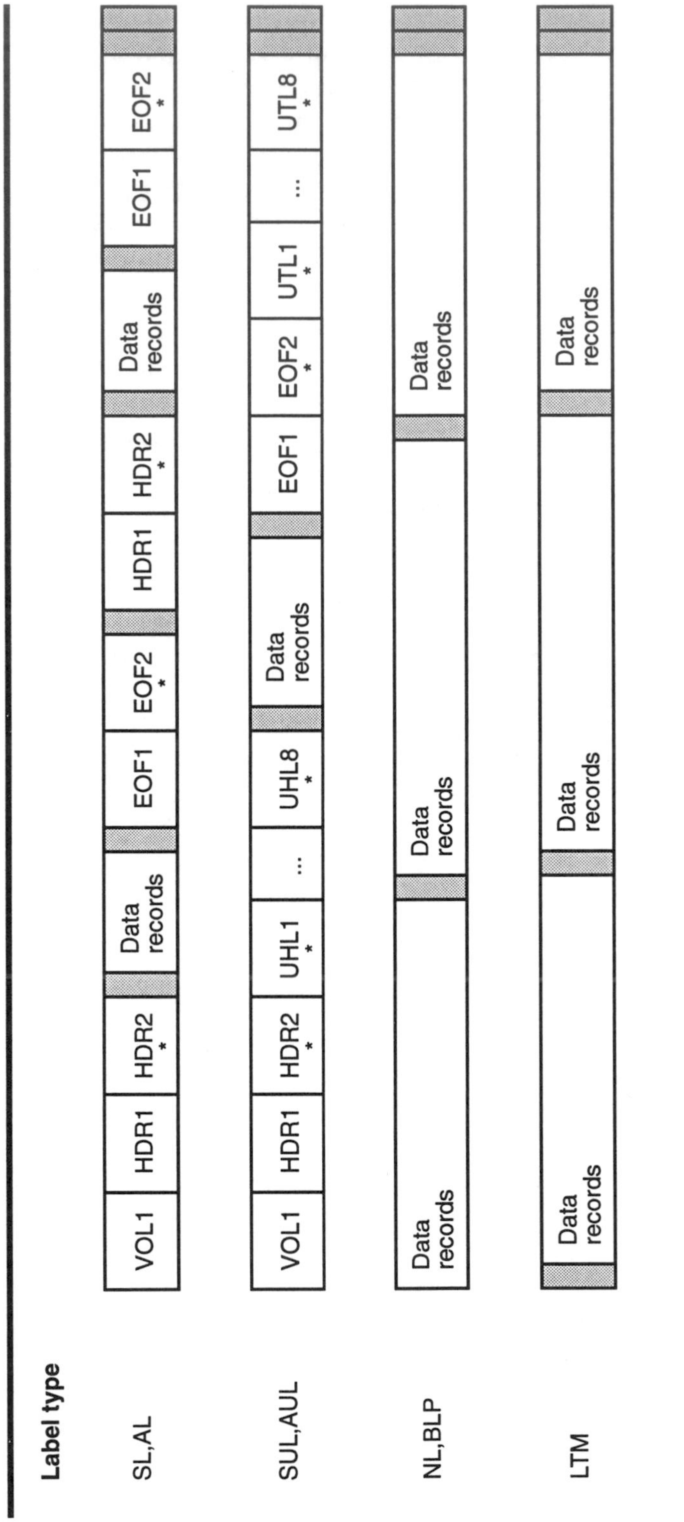

Label type

Note: shading indicates position of tape marks; * indicates an optional label

Figure 11-3   Anticipated positions of labels, data, and tape marks for various label formats

The UNIT parameter

```
{ UNIT=(unit[,count][,DEFER]) }
{ UNIT=AFF=ddname           }
```

Explanation

unit	Specifies the unit as a generic name, group name, or device address.
count	Specifies how many of the requested unit type should be allocated.
DEFER	Specifies that the unit should be allocated when the step is initialized, but the requested volume should not be mounted on the unit until the data set is opened.
AFF	Specifies unit affinity; the unit information is obtained from the specified ddname.

Figure 11-4   The UNIT parameter of the DD statement

before them to mark missing positional subparameters. As a result, this is a valid LABEL parameter:

```
LABEL=(2,RETPD=30)
```

Here, a file will be created as the second file on the tape with a retention period of 30 days. This is valid too:

```
LABEL=RETPD=45
```

Since both of the positional subparameters are omitted, the parentheses aren't required.

The UNIT parameter

When you allocate a tape file, you can code several subparameters on the UNIT parameter to control how tape units are used to process the file. Figure 11-4 shows the format of the UNIT parameter. You already know how to code the first subparameter, unit; for it, you specify a device address, generic name, or group name to identify the device that will be allocated. For tape files, you can usually specify the group name TAPE.

How to allocate more than one unit   The count subparameter lets you allocate more than one device to a single file. When you process a tape data set that requires more than one volume, it's common to allocate two tape drives to the data set. That way, the program can read or write records on a tape volume mounted on one of the drives while the tape on the other drive is rewound, unloaded, and perhaps replaced by the next volume in sequence. In this way, the two tape drives alternate; one of them processes the data on one volume, while the other one prepares to process the data on the next volume.

To allocate two tape drives to a data set, you code the UNIT parameter like this:

```
UNIT=(TAPE,2)
```

Although you can allocate more than two tape drives, there's little reason to. Since tape data must be processed sequentially, your program can't read the records of a data set from more than one tape drive at once.

How to defer volume mounting   The DEFER subparameter is for files that must be allocated but might not actually be processed. It tells MVS to allocate the unit, but the operator isn't instructed to mount the tape volume until the program opens the data set. If the program never opens the file, the tape is never mounted. And that saves time. But if the program does open the file, the operator is instructed to mount the tape. Then, the program and the resources allocated to it must wait until the tape is mounted. Because it's more efficient to mount the tape volume during step allocation than during program execution, I suggest you code DEFER only when there's a good chance the data set won't be used.

How to request unit affinity   In some cases, an application program processes two or more tape files on separate volumes one after another. In other words, the program opens one tape file, processes all of its records, and closes it. Then, the program opens another tape file, processes its records, and closes it. And so on. Although several tape volumes are required, they are processed one at a time.

If you specified UNIT=TAPE in the DD statement of each tape file processed like this, each file is assigned to a separate unit. In some cases, that's appropriate. However, it might be better to use the same tape drive for each data set. Or, you might want to allocate two tape drives to process two or more tape volumes, so that while one volume is being processed, the operator can mount the next volume in sequence. In both cases, the idea is to reduce the number of tape drives required by the program.

To allocate the same tape unit or units to two or more DD statements within a job step, you use the AFF subparameter of the UNIT parameter, like this:

```
UNIT=AFF=TAPEDD1
```

The AFF subparameter says to allocate the same unit or units that are allocated to the specified DD statement; in this case, the one identified by the ddname TAPEDD1. When two or more DD statements share a unit allocation like this, they have *unit affinity*.

To use unit affinity, there are two rules you must remember. First, the AFF subparameter must refer to a ddname within the

---

The VOLUME parameter

```
VOL=([PRIVATE][,RETAIN][,volume-sequence][,volume-count]
        [,SER=(serial,serial...)])
```

Explanation

PRIVATE	Specifies that a private volume should be used. The volume will be dismounted when the step completes (unless RETAIN or DISP =(,PASS) is also coded), and the volume will not be used again unless specifically requested.
RETAIN	Specifies that the volume should remain mounted when the job step completes. RETAIN is usually coded with PRIVATE when a later job step requires the volume.
volume-sequence	For an existing multi-volume data set, indicates that processing is to begin at other than the first volume. Ignored for a new data set.
volume-count	Specifies the maximum number of volumes that a multi-volume output data set will require. MVS rounds the number you specify, as follows: If you omit volume-count or specify 5 or less, MVS assumes 5; if you specify a value between 6 and 20, MVS uses 20; if you specify a value greater than 20, MVS uses a multiple of 15 plus 5 (35, 50, 65, and so on, up to 255).
SER	Specifies one or more volume serial numbers for a specific volume request.

Figure 11-5   The VOLUME parameter of the DD statement

same job step. That makes sense, because units are allocated only for the duration of a job step. Second, the program must open and process the data sets that share unit affinity one at a time. If the program tries to open two data sets that share unit affinity, an allocation conflict will occur and the program will be terminated.

Incidentally, unit affinity is implied if you allocate two or more tape data sets that reside on the same volume. Whenever MVS encounters two or more DD statements that specify the same vol-ser within a job step, they are allocated to the device. So you don't have to specify UNIT=AFF in this case.

The VOLUME parameter

As you already know, the VOLUME parameter lets you specify the volume serial number for one or more volumes required by a data set. Several subparameters of the VOLUME parameter are related to tape volumes. Figure 11-5 shows those subparameters, and figure 11-6 gives several examples of their use. I'll describe the volume-count subparameter first, then the PRIVATE and RETAIN subparameters, and finally, the volume-sequence subparameter.

Example 1

```
VOL=SER=(163013,163014,163015,163016)
```

A specific volume request for the four named volumes.

Example 2

```
VOL=(,,,20)
```

A non-specific volume request for up to 20 volumes.

Example 3

```
VOL=(PRIVATE,SER=(MMA301,MMA302))
```

A specific volume request for the two named private volumes.

Example 4

```
VOL=(PRIVATE,RETAIN,SER=MMA400)
```

A specific volume request for the named private volume; the volume is not dismounted at step completion.

Example 5

```
VOL=(,,3)
```

A request for the third volume of a multi-volume data set.

Figure 11-6   Examples of the VOLUME parameter

How to request multiple volumes   In example 1 in figure 11-6, I allocated four volumes to a tape file using a specific volume request. Suppose I also specified UNIT=(TAPE,2) in the same DD statement. Then, during step allocation, MVS would acquire two tape drives and instruct the operator to mount volume 163013 on one and 163014 on the other. The program would then process the data set on volume 163013. When the end of that volume was reached, the program would automatically switch to volume 163014 on the other drive. While that tape was being processed, MVS would rewind the first tape and tell the operator to remove it and mount volume 163015. This process would continue until each of the volumes were processed or the end of the file was reached. (Not all of the volumes you list in the VOLUME parameter have to be used.)

To create a tape data set, you don't have to request a specific volume. In fact, you don't have to code a VOLUME parameter at all.

If you omit the VOLUME parameter, MVS tells the operator to mount a scratch tape—that is, a tape that doesn't have important data on it—on each of the units you allocate. Your tape file can use up to five volumes in this way.

If you know your file will require more than five tape volumes, you can code the volume-count subparameter, as in example 2 in figure 11-6. Here, I specified that up to 20 tape volumes can be used for the file. Again, not all 20 have to be used. Notice that three commas are required to mark the locations of the three omitted positional parameters.

When you code a volume-count subparameter, MVS rounds the number you specify according to a confusing scheme. If you specify a number that's 5 or less, MVS uses 5 as the volume count. That's why you can omit the VOLUME parameter altogether if you need 5 or fewer non-specific volumes; 5 is the default. If you specify a number that's greater than 5, MVS rounds the number up to the next higher multiple of 15 plus 5: 20, 35, 50, 65, and so on, up to a maximum of 255. In other words, if you specify 6, MVS rounds the volume count up to 20; if you specify 22, MVS rounds it up to 35.

How to request a private volume   The PRIVATE subparameter lets you mark a volume as private. Once marked as private, the volume can't be used by a non-specific request; it must be specifically requested in a VOLUME parameter. Furthermore, PRIVATE causes MVS to rewind and unload the tape at the end of the job step. If a subsequent job step requires the tape, the operator will be told to remount it. Example 3 shows how to code PRIVATE for a specific request.

If you code RETAIN as well as PRIVATE, the volume won't be rewound and unloaded at the end of the step. That way, a subsequent job step can access data on the private volume. Example 4 shows how to specify PRIVATE and RETAIN.

How to specify a volume sequence number   On rare occasions, you'll want to process a multi-volume data set beginning with a volume other than the first. To do that, you specify the volume sequence number, the third positional subparameter of the VOLUME parameter. In example 5 of figure 11-6, I specify that processing should begin with the third volume of a multi-volume data set. As I said, this type of processing isn't common.

The DCB parameter

When you process a tape file, you may need to code the DCB parameter on the file's DD statement. In particular, if you're creating a new

---

DCB subparameters for tape processing

```
OPTCD=[B][Q]

DEN=n

TRTCH={COMP   }
      {NOCOMP }
```

Explanation

OPTCD   Specifies various processing options. For tape, B means that end-of-file records should be treated as end-of-volume records, and Q means that tapes should be read and written in ASCII format.

DEN   Specifies the recording density. Code a single digit, as follows:

1   556 bpi

2   800 bpi

3   1600 bpi

4   6250 bpi

If omitted, the default depends on the unit type.

TRTCH   Specifies whether or not data compaction is used for cartridge tape drives. The default is NOCOMP.

Figure 11-7   DCB subparameters for tape processing

tape file, processing an unlabelled tape, or using the BLP label option, you'll probably need to code the DCB parameter. That's because, in these cases, MVS can't obtain DCB information from the data set's label.

The basic DCB subparameters you already know (DSORG, RECFM, LRECL, and BLKSIZE) provide information that applies to QSAM files whether they reside on tape or DASD. In addition, there are three subparameters that provide information specific to tape processing: OPTCD, DEN, and TRTCH. The OPTCD parameter specifies a variety of processing options, two of which are for tape only. The DEN parameter lets you specify the recording density to use for a dual density tape drive. And the TRTCH parameter lets you specify whether data compaction is used for cartridge tape drives. All three subparameters are described in figure 11-7.

How to process unlabelled ASCII tapes   As you may know, IBM mainframe computers use a code called EBCDIC to represent characters. Most other computer systems do, too. However, some computer systems use a code called ASCII. Although EBCDIC and ASCII are similar in concept, they are incompatible with one another. As a result, if you're processing a tape that's recorded using ASCII rather than EBCDIC, you have to make sure that the characters are translated properly so they can be processed.

Tapes that use IBM standard labels are always recorded in EBCDIC; tapes that use ISO/ANSI labels are always recorded in ASCII (in fact, that's the main difference between IBM and ISO/ASCII labels). As a result, if you specify AL or AUL in the LABEL parameter, MVS automatically converts data between ASCII and EBCDIC when processing the tape. So, if you create a tape using ISO/ANSI labels, data is written on the tape in ASCII format. If you read data from an ISO/ANSI tape, the ASCII data is automatically translated into EBCDIC.

Sometimes, however, you may want to process an unlabelled tape using ASCII. To do that, you specify OPTCD=Q in the DCB parameter of the DD statement for the tape file. Then, the data will be converted to ASCII when it's written to the tape. And data that's read from the tape will be converted back to EBCDIC. Remember that you must code OPTCD=Q only for unlabelled ASCII tapes; for tapes processed with ISO/ANSI labels, ASCII translation is automatic.

How to process multi-volume tape files out of sequence   The other OPTCD option that relates to tape processing is B; it lets you read the volumes of a multi-volume tape file in a sequence other than the sequence in which they were written. It does that by ignoring any end-of-file labels it finds, treating them instead as end-of-volume labels. So, even if an end-of-file label is encountered, the operator is instructed to mount another volume, and processing continues until all of the volumes specified in the VOL=SER parameter have been processed.

Although you might think that the OPTCD=B facility is related to the VOLUME parameter's volume-sequence subparameter, the two actually provide quite different functions. The volume-sequence subparameter of the VOLUME parameter lets you specify which volume of a multi-volume file should be mounted first; after that, however, the remaining volumes must be processed in sequence. In contrast, the OPTCD=B facility lets you ignore the file's volume sequence altogether, processing all of the file's volumes in any order.

I don't think you'll use OPTCD=B very often. After all, most applications that are suitable for tape processing are suitable because they are sequential in nature. And OPTCD=B isn't appropriate for tape files that are inherently sequential.

How to specify a recording density   *Recording density* refers to the compactness of data written on a tape. It's measured in *bytes per inch*, or *bpi*. Most reel tapes today are written in one of two densities: 1600 bpi or 6250 bpi. And many tape drives have a dual density feature that lets them switch from one density to another. Older dual density tape drives record data using 800 or 1600 bpi. And MVS still supports tape drives that record data using 556 bpi.

When reading a tape, a dual density drive is able to determine the recording density of the input tape. For output, though, you must code the DEN DCB subparameter if you want to record data using a density other than the drive's default density. In the DEN subparameter, you code a single digit to represent the recording density, as figure 11-7 indicates. Realistically, the only time you'll code the DEN subparameter is when you want to create a 1600 bpi tape on a 1600/6250 dual density tape drive. To do that, you must specify DEN=3 in the DCB parameter. If the tape drive you're using doesn't have a dual density feature, you don't have to worry about DEN at all.

How to specify data compaction for cartridge tapes   Many 3480 and 3490 cartridge tape drives support a feature called *data compaction* that allows MVS to store data on the tape more efficiently. When MVS reads a cartridge tape data set, it automatically determines whether or not data compaction is used. When you create a tape data set on a 3480 or 3490 drive that supports data compaction, you can use the TRTCH subparameter to specify whether or not data compaction should be used. Specify TRTCH=COMP if you want to use data compaction and TRTCH=NOCOMP if you don't. The default is TRTCH=NOCOMP.

Examples of DD statements for tape files

Now that I've described the DD statement parameters that relate directly to tape processing, the examples in figure 11-8 should help you understand how they work together with the DD statement parameters you already know.

Example 1 shows how to allocate an existing cataloged tape file. In this case, you can't distinguish the DD statement from the DD statement for a DASD file. That's because the UNIT and VOLUME information are obtained from the file's catalog entry.

Example 2 shows how you might code the same DD statement for an existing uncataloged single-volume file. Here, I specify UNIT=TAPE and VOL=SER=300123.

Example 1

```
//JOURNAL   DD    DSNAME=MMA2.AR.JOURNAL,DISP=OLD
```

Allocate an existing cataloged data set.

Example 2

```
//JOURNAL   DD    DSNAME=MMA2.AR.JOURNAL,DISP=OLD,
//                UNIT=TAPE,VOL=SER=300123
```

Allocate an existing uncataloged data set.

Example 3

```
//JOURNAL   DD    DSNAME=MMA2.AR.JOURNAL,DISP=OLD,
//                UNIT=(TAPE,2),
//                VOL=SER=(300123,300124,300125,300126)
```

Allocate an existing uncataloged multi-volume data set using two tape units.

Example 4

```
//JOURNAL   DD    DSNAME=MMA2.AR.JOURNAL,DISP=(NEW,CATLG),
//                UNIT=(TAPE,2),VOL=(PRIVATE,,,10),
//                LABEL=RETPD=100,DCB=BLKSIZE=8192
```

Allocate a new multi-volume data set using 2 tape units, up to 10 volumes, and a retention period of 100 days.

Example 5

```
//SYSUT1    DD    DISP=OLD
//                UNIT=TAPE,VOL=SER=SYD0E01,
//                LABEL=(5,BLP),
//                DCB=(DSORG=PS,RECFM=FB,LRECL=80,BLKSIZE=1600)
```

Allocate the fifth data set on the volume, bypassing label processing.

Example 6

```
//SYSUT1    DD    DISP=OLD,
//                UNIT=TAPE,VOL=SER=111222,
//                LABEL=(,NL),
//                DCB=(DSORG=PS,RECFM=FB,LRECL=80,BLKSIZE=1600,OPTCD=Q)
```

Allocate an unlabelled tape.

Figure 11-8   Examples of DD statements for tape files

Example 3 shows a DD statement for an existing uncataloged multi-volume file. Here, the UNIT parameter allocates two tape drives. And the VOLUME parameter names each of the tape volumes that might be required.

Example 4 shows how to create a multi-volume file using a non-specific request for private tape volumes. Again, the UNIT parameter requests two tape drives. In the VOLUME parameter, I specify PRIVATE to request private volumes and a volume count of 10 to request multiple volumes. Because of the way MVS rounds the volume-count subparameter, however, the data set will actually be allowed to occupy up to 20 volumes. The LABEL parameter specifies a retention period of 100 days, and the DCB parameter supplies a block size of 8192 bytes.

Example 5 illustrates bypass label processing. Here, the operator is instructed to mount tape volume SYDOE01. Then, the fifth file on that volume is processed using the characteristics supplied in the DCB parameter.

Example 6 shows how to process an unlabelled ASCII tape. OPTCD=Q is coded in the DCB parameter, and NL is coded as the label-type subparameter of LABEL.

Discussion

One of the factors that makes tape processing under MVS difficult to learn is that the JCL parameters are closely related to operational procedures. And, in the typical MVS environment, programmers are far removed from operations; at many installations, the machine room is strictly off-limits for programmers. Nevertheless, if you work in a shop that does heavy tape processing, you'll probably use the facilities this topic presents frequently. And you'll quickly become proficient with them. If, on the other hand, your shop doesn't do significant tape processing, you'll probably seldom find opportunity to use the facilities presented in this topic.

Terminology

volume label
file-header label
end-of-file label
file-trailer label
VOL1 label
HDR1 label
EOF1 label

multi-file volume
multi-volume file
end-of-volume label
EOV1 label
IBM standard labels
ISO/ANSI labels
unlabelled tape

non-standard labels   unit affinity
data set sequence number   recording density
user label   bytes per inch
tape mark   bpi
expiration date checking   data compaction

Objective

Code the JCL necessary to allocate a tape data set using one or two units and one or more specific or non-specific volumes and whatever form of label processing is appropriate for the tape.

Exercises

1. Code a DD statement that creates a tape data set named X401.JOURNAL on a single non-specific private tape volume. Specify a block size of 16,384.

2. Code a DD statement to allocate the first data set on a labelled tape whose volume serial number is 555123. The data set is sequential with fixed-length 80-byte records blocked in 16,000-byte blocks.

**Chapter
12**

How to manage generation data groups

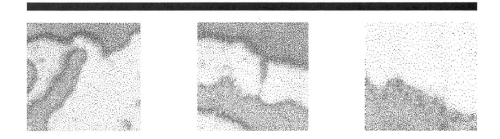

In this chapter, you'll learn how to manage and use generation data groups, which are collections of chronologically related data sets. First, I'll explain what generation data groups are and how MVS keeps track of them. Then I'll show you how to process a generation data group. After that, I'll show you how to create a generation data group.

Generation data group concepts

Although there are many different uses for sequential data sets, many sequential files have one characteristic in common: They are used in cyclical applications. For example, a sequential data set that contains transactions posted daily against a master file is cyclical; each day's transactions, along with the processing required to post them, form one cycle. Similarly, a sequential data set used to hold a backup copy of a master file is cyclical too; each time a new backup copy is made, a new cycle is begun.

In most cyclical applications, it's a good idea to maintain versions of the files used for several cycles. That way, if something goes wrong, you can recreate the processing that occurred during previous cycles to restore the affected files to a known point. Then, processing can continue from that point.

If you had to create your own procedure for doing this, you would begin by establishing naming conventions that would let you identify successive versions, or *generations*, of a single file. MVS provides a facility, called generation data groups, that does just that. Simply put, a *generation data group*, or *GDG*, is a collection of two or more chronologically related versions of the same file. Each version

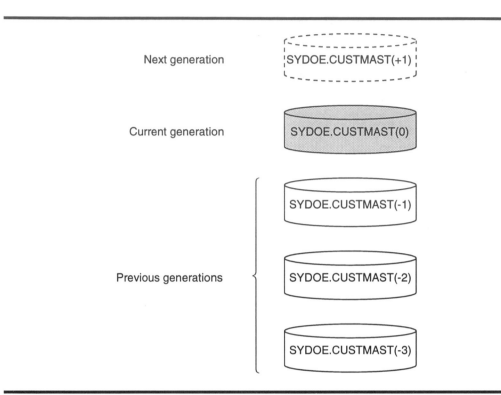

Next generation   SYDOE.CUSTMAST(+1)

Current generation   SYDOE.CUSTMAST(0)

Previous generations   SYDOE.CUSTMAST(-1)

SYDOE.CUSTMAST(-2)

SYDOE.CUSTMAST(-3)

Figure 12-1   Generation data groups let you refer to several generations of a data set by numbering them relative to the current generation

of the file, or member of the generation data group, is called a *generation data set*. A generation data set may reside on tape or DASD. It may be a sequential (QSAM) or direct (BDAM) file, but QSAM is by far the more commonly used because of difficulties associated with using BDAM files. ISAM and VSAM files can't be used in a generation data group.

As each processing cycle occurs, a new generation of the data set is added to the generation data group. This new version becomes the *current generation*; it replaces the old current generation, which becomes a *previous generation*. A previous generation can be re- trieved and processed if necessary. Usually, though, it's the current generation that's retrieved during the next processing cycle.

Figure 12-1 illustrates the structure of a generation data group. Here, the current generation is shaded. There are three previous generations, and the next generation is indicated by a dashed outline. Notice that the generations are numbered relative to the

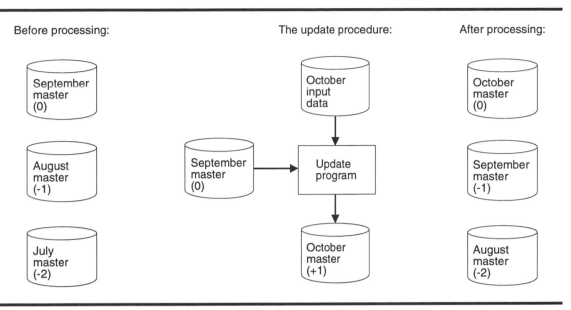

Before processing:

The update procedure:

After processing:

Figure 12-2   Relative positions of generation data sets

current generation, SYDOE.CUSTMAST(0). So the previous generations have *relative generation numbers* of -1, -2, and -3. And the next generation is +1. Relative generation numbers are adjusted when each processing cycle completes so that the current generation (that is, the most recently created member of the group) is always referred to as relative generation 0.

MVS uses the generation data group's catalog entry to keep track of relative generation numbers. As a result, generation data groups must be cataloged. And each generation data set that's a part of the group must be cataloged too. (I'll show you how to catalog a generation data group in a moment.)

When you create a generation data group's catalog entry, you specify how many generations should be maintained. For example, you might specify that five generations, including the current generation, should be maintained. Then, following each processing cycle, the new version of the file becomes the current generation; the fifth-oldest generation is automatically removed from the group.

To help you understand how generation data groups are processed, figure 12-2 shows a typical application that uses a GDG. Here, three generations of a master file are maintained. Transactions collected during the month of October are used to update the previous month's (September's) master file; the result is a new current master file for October. When the processing cycle is completed, the July master file will be removed from the group.

When the processing begins in figure 12-2, September is generation 0, August is generation -1 (one generation before the current generation), and July is generation -2 (two generations before the current generation). During processing, transactions are applied to generation 0 to produce generation +1, which is one generation after the current generation. Then, when processing completes, the relative generation numbers are brought up to date: The October master file becomes generation 0, the September master file becomes generation -1, the August master file becomes generation -2, and the July master file is removed. As a result, during the next processing cycle (in November), the October master file will be retrieved as generation 0.

Although MVS lets you use relative generation numbers to simplify cyclical processing, MVS uses *absolute generation numbers* in the form G*nnnn*V00 to identify each generation data set uniquely. G*nnnn* represents the chronological sequence number of the generation, beginning with G0000. V00 is a *version number*, which lets you maintain more than one version of a generation.

Each time a new generation data set is created, MVS adds one to the sequence number. The sequence and version numbers are stored as a part of the file's data set name, like this:

```
filename.GnnnnV00
```

So, if the file name is PAYROLL.TRANS, its first generation would be named PAYROLL.TRANS.G0000V00. When a new generation is created, it will be named PAYROLL.TRANS.G0001V00. And so on. Because the generation and version numbers require 9 characters (including the preceding period), the data set name of the generation data group is limited to 35 characters; that's 9 less than the MVS data set name limit of 44 characters.

Figure 12-3 should help you understand how absolute generation numbers relate to relative generation numbers. Here, you can see the absolute generation numbers of a master file before and after a new generation is created. Before processing, the current master file is generation 12. After processing, the current master file is generation 13. MVS keeps track of the absolute generation number of the current generation; that's how it knows which file to access when you supply a relative generation number like 0 or -1.

What about the version component of the absolute generation number? As I said, it lets you maintain several copies of a particular generation. For example, if you want to change the data in a generation but don't want the sequence number changed, you can create a

Before processing:

Current master file	PAYFILE.G0012V00
1st previous master file	PAYFILE.G0011V00
2nd previous master file	PAYFILE.G0010V00
3rd previous master file	PAYFILE.G0009V00

The update procedure:

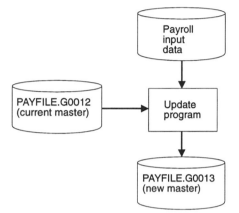

After processing:

Current master file	PAYFILE.G0013V00
1st previous master file	PAYFILE.G0012V00
2nd previous master file	PAYFILE.G0011V00
3rd previous master file	PAYFILE.G0010V00

Figure 12-3   Chronological order of generation data sets

file using the same generation number, but changing the version to V01. Only one version of a generation data set—the version with the highest version number—is considered to be a part of the generation data group. Other versions of a generation must be accessed explicitly by specifying the complete data set name, including the absolute generation and version numbers.

How to process a generation data group

To retrieve an existing generation data set or create a new one, you code the name of the generation data group followed by a relative

```
//SYDOEJ     JOB   USER=SYDOE,PASSWORD=XXXXXXXX
//           EXEC  PGM=PAY3200
//OLDMAST    DD    DSNAME=SYDOE.PAYROLL.MASTER(0),DISP=OLD
//NEWMAST    DD    DSNAME=SYDOE.PAYROLL.MASTER(+1),DISP=(NEW,CATLG),
//                 UNIT=SYSDA,VOL=SER=MPS8BV,
//                 SPACE=(CYL,(10,1)),
//                 DCB=(LRECL=80,BLKSIZE=1600)
//PAYTRAN    DD    DSNAME=SYDOE.PAYROLL.TRANS,DISP=OLD
//PAYLIST    DD    SYSOUT=*
```

Figure 12-4   A job that creates a new member of a generation data group

generation number in parentheses in the DSNAME parameter of a DD statement. For example, to refer to the current generation of a group named PAYROLL.MASTER, you code

```
DSNAME=PAYROLL.MASTER(0)
```

To refer to the most recent previous generation, you code

```
DSNAME=PAYROLL.MASTER(-1)
```

And to create a new generation, you code

```
DSNAME=PAYROLL.MASTER(+1)
```

Figure 12-4 shows a typical job that uses a generation data group. It reads transaction data from an in-stream file and posts it to the current master file, SYDOE.PAYROLL.MASTER(0). In the process, it creates a new master file, SYDOE.PAYROLL.MASTER(+1). Each time this job is run, it uses the new master file from the last execution of the job as the current master file.

Relative generation numbers are updated after the completion of the job, not the completion of a job step. As a result, any step that refers to a generation created in preceding steps must refer to it in relation to the generation that was current when the job began. In other words, if the first step of a job creates a new generation (+1), and the next step is to print data from that file, the new generation must be referred to as (+1) in the second step also. However, if the print program is run in a separate job, it would refer to the new generation as (0). That's because the relative generation number is updated when the job finishes.

Figure 12-5 should help clarify this confusing point. The first example shows a two-step job that creates a new generation in the first step and retrieves it in the second. The second example shows the same processing, only this time as two separate jobs. In the

One two-step job

```
//SYDOEJ    JOB   USER=SYDOE,PASSWORD=XXXXXXXX
//UPDATE    EXEC  PGM=PAY3200
//OLDMAST   DD    DSNAME=SYDOE.PAYROLL.MASTER(0),DISP=OLD
//NEWMAST   DD    DSNAME=SYDOE.PAYROLL.MASTER(+1),DISP=(NEW,CATLG),
//                UNIT=SYSDA,VOL=SER=MPS8BV,
//                SPACE=(CYL,(10,1)),
//                DCB=(LRECL=80,BLKSIZE=1600)
//PAYTRAN   DD    DSNAME=SYDOE.PAYROLL.TRANS,DISP=OLD
//PAYLIST   DD    SYSOUT=*
//REPORT    EXEC  PGM=PAY3300
//PAYMAST   DD    DSNAME=SYDOE.PAYROLL.MASTER(+1),DISP=OLD
//PAYRPT    DD    SYSOUT=*
```

Two one-step jobs

```
//SYDOEJ    JOB   USER=SYDOE,PASSWORD=XXXXXXXX
//UPDATE    EXEC  PGM=PAY3200
//OLDMAST   DD    DSNAME=SYDOE.PAYROLL.MASTER(0),DISP=OLD
//NEWMAST   DD    DSNAME=SYDOE.PAYROLL.TRANS,DISP=(NEW,CATLG),
//                UNIT=SYSDA,VOL=SER=MPS8BV,
//                SPACE=(CYL,(10,1)),
//                DCB=(LRECL=80,BLKSIZE=1600)
//PAYTRAN   DD    DSNAME=SYDOE.PAYROLL.TRANS,DISP=OLD
//PAYLIST   DD    SYSOUT=*

//SYDOEK    JOB   USER=SYDOE,PASSWORD=XXXXXXXX
//REPORT    EXEC  PGM=PAY3300
//PAYMAST   DD    DSNAME=SYDOE.PAYROLL.MASTER(0),DISP=OLD
//PAYRPT    DD    SYSOUT=*
```

Figure 12-5   Relative generation numbers are updated at the end of a job, not at the end of a job step

second example, the relative generation numbers are updated at the
completion of the first job, so the second job treats the file as the
current generation (0).

How to create a generation data group

Before you can process jobs that create and retrieve generation data
sets, you must create the generation data group. To do that, you
must do two things. First, you must create a catalog entry for the
generation data group. Second, you must create or locate an existing
model data set control block.

How to create a generation data group catalog entry   All generation
data groups must be cataloged in a master or user catalog. To create a
generation data group catalog entry, you invoke the VSAM utility

The DEFINE GDG command

```
DEFINE GDG    ( NAME(entry-name)
                LIMIT(limit)
              [ EMPTY | NOEMPTY ]
              [ SCRATCH | NOSCRATCH ]
              [ OWNER(owner-id) ]
              [ TO(date) | FOR(days) ] )
```

Note: GDG is an abbreviation for GENERATIONDATAGROUP.

Explanation

NAME	Specifies the name of the generation data group; this name follows normal MVS naming conventions but is limited to 35 characters.
LIMIT	Specifies how many generation data sets are to be maintained in the group.
EMPTY NOEMPTY	Specifies what action MVS should take when the LIMIT value is reached: EMPTY means that all generations should be removed from the group; NOEMPTY means that just the oldest generation should be removed. NOEMPTY is the default.
SCRATCH NOSCRATCH	Specifies whether or not MVS should scratch generation data sets as they're removed from the group. NOSCRATCH is the default.
OWNER	Specifies a one- to eight-character owner-id for the generation data group.
TO FOR	Specifies an expiration date (in the format yyddd) or a retention period (in the format dddd) for the generation data group.

Figure 12-6   The DEFINE GDG command

program IDCAMS and issue a DEFINE GDG command. You learned how to invoke IDCAMS and use it for various VSAM functions in chapter 10, so I won't cover it in detail here. Instead, I'll just show you an example of defining a GDG entry so you'll see how it's done.

Figure 12-6 shows the format of the DEFINE GDG command, and figure 12-7 shows a complete job to create a GDG catalog entry. The MODEL DD statement defines the model DSCB. I'll explain how to do that next, so you can ignore this statement for now. It's the DEFINE GDG command I want you to study here.

The NAME parameter of the DEFINE GDG command supplies the name of the generation data group: SYDOE.PAYROLL.MASTER in this example. Remember, the system adds the *Gnnnn*V00 qualifier to the end of the name you supply, so the name of a generation data group can't be more than 35 characters long.

The LIMIT parameter indicates how many generation data sets should be maintained in the group. The minimum is 1 and the maximum is 255. The number you code includes the current generation. So,

```
//SYDOEJ    JOB   USER=SYDOE,PASSWORD=XXXXXXXX
//          EXEC  PGM=IDCAMS
//SYSPRINT  DD    SYSOUT=*
//MODEL     DD    DSNAME=SYDOE.PAYROLL.MASTER,DISP=(NEW,KEEP),
//                UNIT=SYSDA,VOL=SER=MPS800,
//                SPACE=(TRK,0),
//                DCB=(DSORG=PS,RECFM=FB)
//SYSIN   DD   *
  DEFINE  GDG  ( NAME(SYDOE.PAYROLL.MASTER) -
                 LIMIT(5)                    -
                 NOEMPTY                     -
                 SCRATCH )
 /*
```

Figure 12-7   A job that defines a generation data group and allocates a model DSCB

to maintain the current generation and four previous generations, you code LIMIT(5).

NOEMPTY specifies that when the number of generation data sets belonging to the group exceeds the limit, the oldest generation is to be removed from the group. If you specify EMPTY instead of NOEMPTY, *all* generations (except the current generation) are removed from the group when the limit is exceeded. In most cases, you'll specify NOEMPTY or let it default.

SCRATCH works along with EMPTY/NOEMPTY to indicate what MVS should do with generation data sets residing on DASD that are removed from the group. If you specify SCRATCH, a generation data set is actually deleted from the DASD volume where it resides; if you omit SCRATCH or specify NOSCRATCH, the data set is uncataloged (removed from the group), but not actually deleted. You'll probably specify SCRATCH most of the time. If you really want to keep data sets that are no longer a part of the group, you should consider specifying a larger limit instead. SCRATCH has no meaning for tape data sets.

How to create a model DSCB   The second requirement for processing a generation data group is that there must be a *model data set control block* (*DSCB*) on the same volume as the catalog that contains the GDG entry. The model DSCB is a data set that's used to obtain DCB information for new generations of the group. Usually, no space is allocated to the model DSCB. So, the model DSCB is a VTOC entry that doesn't have any space allocated to it.

The MODEL DD statement in figure 12-7 creates the model DSCB for the generation data group defined by the DEFINE GDG command. The ddname can be any name you wish, but the data set name for the model DSCB should be the same as for the generation data group (unless it's a general-purpose model DSCB, which I'll discuss in a moment). That way, MVS can use this data set as a model without any special coding. Because the name is the same as the generation data group, however, the model DSCB can't be cataloged; if you tried to catalog it, a duplicate entry would occur.

As you can see, no space is allocated to the model DSCB; I specified SPACE=(TRK,0) in the DD statement. (The SPACE parameter is required on a DD statement for a DASD file, so you can't omit it even if you don't allocate any space.) The VOLUME parameter specifies the vol-ser for the volume that contains the user catalog the generation data group is defined in. And the DCB parameter defines the characteristics of each generation data set: DSORG=PS and RECFM=FB. You can also specify the LRECL, BLKSIZE, OPTCD, KEYLEN, and RKP subparameters of DCB for a generation data set. (You'll learn about the RKP parameter in chapter 13.)

As I mentioned a moment ago, the name of the model DSCB doesn't have to be the same as the name of the generation data group. Instead you can create a general-purpose model DSCB that can be used by many generation data groups. In that case, since the model DSCB name isn't the same as the generation data group name, you have to code it in the DCB parameter of the DD statement that allocates a new generation data set, like this:

```
DCB=(MODLDSCB,LRECL=80,BLKSIZE=1600)
```

Here, MODLDSCB is the data set name of a model DSCB; the LRECL and BLKSIZE subparameters coded here override the values obtained from the model.

Terminology

generation
generation data group
GDG
generation data set
current generation
previous generation
relative generation number
absolute generation number
version number
model data set control block
model DSCB

Objectives

1. Code the JCL necessary to create or retrieve generations of a generation data group.

2. Using figure 12-7 as a model, code a job that creates a model DSCB and defines a generation data group.

Exercises

1. In the following job stream, fill in the missing blanks:

```
//jobname   JOB   USER=user-id,PASSWORD=xxxxxxxx
//EXTRU     EXEC  PGM=TRUNEV
//TRUDATA   DD    *
   (input data)
//TRUFILE   DD    DSN=_____,      Current generation of X401.MASTER
//          DISP=SHR
//TRUFILE2  DD    DSN=_____,      New generation of X401.MASTER
//          DISP=(NEW,CATLG),
//          UNIT=SYSDA,VOL=SER=TSO001,
//          SPACE=(CYL,(100,5)),
//          DCB=(MODLDSCB,LRECL=1300,BLKSIZE=1300,RECFM=F)
//RPTTRU    EXEC  PGM=TRPT001
//TRUFILE   DD    DSN=_____,      Generation created in previous step
//          DISP=OLD
//TRURPT    DD    SYSOUT=A
```

2. Code a job that creates a model DSCB and defines a generation data group. The generation data group is named X401.PROJ.JOURNAL and resides on a SYSDA volume named TSO001. Allow for up to 10 generations, and scratch the oldest generation when a new generation is created (assuming that 10 generations already exist). In the model DSCB, do not specify any DCB options.

**Chapter
13**

How to manage ISAM data sets

ISAM, which stands for *Indexed Sequential Access Method*, is both a file organization and an access method. As a file organization, ISAM provides a defined way of storing data so that it can be processed in one of two ways: sequentially, as if it were a physical sequential data set, and randomly, retrieving individual records on request based on a key value that uniquely identifies each record in the file. As an access method, ISAM comes in two forms: *BISAM* (*Basic Indexed Sequential Access Method*) processes ISAM files randomly; *QISAM* (*Queued Indexed Sequential Access Method*) processes ISAM files sequentially. An application program can invoke the services of either access method, or both, depending on how it needs to process the file.

Although still supported, ISAM is considered obsolete today. That's because VSAM key-sequenced data sets provide the same capabilities and are more efficient. Still, you'll occasionally come across an application that hasn't been converted to VSAM. So, the information in this chapter might be helpful to you.

ISAM file organization

To code the JCL to create and retrieve ISAM files, you need to understand how an ISAM file is organized. An ISAM file is divided into three distinct kinds of areas: prime data areas, index areas, and overflow areas.

The prime data area   The *prime data area* of an ISAM file contains the bulk of the file's data records. Within the prime data area, records are stored sequentially based on their key values. When a record is inserted into the prime data area, it is inserted in its proper key-sequence location and other records are moved accordingly. If, as often happens, ISAM can't find room for the record in its proper location, the record is stored in an overflow area, which you'll learn about in a few moments. As a result, the prime data area doesn't always contain all of the file's records; some records may be in an overflow area.

Within the prime data area (and in an overflow area too), data may be marked as deleted by placing hexadecimal FF in the first byte of the record. When this is done, the record is said to be *logically deleted*. A logically deleted record is eligible to be *physically deleted*. That can happen in one of two ways. First, if you try to insert a record at a nearby location, ISAM may physically delete the logically deleted record to make room for the new record. Second, if you copy the file sequentially, records that have been marked as logically deleted won't be included in the new copy.

Index areas   To let you retrieve records at random, ISAM uses an index structure. Every ISAM file uses two kinds of indexes to locate specific records: a *cylinder index* and *track indexes*. In addition, large ISAM files may use a third type of index: a *master index*. After I describe cylinder and track indexes, I'll describe the master index.

The cylinder index contains one entry for each cylinder in the prime data area. Each entry contains two elements: (1) the highest key value of the records stored in the cylinder and (2) the address of a lower level index for that cylinder, the track index. The track index, located at the beginning of each cylinder in the prime data area, contains one entry for each track within that cylinder. Like the entries in the cylinder index, each track index entry contains two elements: (1) the highest key value of the records stored on the track and (2) the track number itself.

If an ISAM file is large, the cylinder index may require several tracks. When that's the case, the time required to locate an entry can be reduced by an optional master index. The master index is structured much like the cylinder and track indexes, except that each entry points to a track of the cylinder index. As a result, the time required to search the cylinder index is reduced.

Overflow areas   ISAM files can include *overflow areas* that are used when records are added to the file. As a result, the entire file doesn't have to be rewritten when records are added to the prime data area. When records are added to an overflow area, the index structure is updated so records can still be retrieved in key sequence. There are two kinds of overflow areas: cylinder overflow areas and the independent overflow area.

One way to allow for file additions is to provide *cylinder overflow areas*. When you use this approach, part of each cylinder in the prime data area is reserved for inserted records. Because the DASD unit's access mechanism doesn't have to move to access a cylinder overflow area, this is a relatively efficient way to handle insertions. You indicate how many tracks of each cylinder should be reserved for cylinder overflow areas in the JCL that creates the ISAM file.

The other type of overflow area is a separate disk extent called the *independent overflow area*. You may use it instead of or in addition to cylinder overflow areas. An independent overflow area can provide more space for insertions than is available in cylinder overflow areas. However, because the DASD unit's access mechanism must move to access it, it's less efficient than cylinder overflow areas. As a result, most ISAM files provide both types of overflow areas.

As records are added to overflow areas, the areas begin to fill up. As more and more records are stored in the independent overflow area, both sequential and random processing become less and less efficient because additional DASD reads are required to locate overflow records. So, ISAM files are periodically reorganized. When a file is reorganized, records from the overflow areas are moved into the prime data area and the index structure is rebuilt. Although this reorganization process takes time, it's necessary not only to improve processing efficiency, but to allow for future additions as well.

How to code DD statements to create ISAM files

When you code a job that creates an ISAM file, you must provide one or more DD statements that identify the characteristics of the file and allocate space to it. For all but the smallest of ISAM files, you code three DD statements: one for the index area that contains the master and cylinder indexes, one for the prime data area, and one for the independent overflow area. You code these DD statements as if you were concatenating them. In other words, you specify the ddname only on the first DD statement (for the index). Then, you code additional DD statements for the prime data area and the overflow area, omitting the ddname.

The DD statements for the index and independent overflow areas are optional. If you omit one, the appropriate area is imbedded in the prime data area; MVS determines how much of the prime data area to allocate to the area. Whichever of the three DD statements you code, you must always code them in this sequence: index, prime data, and overflow.

The DSNAME parameter   In the DSNAME parameter, you provide not only the name of the data set, but the area being defined. You specify the area, which may be INDEX, PRIME, or OVFLOW, in parentheses following the data set name. To illustrate, suppose you use three DD statements to create an ISAM file named SYDOE.CUSTOMER.MASTER. The first DD statement identifies the index; you code its DSNAME parameter like this:

```
DSNAME=SYDOE.CUSTOMER.MASTER(INDEX)
```

The second DD statement identifies the prime data area; you code its DSNAME parameter like this:

```
DSNAME=SYDOE.CUSTOMER.MASTER(PRIME)
```

Finally, the third DD statement should contain this DSNAME parameter:

```
DSNAME=SYDOE.CUSTOMER.MASTER(OVFLOW)
```

It defines the independent overflow area.

If you imbed both the index and the overflow area in the prime data area, you use just one DD statement. Then, the PRIME area indicator is optional. So, you can specify SYDOE.CUSTOMER.MASTER(PRIME) or just SYDOE.CUSTOMER.MASTER as the data set name.

The DISP parameter   To create an ISAM file, you code the DISP parameter like this:

```
DISP=(NEW,KEEP)
```

That way, new space will be allocated and the ISAM file will be retained. Although you can catalog an ISAM file, you can only catalog it using the DISP parameter if you define it with a single DD statement. If you use two or three DD statements to define your ISAM file, you use the VSAM utility program, IDCAMS, to catalog the file after you've created it. Since that's an uncommon requirement, I won't show you how to do it. If you need to know, you can consult the IBM VSAM reference manuals.

The UNIT and VOLUME parameters   You use the UNIT and VOLUME parameters to specify which devices and volumes are to contain the file. If you use three separate DD statements to create your ISAM file, the three areas may or may not reside on the same volume. In addition, the prime data area may be multi-volume; in other words, you can specify more than one volume in the DD statement for the prime data area.

If you use more than one volume for your ISAM file, it's a good idea to use volumes of the same device type. Otherwise, as you'll see later, you'll have to code more than one DD statement to retrieve the file. If the file resides on volumes of the same type, you can retrieve it with a single DD statement even if you used two or three DD statements to create the file.

The SPACE parameter   There are some restrictions on how you can code the SPACE parameter for an ISAM file. First, the space allocation must be in terms of cylinders; you can't code TRK or specify a block or record size in the SPACE parameter. Second, you can't specify a secondary allocation amount. So, once an ISAM file has filled its primary space, you must recreate it with additional primary space.

The SPACE allocation parameter for an ISAM file includes a positional subparameter that lets you specify how many cylinders of the prime data area are allocated for the index. You use this subparameter only when you imbed the index; that is, when you don't code a DD statement for the index area. The index space subparameter is in the same position as the directory-block allocation subparameter for a partitioned data set. You code it like this:

```
SPACE=(CYL,(20,,1))
```

Here, I allocated 20 cylinders to the prime data area, with one cylinder allocated to the imbedded index. Notice that I coded two consecutive commas to mark the place of the omitted secondary allocation amount.

The CONTIG option is often specified in the SPACE parameter for an ISAM file. CONTIG, which I introduced in chapter 6, causes MVS to allocate contiguous extents for the primary allocation. That usually results in more efficient processing for ISAM files.

The DCB parameter   In the DCB parameter, you supply information that ISAM uses to control the format of the file. If you use more than one DD statement to create the file, all of them must have the same DCB parameter. So, I suggest you use a referback in the second and third DD statements. You'll see an example of that in a few moments.

Figure 13-1 gives the format of the DCB subparameters for ISAM files. The first subparameter, DSORG=IS, is always required when you process an ISAM file, even if it's also supplied by your program. DSORG=IS indicates that the file is stored in the ISAM format. You can omit the other DCB specifications shown in figure 13-1 if your program supplies them.

DCB subparameters for ISAM files

```
DSORG=IS
RECFM=format
LRECL=length
BLKSIZE=size
KEYLEN=key-length
RKP=key-position
NTM=master-index-size
CYLOFL=cyl-overflow-size
OPTCD=options
```

Explanation

DSORG	Specifies ISAM data set organization.
RECFM	Specifies the record format: F=fixed, FB=fixed blocked, VB=variable blocked.
LRECL	Specifies the record length.
BLKSIZE	Specifies the block size.
KEYLEN	Specifies the key length in bytes.
RKP	Specifies the starting position of the key relative to the first byte of the record. (The first byte is key position 0.)
NTM	Specifies the number of tracks to reserve for the master index; you must also specify OPTCD=M.
CYLOFL	Specifies the number of tracks to reserve for the cylinder overflow areas. To use those areas, specify OPTCD=Y.
OPTCD	Specifies one or more optional processing features; see figure 13-2 for details.

Figure 13-1   DCB subparameters for ISAM files

The next three DCB subparameters, RECFM, LRECL, and BLKSIZE, specify the characteristics of the file's records. You code these subparameters the same as you would for a sequential file.

The next two subparameters, KEYLEN and RKP, specify the length and location of the file's key field. The KEYLEN subparameter specifies the length of the key field. For example, if the key field is a five-byte customer number, you code KEYLEN=5. The RKP subparameter specifies the position of the key field relative to the first byte of the record. If the key field starts in the first byte, you code RKP=0; if it starts in the second byte, you code

RKP=1. For most ISAM files, you shouldn't put the key field in the first byte of the records. That's because the first byte is used for the delete byte.

The NTM subparameter specifies how many tracks of the cylinder index area should be reserved for a master index. If you want your ISAM file formatted with a master index, you must code NTM. In addition, you must code the M option in the OPTCD subparameter.

The CYLOFL subparameter is similar to the NTM subparameter; it specifies how many tracks of each prime data area cylinder should be reserved for the cylinder overflow area. For example, if you specify CYLOFL=3, three tracks of each cylinder are reserved. Like NTM, CYLOFL has a corresponding OPTCD option: Y. However, you don't have to specify OPTCD=Y when you code CYLOFL; if you don't, the cylinder overflow tracks are reserved but not used. That might be useful when you're initially loading records into the file.

The OPTCD subparameter specifies several processing options related to ISAM. Figure 13-2 lists the options you can specify and explains the meaning of each one. I want you to notice two things in particular. First, you should specify both I and Y if you want both types of overflow areas to be used; I indicates that the independent overflow area should be used. When both overflow areas are active, ISAM first tries to put an inserted record in the cylinder overflow area; the independent overflow area is used only if there's no room in the cylinder overflow area. Second, you should specify the L option if deleted records will be marked with hex FF in the first byte.

Examples of DD statements to create ISAM files Now that you've seen each of the DD statement parameters that apply to ISAM files, figures 13-3 and 13-4 show two examples of how ISAM files are created. In figure 13-3, a single DD statement is used to create an ISAM file with imbedded index and overflow areas. Here, I allocated 14 cylinders of primary space, specifying that one of the 14 cylinders should be used for the cylinder index. I also specified that one track of each cylinder should be reserved for the cylinder overflow area.

Figure 13-4 shows a more complicated ISAM file that's defined with three DD statements. The first DD statement allocates one cylinder to the index. Because I specified NTM=1 and OPTCD=M, the first track of the index area is used as the master index; the remaining tracks of the index area are available for the cylinder index.

OPTCD code	Meaning
I	Specifies that an independent overflow area, if provided, should be used for overflow records.
L	Specifies that any records containing hex FF in the first byte represent deleted records. Deleted records are ignored during sequential retrieval and may be physically deleted when ISAM needs the space they occupy.
M	Specifies that a master index is to be used. You must also code the NTM subparameter to specify the size of the master index.
R	Specifies that ISAM is to record the status of cylinder overflow areas. This information can be used to determine when to reorganize the data set. R is assumed if you omit the OPTCD subparameter altogether. If you code OPTCD, however, you must specify R if you want the statistics recorded.
U	Specifies that track indexes are to be maintained in virtual storage and written to DASD only as needed; if U is omitted, a DASD write operation is performed each time a record is written to the file. OPTCD=U can improve performance for sequential output allocations. Valid only for fixed-length records.
Y	Specifies that overflow records should be written to the cylinder overflow area, whose size is indicated by the CYLOFL subparameter.

Figure 13-2   OPTCD options for ISAM files

The second DD statement in figure 13-4 allocates 15 cylinders to the prime data area. Notice that this DD statement doesn't include a ddname. Notice also that the DCB parameter specifies a referback to the CUSTMAST DD statement. That way, the DCB subparameters for each area of the ISAM file are the same. If you look back at the DCB parameter, you'll see that I reserved one track of each cylinder in the prime data area for the cylinder overflow area.

The third DD statement in figure 13-4 allocates three cylinders to the independent overflow area. Like the second DD statement, it omits the ddname field and uses a referback in the DCB parameter.

How to code DD statements to retrieve ISAM files

In contrast to creating ISAM files, the DD statement requirements for retrieving existing ISAM files are easy to learn. Figure 13-5 shows four examples. Example 1 is the simplest case; it shows you how to retrieve an existing cataloged ISAM file. DSORG=IS is required to identify the file as an ISAM file.

```
//CUSTMAST DD     DSNAME=SYDOE.CUSTOMER.MASTER,DISP=(NEW,CATLG),
//                UNIT=SYSDA,VOL=SER=MPS800,
//                SPACE=(CYL,(14,,1)),
//                DCB=(DSORG=IS,RECFM=F,LRECL=100,KEYLEN=6,RKP=3,
//                CYLOFL=1,OPTCD=Y)
```

Figure 13-3   Allocating an ISAM file with imbedded index and overflow areas

```
//CUSTMAST DD     DSNAME=SYDOE.CUSTOMER.MASTER(INDEX),DISP=(NEW,KEEP),
//                UNIT=SYSDA,VOL=SER=MPS800,
//                SPACE=(CYL,1),
//                DCB=(DSORG=IS,RECFM=F,LRECL=100,KEYLEN=6,RKP=3,
//                NTM=1,CYLOFL=1,OPTCD=MYI)
//         DD     DSNAME=SYDOE.CUSTOMER.MASTER(PRIME),DISP=(NEW,KEEP),
//                UNIT=SYSDA,VOL=SER=MPS800,
//                SPACE=(CYL,15),
//                DCB=*.CUSTMAST
//         DD     DSNAME=SYDOE.CUSTOMER.MASTER(OVFLOW),DISP=(NEW,KEEP),
//                UNIT=SYSDA,VOL=SER=MPS800,
//                SPACE=(CYL,3),
//                DCB=*.CUSTMAST
```

Figure 13-4   Allocating an ISAM file with separate index and overflow areas

Example 2 is only slightly more complicated; it's for an uncataloged ISAM file. Because the file is uncataloged, I included UNIT and VOLUME information. As in example 1, the DD statement in example 2 specifies DSORG=IS.

The DD statements shown in examples 1 and 2 are usually sufficient to allocate the ISAM file even if more than one DD statement was used to create it. However, there's one case where a single DD statement isn't adequate: when the index or overflow area is on a different type of device than the prime data area. For example, if the prime data area is on a 3390 DASD and the index is on a 3380, you must supply separate DD statements to retrieve them. That's just what example 3 in figure 13-5 shows. Notice that you don't have to specify the area type in the DSNAME parameter; ISAM can determine that from the data set labels. Also, be aware that these DD statements must appear in the same sequence as when the ISAM file was created: index, prime data, and overflow.

Example 1

```
//CUSTMAST  DD    DSNAME=SYDOE.CUSTOMER.MASTER,DISP=OLD,
//                DCB=DSORG=IS
```

Allocate an existing cataloged ISAM file.

Example 2

```
//EMPMAST   DD    DSNAME=SYDOE.EMPLOYEE.MASTER,DISP=OLD,
//                UNIT=SYSDA,VOL=SER=MPS800,
//                DCB=DSORG=IS
```

Allocate an existing uncataloged ISAM file.

Example 3

```
//PAYMAST   DD    DSNAME=SYDOE.PAYROLL.MASTER,DISP=OLD,
//                UNIT=3380,VOL=SER=PD8100,
//                DCB=DSORG=IS
//           DD    DSNAME=SYDOE.PAYROLL.MASTER,DISP=OLD,
//                UNIT=3390,VOL=SER=PD9310,
//                DCB=DSORG=IS
```

Allocate an existing uncataloged ISAM file that resides on different device types.

Example 4

```
//CUSTMAST  DD    DSNAME=SYDOE.CUSTOMER.MASTER,DISP=OLD,
//                DCB=(DSORG=IS,OPTCD=L)
```

Allocate an existing ISAM file specifying that deleted records should be ignored.

Figure 13-5   Examples of DD statements to retrieve existing ISAM files

Example 4 in figure 13-5 shows that you can change DCB parameters when you retrieve an existing ISAM file. In particular, this example specifies OPTCD=L in the DCB parameter so that logically deleted records will be ignored as the file is processed and may be physically deleted. You can override other DCB subparameters as well, although you can't change the basic characteristics of the file such as the key length and position.

Discussion

As I mentioned at the start of this chapter, VSAM has all but replaced ISAM for application processing. In fact, ISAM is an optional component of MVS and may not even be available at your installation.

Terminology

ISAM
Indexed Sequential Access Method
BISAM
Basic Indexed Sequential Access Method
QISAM
Queued Indexed Sequential Access Method
prime data area
logically deleted
physically deleted
cylinder index
track index
master index
overflow areas
cylinder overflow area
independent overflow area

Objectives

1. Code a DD statement to create an ISAM file using separate or imbedded index and overflow areas and specifying any of the DCB options covered in this topic.

2. Code a DD statement to retrieve an existing ISAM file, cataloged or uncataloged.

Exercises

1. Code a DD statement that creates a cataloged ISAM file named X401.MASTER on a SYSDA volume named TSO001. Allocate 50 cylinders of space and 2 cylinders for the index. The file contains fixed-length records of 300 bytes each with 8-byte keys starting in the second byte of each record. Provide for a 10-cylinder independent overflow area.

2. Code a DD statement to allocate the ISAM file created in exercise 1.

Chapter 14

How to manage BDAM data sets

DCB subparameters for BDAM files
    The DSORG subparameter
    The BLKSIZE and RECFM subparameters
    The KEYLEN and LIMCT subparameters
    The OPTCD subparameter
Examples of DD statements for BDAM files

BDAM (*Basic Direct Access Method*) files, like ISAM files, let you access records directly and sequentially. Unlike ISAM, however, BDAM does not maintain an index structure to enable direct access. Instead, BDAM provides direct access to records based on the records' positions in the file. As a result, BDAM files are often called *direct files*.

To access a record in a BDAM file, you can supply the record's position in one of three formats. First, you can specify the actual DASD address of the record. In a *DASD address*, you identify the cylinder number, track number, and record number. That's not so good, though, because it ties the file to a particular DASD location. Files addressed in this way are called *unmovable files* because if they are moved from one DASD location to another, the DASD addresses used for the previous file location are invalid.

The second way to address records in a direct file is by *relative track address*. A relative track address specifies a track number relative to the first track in the file, along with a record number that indicates which record on the track is being accessed. When you use relative track addresses, you can copy the file to another location on the volume, or to another volume of the same DASD type, without invalidating the file. You can't copy it to another DASD type, however, because the structure of the file depends on the track capacity of the device where it's stored.

The third way to address records in a direct file is by *relative block address*, which indicates the number of a particular data block relative to the first data block in the file. BDAM treats all files as unblocked, so as far as BDAM is concerned, there's just one record in each block. As a result, the term *relative record number* is sometimes used instead of relative block address. In any event, a file that's accessed in this way is often called a *relative file*. When you use relative block addressing, the file is less dependent on its DASD location and type than it is when you use relative track addressing or actual DASD addresses.

The programming requirements for applications that use direct files can be unreasonably complex. Complex enough, in fact, that avoiding them was one of the main reasons ISAM (and, subsequently, VSAM) was developed. Fortunately, the complexities don't significantly affect the way you code JCL to create or retrieve BDAM files. In fact, you code all of the DD statement parameters for a BDAM file the same as you do for a sequential file, except for the DCB parameter. So, after I describe the DCB subparameters that apply to BDAM files, I'll show you a few examples of DD statements that create and retrieve BDAM data sets.

DCB subparameters for BDAM files

Figure 14-1 shows the DCB subparameters that apply to BDAM files. Most of them are familiar, but some of them have special implications for BDAM.

The DSORG subparameter   When you create a BDAM file, you should specify the DSORG subparameter to indicate that the file has direct organization. Code DSORG=DAU if the records will be accessed using DASD addresses; that makes the file unmovable. Otherwise, code DSORG=DA.

The BLKSIZE and RECFM subparameters   As I already mentioned, all BDAM files are unblocked. As a result, there's no LRECL subparameter in figure 14-1. You use the BLKSIZE subparameter to specify the size of each data block, and you use the RECFM subprameter to indicate whether the blocks are fixed-length (F) or variable-length (V).

That doesn't mean that each BDAM data block must contain just one logical record. It simply means that BDAM doesn't provide any blocking or deblocking functions. If you want to store blocked data in a BDAM file, you have to provide for blocking and deblocking in the application programs that process the file.

The KEYLEN and LIMCT subparameters   Although BDAM doesn't maintain indexes to access keyed records directly, BDAM does provide a crude form of keyed access. Specifically, BDAM lets you store key information in the key portion of the CKD (count-key-data) DASD storage layout. To access a record by key, however, you must still

---

DCB subparameters for BDAM files

```
DSORG={DA | DAU}
RECFM=format
BLKSIZE=size
KEYLEN=key-length
LIMCT=count
OPTCD=options
```

Explanation

DSORG	Specifies BDAM data set organization. If you specify DAU, the file is unmovable.
RECFM	Specifies the record format: F=fixed, V=variable.
BLKSIZE	Specifies the block size.
KEYLEN	Specifies the key length in bytes, if keys are to be recorded.
LIMCT	Specifies how many additional blocks or tracks will be searched for the requested key.
OPTCD	Specifies one or more optional processing features; see figure 14-2 for details.

Figure 14-1   DCB subparameters for BDAM files

provide a relative track or block address. The KEYLEN subparameter lets you specify the length of the keys, if you want to use them.

The LIMCT subparameter extends this capability by letting BDAM search more than one block or track to locate a keyed record. LIMCT identifies how many blocks or tracks beyond the first block or track should be searched. For example, suppose you specify LIMCT=2, and you want to retrieve a record with a key of 5560 using relative track addressing. If you begin the search at track 5 of cylinder 40 and the record isn't found on that track, BDAM will search track 6. If the record still isn't found, BDAM searches track 7. If the record isn't found on track 7, the search is terminated. Whether or not you need to code this subparameter depends on the requirements of your application. If you do code it, however, you should also code OPTCD=E.

The OPTCD subparameter   As you already know, OPTCD lets you specify a variety of processing options that are applied to the file. Figure 14-2 shows the OPTCD options that relate to BDAM files. The first two, which specify how records are accessed, are mutually exclusive. If you specify OPTCD=A, DASD addresses are

OPTCD code	Meaning
A	Specifies that the program will use actual device addresses to locate data blocks.
R	Specifies that the program will use relative block addresses to locate data blocks. Do not code R and A together. If you omit both R and A, the program refers to data blocks using relative track addresses.
E	Specifies that more than one track or block should be searched for a requested record. If you specify OPTCD=E, you must also code the LIMCT subparameter.
F	Specifies that the program can request feedback information from BDAM.

Figure 14-2   OPTCD options for BDAM files

used; if you specify OPTCD=R, relative block addresses are used; if you omit A and R, relative track addresses are used.

OPTCD=E specifies that the extended search option is to be used. It should be coded along with the LIMCT subparameter. OPTCD=F enables a special form of assembler language operations that requests information about the layout of tracks and records in a BDAM file.

Examples of DD statements for BDAM files

Figure 14-3 shows three examples of DD statements for BDAM files. As you study these examples, you'll see that the JCL requirements for BDAM files are minimal.

Example 1 shows how to create a BDAM file. It specifies the file's name, disposition, unit and volume information, space allocation, and organization. In this example, the application program that loads records into the file will supply additional DCB information such as block length, record format, and so on. That's why I specified only DCB=DSORG=DA.

Example 2 shows that to retrieve an existing cataloged BDAM file, you code just the DSNAME and DISP parameters. If the file was uncataloged, I would have included the UNIT and VOLUME parameters as well. The DCB information for a BDAM file can be obtained from the data set label, so a DCB parameter isn't required.

In example 3, I create a BDAM file and supply DCB information. Here, the blocks are fixed length and contain 400 bytes each. The records will be written with six-byte keys, and the extended search option will be used.

Example 1

```
//EMPMAST   DD    DSNAME=SYDOE.EMPLOYEE.MASTER,DISP=(NEW,CATLG),
//                UNIT=SYSDA,VOL=SER=MPS800,
//                SPACE=(CYL,20),
//                DCB=DSORG=DA
```
Allocate a new BDAM file.

Example 2

```
//EMPMAST   DD    DSNAME=SYDOE.EMPLOYEE.MASTER,DISP=OLD
```
Allocate an existing cataloged BDAM file.

Example 3

```
//INVMAST   DD    DSNAME=SYDOE.INVENTRY.MASTER,DISP=(NEW,CATLG),
//                UNIT=SYSDA,VOL=SER=MPS800,
//                SPACE=(CYL,40),
//                DCB=(DSORG=DA,RECFM=F,BLKSIZE=400,
//                KEYLEN=6,LIMCT=2,OPTCD=E)
```
Allocate a new BDAM file and specify DCB information.

Figure 14-3   Examples of the DD statement for BDAM files

Discussion

BDAM is seldom used today for application processing because the programming difficulties it imposes make it a poor choice for most applications. Instead, VSAM files are now used in situations for which BDAM would have been appropriate in the past. Nevertheless, BDAM is a standard component of MVS (unlike ISAM, which is optional) because it's used for some operating system functions.

Terminology

BDAM
Basic Direct Access Method
direct file
DASD address
unmovable file

relative track address
relative block address
relative record number
relative file

Objective

Code a DD statement to create or retrieve a BDAM file.

Exercises

1. Code a DD statement that creates a cataloged BDAM file named X401.MASTER on a SYSDA volume named TSO001. Allocate 50 cylinders to the file.

2. Code a DD statement to allocate the file created in exercise 1.

Section 5

Program development and utilities

The three chapters in this section show you how to use MVS facilities that help you produce programs and job streams for production applications. Chapter 15 shows you how to use MVS program development facilities to compile, link-edit, and execute programs. Chapter 16 shows you how to use the standard utility programs that are available with MVS. And chapter 17 shows you how to use the sort/merge program. These chapters are independent of each other, so you can read them in any order you wish.

Chapter
15

Program development

Most people who use JCL are involved in one form of program development or another. You may be an applications programmer who works mostly in COBOL or a systems programmer who works mostly in assembler language. Or, you might develop programs for one of the major MVS subsystems, like CICS or IMS. In any event, it's likely that the main reason you need to know JCL is to support your program development activities.

In this chapter, you'll learn how to code program development jobs. You won't learn how to code source programs in any particular programming language, but you will learn how to use the MVS facilities that support program development, including the compilers, the linkage editor, and the loader. Because the bulk of program development today is done in COBOL, this chapter emphasizes COBOL program development.

The end result of COBOL program development is a program you can execute directly using a JCL EXEC statement. A program like that is called a "batch program" because it's designed to operate within the context of MVS batch job processing facilities. The COBOL program development concepts you'll learn in this chapter apply to batch program development in any programming language. For online programs that execute under the control of a subsystem like CICS, however, the program development process is different and beyond the scope of this book.

Before I begin, I want to point out that all of the tasks I'll describe in this chapter can probably be done more easily using the interactive facilities of TSO and ISPF. In particular, ISPF lets you invoke the compilers and the linkage editor and loader by making simple menu selections. I won't describe TSO and ISPF program development facilities here. But my book, *MVS TSO, Part 1: Concepts and ISPF*, contains a complete description of how those facilities work.

Program development concepts

As I've already mentioned, the final result of program development is an executable program, called a *load module* in MVS terminology. The most straightforward way to create a load module is to execute a *compile-link-and-go job*, as illustrated in figure 15-1. Here, a *source module*, which contains program statements coded in text form, is compiled or assembled to produce an *object module*, which contains the machine language equivalent of the source module. Then, a program called the *linkage editor* processes the object module to create a load module, which is then executed by an EXEC statement.

During program development, it's common to use a simpler type of job, called a *compile-and-go job*. In figure 15-2, you can see that a compile-and-go job uses a program called the *loader* to combine the functions of link-editing and program execution. In other words, the loader processes the object module created by the compiler and executes it directly; no load module is created. A compile-and-go job is useful during program development because until a program is ready for production, there's no need for a permanent load module.

Two other types of jobs are commonly used during program development. A *compile-only job* simply produces an object module; no linkage editor or loader step is involved. And a *compile-and-link job* compiles and link-edits a program without actually executing the resulting load module.

Because the compilers and the linkage editor and loader are used frequently, IBM supplies cataloged procedures to invoke them in various combinations. So, you don't have to code the JCL to invoke a compiler and the loader for a compile-and-go job; instead you just invoke the compile-and-go cataloged procedure for the programming language you're using. Later in this chapter, I'll describe the details of how you use those procedures. First, though, I want you to learn more about the compilers, the linkage editor, and the loader.

The compilers and the assembler

Strictly speaking, a *compiler* converts the statements of a high-level programming language like COBOL or PL/I into equivalent machine-executable instructions. This conversion is usually one-to-many; in other words, one high-level programming language statement may

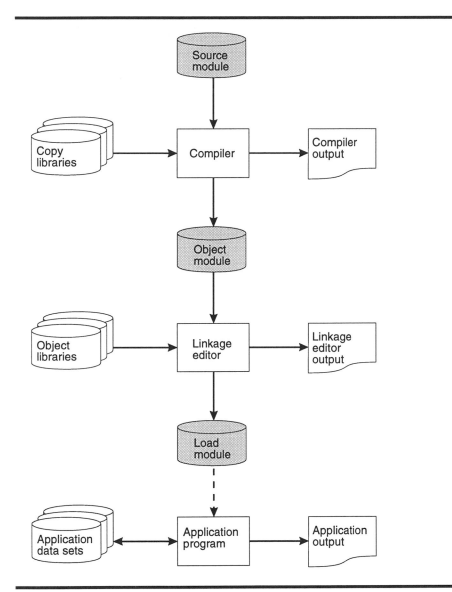

Figure 15-1   Program development under MVS using the linkage editor

result in many machine instructions. In contrast, an *assembler* processes assembler language statements, which usually have a one-to-one correspondence to machine instructions. Other than the nature of the source language statements processed by each, there's little difference between a compiler and an assembler. They both convert a source module containing instructions written according to the rules of a

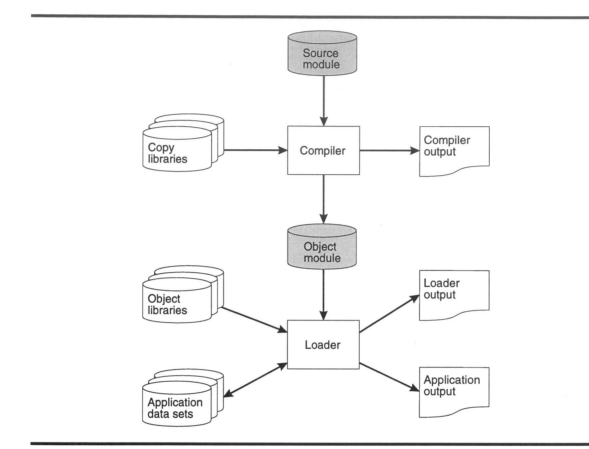

Figure 15-2   Program development under MVS using the loader

programming language into an object module. Throughout the rest of this chapter, then, I'll use the term compiler to mean either a high-level language compiler or an assembler.

As figures 15-1 and 15-2 indicate, a compiler has two inputs and outputs. The main input to a compiler is the source program, called a source module. And the main output is the object module. A compiler can process additional source input in the form of source libraries. And each compiler produces a listing that contains many items of information about the source program.

The source program contains program statements coded in text form according to the rules of one of the programming languages supported under MVS. It's stored in card-image format (80-character records), and can be supplied to the compiler as in-stream data or, more likely, as a member of a partitioned data set. Usually, you'll use an interactive text editor like ISPF's edit option to create and maintain the source program.

Most programming languages let you copy source statements from a *source statement library*. In COBOL, you do that by coding a COPY statement; the COBOL compiler locates the member specified in the COPY statement and copies it into your program. Other languages provide similar facilities.

All of the compilers produce printed output that includes a listing of the source program plus additional useful information. Later on, I'll show you how to tell the compiler what kind of information to include in this listing.

The primary output of a compiler is an object module. It's produced in card-image format, usually as a temporary sequential data set or as a member of a partitioned data set. Although an object module contains the machine instructions that correspond to the source statements in the source program, the object module can't be executed directly. That's because it contains references to other object modules, either invoked by statements you coded in the source program or by instructions inserted by the compiler to perform I/O or other types of processing functions. Either way, the object module must be combined with any other object modules it refers to before it can be executed. You can do that using the linkage editor or the loader.

The linkage editor

The basic function of the linkage editor is to convert an unexecutable object module into an executable load module. In figure 15-1, you can see that the basic input to the linkage editor is an object module produced by a compiler, and the basic output is a load module that can be executed. A load module is stored as a member in a partitioned data set.

As I mentioned, the object module produced by a compiler contains references to other object modules. Some of those references are to IBM-supplied modules, and others are to user-written subprograms. Either way, those references should be resolved by providing the referenced object modules as input to the linkage editor. To do that, you just identify the libraries that contain the modules. Then, the linkage editor searches these *object libraries* to locate any required modules.

Like the compilers, the linkage editor produces printed output that contains useful information. In particular, the output listing includes a map of all the object modules included in the load module. That information can be essential in some debugging situations.

The loader

The loader is similar in function to the linkage editor, except that it doesn't actually create a load module as output. Instead, it combines the object module with any other required modules and loads the executable program directly into virtual storage and executes it. In figure 15-2, you can see that the loader uses the same input as the linkage editor. In addition, any data sets required by the application program must be provided to the loader so they'll be available when the loader executes the program.

As I mentioned earlier, the loader is used mostly during program testing. In a production environment, you don't want to perform link-editing functions each time a program is executed, so you should use the linkage editor only when you want to create a permanent load module. Although the linkage editor provides more advanced link-editing functions than the loader, those functions are rarely used for application programs developed in high-level languages. So there's no benefit to using the linkage editor rather than the loader during program testing.

Cataloged procedures for COBOL program development

As I've already mentioned, IBM provides cataloged procedures for each programming language. In general, there are four procedures for each language: compile only, compile-and-link, compile-link-and-go, and compile-and-go. The names of these procedures are formed by combining a code that indicates which compiler is used (like COBU for VS COBOL or ASMF for Assembler H) with letters that represent which of the three possible job steps are included in the procedure: C for compile, L for link, and G for GO. So, the compile-and-go procedure for VS COBOL is COBUCG. And the Assembler H compile-link-and-go procedure is ASMFCLG.

Figure 15-3 lists the cataloged procedures for the major MVS programming languages. Notice that there are three COBOL compilers: the VS COBOL compiler, which followed the 1974 ANSI COBOL standards and is now seldom used; the VS COBOL II compiler, which follows the 1985 ANSI COBOL standards and is the most widely used compiler; and COBOL/370, the newest IBM COBOL compiler. The procedures that use the VS COBOL compiler begin with COBU, the procedures that use the VS COBOL II compiler begin with COB2U, and the procedures that use the COBOL/370 compiler begin with IGYW.

Language	Procedures				Step names		
	Compile only	Compile & link	Compile link & go	Compile & go	Compile	Link	Go
VS COBOL	COBUC	COBUCL	COBUCLG	COBUCG	COB	LKED	GO
VS COBOL II	COB2UC	COB2UCL	COB2UCLG	COB2UCG	COB2	LKED	GO
COBOL/370	IGYWC	IGYWCL	IGYWCLG	IGYWCG	COBOL	LKED	GO
Assembler H	ASMHC	ASMHCL	ASMHCLG	ASMHCG	C	L	G
High Level Asm	HLASMC	HLASMCL	HLASMCLG	HLASMCG	C	L	G
OS PL/I	PLIXC	PLIXCL	PLIXCLG	PLIXCG	PLI	LKED	GO
PL/I MVS & VM	IEL1C	IEL1CL	IEL1CLG	IEL1CG	PLI	LKED	GO
VS Fortran 2	VSF2C	VSF2CL	VSF2CLG	VSF2CG	FORT	LKED	GO
C/370	EDCC	EDCCL	EDCCLG	(n/a)	COMPILE	LKED	GO

Note: *Some C/370 programs may require a pre-link step that is provided by the cataloged procedure EDCCPLG. The step name for the pre-link step is PLKED.*

Figure 15-3   Cataloged procedures for batch program development in COBOL, assembler language, PL/I, FORTRAN, and C

Similarly, two assemblers and two PL/I compilers are listed in figure 15-3. The procedures for Assembler H begin with ASMH, and the procedures for the more powerful High Level Assembler begin with HLASM. The procedures for OS PL/I begin with PLIX, and the procedures for PL/I MVS & VM begin with IEL1.

Besides the procedure names, figure 15-3 shows the names of the job steps included in each of the procedures. For the COBOL procedures, the compilation step name is COB (for VS COBOL), COB2 (for VS COBOL II), or COBOL (for COBOL/370). The link-edit step name is LKED, and the execution step name is GO for all of the procedures except the assembler procedures; for those, the step names are L and G. In the compile-and-go procedures, the GO (or G) step invokes the loader; in the compile-link-and-go procedures, the GO (or G) step invokes the load module produced by the LKED (or L) step.

You need to know the step names in each procedure because when you invoke the procedure, you'll probably need to add or override DD statements. Figure 15-4 shows the DD statements you need to know about for each step of the COBOL procedures. In the

Step	ddname	Function
COB/COB2/COBOL	SYSIN	Source program input for the COBOL compiler.
	SYSLIB	A library that's searched for members specified in COPY statements.
	SYSLIN	Object module output (supplied in all procedures except COBUC, COB2UC, and IGYWC).
LKED *	SYSLIB	Subprogram library.
	SYSLIN	Object module input (supplied in all procedures that have a LKED step).
	SYSIN	Additional object module input.
	SYSLMOD	Load module output (supplied in all procedures that have a LKED step).
GO	SYSOUT	Output from DISPLAY, EXHIBIT, and TRACE statements.
	SYSIN	Input for ACCEPT statements.
	SYSDBOUT	Symbolic debugging output, including formatted dump output.
	SYSUDUMP SYSABEND	Abnormal termination dump output.

For the COBUCG, COB2UCG, and IGYWCG procedures, which use the loader rather than the linkage editor, data sets specified here for the LKED step are used with the GO step instead.

Figure 15-4   Important DD statements for the COBOL program development procedures

COB/COB2/COBOL step, for example, SYSIN provides the source program input, SYSLIB identifies COPY libraries, and SYSLIN provides object module output that's passed on to the LKED step. I'll have more to say about these DD statements as I describe the procedures individually. As I describe the procedures, I'll refer specifically to the VS COBOL II procedures. With only a few exceptions, the variations for the other compilers aren't significant.

The COBOL compile-only procedures

Sometimes, you want to invoke the COBOL compiler by itself without link-editing or executing the application program. One reason for doing that is to let the COBOL compiler point out any syntax errors so you can correct them before you submit a compile-link-and-go or compile-and-go job to compile and execute the

The **COB2UC** procedure

```
//COB2UC        PROC      CMP='SYS1.COB2COMP'
//*                       PROC FOR COBOL II-COMPILE ONLY
//COB2          EXEC      PGM=IGYCRCTL,PARM='OBJECT,MAP',
//                        REGION=1024K
//STEPLIB       DD        DSNAME=&CMP,DISP=SHR
//SYSPRINT      DD        SYSOUT=A
//SYSLIN        DD        DSNAME=&&LOADSET,UNIT=SYSDA,
//                        DISP=(MOD,PASS),SPACE=(TRK,(3,3)),
//SYSUT1        DD        UNIT=SYSDA,SPACE=(CYL,(1,1))
//SYSUT2        DD        UNIT=SYSDA,SPACE=(CYL,(1,1))
//SYSUT3        DD        UNIT=SYSDA,SPACE=(CYL,(1,1))
//SYSUT4        DD        UNIT=SYSDA,SPACE=(CYL,(1,1))
//SYSUT5        DD        UNIT=SYSDA,SPACE=(CYL,(1,1))
//SYSUT6        DD        UNIT=SYSDA,SPACE=(CYL,(1,1))
//SYSUT7        DD        UNIT=SYSDA,SPACE=(CYL,(1,1))
```

Invoking JCL

```
//SYDOEJ    JOB   USER=SYDOE,PASSWORD=XXXXXXXX
//          EXEC COB2UC,PARM.COB2='APOST,OBJECT'
//COB2.SYSIN  DD DSNAME=SYDOE.PAYROLL.COBOL(PAY4000),DISP=SHR
//COB2.SYSLIB DD DSNAME=SYDOE.COPYLIB.COBOL,DISP=SHR
//COB2.SYSLIN DD DSNAME=SYDOE.PAYROLL.OBJLIB(PAY4000),DISP=SHR
```

Figure 15-5   The COB2UC procedure

program. Another reason is to compile a subprogram you want stored in an object library. To do either, you use the COBUC, COB2UC, or IGYWC procedure. Figure 15-5 shows the procedure for VS COBOL II: COB2UC.

You can see in figure 15-5 that the name of the VS COBOL II compiler is IGYCRCTL. This program is stored in the system program library named SYS1.COB2COMP, which is specified in the PROC statement as the default value of the symbolic parameter named &CMP. This symbolic parameter is referred to in the DSNAME parameter of the STEPLIB DD statement.

The COBOL compiler expects to find the source program in a sequential data set or a partitioned data set member identified by a DD statement named SYSIN. Since the procedure doesn't include SYSIN, you must supply it along with the JCL that invokes the procedure. You'll also want to supply a SYSLIB DD statement if your program uses any COPY statements.

The SYSLIN DD statement specifies that a temporary data set should be used for the object module. If you want to save the object module, you'll need to override the SYSLIN DD statement to identify the data set where you want the object module saved. By the way, don't let the temporary data set name that's used in the procedure (&&LOADSET) confuse you; the SYSLIN DD statement identifies an object module, not a load module.

The other DD statements in the COB2UC procedure—SYSUT1, SYSUT2, SYSUT3, SYSUT4, SYSUT5, SYSUT6, and SYSUT7—allocate work files that are required by the compiler. Because these DD statements specify only UNIT and SPACE information, they'll probably be processed in virtual storage using VIO.

The bottom part of figure 15-5 shows typical JCL used to invoke the COB2UC procedure. Here, SYSIN names a PDS member as the source program, SYSLIB identifies a copy library named SYDOE.COPYLIB.COBOL, and SYSLIN overrides the temporary data set specified in the procedure, storing the object module in SYDOE.PAYROLL.OBJLIB(PAY4000). The PARM parameter on the EXEC statement supplies compiler options; I'll explain it later in this chapter.

As shipped from IBM, the VS COBOL version of the compile-only procedure (COBUC) is designed for syntax checking only; it doesn't produce an object module. To invoke COBUC to produce an object module, you must do two things. First, you must tell the COBOL compiler to produce an object module by specifying PARM.COB='LOAD' on the EXEC statement that invokes the procedure. (I'll explain how and why you pass parameters to the COBOL compiler later in this chapter.) Second, you must supply a DD statement for SYSLIN just as you do for the COB2UC procedure when you don't want to use the temporary data set specified in the procedure.

The COBOL compile-and-link procedures

The COBUCL, COB2UCL, and IGYWCL procedures each contain two steps: the COB, COB2, or COBOL step compiles a program, and the LKED step link-edits the resulting object module to create a load module. Figure 15-6 shows the COB2UCL procedure and the JCL you typically code to invoke it.

The COB2 step of COB2UCL is the same as the COB2 step of COB2UC. In the LKED step, the object module stored in the &&LOADSET temporary data set is used as input to the linkage editor, whose program name is IEWL. When the LKED step finishes, &&LOADSET is deleted. But the resulting load module, stored as a member named GO in a temporary partitioned data set

The COB2UCL procedure

```
//COB2UCL    PROC     CMP='SYS1.COB2COMP',LIB='SYS1.COB2LIB'
//*                   PROC FOR COBOL II-COMPILE AND LINK
//COB2       EXEC     PGM=IGYCRCTL,PARM='OBJECT',REGION=1024K
//STEPLIB    DD       DSNAME=&CMP,DISP=SHR
//SYSPRINT   DD       SYSOUT=A
//SYSLIN     DD       DSNAME=&&LOADSET,UNIT=SYSDA,DISP=(MOD,PASS),
//                    SPACE=(TRK,(3,3))
//SYSUT1     DD       UNIT=SYSDA,SPACE=(CYL,(1,1))
//SYSUT2     DD       UNIT=SYSDA,SPACE=(CYL,(1,1))
//SYSUT3     DD       UNIT=SYSDA,SPACE=(CYL,(1,1))
//SYSUT4     DD       UNIT=SYSDA,SPACE=(CYL,(1,1))
//SYSUT5     DD       UNIT=SYSDA,SPACE=(CYL,(1,1))
//SYSUT6     DD       UNIT=SYSDA,SPACE=(CYL,(1,1))
//SYSUT7     DD       UNIT=SYSDA,SPACE=(CYL,(1,1))
//LKED       EXEC     PGM=IEWL,PARM='LIST,XREF,LET,MAP',COND=(5,LT,COB2),
//                    REGION=512K
//SYSLIN     DD       DSNAME=&&LOADSET,DISP=(OLD,DELETE)
//           DD       DDNAME=SYSIN
//SYSLMOD    DD       DSNAME=&&GOSET(GO),DISP=(,PASS),UNIT=SYSDA,
//                    SPACE=(CYL,(1,1,1))
//SYSLIB     DD       DSNAME=&LIB,DISP=SHR
//SYSUT1     DD       UNIT=SYSDA,SPACE=(CYL,(1,1))
//SYSPRINT   DD       SYSOUT=A
```

Invoking JCL

```
//SYDOEJ     JOB      USER=SYDOE,PASSWORD=XXXXXXXX
//           EXEC     COB2UCL,PARM.COB2='APOST,OBJECT'
//COB2.SYSIN    DD    DSNAME=SYDOE.PAYROLL.COBOL(PAY4000),DISP=SHR
//COB2.SYSLIB   DD    DSNAME=SYDOE.COPYLIB.COBOL,DISP=SHR
//LKED.SYSLMOD  DD    DSNAME=SYDOE.PAYROLL.LOADLIB(PAY4000),DISP=SHR
//LKED.SYSLIB   DD
//             DD     DSNAME=SYDOE.PAYROLL.OBJLIB,DISP=SHR
```

Figure 15-6   The COB2UCL procedure

named &&GOSET, is passed to the next job step. Usually, you'll
want to store the load module in a permanent load library, so be
sure to override the SYSLMOD DD statement to indicate the member and library. In the bottom part of figure 15-6, I store the load
module in SYDOE.PAYROLL.LOADLIB(PAY4000).

The SYSLIB DD statement in the LKED step identifies any object
libraries used to resolve subprogram references. As you can see, the
procedure supplies one subprogram library; SYS1.COB2LIB. (This
library is coded as the default value for the &LIB symbolic parameter, which is referred to in the SYSLIB DD statement.) This library
contains essential COBOL subroutines, so it must be available when
the object module is link edited. To concatenate another object

library to SYS1.COB2LIB, you code two DD statements in the invoking JCL, like this:

```
//LKED.SYSLIB  DD
//             DD  DSNAME=SYDOE.PAYROLL.OBJLIB,DISP=SHR
```

Here, I didn't code any parameters on the first DD statement. That way, its parameter information will be copied from the procedure. Then, the second DD statement concatenates my private object library, SYDOE.PAYROLL.OBJLIB, with SYS1.COB2LIB.

Notice that the EXEC statement in the LKED step specifies conditional execution using this COND parameter:

```
COND=(5,LT,COB2)
```

Because of this parameter, the linkage editor is not invoked if 5 is less than the return code from the COB2 step. In other words, if the COBOL compiler issues a return code of 5 or more, which indicates a serious error, the linkage editor isn't executed.

The COBOL compile-link-and-go procedures

To compile, link-edit, and execute a COBOL program, you use COBUCLG, COB2UCLG, or IGYWCLG; figure 15-7 shows the VS COBOL II version, COB2UCLG. The COB2 and LKED steps are the same as in the other procedures. In the GO step, the PGM parameter of the EXEC statement uses a backwards reference to execute the program defined by the SYSLMOD DD statement in the LKED step.

The EXEC statement in the GO step includes a COND parameter that specifies these conditions:

```
COND=((5,LT,LKED),(5,LT,COB2))
```

In other words, the load module isn't executed if the LKED or COB2 step issues a return code of 5 or greater.

In the invoking JCL shown in the bottom part of figure 15-7, you can see that I supplied several DD statements for the GO step. The first, SYSOUT, defines the output data set used to print messages produced by COBOL DISPLAY statements. The others, PAYTRAN and PAYRPT, allocate files processed by the program.

The COBOL compile-and-go procedures

For most program development purposes, you can use the simpler compile-and-go procedures rather than the compile-link-and-go procedures. For COBOL, the compile-and-go procedures are COBUCG, COB2UCG, and IGYWCG. Figure 15-8 shows COB2UCG.

The COB2UCLG procedure

```
//COB2UCLG   PROC  CMP='SYS1.COB2COMP',LIB='SYS1.COB2LIB'
//*                PROC FOR COBOL II COMPILE, LINK AND GO
//COB2       EXEC  PGM=IGYCRCTL,PARM='OBJECT',REGION=1024K
//STEPLIB    DD    DSNAME=&CMP,DISP=SHR
//SYSPRINT   DD    SYSOUT=A
//SYSLIN     DD    DSNAME=&&LOADSET,UNIT=SYSDA,DISP=(MOD,PASS),
//                 SPACE=(TRK,(3,3)),DCB=(BLKSIZE=80,LRECL=80,RECFM=FB)
//SYSUT1     DD    UNIT=SYSDA,SPACE=(CYL,(1,1))
//SYSUT2     DD    UNIT=SYSDA,SPACE=(CYL,(1,1))
//SYSUT3     DD    UNIT=SYSDA,SPACE=(CYL,(1,1))
//SYSUT4     DD    UNIT=SYSDA,SPACE=(CYL,(1,1))
//SYSUT5     DD    UNIT=SYSDA,SPACE=(CYL,(1,1))
//SYSUT6     DD    UNIT=SYSDA,SPACE=(CYL,(1,1))
//SYSUT7     DD    UNIT=SYSDA,SPACE=(CYL,(1,1))
//LKED       EXEC  PGM=IEWL,PARM='LIST,XREF,LET,MAP',COND=(5,LT,COB2),
//                 REGION=512K
//SYSLIN     DD    DSNAME=&&LOADSET,DISP=(OLD,DELETE)
//           DD    DDNAME=SYSIN
//SYSLMOD    DD    DSNAME=&&GOSET(GO),DISP=(,PASS),UNIT=SYSDA,
//                 SPACE=(CYL,(1,1,1))
//SYSLIB     DD    DSNAME=&LIB,DISP=SHR
//SYSUT1     DD    UNIT=SYSDA,SPACE=(CYL,(1,1))
//SYSPRINT   DD    SYSOUT=A
//GO         EXEC  PGM=*.LKED.SYSLMOD,COND=((5,LT,LKED),(5,LT,COB2))
//STEPLIB    DD    DSNAME=&LIB,DISP=SHR
//SYSABOUT   DD    SYSOUT=A
//SYSDBOUT   DD    SYSOUT=A
//SYSUDUMP   DD    SYSOUT=A
```

Invoking JCL

```
//SYDOEJ     JOB   USER=SYDOE,PASSWORD=XXXXXXXX
//           EXEC  COB2UCLG,PARM.COB2='APOST,OBJECT'
//COB2.SYSIN    DD DSNAME=SYDOE.PAYROLL.COBOL(PAY4000),DISP=SHR
//COB2.SYSLIB   DD DSNAME=SYDOE.COPYLIB.COBOL,DISP=SHR
//LKED.SYSLMOD  DD DSNAME=SYDOE.PAYROLL.LOADLIB(PAY4000),DISP=SHR
//LKED.SYSLIB   DD
//             DD DSNAME=SYDOE.PAYROLL.OBJLIB,DISP=SHR
//GO.SYSOUT     DD SYSOUT=A
//GO.PAYTRAN    DD DSNAME=SYDOE.PAYROLL.TRANS,DISP=SHR
//GO.PAYRPT     DD SYSOUT=A
```

Figure 15-7   The COB2UCLG procedure

As you can see, the COB2 step in the COB2UCG procedure is the same as it is in the COB2UCLG procedure. However, the GO step combines the functions performed by the LKED and GO steps in COB2UCLG. In the EXEC statement, the program name is LOADER; it's executed only if the COBOL compiler issues a return code that's less than 5.

The COB2UCG procedure

```
//COB2UCG     PROC      CMP='SYS1.COB2COMP',LIB='SYS1.COB2LIB'
//*                     PROC FOR COBOL II COMPILE AND GO
//COB2        EXEC      PGM=IGYCRCTL,PARM='OBJECT',REGION=1024K
//STEPLIB     DD        DSNAME=&CMP,DISP=SHR
//SYSPRINT    DD        SYSOUT=A
//SYSLIN      DD        DSNAME=&&LOADSET,UNIT=SYSDA,DISP=(MOD,PASS),
//                      SPACE=(TRK,(3,3))
//SYSUT1      DD        UNIT=SYSDA,SPACE=(CYL,(1,1))
//SYSUT2      DD        UNIT=SYSDA,SPACE=(CYL,(1,1))
//SYSUT3      DD        UNIT=SYSDA,SPACE=(CYL,(1,1))
//SYSUT4      DD        UNIT=SYSDA,SPACE=(CYL,(1,1))
//SYSUT5      DD        UNIT=SYSDA,SPACE=(CYL,(1,1))
//SYSUT6      DD        UNIT=SYSDA,SPACE=(CYL,(1,1))
//SYSUT7      DD        UNIT=SYSDA,SPACE=(CYL,(1,1))
//GO          EXEC      PGM=LOADER,PARM='MAP,LET',COND=(5,LT,COB2)
//SYSLIB      DD        DSNAME=&LIB,DISP=SHR
//SYSLIN      DD        DSNAME=*.COB2.SYSLIN,DISP=(OLD,DELETE)
//SYSLOUT     DD        SYSOUT=A
//SYSABOUT    DD        SYSOUT=A
//SYSDBOUT    DD        SYSOUT=A
//SYSUDUMP    DD        SYSOUT=A
```

Invoking JCL

```
//SYDOEJ    JOB   USER=SYDOE,PASSWORD=XXXXXXX
//          EXEC COB2UCG,PARM.COB2='APOST,OBJECT'
//COB2.SYSIN  DD   DSNAME=SYDOE.PAYROLL.COBOL(PAY4000),DISP=SHR
//COB2.SYSLIB DD   DSNAME=SYDOE.COPYLIB.COBOL,DISP=SHR
//GO.SYSLIB   DD
//            DD   DSNAME=SYDOE.PAYROLL.OBJLIB,DISP=SHR
//GO.SYSOUT   DD   SYSOUT=A
//GO.PAYTRAN  DD   DSNAME=SYDOE.PAYROLL.TRANS,DISP=SHR
//GO.PAYRPT   DD   SYSOUT=A
```

Figure 15-8   The COB2UCG procedure

SYSLIN identifies the primary input to the loader; in this case, a backwards reference is used to indicate that the object module output (SYSLIN) from the COB2 step should be used. The SYSLIB DD statement required for the LKED step in figure 15-7 is supplied to the loader in the GO step in figure 15-8. The DD statements required by the COBOL program (PAYTRAN and PAYRPT) are supplied in the GO step as well.

Compiler options

Compiler options control various optional functions of a compiler or assembler. For example, you can specify a compiler option to indicate

Category	VS COBOL	VS COBOL II and COBOL/370	Function
Object module	LOAD DECK	OBJECT DECK	Writes object module output to SYSLIN. Writes object module output to SYSPUNCH.
Delimiter	QUOTE APOST	QUOTE APOST	Use the ANSI standard quotation mark ("). Use the apostrophe (').
Source library	LIB	LIB	Allow COPY statements.
Compiler listing	SOURCE CLIST PMAP DMAP XREF SXREF	SOURCE OFFSET LIST MAP XREF	Print source listing. Print offset of each Procedure Division verb. Print assembler listing of object module. Print offset of each Data Division field. Print Data Division/Procedure Division cross reference. Print sorted cross reference.
Testing	TEST SYMDMP STATE FLOW	TEST FDUMP	Allow interactive debugging. Provide formatted dump at abend. Print statement number at abend. Print a program execution trace.

Figure 15-9   Commonly used compiler options for VS COBOL, VS COBOL II, and COBOL/370

whether or not you want the compiler to produce an object module. Another compiler option specifies whether or not you want the compiler to print a listing of the source program. And so on. To give you some idea of how to use these options, I'll briefly describe the compiler options you're likely to use for the COBOL compilers; although the other compilers may use different options, they provide similar functions. Then, I'll show you how to specify the compiler options you want to use.

COBOL compiler options

Figure 15-9 shows some of the more commonly used compiler options for the VS COBOL, VS COBOL II, and COBOL/370 compilers. There are others, but they aren't used as often. I've listed the options for all three compilers here so you can see that different keywords are used to represent similar options.

To turn off one of the options shown in figure 15-9, you code NO in front of the option keyword. In other words, if you don't want a source listing, you specify NOSOURCE. (An exception to that rule is the QUOTE/APOST option, which I'll explain in a few moments.)

Options to control object code generation   If you want the compiler to write an object module to the SYSLIN data set, you should make sure the LOAD (VS COBOL) or OBJECT (VS COBOL II or COBOL/370) option is specified. If NOLOAD or NOOBJECT is specified, an object module isn't written to SYSLIN.

As an alternative to creating an object module in a DASD data set, the DECK option lets you create a card-image object module that's written to a file identified by the SYSPUNCH DD statement. Practically speaking, there's no difference between the SYSPUNCH object module and the SYSLIN object module. So the DECK option isn't used much.

Option to set the literal delimiter   Officially, the ANSI COBOL standards require that all alphanumeric literals be delimited by quotes ("). IBM COBOL compilers, however, provide an option that lets you specify whether you're using quotes or apostrophes (') to mark literals. And, for historical reasons, most IBM installations have used apostrophes regardless of the standards. IBM ships the COBOL compiler with QUOTE as the default setting, so you'll probably need to change it to APOST.

Unlike the other compiler options, QUOTE and APOST have no negative forms. In other words, you can't code NOQUOTE or NOAPOST. In addition, QUOTE and APOST are mutually exclusive; you can only code one or the other.

Option to control COPY library usage   The LIB option indicates whether or not you want the compiler to process COPY statements. Surprisingly, the default setting for this option is NOLIB, which prohibits COPY statements. So, if you use COPY statements in your programs, be sure the LIB option is activated.

Options for compiler output   The COBOL compilers can produce several different kinds of output that can be useful as you test your program. The main form of output is a simple listing of the source program; it's produced if the SOURCE option is in effect.

The CLIST (VS COBOL) and OFFSET (VS COBOL II and COBOL/370) options produce a listing that indicates the relative address (or offset) within the object module for each Procedure Division statement. Using this listing, along with information supplied in a storage dump, you can locate the last statement that was executed before an abend occurred. A similar listing is produced when you specify PMAP (VS COBOL) or LIST (VS COBOL II and COBOL/370). This listing, however, shows not just the offset of each Procedure Division statement, but lists each of the assembler language instructions generated for the statement as well. For most uses, the CLIST/OFFSET listing is sufficient.

The DMAP (VS COBOL) and MAP (VS COBOL II and COBOL/370) options produce a map of the Data Division that includes the characteristics and offset of each data field. Like the CLIST/OFFSET listing, this listing can be invaluable when an abend occurs.

The XREF and SXREF options help you trace how variables are used in Procedure Division statements. They produce a listing of each field defined in the Data Division and each Procedure Division statement that references the field. SXREF for VS COBOL is the same as XREF for VS COBOL II and COBOL/370; the listing is printed in alphabetical order by field name. For VS COBOL, XREF produces an unsorted listing that's not as useful.

Options used for symbolic debugging   COBOL provides two basic forms of debugging information that can dramatically simplify the debugging process. The TEST option lets you use an interactive debugging tool that lets you monitor the progress of your program's execution from a TSO terminal. You're more likely to use this option when you compile your program directly from TSO, however.

The SYMDMP, STATE, and FLOW options for VS COBOL and the FDUMP option for VS COBOL II and COBOL/370 provide information that's helpful when your program abends. SYMDMP produces a formatted listing of the contents of each Data Division field. STATE identifies by statement number the Procedure Division statement that was last executed before the abend. And FLOW provides a trace of your program's execution. For VS COBOL II and COBOL/370, the FDUMP option provides similar information. For any of these options to work, you must provide a SYSDBOUT DD statement in the procedure's GO step.

How to specify compiler options

To select a compiler option, you use the PARM parameter on the EXEC statement that invokes the procedure, specifying the compiler's step name. For example, the statement

```
//              EXEC PROC=COB2UC,PARM.COB='OBJECT,XREF'
```

specifies that the OBJECT and XREF options should be used.

When you code a PARM parameter on an EXEC statement that invokes a procedure, you need to be aware that there are two previous levels at which compiler options can be set. First, when the compiler is installed, each option is given a default setting. Although IBM recommends specific defaults for each option, an installation can change those defaults to meet its own needs.

Second, the cataloged procedures themselves contain PARM parameters on the EXEC statements that invoke the compilers. In other words, each procedure overrides some of the compiler options to meet the processing needs of the procedure. In figure 15-8, for example, you can see that the EXEC statement that invokes the COBOL compiler specifies PARM='OBJECT' so that an object module will be created.

Whenever you code the PARM parameter in a procedure-invoking EXEC statement, your PARM values replace the ones in the procedure you invoke. So if you want one or more of the options specified in the procedure to remain in effect, you must code them in your PARM parameter; otherwise, they'll revert to their default values.

To illustrate, suppose you want the APOST option to be in effect when you invoke the COB2UCG procedure. If you just specify PARM.COB='APOST', the OBJECT option specified in the procedure will revert to its default: NOOBJECT. So you must specify PARM.COB2='APOST,OBJECT' so that both APOST and OBJECT will be in effect. That's just what I did in figure 15-8.

Sometimes, it's helpful to know what a compiler's default option settings are. To find that out, you can invoke the compiler's procedure and specify PARM=''. That way, the compiler options in the procedure will be ignored. In the compiler listing, you'll find an indication of which options were used; all of them represent default options for the compiler.

Incidentally, the linkage editor and the loader both let you specify options, too. Since you don't normally need to change those options, I won't describe them here.

Discussion

This chapter has focused on the JCL requirements for compiling and executing batch COBOL programs. The JCL requirements for compiling and executing batch programs written in other languages, like PL/I or assembler language, are similar. But if you're developing a program that will execute under the control of a subsystem like CICS, the JCL requirements are altogether different. You'll have to refer to IBM literature or other training materials to learn those requirements.

Of course, the purpose of this chapter has been to teach you JCL for program development rather than to teach you how to code programs in any specific programming language. Mike Murach and Associates, Inc. publishes a variety of books on programming languages, including COBOL and assembler language. If you're interested in learning more about these languages, you'll find those books listed on the order form that's at the back of this book.

Terminology

load module	compile-only job
compile-link-and-go job	compile-and-link job
source module	compiler
object module	assembler
linkage editor	source statement library
compile-and-go job	object library
loader	compiler option

Objectives

1. Describe the differences between a source module, an object module, and a load module.

2. Describe the functional difference between the linkage editor and the loader.

3. Code the JCL necessary to invoke the VS COBOL, VS COBOL II, or COBOL/370 program development cataloged procedures, supplying any DD statements that might be necessary to allocate required data sets.

4. List the more commonly used options for the VS COBOL, VS COBOL II, or COBOL/370 compilers, and explain how to specify them when you invoke a program development procedure.

Exercise

Code a job that compiles and link-edits a member named X401RPT in a source library named X401.MASTER.COBOL and stores the resulting load module in X401.MASTER.LOAD. Any copy members required by the program are contained in X401.COPYLIB.COBOL or SYS3.COPYLIB.COBOL, and the program may call subprograms contained in X401.MASTER.OBJLIB or SYS3.COBOL.OBJLIB.

Chapter 16

Utility programs

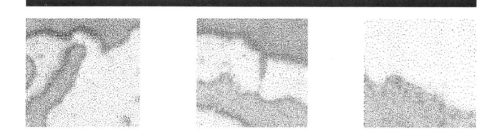

Utility programs (or just *utilities*) are generalized programs that can be used for common data processing functions. For example, computer installations frequently copy sequential files. To write a separate program to copy each file would be a waste of programmer effort. So, MVS includes a utility program that can copy any sequential file.

This chapter introduces you to the utility programs that are available under MVS. First, I'll describe the types of utility programs so you'll have an idea of what's available. Then, I'll show you how to use each of the utility programs.

Types of MVS utility programs

Many utility programs are available under MVS. Some are supplied by IBM as a part of MVS, some are licensed separately from IBM, and some are available from independent software developers. Many of them duplicate the functions of another, and many of them are provided for the sake of compatibility with other systems or with earlier OS or MVS systems, even though there may be better utility programs to perform a given function.

MVS comes with a set of utility programs called simply *MVS utilities*. These programs have been available in the same basic form for years. As a result, many of them provide functions that are either obsolete or better handled by other, more recently developed utility programs. But some of them are still commonly used, so you need to be familiar with them. Figure 16-1 lists the MVS utilities that are covered in this chapter.

In chapter 10, you learned how to use another utility program: the VSAM multi-function utility program, Access Method Services.

Program	Function
IEBGENER	Copies sequential data sets.
IEBPTPCH	Prints and punches sequential data sets.
IEBCOPY	Copies, merges, and compresses partitioned data sets.
IEBDG	Generates test data.
IEBCOMPR	Compares the contents of sequential data sets.
IEBUPDTE	Updates PDS members.
IEHLIST	Lists system information: PDS directories, VTOC entries, and obsolete CVOL entries.
IEHMOVE	Copies and moves DASD data.
IEHPROGM	Maintains catalog entries.

Figure 16-1   Major MVS utilities

For VSAM files, IDCAMS performs many of the same utility functions performed for non-VSAM files by the MVS utilities. And you can use some IDCAMS functions, like copying and printing, for non-VSAM files. Like the MVS utilities, IDCAMS is a standard part of MVS.

Another commonly used utility program is the sort/merge program, called DFSORT. This program sorts or merges the records of sequential files. Sort/merge played a major role in the past, when batch processing was the norm. In today's online systems, however, sorting is less important; VSAM key-sequenced data sets reduce the need for sorting by maintaining data sets in key sequence automatically. But you need to know how to use sort/merge because there are still many applications that require data to be sorted. Although sort/merge is an optional, separately licensed program, it (or compatible programs from independent software developers) is used almost universally. DFSORT is covered in detail in the next chapter.

How to copy or print a data set: the IEBGENER program

One of the most commonly required utility functions is copying or printing data sets. Copying and printing a data set are essentially the same thing: To print a file, you simply copy it to a SYSOUT data set; JES2/JES3 takes care of the actual printing.

```
//COPYFILE EXEC  PGM=IEBGENER
//SYSPRINT DD    SYSOUT=*
//SYSUT1    DD    DSNAME=SYDOE.TEST.CUSTMAST,DISP=OLD
//SYSUT2    DD    DSNAME=SYDOE.CUSTMAST.BACKUP,DISP=(NEW,CATLG),
//                UNIT=SYSDA,VOL=SER=MPS8BV,
//                SPACE=(CYL,(1,1))
//SYSIN     DD    DUMMY
```

Figure 16-2   An IEBGENER job step to copy a sequential file

In chapter 10, you learned how to use the IDCAMS REPRO and PRINT statements to copy and print VSAM and non-VSAM files. So I won't repeat that information here. Instead, I'll concentrate on the MVS utility that copies data sets: IEBGENER. (Another MVS utility, IEBPTPCH, is designed to print data sets. It's covered later in this chapter.)

Figure 16-2 shows a simple IEBGENER job step. Here, IEBGENER is invoked to copy the contents of a sequential file named SYDOE.TEST.CUSTMAST to a new data set named SYDOE.CUSTMAST.BACKUP.

As you can see, IEBGENER requires four DD statements: SYSPRINT defines an output message file, SYSUT1 defines the input file, SYSUT2 defines the output file, and SYSIN defines a control file. In figure 16-2, SYSIN is a DUMMY data set; no control statements are supplied. When IEBGENER is invoked without control statements, a simple copy operation is performed; each record in the input file is written unchanged to the output file.

In the SYSIN file, you can include control statements that let you modify the format of the input records by rearranging fields or converting data to different formats. For example, a zoned-decimal field that appears in one input record location can be converted to packed-decimal and placed in a different output record location. In my experience, however, I've found that the capabilities of IEBGENER are inadequate for most applications where I've needed to reformat data, so I've ended up writing COBOL programs to do the reformatting anyway. As a result, I won't show you how to use the IEBGENER control statements.

One final point about IEBGENER: In figure 16-2, IEBGENER performs a copy operation by copying the input file to a DASD data set. You can also use IEBGENER to print a data set simply by allocating the output file as a SYSOUT data set. In fact, the first job I presented in this book did just that. Although it's the simplest way to print a data set under MVS, there are three problems with it. First, IEBGENER doesn't realize that it's writing data to a SYSOUT data set, so it pays no attention to page divisions. In other words, printed output from IEBGENER will print right over the perforation between pages. The second and third problems are more serious: IEBGENER can't print unprintable data (like packed-decimal fields); and if the input records are too long to be printed on a single line, IEBGENER truncates any excess characters. To print files that have unprintable data or long records, you should use IEBPTPCH or IDCAMS rather than IEBGENER.

How to print or punch data: the IEBPTPCH program

Although you can use the IEBGENER program to copy a file to a SYSOUT data set, the resulting output is completely unformatted. To produce a formatted listing of a data set, you can use IEBPTPCH, the Print/Punch utility. IEBPTPCH adds titles and page numbers to the output.

Like IEBGENER, IEBPTPCH requires that you allocate the input data set using the ddname SYSUT1 and the output data set using the ddname SYSUT2. Unlike IEBGENER, however, IEBPTPCH requires that you provide at least one control statement via a SYSIN DD statement. At the minimum, the SYSIN input stream should contain either a PRINT or a PUNCH statement. Other statements you can use are TITLE, MEMBER, and RECORD.

The PRINT and PUNCH statements

Figure 16-3 shows the format of the PRINT and PUNCH statements. The PRINT statement is the primary control statement for IEBPTPCH. For printing operations, it must be the first statement in the SYSIN file. In its simplest form, it is coded like this:

```
PRINT
```

Here, no parameters are coded. When PRINT is used without parameters, data from the input file is printed in groups of eight characters with each group separated by two blanks. Up to 112 characters (12 groups of eight) can be printed on one line. If the input record contains more than 112 characters, the data is wrapped to additional lines.

The PRINT statement

```
PRINT   [ PREFORM={A|M} ]
        [ ,TYPORG={PS|PO} ]
        [ ,TOTCONV={XE|PZ} ]
        [ ,CNTRL={1|2|3} ]
        [ ,STRTAFT=n ]
        [ ,STOPAFT=n ]
        [ ,SKIP=n ]
        [ ,MAXNAME=n ]
        [ ,MAXFLDS=n ]
        [ ,INITPG=n ]
        [ ,MAXLINE=n ]
```

The PUNCH statement

```
PUNCH   [ PREFORM={A|M} ]
        [ ,TYPORG={PS|PO} ]
        [ ,TOTCONV={XE|PZ} ]
        [ ,CNTRL={1|2|3} ]
        [ ,STRTAFT=n ]
        [ ,STOPAFT=n ]
        [ ,SKIP=n ]
        [ ,MAXNAME=n ]
        [ ,MAXFLDS=n ]
        [ ,CDSEQ=n ]
        [ ,CDINCR=n ]
```

Explanation

PREFORM	Specifies that the input file already contains printer-control characters in the first byte of each record. A indicates ASA characters; M indicates machine characters. If you specify PREFORM, do not specify any other PRINT/PUNCH options.
TYPORG	Indicates the input file organization: PS for sequential files, PO for partitioned files. The default is PS.
TOTCONV	Indicates conversion of the entire input record (as opposed to conversion of individual fields specified by the RECORD statement). XE means to convert to hexadecimal; PZ means to unpack packed-decimal fields. If TOTCONV is omitted, no conversion is done.
CNTRL	Specifies the line spacing for the output listing. The default is 1.
STRTAFT	Indicates how many records to skip before printing.
STOPAFT	Indicates the number of records to be printed.
SKIP	Indicates that only every nth record is to be printed.
MAXNAME	Specifies the number of MEMBER statements in the SYSIN file.
MAXFLDS	Specifies the number of FIELD parameters in subsequent RECORD statements.
INITPG	Specifies the starting page number. The default is 1.
MAXLINE	Specifies the number of lines to print on each page. The default is 50.
CDSEQ	Specifies the starting value for sequence numbers punched in columns 73-80.
CDINCR	Specifies the increment for the sequence numbers. The default is 10.

Figure 16-3   The PRINT and PUNCH statements of IEBPTPCH

If you don't like the way the PRINT statement prints the input data in groups of eight characters, you can use the PUNCH statement instead. IEBPTPCH was designed back in the days when most computer installations had card punch devices and punched cards were commonly used. Although punched cards are now long obsolete, the PUNCH statement is still useful for printing files without the annoying eight-character groupings used by the PRINT statement.

You use the TOTCONV parameter to convert the input data from one format to another. For example, the PRINT statement

```
PRINT TOTCONV=XE
```

prints the input file in hexadecimal format. Unfortunately, the hexadecimal format used by IEBPTPCH isn't very readable. If you want to print data in hexadecimal form, I suggest you use the IDCAMS PRINT command instead. It is described in chapter 10.

If you want to print just a certain range of input records, you can use the STRTAFT, STOPAFT, and SKIP parameters. For example, the PRINT statement

```
PRINT STRTAFT=100,STOPAFT=300
```

prints 300 records starting at the 100th record in the file. And the statement

```
PRINT SKIP=10
```

prints only every tenth record in the file.

Two of the PRINT parameters, MAXNAME and MAXFLDS, are used in conjunction with other control statements. For example, if the SYSIN file contains three MEMBER statements, the PRINT command must contain a MAXNAME parameter, like this:

```
PRINT MAXNAME=3
```

Otherwise, IEBPTPCH will terminate with an error. You must similarly indicate the number of FIELD parameters you code on RECORD statements with the MAXFLDS parameter.

Two of the parameters listed in figure 16-3 apply only to PUNCH statements: CDSEQ and CDINCR. Both are used to insert sequence numbers into the output file. CDSEQ provides the starting value for the sequence numbers, and CDINCR provides the increment value. If you use either of these parameters, sequence numbers are placed in columns 73 through 80 of the output records. Otherwise, the sequence numbers are omitted.

The TITLE statement

```
TITLE  ITEM=('literal'[,out-loc])
```

literal   The title to be printed.

out-loc   The starting position of the literal in the title line. The default is 1.

The MEMBER statement

```
MEMBER NAME=name
```

name   The name of the member to be printed or punched.

The RECORD statement

```
RECORD    FIELD=(length[,in-loc][,conv][,out-loc])
          [,FIELD=(length[,in-loc][,conv][,out-loc])]...
```

length   The length of the field.

in-loc   The position of the field in the input record. The default is 1.

conv   The conversion operation to be performed on the field. Specify XE to convert to hexadecimal or PZ to unpack packed-decimal fields. If omitted, no conversion is done.

out-loc   The position where the field should begin in the output record. The default is 1.

Figure 16-4   Other IEBPTPCH control statements

Other IEBPTPCH control statements

In addition to the PRINT and PUNCH statements, IEBPTPCH lets you code three other control statements: TITLE, MEMBER, and RECORD. These control statements are summarized in figure 16-4.

The TITLE statement   The TITLE statement specifies a literal that is printed at the beginning of the listing. For example, the TITLE statement

```
TITLE ITEM=('LISTING OF TRANSACTION FILE',20)
```

says to print "LISTING OF TRANSACTION FILE" beginning in column 20.

If you use a TITLE statement, it must immediately follow the PRINT or PUNCH statement. If you want to print two title lines, you can use two TITLE statements.

The MEMBER statement   The MEMBER statement is used when the input file (SYSUT1) is a partitioned data set. It specifies the name of a member you want to print. For example, the MEMBER statement

```
MEMBER NAME=TRANREC
```

prints the member named TRANREC.

If you want to print more than one member, you simply code more than one MEMBER statement. To print three members, for example, you code three MEMBER statements, like this:

```
PRINT TYPORG=PO,MAXNAME=3
MEMBER NAME=TRANREC
MEMBER NAME=ORDREC
MEMBER NAME=ACRCREC
```

Notice that I coded TYPORG=PO on the PRINT statement to tell IEBPTPCH that the input file is a partitioned data set, and I coded MAXNAME=3 to indicate that three MEMBER statements follow.

The RECORD statement   The RECORD statement lets you specify formatting and conversion instructions for various fields in the input records. For example, the following statements print three fields from the input records:

```
PRINT MAXFLDS=3
RECORD FIELD=(5,1,,1),FIELD=(5,6,,8),FIELD=(6,11,,15)
```

Here, the first field is 5 bytes long, begins in byte 1 of the input record, and is printed starting in byte 1 of the output record. The second field is 5 bytes long, begins in byte 6 of the input record, and is printed starting in byte 8 of the output record. And the third field is 6 bytes long, begins in byte 11 of the input record, and is printed starting in byte 15 of the output record. (Notice how I used the MAXFLDS parameter in the PRINT statement to indicate how many FIELD parameters appear on the RECORD statement.)

Although the RECORD statement can be used to create elaborate output formats, it can also be used to create simple formats. For example, consider these statements:

```
PRINT MAXFLDS=1
RECORD FIELD=(80)
```

In this example, the first 80 bytes of each input record is printed without the 8-character groupings normally created by IEBPTPCH. Because I omitted the in-loc and out-loc subparameters, their default values of 1 were used.

```
//PRINT     EXEC  PGM=IEBPTPCH
//SYSPRINT  DD    SYSOUT=*
//SYSUT1    DD    DSN=SYDOE.COBOL.COPYLIB,DISP=SHR
//SYSUT2    DD    SYSOUT=*
//SYSIN     DD    *
 PRINT TYPORG=PO,MAXNAME=3,MAXFLDS=1
 RECORD FIELD(80)
 MEMBER NAME=TRANREC
 MEMBER NAME=ORDREC
 MEMBER NAME=ACRCREC
/*
```

Figure 16-5   An IEBPTPCH job step to print three members of a partitioned data set

A sample IEBPTPCH job step

Figure 16-5 shows the JCL for an IEBPTPCH job step. In this example, three members from a partitioned data set are printed. A RECORD statement prints the first 80 characters of each input record without breaking the data into 8-character groups.

How to copy and compress partitioned data sets: the IEBCOPY program

The IEBCOPY utility is used to make copies of partitioned data sets. Specifically, IEBCOPY can be used to make a backup copy of a PDS, merge two or more partitioned data sets, copy a PDS to a sequential file in a special *unloaded* format for archival purposes, reload an unloaded PDS, or compress a PDS to reclaim unused space trapped within the PDS.

Figure 16-6 lists the control statements used by IEBCOPY. As you can see, these statements are straightforward enough. The COPY statement simply identifies the ddnames of the input and output files, and the SELECT and EXCLUDE statements list members to be included or excluded from the operation.

IEBCOPY determines the type of copy operation to be performed based on the types of data sets you specify in the COPY statement. For example, if INDD refers to an existing PDS and OUTDD allocates a new PDS, IEBCOPY copies members from the existing PDS to the new PDS. On the other hand, if OUTDD refers to an existing PDS, IEBCOPY merges members from the INDD PDS into the OUTDD PDS.

The COPY statement

```
COPY OUTDD=ddname,INDD=ddname[,ddname...]
```

OUTDD   Specifies the ddname of the data set to be created.

INDD   Specifies the ddnames of one or more input files.

The SELECT statement

```
SELECT MEMBER=member[,member...]
```

MEMBER   Specifies the names of one or more members to be included.

The EXCLUDE statement

```
EXCLUDE MEMBER=member[,member...]
```

MEMBER   Specifies the names of one or more members to be excluded.

Figure 16-6   IEBCOPY control statements

If OUTDD refers to a sequential file, IEBCOPY unloads the INDD PDS to the sequential file, which would normally be a tape data set for off-line storage. Similarly, if INDD refers to a sequential file, IEBCOPY reloads the unloaded PDS into the PDS referred to in the OUTDD parameter.

If both INDD and OUTDD refer to the same DD statement, IEBCOPY compresses the partitioned data set to reclaim unused space that has become trapped within the PDS. It is important to do this periodically, because partitioned data sets quickly build up unusable space whenever you modify members.

Figure 16-7 shows a sample IEBCOPY job step that compresses a PDS named SYDOE.COPYLIB.COB. As you can see, the COPY statement specifies the same DD statement for both INDD and OUTDD. Also notice the SYSUT3 and SYSUT4 DD statements in figure 16-7. These DD statements, which are required by IEBCOPY, define work files. They don't have to be very big, so one track of space is usually sufficient for each file. (A secondary allocation of one track helps assure that the work files will have sufficient space.)

How to generate data: the IEBDG program

IEBDG is a data generator you can use to create a sequential or ISAM file that contains data extracted from other files or data generated by

```
//COMPRESS EXEC  PGM=IEBCOPY
//SYSPRINT DD    SYSOUT=*
//COMPFILE DD    DSN=SYDOE.COPYLIB.COB,DISP=OLD
//SYSUT3   DD    UNIT=SYSDA,SPACE=(TRK,(1,1))
//SYSUT4   DD    UNIT=SYSDA,SPACE=(TRK,(1,1))
//SYSIN    DD    *
 COPY OUTDD=COMPFILE,INDD=COMPFILE
/*
```

Figure 16-7   An IEBCOPY job to compress a partitioned data set

the program itself based on specifications you provide in control statements. When you use IEBDG to generate data, the data can be created for each output record according to a pattern you supply. For example, you could specify that a three-digit number field is given an initial value of zero and is increased by one for each output record. Or, you could define an alphanumeric field with a certain initial value and specify that its value is changed in various ways for each output record.

JCL requirements for IEBDG

Figure 16-8 shows an IEBDG job step that creates 50 records using data generated by the program. As you can see, SYSPRINT is used for message output, and SYSIN is used for control statement input. You can use any ddnames you wish for the input and output files. Then, you specify those names in control statements to tell IEBDG what files to use. In figure 16-8, the OUTDD DD statement allocates the new SYDOE.TEST.CUSTMAST file, a sequential data set with 150-byte records.

IEBDG control statements

Look at the control statements I supplied to IEBDG in figure 16-8. There are four different statements: DSD, FD, CREATE, and END. In the DSD (Data Set Definition) statement, the OUTPUT parameter names the data set used; in this case, the output file is defined by the OUTDD DD statement. If data were copied from one or more input files, the DSD statement would include an INPUT parameter as well. Figure 16-9 shows the complete format of the DSD statement.

Figure 16-10 shows a partial format for the FD (Field Definition) statement, which is used to define the data that will appear in each

```
//CREATE    EXEC  PGM=IEBDG
//SYSPRINT  DD    SYSOUT=*
//OUTDD     DD    DSNAME=SYDOE.TEST.CUSTMAST,DISP=(NEW,CATLG),
//                UNIT=SYSDA,VOL=SER=MPS8BV,
//                SPACE=(CYL,(1,1)),
//                DCB=(DSORG=PS,RECFM=FB,BLKSIZE=3000,LRECL=150)
//SYSIN      DD    *
 DSD      OUTPUT=(OUTDD)
 FD       NAME=KEY,LENGTH=5,FORMAT=ZD,INDEX=1
 FD       NAME=FILLER1,LENGTH=100,FORMAT=AN,ACTION=RP
 FD       NAME=FILLER2,LENGTH=7,PICTURE=7,'CA93711'
 FD       NAME=FILLER3,LENGTH=38,FILL='X'
 CREATE QUANTITY=50,NAME=(KEY,FILLER1,FILLER2,FILLER3)
 END
/*
```

Figure 16-8   An IEBDG job step to create a sequential file

output record. Each of the four FD statements in figure 16-8 includes a NAME parameter, which associates a name with the data field. In this case, the names I used are KEY, FILLER1, FILLER2, and FILLER3. Each FD statement also includes a LENGTH parameter, which specifies the field's length in the output record.

The first FD statement is this:

```
FD   NAME=KEY,LENGTH=5,FORMAT=ZD,INDEX=1
```

The FORMAT parameter specifies that I want IEBDG to fill the field with data according to a specified pattern; in this case, ZD says to use the zoned-decimal data format. (Figure 16-11 shows other patterns you can specify in the FORMAT parameter along with their initial values.) The INDEX parameter tells IEBDG to add 1 to the value of the field after each record is written. As a result, the five-byte KEY field will begin with an initial value of 00001, and it will be incremented by 1 for each record.

The second FD statement in figure 16-8 is this:

```
FD   NAME=FILLER1,LENGTH=100,FORMAT=AN,ACTION=RP
```

Here, the alphanumeric format (AN) is used. To vary the data in this field for each record, I specified an ACTION parameter; in this case, RP specifies that the data should be "rippled." (RP causes data to be shifted to the left in each successive output record. There are other actions you can specify for a field, but RP is probably the one you'll use most.)

The DSD statement

```
DSD    OUTPUT=(ddname)
       [ ,INPUT=(ddname[,ddname...])]
```

Explanation

OUTPUT   Specifies the ddname of the output file.

INPUT   Specifies the ddnames of one or more optional input files.

Figure 16-9   The DSD statement of IEBDG

The FD statement

```
FD    NAME=name
      ,LENGTH=length
          fFORMAT=pattern
      [ ,{ PICTURE=length,[P]'literal'} ]
      [ ,ACTION=action ]
      [ ,INDEX=number ]
      [ ,FILL={'character' | X'hex-constant'} ]
```

Explanation

NAME   Specifies the name of the field.

LENGTH   Specifies the length of the field.

FORMAT   Specifies an IBM-supplied data format. See figure 16-11 for details.

PICTURE   Specifies a user-supplied picture. *Length* is the number of characters between the
                quotes. For a packed-decimal number, code a P before the first quote mark.

ACTION   Specifies what action is to be applied to the field for each record. If omitted, the
                field remains constant. To vary the data for each record, code ACTION=RP.

INDEX   Specifies a number that's added to the field for each record.

FILL   Specifies a single-character alphanumeric literal or a two-character hexadecimal
                literal used to fill this field in each output record. If omitted, FILL=X'00' (hex zero)
                is assumed.

Figure 16-10   The FD statement of IEBDG

FORMAT	Name	Description	Initial value (5-byte field)
AN	Alphanumeric	Letters A-Z, digits 0-9	A B C D E
AL	Alphabetic	Letters A-Z	A B C D E
ZD	Zoned decimal	Digits 0-9	00001
PD	Packed decimal	Packed number	(Hex) 00 00 00 00 1C
BI	Binary pattern	Binary number	(Hex) 00 00 00 00 01
CO	Collating sequence	Special characters: b.<(+|&!$*);~ -/,%_>?:#@'=" letters A-Z, digits 0-9 (where *b* is one blank)	b.<(+ (where *b* is one blank)
RA	Random pattern	Random hexadecimal digits	(Hex) 4F 38 2D A5 A0

Figure 16-11   Patterns for the FORMAT parameter of the IEBDG FD statement

In the third FD statement, I specified a PICTURE parameter:

```
FD    NAME=FILLER2,LENGTH=7,PICTURE=7,'CA93711'
```

Here, the PICTURE parameter specifies the length (7) and is immediately followed by a 7-character literal value. This value is used in each output record. The last FD statement in figure 16-8 is similar, but it uses a FILL parameter to specify that all 38 bytes of the field should contain the letter X.

Following the four FD statements is a CREATE statement. It's the CREATE statement that tells IEBDG to generate records in the output file. Figure 16-12 shows its format. The first parameter, QUANTITY, specifies how many records should be generated. The INPUT and FILL parameters specify how you want undefined character positions to be handled. If you specify INPUT, records read from the specified file are used as the basis for the output records, so data that's not overridden by FD statements remains unchanged. If you specify FILL, the literal you supply is used to fill any character positions not defined by DD statements.

The last parameter on the CREATE statement, NAME, lists the names of the fields defined by FD statements to include in the output records. In figure 16-8, the NAME parameter names all four of the fields defined by FD statements. As a result, each output record will be constructed using data derived from the specifications in the four FD statements. Following the CREATE statement, an END statement is required to indicate the end of the control statements. It has no parameters.

The CREATE statement

```
CREATE    QUANTITY=number
       [ ,INPUT=ddname ]
       [ ,FILL={'character' | X'hex-constant'} ]
       [ ,NAME=(name[,name...]) ]
```

Explanation

QUANTITY   Specifies the number of records to be generated.

INPUT   Specifies an input file from which records are read and used as the basis for modification by fields selected with the NAME parameter. If omitted, records are created by IEBDG and filled with the character specified in FILL.

FILL   Specifies a single-character alphanumeric literal or a two-character hexadecimal literal used to fill undefined character positions in each output record. If omitted, FILL=X'00' (hex zero) is assumed.

NAME   Names one or more fields defined in FD statements that are used to build the output record.

Figure 16-12   The CREATE statement of IEBDG

I hope you can appreciate the value of IEBDG. It's most useful during program development when you need large volumes of test data. I think you'll agree, however, that IEBDG is awkward to use and difficult to learn. As a result, you should consider other ways of creating test data before you use IEBDG. In many cases, you can use the ISPF editor to create test data. In other cases, you can copy data from an actual production file. When neither of these alternatives will do, however, IEBDG may be your best bet.

How to compare data sets: the IEBCOMPR program

IEBCOMPR is designed to compare data sets and produce output detailing any differences that are found. It is typically used to compare two versions of a file that you suspect might be identical. The files can be sequential or partitioned, but both files must have the same record length and record format.

Figure 16-13 shows two job steps that use IEBCOMPR. The first compares two sequential data sets. The files to be compared are allocated using the SYSUT1 and SYSUT2 DD statements. SYSIN is required, but can be allocated as a DUMMY data set since no control statements are required to compare sequential data sets. In the second example, you can see that I included a COMPARE

Example 1:	Comparing sequential data sets

```
//COMPSEQ   EXEC  PGM=IEBCOMPR
//SYSPRINT  DD    SYSOUT=*
//SYSUT1    DD    DSN=SYDOE.CPMAST1,DISP=OLD
//SYSUT2    DD    DSN=SYDOE.CPMAST2,DISP=OLD
//SYSIN     DD    DUMMY
```

Example 2:	Comparing partitioned data sets

```
//COMPPDS   EXEC  PGM=IEBCOMPR
//SYSPRINT  DD    SYSOUT=*
//SYSUT1    DD    DSN=SYDOE.SRCLIB.P42A.COB,DISP=OLD
//SYSUT2    DD    DSN=SYDOE.SRCLIB.P43A.COB,DISP=OLD
//SYSIN     DD    *
 COMPARE  TYPORG=PO
/*
```

Figure 16-13   IEBCOMPR job steps

TYPORG=PO statement in the SYSIN input stream to tell IEBCOPY that the files are partitioned data sets.

When you run the IEBCOMPR program, you'll have to review the output (SYSPRINT) to determine whether the data sets are identical. If they are not, the SYSPRINT listing will indicate the differences.

How to edit partitioned data sets: the IEBUPDTE program

IEBUPDTE is designed to edit and maintain partitioned data sets. It was developed before online terminals and TSO/ISPF were in widespread use, so its function is now largely obsolete. However, it is still used occasionally to update source code libraries, so a general understanding of how it works is helpful.

Figure 16-14 shows an example of an IEBUPDTE job step that adds a member named TRANREC to a partitioned data set named SYDOE.SRCLIB.COBOL. In the JCL, the library to be updated is allocated to two DD statements: SYSUT1 and SYSUT2. Although you can allocate different libraries to SYSUT1 and SYSUT2, that's not usually necessary.

The SYSIN input for IEBUPDTE in figure 16-14 includes three control statements: ADD, NUMBER, and ENDUP. The ADD statement instructs IEBUPDTE to create a new member using the data that

```
//ADDMEM    EXEC  PGM=IEBUPDTE
//SYSPRINT  DD    SYSOUT=*
//SYSUT1    DD    DSN=SYDOE.SRCLIB.COBOL,DISP=SHR
//SYSUT2    DD    DSN=SYDOE.SRCLIB.COBOL,DISP=SHR
//SYSIN     DD    *
./  ADD     NAME=TRANREC,LIST=ALL
./  NUMBER  NEW1=1000,INCR=100
        01  TRAN-RECORD.
      *
            05  TR-ITEM-NO          PIC X(10).
            05  TR-VENDOR-NO        PIC X(6).
            05  TR-RECEIPT-DATE     PIC X(6).
            05  TR-RECEIPT-QTY      PIC S9(5)   COMP-3.
            05  FILLER              PIC X(148).
./  ENDUP
/*
```

Figure 16-14   An IEBUPDTE job that adds a member

follows. The NUMBER statement tells IEBUPDTE to insert sequence numbers in columns 73 through 80 of the new member. The sequence numbers will start with 1000 and be incremented by 100 for each record. You can also use the NUMBER statement to insert records into a member and renumber existing records by including INSERT=YES on the statement. The ENDUP control statement indicates the end of the control file. Notice that all three of these statements are coded with a period in column 1 and a slash in column 2. This distinguishes the control statements from any data in the control file.

Figure 16-15 shows the formats of the ADD and NUMBER statements as well as several other useful IEBUPDTE control statements. The CHANGE statement tells IEBUPDTE that data records that follow are to replace existing records in the specified member. IEBUPDTE matches sequence numbers in the input records with sequence numbers in the member to decide which records are to be updated. The REPLACE statement directs IEBUPDTE to replace the specified member with the data records that follow in the input stream. And the DELETE statement lets you delete specific lines from a member. It is used following a CHANGE statement that specifies the member it applies to.

Notice that the ADD, CHANGE, and REPLACE statements let you specify LIST=ALL. I highly recommend that you use this option, because it lets you verify that the library members were updated as you intended.

The ADD statement

```
./ ADD NAME=name[,LIST=ALL]
```

The CHANGE statement

```
./ CHANGE NAME=name[,LIST=ALL]
```

The REPLACE statement

```
./ REPL NAME=name[,LIST=ALL]
```

The NUMBER statement

```
./ NUMBER [ SEQ1={number|ALL} ]
          [ ,SEQ2=number ]
          [ ,NEW1=number ]
          [ ,INCR=number ]
          [ ,INSERT=YES ]
```

The DELETE statement

```
./ DELETE SEQ1=number,SEQ2=number
```

Explanation

NAME	Specifies the name of the member to be processed.
LIST	When LIST=ALL is specified, each updated member is listed along with the control statements. If LIST is omitted, only the control statements and the updated records are listed.
SEQ1	Specifies the number of the first record the NUMBER or DELETE statement applies to. If ALL is coded, the operation applies to all of the input records.
SEQ2	Specifies the number of the last record the NUMBER or DELETE statement applies to. Not valid if SEQ1=ALL is coded.
NEW1	Specifies the starting number for the updated member.
INCR	Specifies the increment used when renumbering records.
INSERT	If INSERT=YES is specified, the data records that follow are inserted in the updated library.

Figure 16-15   IEBUPDTE control statements

How to list VTOC and PDS directory entries: the IEHLIST program

In chapter 10, I showed you how to use the IDCAMS LISTCAT command to print the entries in a VSAM or ICF catalog. For VSAM files, the LISTCAT output shows you everything you might want to know about a file: its size, DASD location, and characteristics (like organization and record size). Detailed information about non-VSAM files, however, can't be found in a catalog. Instead that information is stored in the DASD volume's VTOC entry for the file. As a result, you'll sometimes want to print information from a VTOC rather than from a catalog. The IEHLIST utility program lets you do just that.

Just as you'll sometimes want to list VTOC entries, you'll also sometimes need to list the entries in a partitioned data set directory. In other words you'll want a listing of the names of the members in a partitioned data set. IEHLIST lets you do that, too.

Frankly, the interactive facilities of ISPF under TSO let you perform both of these functions without the bother of coding JCL and control statements and submitting a job. So, if you need to look at a VTOC or PDS directory listing just to find the name or location of a single file or member, I suggest you use ISPF instead of the IEHLIST utility. However, if you want to print a listing of an entire VTOC or PDS directory and you suspect the listing will be long, IEHLIST might be a better choice.

IEHLIST has a third function: It lists the contents of CVOL-format catalogs. Since CVOL-format catalogs are seldom used today, though, I won't show you how to use that IEHLIST function.

JCL requirements for IEHLIST

The JCL to invoke IEHLIST is simple. After specifying IEHLIST in the PGM parameter of an EXEC statement, you usually code three or more DD statements: SYSPRINT, SYSIN, and additional DD statements with any ddnames you wish. SYSPRINT identifies the output file, so it usually allocates a SYSOUT data set. SYSIN contains the control statements, so it's usually in-stream data.

The additional DD statements allocate the volumes that contain the VTOCs or PDS directories you want to list. You should include one DD statement for each different volume that contains a VTOC or PDS you want to process. You can use any ddname you wish for these DD statements, and all you need to specify on it is UNIT, VOL, and DISP. For example, consider this DD statement:

```
//DD1      DD    UNIT=SYSDA,VOL=SER=TSO001,
                 DISP=OLD
```

Here, the SYSDA volume named TSO001 is allocated. Notice that I didn't specify the DSNAME parameter in the DD statement. If you're listing a partitioned data set directory, you'll specify the data set name in an IEHLIST control statement.

IEHLIST control statements

Figure 16-16 shows the control statements you use to direct IEHLIST's processing. To list a VTOC entry, you code a LISTVTOC statement; to list a PDS directory, you code a LISTPDS statement. You can include as many of these control statements as you wish in a single execution of IEHLIST.

The LISTVTOC statement   You use the LISTVTOC statement to list entries in a VTOC. In the VOL parameter, you identify the volume whose VTOC you want to list; in it, you include the unit specification as well as the volume serial number, like this:

```
LISTVTOC VOL=SYSDA=TSO001
```

Here, the VTOC on the SYSDA volume named TSO001 will be listed. The volume you specify must be allocated by a DD statement, but the ddname you use doesn't matter.

The DATE parameter tells IEHLIST to highlight expired files. IEHLIST checks each data set's expiration date (which is stored in the file's VTOC entry) against the date you specify in the DATE parameter. If the file has expired or will expire as of the date specified, an asterisk is printed next to it on the listing.

You use the DSNAME parameter to generate a listing of selected VTOC entries. For example,

```
LISTVTOC VOL=SYSDA=TSO001,DSNAME=SYDOE.CUSTMAST
```

says to list the VTOC entry for the file named SYDOE.CUSTMAST on volume TSO001. You can list up to 10 data set names in the DSNAME parameter; if you list more than one, you must enclose the entire list in parentheses. If you need to list more than 10 specific VTOC entries, just include more than one LISTVTOC statement. If you omit the DSNAME parameter, IEHLIST lists all of the VTOC entries.

IEHLIST can print VTOC entries in one of three formats. The default format is an abbreviated listing that lists one line per data set. The abbreviated listing includes the data set name, creation and

---

The LISTVTOC statement

```
LISTVTOC    VOL=unit=serial

         [ ,DATE=dddyy ]

         [ ,DSNAME=(name[,name...]) ]

         [ ,{FORMAT} ]
            {DUMP  }
```

The LISTPDS statement

```
LISTPDS DSNAME=(dsname[,dsname...])
        ,VOL=unit=serial
```

Explanation

VOL	Specifies the unit (such as SYSDA) and serial number for the volume to be processed. The volume must be allocated with a DD statement.
DATE	Specifies that files that are or will be expired on the date specified should be flagged with asterisks.
DSNAME	Specifies one or more data set names. For LISTVTOC, only the VTOC entries for those data sets are listed. For LISTPDS, only the directories of the specified data sets are listed. If you specify only one data set name, you can omit the parentheses.
FORMAT DUMP	FORMAT specifies that complete VTOC information should be printed in a readable format. DUMP specifies that the VTOC labels should be dumped in hexadecimal format. If you omit both FORMAT and DUMP, an abbreviated listing is produced.

Figure 16-16   The LISTVTOC and LISTPDS statements of IEHLIST

expiration dates, file type, number of extents, and a few other items that aren't as meaningful. This is the easiest VTOC listing format to work with, so I recommend you use it unless you need more information. Figure 16-17 shows a job step that produces an abbreviated VTOC listing, as well as a portion of the resulting output.

The second format lists in detail the information contained in the Data Set Control Blocks (DSCBs) for the files specified. This includes the data set name, DCB information like DSORG, RECFM, and BLKSIZE, and space allocation information. To obtain this output, code the FORMAT parameter on the LISTVTOC statement, like this:

```
LISTVTOC VOL=SYSDA=TSO001,DSNAME=SYDOE.CUSTMAST.DATA,FORMAT
```

Figure 16-18 shows a formatted VTOC listing. Be careful about specifying FORMAT when you're listing the entire VTOC of a

JCL

```
//LVTOC    EXEC PGM=IEHLIST
//SYSPRINT DD   SYSOUT=*
//DD1      DD   UNIT=SYSDA,VOL=SER=TS0001,DISP=SHR
//SYSIN    DD   *
  LISTVTOC VOL=SYSDA=TS0001
```

Resulting output

```
                              SYSTEMS SUPPORT UTILITIES--IEHLIST                           PAGE    1

DATE: 1994.129  TIME: 23.09.04
        CONTENTS OF VTOC ON VOL TS0001
    THERE IS A  2 LEVEL VTOC INDEX
    DATA SETS ARE LISTED IN ALPHANUMERIC ORDER
------------DATA SET NAME------------   CREATED   PURGE     FILE TYPE    EXTENTS  FILE SERIAL  VOL. SEQ.  SECURITY
CICSTEST.PANLINK.LOADLIB                1985.130  00.000  PARTITIONED    00001    TS0001       00001      NONE
CICSTEST.PANLINK.TLUSERS.DATA           1993.255  1999.365  VSAM         00001    TS0001       00001      PWD
CICSTEST.PANLINK.TLUSERS.INDEX          1993.255  1999.365  VSAM         00001    TS0001       00001      PWD
IAACF.ISPEDA                            1994.031  00.000  SEQUENTIAL     00001    TS0001       00001      NONE
IAAXK.ISPEDA                            1994.126  00.000  SEQUENTIAL     00001    TS0001       00001      NONE
IAJAP.ISPPROF                           1994.119  00.000  PARTITIONED    00001    TS0001       00001      NONE
IAKEJ.ISPEDA                            1994.119  00.000  SEQUENTIAL     00001    TS0001       00001      NONE
IARYW.ISPEDA                            1994.073  00.000  SEQUENTIAL     00001    TS0001       00001      NONE
IDAXJ.USER.CLIST                        1993.258  00.000  PARTITIONED    00001    TS0001       00001      NONE
IDBBW.ISPEDA                            1994.074  00.000  SEQUENTIAL     00001    TS0001       00001      NONE
IDCGM.ISPEDB                            1994.123  00.000  SEQUENTIAL     00001    TS0001       00001      NONE
IDCKY.ISPEDB                            1994.123  00.000  SEQUENTIAL     00001    TS0001       00001      NONE
IDFLW.ISPFPLIB                          1994.003  00.000  PARTITIONED    00001    TS0001       00001      NONE
IDFLW.LIB                               1994.116  00.000  PARTITIONED    00001    TS0001       00001      NONE
IDFLW.ROSCOE.CNVTLIB                    1994.116  00.000  PARTITIONED    00001    TS0001       00001      NONE
IDJWC.PDS.CNTL2                         1994.097  00.000  PARTITIONED    00001    TS0001       00001      NONE
IDLLJ.SPFLOG4.LIST                      1994.125  00.000  SEQUENTIAL     00001    TS0001       00001      NONE
IDLMA.ISPPROF                           1994.123  00.000  PARTITIONED    00001    TS0001       00001      NONE
IDPUB.CNT.UPDFILEX                      1994.126  00.000  SEQUENTIAL     00001    TS0001       00001      NONE
IDPUB.LNS0000.CNT00000                  1994.126  00.000  SEQUENTIAL     00001    TS0001       00001      NONE
IDPUB.NOI.LETSORTN                      1994.125  00.000  SEQUENTIAL     00001    TS0001       00001      NONE
IDPUB.X000000.LOANMAST.LATECHG          1994.104  00.000  SEQUENTIAL     00001    TS0001       00001      NONE
IDPUB.XLNN0000.CNT00000                 1994.101  00.000  SEQUENTIAL     00001    TS0001       00001      NONE
IDRBF.ISPEDA                            1994.123  00.000  SEQUENTIAL     00001    TS0001       00001      NONE
```

Figure 16-17   An IEHLIST job step to list VTOC entries

```
                    SYSTEMS SUPPORT UTILITIES---IEHLIST                    PAGE    1

DATE: 1994.129  TIME: 23.09.09
                CONTENTS OF VTOC ON VOL TSO001

-----------DATA SET NAME--------------  SER NO  SEQNO  DATE.CRE  DATE.EXP  DATE.REF  EXT DSORG RECFM CPTCD BLKSIZE
SYDOE.CUSTMAST.DATA                      TSO001    1    1994.129  1999.365  1994.129   1   VS    U     80    4096

    LRECL  KEYLEN  INITIAL ALLOC  2ND ALLOC/LAST BLK PTR(T-R-L)  USED PDS BYTES  FMT 2 OR 3(C-H-R)/DSCB(C-H-R)
      0      0         CYLS              1         0  58786          0   0            1    6    25

    EXTENTS  NO  LOW(C-H)   HIGH(C-H)
             0  362   0      362  14
                         ----UNABLE TO CALCULATE EMPTY SPACE.
```

Figure 16-18   Output from an IEHLIST LISTVTOC statement with the FORMAT parameter

volume that contains many files. The resulting output can be surprisingly large.

The third format is one you probably won't use; it prints an unformatted hexadecimal listing of the DSCBs. You get that format by specifying DUMP instead of FORMAT on the LISTVTOC statement.

The LISTPDS statement   The LISTPDS statement, used to list the directory of a partitioned data set, has only two parameters. The DSNAME parameter identifies the data set names of the partitioned data set directories you want listed; if you're listing only one PDS directory, you can omit the parentheses. The VOL parameter identifies the unit and volume containing the PDS; you code it as you do for LISTVTOC. The volume must be allocated with a DD statement, but the DD statement's ddname doesn't matter.

The top part of figure 16-19 shows the JCL and control statement required to print the contents of the directory of a partitioned data set named SYS1.COBLIB that resides on a volume named MVS002. The bottom part shows a portion of the resulting output.

How to copy and move data sets: the IEHMOVE program

IEHMOVE is a utility used to copy or move sequential, direct, or partitioned data sets. It combines the functions of IEBCOPY and IEBGENER, but has a distinct advantage over those utilities: It can automatically determine the space allocation for its output files from the space allocated to its input files. In contrast, both IEBCOPY and IEBGENER require that you specify the space requirements for output files in the SYSUT2 DD statement.

Before I show you how to use the IEHMOVE utility, I want to explain the difference between a move and a copy operation. To copy a data set means to reproduce it in another location. After a file has been copied, there are two versions of it—the original version and the copy. To move a data set, however, means to copy the file and delete the original, so only one version remains. It's important to remember this distinction when you use IEHMOVE, because the utility can perform either function.

JCL requirements for IEHMOVE

IEHMOVE has several peculiar JCL requirements that need some explanation. In addition to the usual EXEC PGM=IEHMOVE and

JCL

```
//LPDS     EXEC PGM=IEHLIST
//SYSPRINT DD   SYSOUT=*
//DD1      DD   UNIT=SYSDA,VOL=SER=MVS002
//SYSIN    DD   *
  LISTPDS DSNAME=SYS1.COBLIB,VOL=SYSDA=MVS002
/*
```

Resulting output

```
DATE: 1994.129  TIME: 23.09.10
DIRECTORY INFO FOR SPECIFIED PDS ON VOL MVS002
SYS1.COBLIB
```

```
                                   SYSTEMS  SUPPORT  UTILITIES---IEHLIST

MEMBERS    TTRC       VARIABLE USER DATA ---(USER DATA AND TTRC ARE IN HEX)
BLDQS      001415B1   00141B0000 000000002E2 0018981898 0000000800 0100000000C9 D3C2D6D8E2 E4400100
EOFINPUT   0004088B3  0004100000 000000002C2 0097681FF0 0090DE9800 0800001C8C9 D2C6C3C2D3 F8F0011127 200100
EOFQUEUE   0004088B3  0004100000 000000002C2 0097681FF0 0092AA9800 0800001C8C9 D2C6C3C2D3 F8F0011127 200100
IKFCBL00   00060042E  00060A0000 000000002C2 0043182588 0018389800 0300011111 520100
IKFCBL01   0014042C   0014090000 000000002E2 0000D000D0 0000008800 01010000
IKFCBL02   0006122E   0007010000 000000002C2 0038F826C8 0000409800 0300011111 520100
IKFCBL03   00011C2C   0001220000 000000002C2 0004D004D0 0003188800 01010000
IKFCBL04   0007072E   0007000000 000000002E2 0034683468 0000009800 0100011111 520100
IKFCBL05   0007102E   0008010000 000000002C2 0043F843F8 0030EC9800 0100011111 520100
IKFCBL06   00011252C  00012B0000 000000002C2 000E480E48 0002648800 01010000
IKFCBL08   00050082E  0006010000 000000002C2 0046604660 0007809800 0100011170 510100
IKFCBL1B   0013042E   00130A0000 000000002C2 0088804508 0008F09800 0200011161 580100
IKFCBL10   00080042E  00080B0000 000000002C2 00A3305300 00003C9800 0200011111 520100
IKFCBL12   00090042E  00090B0000 000000002C2 0089604F70 00003C9800 0200011111 520100
IKFCBL20   000A042E   000A0A0000 000000002C2 00635050D8 0100011111 520100
IKFCBL21   000A102E   000B010000 000000002C2 005BB05100 0008F09800 0100011111 520100
IKFCBL22   000B062E   000B0C0000 000000002C2 007E484D50 0010989800 0100011111 520100
IKFCBL25   00012E2C   0002010000 000000002C2 001A981A98 0007808800 01010000
IKFCBL30   0013102E   0014010000 000000002E2 0044A844A8 0000009800 0100011181 080100
IKFCBL35   0002042C   00020A0000 000000002E2 0020B020B0 0000008800 01010000
IKFCBL40   000C052E   000C0B0000 000000002C2 00DA504728 00D9209800 0100011111 520100
IKFCBL45   000D082E   000D0E0000 000000002C2 0017081708 00003C9800 0100011111 520100
IKFCBL50   0012062E   00120D0000 000000002C2 00A6D84A98 009CB89800 0100011140 880100
IKFCBL51   000D112E   000E010000 000000002C2 00CA804B48 00B7689800 0100011111 520100
```

Figure 16-19   An IEHLIST job step to list the contents of a partitioned data set's directory

SYSPRINT and SYSIN DD statements, IEHLIST requires that you allocate a work volume using a DD statement similar to this:

```
//SYSUT1    DD    UNIT=SYSDA,VOL=SER=WORK01,DISP=OLD
```

Of course, you should adjust the UNIT and VOL parameters so that they refer to an available work volume at your installation. IEHMOVE will use about 50 tracks of space on this volume.

Next, IEHMOVE requires a DD statement that allocates the system residence volume. Since the volume serial number of the system residence volume varies from shop to shop, the easiest way to allocate it is to use a VOL=REF parameter to refer to a data set that you know resides on the system residence volume, like this:

```
//SYSRES    DD    UNIT=SYSDA,VOL=REF=SYS1.SVCLIB,DISP=OLD
```

Note that the ddname for this DD statement doesn't matter. I picked SYSRES to make the purpose of the DD statement clear, but you can use any ddname you wish.

Finally, IEHMOVE requires that you provide a DD statement to allocate each volume you process. These DD statements should look something like this:

```
//DD1       DD    UNIT=device,VOL=SER=volser,DISP=OLD
```

You can use any ddname you wish for these DD statements. You do not have to supply the names of the files processed by IEHMOVE on these DD statements; the file names will be specified on IEHMOVE control statements.

IEHMOVE control statements

IEHMOVE lets you include several control statements in the SYSIN input stream. You should include at least one COPY or MOVE statement to initiate a copy or move operation. The COPY or MOVE statement specifies the name of the data set to be moved, the volume that contains the data set (required only if the data set is not cataloged), and the volume the data set is to be moved or copied to. You can also direct IEHMOVE to uncatalog or rename the data set or create additional space in a partitioned data set's directory. Figure 16-20 shows the format of the COPY and MOVE statements.

When the file being copied is a partitioned data set, you can also provide one or more SELECT or EXCLUDE statements to copy or move only specific members or to exclude specific members from the operation. The SELECT and EXCLUDE statements are mutually exclusive and should immediately follow the COPY or MOVE statement they apply to. The SELECT and EXCLUDE statements are described in figure 16-21. Notice that you can code one or more

The COPY and MOVE statements

```
{COPY}  { DSNAME=data-set-name }
{MOVE}  { PDS=library-name     }
        { DSGROUP=name         }
          ,TO=unit=serial
     [ ,FROM=unit=serial ]
     [ ,UNCATLG ]
     [ ,RENAME=new-name ]
     [ ,EXPAND=number ]
```

Explanation

DSNAME	Specifies the input data set name (sequential).
PDS	Specifies the input data set name (partitioned).
DSGROUP	Specifies one or more data set name qualifiers used to identify a data set group. All data sets on the volume named with the same qualifiers are copied or moved.
TO	Specifies the output volume.
FROM	Specifies the input volume.
UNCATLG	Uncatalogs the input file.
RENAME	Specifies the name of the output file if different from the input file.
EXPAND	Specifies a number of additional directory blocks to be inserted into the directory of a partitioned data set.

Figure 16-20   The COPY and MOVE statements of IEHMOVE

The SELECT statement

```
SELECT MEMBER=(name[,name...])
```

MEMBER   Specifies the names of one or more members to be included.

The EXCLUDE statement

```
EXCLUDE MEMBER=(name)
```

MEMBER   Specifies the name of a member to be excluded. You can code only one member in an EXCLUDE statement, but you may code as many EXCLUDE statements as you need.

Note: You cannot code a SELECT and an EXCLUDE statement together. You can use only one or the other.

Figure 16-21   The SELECT and EXCLUDE statements of IEHMOVE

Example 1: Copying a sequential file

```
//COPYSEQ   EXEC  PGM=IEHMOVE
//SYSPRINT  DD    SYSOUT=*
//SYSUT1    DD    UNIT=SYSDA,VOL=SER=WORK01,DISP=OLD
//SYSRES    DD    UNIT=SYSDA,VOL=REF=SYS1.SVCLIB,DISP=OLD
//TSO001    DD    UNIT=SYSDA,VOL=SER=TSO001,DISP=OLD
//TSO002    DD    UNIT=SYSDA,VOL=SER=TSO002,DISP=OLD
//SYSIN     DD    *
 COPY DSNAME=SYDOE.MARTRAN,FROM=SYSDA=TSO001,TO=SYSDA=TSO002
/*
```

Example 2: Copying and renaming a partitioned data set, excluding members

```
//COPYPDS   EXEC  PGM=IEHMOVE
//SYSPRINT  DD    SYSOUT=*
//SYSUT1    DD    UNIT=SYSDA,VOL=SER=WORK01,DISP=OLD
//SYSRES    DD    UNIT=SYSDA,VOL=REF=SYS1.SVCLIB,DISP=OLD
//TSO001    DD    UNIT=SYSDA,VOL=SER=TSO001,DISP=OLD
//TSO002    DD    UNIT=SYSDA,VOL=SER=TSO002,DISP=OLD
//SYSIN     DD    *
 COPY DSNAME=SYDOE.COPYLIB.COB,FROM=SYSDA=TSO001,TO=SYSDA=TSO002,      X
                RENAME=SYDOE.SAVELIB.COB
 EXCLUDE MEMBER=PRODMSTR
 EXCLUDE MEMBER=PROMSTR
 EXCLUDE MEMBER=BFREC
 EXCLUDE MEMBER=TRREC
/*
```

Figure 16-22   IEHMOVE job steps

member names on the SELECT statement, but you can code only one member name on the EXCLUDE statement. To exclude more than one member, then, you have to code one EXCLUDE statement for each member.

IEHMOVE examples

Figure 16-22 shows two examples of IEHMOVE job steps. The first copies a sequential file from volume TSO001 to volume TSO002. The second moves a partitioned data set from TSO001 to TSO002, omitting several members. The second example also shows you how to continue a control statement. Just place a non-blank character in column 72 and begin the continued statement in column 16 of the next line.

How to maintain catalogs: the IEHPROGM program

IEHPROGM is a nearly obsolete utility program that manages catalog entries. With IEHPROGM, you can scratch, rename, catalog, or uncatalog data sets. You can also create an index structure for a generation data group. All of these functions can be performed more easily with the IDCAMS program or interactively through ISPF, so IEHPROGM isn't used as much as it once was. However, you may still run across it in older job streams.

Figure 16-23 lists the control statements you can supply to IEHPROGM through the SYSIN input stream. As with IEHMOVE, you must provide DD statements to allocate the volumes that contain the data sets referred to in these control statements. For example, if you refer to a data set that resides on volume TSO001 in a SCRATCH or RENAME statement, you should include a DD statement similar to this one in the job step:

```
//DD1       DD    UNIT=SYSDA,VOL=SER=TSO001,DISP=OLD
```

The ddname you assign to the volume doesn't matter. Also, like IEHMOVE, IEHPROGM may require access to the system residence volume. So, you should include a DD statement similar to this one in the job step:

```
//SYSRES    DD    UNIT=SYSDA,VOL=REF=SYS1.SVCLIB,DISP=OLD
```

Once again, the ddname you use for this DD statement doesn't matter.

Figure 16-24 shows a sample IEHPROGM job step that scratches three data sets. Note that this same function could be performed by invoking the IEFBR14 dummy program and providing a DD statement that specifies DISP=(,DELETE) for each of the data sets to be deleted.

Discussion

When batch-sequential processing was the rule in data processing installations, the utility programs I've presented in this chapter had greater significance. Today, nearly all of the functions that were once available only through the utility programs are easily accessible from an online terminal through ISPF. As a result, the utility programs I've presented here are useful only in circumstances that require batch processing.

The SCRATCH statement

`SCRATCH DSNAME=name,VOL=unit=serial[,MEMBER=name][,PURGE]`

DSNAME	Specifies the name of the data set to be scratched.
VOL	Specifies the volume that contains the data set.
MEMBER	Specifies the name of a member if you wish to scratch the member rather than the entire partitioned data set.
PURGE	Specifies that the data set is to be scratched even if its expiration date has not elapsed.

The RENAME statement

`RENAME DSNAME=name,VOL=unit=serial,NEWNAME=name[,MEMBER=name]`

DSNAME	Specifies the name of the data set to be renamed.
VOL	Specifies the volume that contains the data set.
NEWNAME	Specifies the new name assigned to the data set or member.
MEMBER	Specifies the name of a member if you wish to rename the member rather than the entire partitioned data set.

The CATLG statement

`CATLG DSNAME=name,VOL=unit=serial`

DSNAME	Specifies the name of the data set to be cataloged.
VOL	Specifies the volume that contains the data set.

The UNCATLG statement

`UNCATLG DSNAME=name`

DSNAME	Specifies the name of the data set to be uncataloged.

The BLDG statement

`BLDG INDEX=name,ENTRIES=number[,{EMPTY|DELETE}]`

INDEX	Specifies the name of the generation data group index.
ENTRIES	Specifies the number of generations to be saved in a generation data group.
EMPTY DELETE	Specifies the action to take when the generation index is filled. EMPTY means to scratch all entries; DELETE means to scratch only the oldest entry. If you omit both EMPTY and DELETE, the oldest entry is uncataloged but not scratched.

Figure 16-23   IEHPROGM control statements

```
//SCRATCH   EXEC  PGM=IEHPROGM
//SYSPRINT  DD    SYSOUT=*
//SYSRES    DD    UNIT=SYSDA,VOL=REF=SYS1.SVCLIB,DISP=OLD
//DD1       DD    UNIT=SYSDA,VOL=SER=TS0001,DISP=OLD
//SYSIN     DD    *
 SCRATCH DSNAME=SYDOE.TEST46.COB,VOL=SYSDA=TS0001
 SCRATCH DSNAME=SYDOE.TEST47.COB,VOL=SYSDA=TS0001
 SCRATCH DSNAME=SYDOE.TEST48.COB,VOL=SYSDA=TS0001
/*
```

Figure 16-24   An IEHPROGM job step that scratches three data sets

Terminology

utility program
utility
MVS utilities

Objectives

1. Code an IEBGENER job to copy or print a sequential data set.

2. Code an IEBPTPCH job to print a data set.

3. Code an IEBCOPY job to copy or compress a partitioned data set.

4. Code an IEBDG job to create a sequential data set. The data in each record can include a numeric field that's incremented by a certain value for each record and fixed data specified by a PICTURE parameter in an FD statement.

5. Code an IEBCOMPR job to compare two data sets.

6. Code an IEBUPDTE job to create a new member in a PDS, re-place or delete existing records in a member, or replace an entire member.

7. Code an IEHLIST job to list VTOC entries or PDS directory entries.

8. Code an IEHMOVE job to copy or move data sets.

9. Code an IEHPROGM job to scratch, rename, catalog, or uncatalog data sets.

Exercises

1. Code an IEBGENER job to copy a cataloged data set named X401.JOURNAL to a new file named X401.JOURNAL.OLD on a SYSDA volume named TSO001. Allocate 10 cylinders of primary space and 2 cylinders of secondary space.

2. Code an IEBPTPCH job to print a data set named X401.JOURNAL.

3. Code an IEBCOPY job to compress a partitioned data set named X401.MASTER.COBOL.

4. Code an IEBDG job to create a sequential data set named X401.MASTER.TEST with 150-byte records in 3000-byte blocks. The records should be created with the following two fields:

Field name	Positions	Format	Test data type
CUSTNO	1-5	Zoned decimal	Sequence numbers starting with 00001 and incremented by 1 for each record
DATA	6-150	Alphanumeric	Ripple

    Generate 5,000 records. Allocate space by blocks to ensure that the correct amount of space is allocated to the data set.

5. Code an IEBCOMPR job to compare two cataloged data sets named X401.JOURNAL and X401.JOURNAL.OLD.

6. Code an IEBUPDTE job to add a member named CUSTREC to a PDS named X401.COPYLIB.COBOL.

7. Code an IEHLIST job to list VTOC entries for the file named X401.JOURNAL, including detailed DSCB information. The file resides on the SYSDA volume TSO001.

8. Code an IEHMOVE job to copy a cataloged data set named X401.JOURNAL to a new file named X401.JOURNAL.OLD on a SYSDA volume named TSO001.

9. Code an IEHPROGM job to scratch a file named X401.JOURNAL.OLD on a SYSDA volume named TSO001.

Chapter 17

Sort/merge

Often, data stored in a file in one sequence needs to be reordered to produce a particular kind of output. For example, a sequential file of employee records stored in employee number sequence might have to be reordered so it's in sequence by employee name, social security number, department, salary, hiring date, date of last promotion, or any other field its records contain. To resequence a file, you use the MVS *sort/merge program*, also known as *DFSORT*.

As its name implies, sort/merge has two functions. The *sort* function assumes that all input records are out of sequence, and it puts them in the sequence you request. The *merge* function assumes that records are in the right sequence, but are stored in separate files. So, it combines them into one file, also in the right sequence. For example, suppose you have three files of general ledger transactions for different accounting periods that are all in account number sequence. If you want to combine them into a single file that's also in account number sequence, you would use the DFSORT merge function.

You can use DFSORT in two ways. First, you can invoke it directly in an EXEC statement just like other MVS utility programs; that's called a *stand-alone sort/merge*. Alternatively, you can invoke it from a program written in a high-level language; that's called an *internal sort/merge*. After I show you how to code the JCL statements DFSORT requires, I'll show you how to code DFSORT control statements and describe two sample job streams. Then, I'll show you how to code the JCL for a program that invokes DFSORT internally.

ddname	Function
SORTLIB	A partitioned data set that contains modules required by the sort/merge program. Normally SYS1.SORTLIB.
SYSOUT	The message listing. Normally a SYSOUT data set.
SYSIN	Control statement input. Normally an in-stream data set.
SORTIN	Input file for a sort operation. If more than one file is to be sorted, concatenate them.
SORTINnn	Input for a merge operation; *nn* should be a consecutive number beginning with 01.
SORTOUT	Output file for a sort or merge operation.
SORTWKnn	Sort work files; *nn* should be a consecutive number beginning with 01. One or two files are usually adequate; the total DASD space allocated to SORTWKnn data sets should be about twice the sum of the input file size.

Figure 17-1   DD statements required by the sort/merge program

JCL requirements for a stand-alone sort/merge

To invoke DFSORT for stand-alone operation, you specify the program's name (SORT) in an EXEC statement. Then, you follow the EXEC statement with DD statements to define the data sets required by DFSORT. Figure 17-1 summarizes those data sets.

The SORTLIB DD statement defines a load library where the DFSORT support modules reside. Usually, the name of this library is SYS1.SORTLIB, but it might be different at your installation. SYSOUT defines the listing produced by DFSORT; it's usually a SYSOUT data set. SYSIN defines the control statement input; I'll describe how you code DFSORT control statements in a moment.

For a sort operation, the SORTIN DD statement defines the input file to be sorted. If you want to sort two or more input files that have similar characteristics into a single output file, you can concatenate them, like this:

```
//SORTIN   DD   DSNAME=SYDOE.TRANFILE.APRIL,DISP=SHR
//         DD   DSNAME=SYDOE.TRANFILE.MAY,DISP=SHR
//         DD   DSNAME=SYDOE.TRANFILE.JUNE,DISP=SHR
```

Here, the transaction files for April, May, and June are treated as a single file to be sorted.

For a merge operation, you code the ddnames for each of the input files in the form SORTINnn, where *nn* is a value between 01 and 16. For example, the DD statements for a three-file merge operation are named SORTIN01, SORTIN02, and SORTIN03. The DD statements you provide must be numbered consecutively. In other words, if you specify SORTIN01, SORTIN02, and SORTIN05, only the first two files are merged; SORTIN05 is ignored because it's not numbered consecutively.

SORTOUT defines the output file where the sorted records are written. It can be a new non-VSAM file with DISP=(NEW,KEEP) or DISP=(NEW,CATLG), an extension of an existing non-VSAM file with DISP=MOD, or a VSAM file.

SORTWKnn DD statements are work files defined on tape or DASD volumes. Because they're inefficient, tape devices are rarely used for sort work files. The *nn* may be a number from 01 to 32, but you usually need to supply only one or two SORTWKnn data sets. A merge-only function doesn't require work files, so you can omit the SORTWKnn DD statements from the JCL for a merge operation.

The amount of space required for the sort work files varies depending on several factors, including the length of the input records, the number of input records, and the lengths of the fields on which the data is sorted. Usually, though, it's safe to figure the required work space as about twice the size of the input file. So, if the input file is 10 cylinders, allocate 20 cylinders of sort work space. It's better to allocate that space in one or two larger files rather than in a greater number of smaller files. And, if possible, you should put the work files on a different volume than the SORTIN and SORTOUT files.

Basic control statements
for a stand-alone sort/merge operation

DFSORT lets you use a variety of control statements to specify the operation you want it to perform. The only statements you'll use regularly are the SORT and MERGE statements, which let you specify the fields on which you want the data sets sorted or merged. Another control statement, RECORD, is required when you use a VSAM input or output file.

The SORT and MERGE statements   If you want DFSORT to perform a sort operation, you have to code a SORT control statement. If you want to perform a merge operation, you code a MERGE control statement. They have similar formats, shown in figure 17-2.

The FIELDS parameter on both statements identifies the field or fields in the input records you want to use to sort the records. For

The SORT and MERGE control statements

```
SORT    { FIELDS=(position,length,format,sequence...)         }
        { FIELDS=(position,length,sequence...),FORMAT=format  }

        [{ ,EQUALS   }]
         { ,NOEQUALS }


MERGE   { FIELDS=(position,length,format,sequence...)         }
        { FIELDS=(position,length,sequence...),FORMAT=format  }
```

Explanation

FIELDS — Specifies the control fields in the input records. Each control field specification consists of four elements: position, length, format, and sequence. The elements are separated by commas.

position — The location of the first byte of the control field in the input record.

length — The length in bytes of the control field. The sum of all control field lengths cannot exceed 4092.

format — A two-character code that identifies the format of the data in the control field. See figure 17-3 for a list of format codes. If all control fields have the same format, you may omit this operand and instead code FORMAT=format to apply to all control fields.

sequence — One of these one-character codes to identify the order in which the control field should be processed:

A   Ascending sequence

D   Descending sequence

EQUALS
NOEQUALS — Specifies whether or not the order of the records in the input files are preserved in the output file when all control fields are equal. Valid only on the SORT statement.

Figure 17-2   The SORT and MERGE control statements

each of those fields, called a *control field* or a *key field*, you specify four things: (1) position, (2) length, (3) format, and (4) sort sequence. DFSORT evaluates the fields you specify to determine the order in which the records will be placed in the output file.

The position value specifies the location of the field's first byte within the input record. If a control field begins at the first byte in the input record, you code 1 for the position. Control fields must be located in the same positions in all the input records, and all of the control fields must be contained within the first 4092 bytes of each record.

Format	Length	Description
CH	1 to 4092 bytes	Character
ZD	1 to 32 bytes	Signed zoned decimal
PD	1 to 32 bytes	Signed packed decimal
FI	1 to 256 bytes	Signed fixed point binary
BI	1 bit to 4096 bytes	Unsigned binary
FL	1 to 256 bytes	Signed normalized floating point
AC	1 to 256 bytes	ASCII characters
CSF	1 to 16 bytes	Numeric with optional leading sign
CSL	2 to 256 bytes	Numeric with leading separate sign
CST	2 to 256 bytes	Numeric with trailing separate sign
CLO	1 to 256 bytes	Numeric with leading overpunch sign
CTO	1 to 256 bytes	Numeric with trailing overpunch sign
ASL	2 to 256 bytes	ASCII numeric with leading separate sign
AST	2 to 256 bytes	ASCII numeric with trailing separate sign

Figure 17-3   Format codes for the SORT and MERGE statements

The second value you code is the length of the control field in bytes. If a field contains signed data, the length should include the sign if it occupies a separate character position. The total length of all the control fields you specify can't exceed 4092.

The third value you specify indicates the format of the data that's stored in the control field. Figure 17-3 shows the most common data representations and the codes you can use for each. If all of the control fields have the same format, you can omit the format value from the control field list and code it in the FORMAT parameter outside the list, as figure 17-2 indicates.

The last value you code for a control field specifies how DFSORT should sequence the output. You may code either A for ascending sequence or D for descending sequence.

The sequence in which you code the control fields affects the way the input records are sorted. The first control field you specify is the *major control field*; it determines the primary sequence of the sorted output. The other control fields are *minor control fields*. They also affect the sequence of the output, but only within the sequence determined by the control fields specified to their left in the SORT or MERGE statement.

You can also code EQUALS or NOEQUALS on a SORT statement to control how DFSORT handles the sequence of records whose major and minor control fields are the same. If you want to preserve the order of those records, specify EQUALS. EQUALS makes DFSORT operate less efficiently, however, so use it only when you need to. NOEQUALS indicates that you don't care if records with equal control fields are maintained in their original input sequence. NOEQUALS is the default.

To understand how the SORT statement works, consider figure 17-4. It shows ten unsorted records, a SORT control statement that specifies how they should be ordered in the output, and the results of the operation: the sorted records. In this example, the file is sorted based on three control fields. Since all of the fields contain character data, I omitted the format values from the list of control fields and coded FORMAT=CH instead. If the three control fields I specified in figure 17-4 had different formats, I would have specified those formats in the FIELDS parameter, like this:

```
SORT FIELDS=(3,6,CH,A,11,3,PD,D,18,3,ZD,A)
```

Here, I specified that the first field contains character data, the second contains packed decimal data, and the third contains zoned decimal data.

According to the FIELDS operand of the SORT control statement in figure 17-4, the program is directed to (1) sort the records in ascending sequence based on the six-byte field that begins in position 3 of each record; (2) within that sequence, sort the records in descending sequence based on the three-byte field that begins in position 11 of each record; and (3) within that sequence, sort the records in ascending sequence based on the three-byte field that begins in position 18 of each record. In the bottom part of figure 17-3, the records are in ascending sequence according to the values in positions 3 through 8. For records that have the same data in that field (012345 and 019412), the records are in descending sequence according to the values in positions 11 through 13. For the records that still have the same control field values (019412 in the first field and 605 in the second), the records are in ascending sequence according to the values in positions 18 through 20.

The MERGE statement works much like the SORT statement. To understand it, consider figure 17-5. It shows two files, already in the desired sequence, that I want to merge into a single sequential file. After DFSORT has finished this merge operation, the output is in the same sequence as the input, but the two files are combined into

Unsorted records

Position	3-8	11-13	18-20
	012345	AAA	012
	012345	ABC	907
	011947	RB2	106
	047693	AAT	999
	142342	BBR	212
	002973	972	660
	112233	617	127
	019412	322	432
	019412	605	692
	019412	605	000

SORT statement

```
SORT   FIELDS=(3,6,A,11,3,D,18,3,A),FORMAT=CH
```

Sorted records

	002973	972	660
	011947	RB2	106
	012345	ABC	907
	012345	AAA	012
	019412	605	000
	019412	605	692
	019412	322	432
	047693	AAT	999
	112233	617	127
	142342	BBR	212

Figure 17-4   Example of the sort operation

one sequential file. As you can see, the format of the FIELDS and FORMAT parameters of MERGE are the same as for SORT.

The RECORD statement   Normally, you need to code just one control statement for DFSORT: a SORT or MERGE statement. If a SORTIN or SORTINnn data set is a VSAM file, however, you must also include a RECORD statement to indicate the format of the VSAM file's records. You can also use a RECORD statement to specify the characteristics of a non-VSAM file with variable-length records, but it's not required.

Figure 17-6 shows the format of the RECORD statement. The TYPE parameter specifies the file's record format; you code F if the records are fixed-length, V if the records are variable-length, and D if you're processing ASCII variable-length records from tape.

The LENGTH parameter supplies information about the length of the file's records. It contains five positional subparameters, but you're only likely to use the last two: min-length and avg-length.

Position	Input file 1		Input file 2	
	1-5	**9**	**1-5**	**9**
	01234	A	01234	B
	02694	A	01234	E
	02694	D	02988	A
	02988	R	06111	T
	05617	B	07122	R
	05617	C	88216	A
	98999	D	98999	A
	98999	E	98999	Z
	99667	X	99500	B
	99999	Z	99999	T

MERGE statement

```
MERGE    FIELDS=(1,5,A,9,1,A),FORMAT=CH
```

Merged file

01234	A
01234	B
01234	E
02694	A
02694	D
02988	A
02988	R
05617	B
05617	C
06611	T
07122	R
88216	A
98999	A
98999	D
98999	E
98999	Z
99500	B
99667	X
99999	T
99999	Z

Figure 17-5   Example of the merge operation

The others either assume correct default values or are used only for advanced processing. If you omit any of these subparameters, don't forget to code the required commas.

The min-length subparameter of LENGTH indicates the size of the smallest record in a variable-length input file. This value must

---

The RECORD statement

```
RECORD    TYPE=type
       [ ,LENGTH=(in-length,E15-length,out-length,min-length,avg-length) ]
```

Explanation

TYPE   Specifies the format of the file's records: F for fixed length, V for variable length, or D for ASCII variable length.

LENGTH   Specifies various length attributes for the file:

    in-length   The length of the input records. Required for VSAM files.

    E15-length   Used only if an E15 sort exit is used to change the input length.

    out-length   The length of the output records. Used only when the SORTOUT DD statement is omitted.

    min-length   When variable-length records are used, specifies the minimum record length.

    avg-length   When variable-length records are used, specifies the average record length.

Figure 17-6   The RECORD statement

be at least as large as the sum of the control field lengths. The avg-length subparameter indicates the average record length for the file. Coding these values correctly helps the sort/merge program optimize its performance.

Other sort/merge control statements

Besides the SORT, MERGE, and RECORD statements, DFSORT provides several additional statements. Figure 17-7 summarizes the ones you're most likely to use.

The MODS statement   The MODS statement lets you set up a special *exit routine* that is executed during the sort. DFSORT provides 16 different *exits*. The two most commonly used exits are E15, which is processed as each input record is read, and E35, which is processed as each sorted record is written. The routines that can be attached to these exits are generally used to modify the input or output records in some way.

The programming requirements for sort exits are well beyond the scope of this book. But if you or someone else has written a sort

The MODS statement

```
MODS exit=(routine,bytes,ddname[,C])
```

exit	The sort exit to be taken, such as E15 (before sort) or E35 (after sort).
routine	The name of the routine to process the exit.
bytes	The size of the exit routine.
ddname	The ddname of the data set that contains the routine.
C	Used to indicate a COBOL routine.

The INCLUDE and OMIT statements

```
{INCLUDE} COND=(field,comparison,field or constant)
{OMIT   }
```

field	A field to be used in a comparison. The field is specified as in the SORT or MERGE statement: *position, length, format*. For example, 6,10,CH is a valid field.
comparison	One of the following comparison operators:

EQ	Equal
NE	Not equal
GT	Greater than
GE	Greater than or equal to
LT	Less than
LE	Less than or equal to

constant	A literal value in one of the following formats:

decimal	5, +104, -39
character	C'CA', C'JONES'
hexadecimal	X'00', X'40404040'

Figure 17-7   Other DFSORT control statements (part 1 of 2)

exit, you must use the MODS statement to activate it. For example, the statement

```
MODS E15=(MYEXIT,2000,EXITLIB)
```

tells DFSORT that the E15 exit should be processed by a routine called MYEXIT. The MYEXIT routine occupies 2,000 bytes and is contained in the data set allocated by the EXITLIB DD statement.

The INCLUDE and OMIT statements   The INCLUDE and OMIT statements let you improve sorting efficiency by telling DFSORT to sort only those records that meet a specified criteria. For example, to sort only records that have the letter A in the first byte, use this INCLUDE statement:

```
INCLUDE COND=(1,1,CH,EQ,C'A')
```

The INREC and OUTREC statements

$\begin{Bmatrix} \texttt{INREC} \\ \texttt{OUTREC} \end{Bmatrix}$ `FIELDS=([constant,]position,length[,align,]...)`

constant	Tells DFSORT to insert a constant value into the output record. *Constant* can be specified in one of the following forms:

nX	Inserts *n* spaces.
nZ	Inserts *n* binary zeros.
C'text'	Inserts the specified text.
X'hex-value'	Inserts the specified hex value.

position	The location of the first byte of the field.
length	The length in bytes of the field.
align	The alignment of the field:

H	Halfword
F	Fullword
D	Doubleword

The SUM statement

`SUM FIELDS=` $\begin{Bmatrix} \texttt{(position,length,format...)} \\ \texttt{NONE} \end{Bmatrix}$

position	The location of the first byte of the field to be summarized.
length	The length in bytes of the field to be summarized.
format	A numeric field format code: BI, FI, PD, or ZD.
NONE	Specifies that no sum is to be calculated. If more than one record with the same sort key is present in the input, only the last one will be written to the output file.

Figure 17-7   Other DFSORT control statements (part 2 of 2)

To omit any records that have an A in the first byte, you would use a similar OMIT statement:

```
OMIT COND=(1,1,CH,EQ,C'A')
```

Note that the INCLUDE and OMIT statements are mutually exclusive. You can use one or the other, but not both.

The INREC and OUTREC statements   The INREC and OUTREC statements let you change the format of records before and after they are sorted. The INREC statement is usually used to eliminate unnecessary information from input records before sorting, and the OUTREC statement is usually used to add literal values to the sorted output records.

The INREC statement tells DFSORT what portions of the input records you want to use in the sort operation. For example, if you want DFSORT to sort only the first 50 characters of each record, you would use an INREC statement like this:

```
INREC FIELDS=(1,50)
```

To use bytes 1 through 50, 75 through 100, and 125 through 175 of each input record, you would use an INREC statement like this:

```
INREC FIELDS=(1,50,75,25,125,50)
```

You can use the OUTREC statement to rearrange sorted records or to add spaces. For example, consider this OUTREC statement:

```
OUTREC FIELDS=(C'ABC',1,50,100X)
```

Here, the output records consist of the letters ABC, followed by the first 50 bytes from the input records, followed by 100 spaces. If you use both INREC and OUTREC together, or if you use an E15 exit to modify the input records, be aware that the position and length specifications in an OUTREC statement refer to the input record *after* it has been reorganized by the INREC statement or the E15 exit.

The SUM statement　The SUM statement lets you summarize sorted data by consolidating information from multiple records with the same sort key. For example, suppose you are sorting a sales file by customer number, and bytes 50 through 55 contain the sales amount in packed-decimal format. With the following SUM statement, you could produce a sorted output file that has only one record per customer with the total sales summed from each of the customer's input records:

```
SUM FIELDS=(50,6,PD)
```

Here, the data in bytes 50 through 55 for each customer are summed to produce the total sales for each output record. The data for the remainder of the output record is copied from the last record for each customer.

Two sample stand-alone DFSORT jobs

To help you understand how DFSORT is used, figures 17-8 and 17-9 present two sample job steps. Both use sequential transaction files from a general ledger system. The control fields are transaction date and account number. The transaction date consists of three two-byte character fields: month beginning at position 29, day at position 31, and year at position 33. The account number is a six-byte character field beginning at position 41.

```
//SORT      EXEC PGM=SORT
//SORTLIB   DD    DSNAME=SYS1.SORTLIB,DISP=SHR
//SYSOUT    DD    SYSOUT=*
//SORTIN    DD    DSNAME=SYDOE.GL.TRANS.APRIL,DISP=SHR
//          DD    DSNAME=SYDOE.GL.TRANS.MAY,DISP=SHR
//          DD    DSNAME=SYDOE.GL.TRANS.JUNE,DISP=SHR
//SORTOUT   DD    DSNAME=SYDOE.GL.TRANS.Q2,DISP=(NEW,CATLG),
//                UNIT=SYSDA,VOL=SER=MPS8BV,
//                SPACE=(CYL,(10,5))
//SORTWK01  DD    UNIT=SYSDA,SPACE=(CYL,(20,5))
//SYSIN     DD    *
 SORT FIELDS=(41,6,CH,A,29,4,CH,A)
/*
```

Figure 17-8   A DFSORT job step to sort three files

```
//SORT      EXEC PGM=SORT
//SORTLIB   DD    DSNAME=SYS1.SORTLIB,DISP=SHR
//SYSOUT    DD    SYSOUT=*
//SORTIN01  DD    DSNAME=SYDOE.GL.TRANS.APRIL,DISP=SHR
//SORTIN02  DD    DSNAME=SYDOE.GL.TRANS.MAY,DISP=SHR
//SORTIN03  DD    DSNAME=SYDOE.GL.TRANS.JUNE,DISP=SHR
//SORTOUT   DD    DSNAME=SYDOE.GL.TRANS.Q2,DISP=(NEW,CATLG),
//                UNIT=SYSDA,VOL=SER=MPS8BV,
//                SPACE=(CYL,(10,5))
//SYSIN     DD    *
 MERGE FIELDS=(41,6,CH,A,29,4,CH,A)
/*
```

Figure 17-9   A DFSORT job step to merge three files

A sort operation   Figure 17-8 shows a job that sorts three general
ledger transaction files: one for April, one for May, and one for
June. To accomplish this, the files are concatenated together using
the ddname SORTIN. To sort just one of the files, you would simply
omit the concatenations. The output from this sort operation will be
in account-number sequence; within each account number, records
will be ordered in date sequence.

The SORT statement specifies two control fields; the major
control field is account number and the minor control field is a four-

byte field that includes the month and the day. I coded the format
subparameter within the FIELDS parameter, but since both control
fields have character format, I could have coded the FORMAT
parameter instead, like this:

```
SORT FIELDS=(41,6,A,29,4,A),FORMAT=CH
```

Either way, the effect is the same.

A merge operation   If the three input files in figure 17-8 were already
in date within account-number sequence, a sort operation would be
wasteful; instead, a merge operation could accomplish the same thing.
Figure 17-9 shows the JCL to merge the three transaction files. Here, the
input files have ddnames SORTIN01, SORTIN02, and SORTIN03. Since
this is a merge operation, there aren't any SORTWKnn files. The
FIELDS parameter in the MERGE statement is the same as in the SORT
statement in figure 17-8; it identifies the account number as the major
control field and the month and day as the minor control field.

JCL requirements for an internal sort/merge

Sometimes, it's better to code an application program that performs
an internal sort/merge rather than invoke DFSORT directly for a
stand-alone sort/merge. When you use DFSORT through an application program, it's invoked by a SORT or MERGE statement coded
according to the conventions of the language you use.

Figure 17-10 shows a job step that executes a COBOL program
that includes an internal sort. Here, the application program is
named GL6725. Following the EXEC statement that executes this
program are the DD statements required to allocate files processed
by the application program. Following these statements are the DD
statements required by DFSORT: SORTLIB and SORTWK01. In
COBOL, the input and output files for DFSORT are intercepted by
the COBOL program, so no SORTIN, SORTINnn, or SORTOUT DD
statements are required. And a SYSIN DD statement isn't needed
because the source program gives the sort/merge specifications.

Discussion

When batch-sequential processing was the rule in data processing
installations, the sort/merge program was used frequently in
transaction processing applications to sort transactions into the
proper sequence and to merge multiple transaction files (often on

```
//GL6725    EXEC  PGM=GL6725
//STEPLIB   DD    DSNAME=SYDOE.GL.LOADLIB,DISP=SHR
//GLTRAN    DD    DSNAME=SYDOE.GL.TRANS.APRIL,DISP=SHR
//          DD    DSNAME=SYDOE.GL.TRANS.MAY,DISP=SHR
//          DD    DSNAME=SYDOE.GL.TRANS.JUNE,DISP=SHR
//GLQTR     DD    DSNAME=SYDOE.GL.TRANS.Q2,DISP=(NEW,CATLG),
//                UNIT=SYSDA,VOL=SER=MPS8BV,
//                SPACE=(CYL,(10,5))
//GLTLIST   DD    SYSOUT=*
//GLTSUM    DD    SYSOUT=*
//SYSOUT    DD    SYSOUT=*
//SORTLIB   DD    DSNAME=SYS1.SORTLIB,DISP=SHR
//SORTWK01  DD    UNIT=SYSDA,SPACE=(CYL,(20,5))
//SYSDBOUT  DD    SYSOUT=*
```

Figure 17-10 A job step to invoke an application program with an internal sort

tape) together so that they could be posted to a master file with a single run. With today's online systems however, transactions are usually posted immediately to their related master files, so batch sorting and posting isn't required. However, there are still plenty of applications that require data to be sorted, so you still need to know how to use the sort/merge program.

Terminology

sort/merge program	control field
DFSORT	key field
sort	major control field
merge	minor control field
stand-alone sort/merge	exit routine
internal sort/merge	exit

Objectives

1. Code a stand-alone sort/merge job that sorts or merges data from one or more files using one or more control fields.

2. Code the JCL necessary to invoke an application program that performs an internal sort/merge.

Exercises

1. Code a stand-alone DFSORT job that sorts the cataloged file
   X401.JOURNAL into ascending sequence using the first 18 bytes
   of each record as the sort key. The output file should be named
   X401.JOURNAL.SORT. Assume that the data to be sorted
   requires 15 cylinders of disk space.

2. Code the JCL necessary to invoke a program named X401RPT
   that requires an internal sort. The program requires DD statements to allocate the following two files:

```
X401JRNL    Input file; X401.JOURNAL
X401RPT     Report output; SYSOUT=A
```

The DFSORT modules are located in SYS1.SORTLIB. Allocate 30
cylinders of primary space and 10 cylinders of secondary space
on a non-specific SYSDA volume for the sort work file.

Appendix A

Reference summary

This appendix presents the formats of the MVS JCL and JES2/JES3 control statements presented in this book. Each statement contains one or more figure references so you can look back to the complete figure if you need a description of the statement's parameters.

JCL statements

The JOB statement

(Figures 5-5 and 6-5)

```
//jobname    JOB  [ accounting information ] [ ,programmer name ]

             [ ,ADDRSPC={ VIRT  } ]
                        { REAL  }

                         ⎧ value                    ⎫
             [ ,BYTES=  ⎨                ⎧ CANCEL  ⎫ ⎬ ]
                         ⎩ ([value][,    ⎨ DUMP    ⎬ ]) ⎭
                                         ⎩ WARNING ⎭

                         ⎧ value                    ⎫
             [ ,CARDS=  ⎨                ⎧ CANCEL  ⎫ ⎬ ]
                         ⎩ ([value][,    ⎨ DUMP    ⎬ ]) ⎭
                                         ⎩ WARNING ⎭

             [ ,CLASS=class ]
             [ ,COND=((value,op)...) ]

                         ⎧ value                    ⎫
             [ ,LINES=  ⎨                ⎧ CANCEL  ⎫ ⎬ ]
                         ⎩ ([value][,    ⎨ DUMP    ⎬ ]) ⎭
                                         ⎩ WARNING ⎭

             [ ,MSGCLASS=class ]
             [ ,MSGLEVEL=(stmt,msg) ]
             [ ,NOTIFY=user-id ]

                         ⎧ value                    ⎫
             [ ,PAGES=  ⎨                ⎧ CANCEL  ⎫ ⎬ ]
                         ⎩ ([value][,    ⎨ DUMP    ⎬ ]) ⎭
                                         ⎩ WARNING ⎭

             [ ,PASSWORD=password ]
             [ ,PERFORM=group ]
             [ ,PRTY=priority ]

             [ ,REGION={ valueK } ]
                        { valueM }

                         ⎧ ([min][,sec]) ⎫
             [ ,TIME=   ⎨ NOLIMIT        ⎬ ]
                         ⎩ MAXIMUM        ⎭

                         ⎧ COPY    ⎫
             [ ,TYPRUN= ⎨ HOLD    ⎬ ]
                         ⎨ JCLHOLD ⎬
                         ⎩ SCAN    ⎭

             [ ,USER=user-id ]
```

The EXEC statement

(Figures 5-10 and 6-4)

```
//stepname EXEC  PGM=program-name
                 [ ,ADDRSPC= { VIRT  } ]
                             { REAL  }

                 [ ,COND=([(value,op,step)...][, { EVEN } ]) ]
                                                 { ONLY }
                 [ ,DPRTY=([value1][,value2]) ]

                 [ ,PARM=information ]

                 [ ,PERFORM=group ]

                 [ ,REGION= { valueK } ]
                            { valueM }

                 [ ,TIME= { ([min][,sec]) } ]
                          { NOLIMIT       }
                          { MAXIMUM       }
```

The IF, ELSE, and ENDIF statements

(Figure 6-17)

```
//[name] IF (relational-expression) THEN
  .
  .
  .
    statements-executed-if-true
  .
  .
  .
//[name] ELSE
  .
  .
  .
    statements-executed-if-not-true
  .
  .
  .
//[name] ENDIF
```

The DD statement for in-stream data sets

(Figure 5-12)

```
//ddname   DD  {*    }
                {DATA }
               [ ,DLM=xx ]
```

The DD statement for SYSOUT data sets

(Figures 5-12 and 6-34)

```
//ddname     DD [ SYSOUT=(class[,writer][,{form-name}]) ]
                                          {code-name}

             [ ,BURST= {YES} ]
                       {NO }

             [ ,CHARS=character-set ]

             [ ,COPIES=nnn(,(group-value[,group-value...])) ]

             [ ,DEST=destination ]

             [ ,FCB=fcb ]

             [ ,FLASH=overlay ]

             [ ,HOLD= {YES} ]
                      {NO }

             [ ,MODIFY=module ]

             [ ,OUTLIM=number ]

             [ ,OUTPUT=name ]

             [ ,SPIN= {UNALLOC} ]
                      {NO     }

             [ ,UCS=character-set ]
```

The DD statement for VSAM data sets

(Figures 9-1 and 9-4)

```
//ddname      DD    { DSNAME=data-set-name }
                    { DUMMY                }

                    [ ,DISP=(status,normal-disp,abnormal-disp) ]

                    [ ,AMP=(option,option...) ]

                    [ ,UNIT=unit ]

                    [ ,VOL=  { SER=vol-ser         } ]
                             { REF=data-set-name    }

                    [ ,SPACE=(unit,(primary,secondary)) ]

                    [ ,AVGREC= { U }  ]
                               { K }
                               { M }

                    [ ,RECORG= { KS } ]
                               { ES }
                               { RR }

                    [ ,LRECL=length ]

                    [ ,KEYLEN=length ]

                    [ ,KEYOFF=offset ]

                    [ ,LIKE=data-set-name ]

                    [ ,STORCLAS=storage-class ]

                    [ ,DATACLAS=data-class ]

                    [ ,MGMTCLAS=management-class ]
```

The DD statement for non-VSAM DASD data sets

(Figures 5-12 and 6-21)

```
//ddname   DD   [ DUMMY ]

               [ ,DSNAME=data-set-name ]

               [ ,DISP=(status,normal-disp,abnormal-disp) ]

               [ ,UNIT=unit ]

               [ ,VOL= {SER=vol=ser        } ]
                       {REF=data-set name  }

               [ ,SPACE=(unit,(prim,sec, {dir  } )[,RLSE][, {CONTIG} ]
                                         {index}             {MXIG  }
                   [,ROUND]) ]                               {ALX   }

               [ ,AVGREC= {U} ]
                          {K}
                          {M}

               [ ,DCB=(option,option...) ]

               [ ,LIKE=data-set-name ]

               [ ,STORCLAS=storage-class ]

               [ ,DATACLAS=data-class ]

               [ ,MGMTCLAS=management-class ]
```

The DD statement for tape data sets

(Figures 11-2, 11-4, and 11-5)

```
//ddname DD    [ DUMMY ]

               [ ,DSNAME=data-set-name ]

               [ ,DISP=(status,normal-disp,abnormal-disp) ]

               [ , {UNIT=(unit[,count][,DEFER]) } ]
                   {UNIT=AFF=ddname            }

               [ ,VOL=([PRIVATE][,RETAIN][,volume-sequence][,volume-count]
                   [,SER=(serial,serial...)]) ]

               [ ,LABEL=([data-set-sequence][,label-type][, {RETPD=nnnn } ]) ]
                                                            {EXPDT=yyddd}

               [ ,DCB=(option,option...) ]
```

The OUTPUT statement

(Figure 6-32)

```
//name     OUTPUT [ ADDRESS= { addr                      } ]
                                (addr[,addr...])

                   [ ,BUILDING=building ]

                   [ ,BURST= { YES } ]
                             { NO  }

                   [ ,CHARS=character-set ]
                   [ ,CLASS=class ]

                                 { PROGRAM }
                   [ ,CONTROL=   { SINGLE  } ]
                                 { DOUBLE  }
                                 { TRIPLE  }

                   [ ,COPIES= { nnn                              } ]
                              { (,(group-value[,group-value...])) }

                   [ ,DEFAULT= { YES } ]
                               { NO  }

                   [ ,DEPT=dept ]
                   [ ,DEST=destination ]
                   [ ,FCB=fcb ]
                   [ ,FLASH=overlay ]
                   [ ,FORMDEF=form-def ]
                   [ ,FORMS=form ]

                              { ALL }
                   [ ,JESDS=  { JCL } ]
                              { LOG }
                              { MSG }
                   [ ,LINECT=count ]
                   [ ,MODIFY=module ]
                   [ ,NAME=name ]
                   [ ,OUTDISP=(normal-disp[,abnormal-disp]) ]
                   [ ,PAGEDEF=page-def ]
                   [ ,PRTY=priority ]
                   [ ,ROOM=room ]
                   [ ,TITLE=title ]
                   [ ,UCS=character-set ]
```

The INCLUDE statement

(Figure 7-14)

```
//          INCLUDE MEMBER=name
```

The JCLLIB statement

(Figure 7-8)

```
//name      JCLLIB ORDER=(library[,library...])
```

The SET statement

(Figure 7-11)

```
//          SET parameter=value[,parameter=value...]
```

JES2 control statements

The /*JOBPARM statement

(Figure 6-7)

```
/*JOBPARM  [ BYTES=value ]
           [ ,CARDS=value ]
           [ ,LINES=value ]
           [ ,PAGES=value ]
           [ ,SYSAFF=(system) ]
           [ ,TIME=value ]
```

The /*MESSAGE statement

```
/*MESSAGE  message
```

The /*NETACCT statement

```
/*NETACCT  account-no
```

The /*NOTIFY statement

```
/*NOTIFY  user-id
```

The /*OUTPUT statement

(Figure 6-36)

```
/*OUTPUT   code
           [ ,BURST={ YES } ]
                    { NO  }

           [ ,CHARS=character-set ]

           [ ,COPIES={ nnn                                          } ]
                     { (nnn[,(group-value[,group-value...])])]) }

           [ ,COPYG=(group-value[,group-value...]) ]

           [ ,DEST=destination ]

           [ ,FCB=fcb-name ]

           [ ,FLASH=overlay ]

           [ ,FORMS=form ]

           [ ,LINECT=count ]

           [ ,MODIFY=module ]

           [ ,UCS=character-set ]
```

The /*PRIORITY statement

```
/*PRIORITY priority
```

The /*ROUTE statement

```
/*ROUTE {XEQ|PRINT} node
```

The /*SETUP statement

```
/*SETUP  volume,volume...
```

The /*SIGNOFF statement

```
/*SIGNOFF
```

The /*SIGNON statement

```
/*SIGNON       REMOTEnnn [password] [new-password] [password2]
```

The /XEQ statement

```
/*XEQ node
```

The /*XMIT statement

```
/*XMIT node [DLM=xx]
```

JES3 control statements

The //*DATASET statement

```
//*DATASET DDNAME=ddname,option,option...
```

The //*ENDDATASET statement

```
//*ENDDATASET
```

The //*ENDPROCESS statement

```
//*ENDPROCESS
```

The //*FORMAT PR statement

(Figure 6-37)

```
//*FORMAT    PR,DDNAME=[ddname-specification]

            [ ,CHARS=character-set ]

                        ⎧PROGRAM⎫
            [ ,CONTROL= ⎨SINGLE ⎬ ]
                        ⎪DOUBLE ⎪
                        ⎩TRIPLE ⎭

            [ ,COPIES= ⎧nnn                             ⎫ ]
                       ⎨(group-value[,group-value...]) ⎬
                       ⎩                               ⎭

            [ ,DEST=destination ]

            [ ,FCB=fcb ]

            [ ,FLASH=overlay ]

            [ ,FORMS=form ]

            [ ,MODIFY=module ]

            [ ,PRTY=priority ]
```

The //*MAIN statement

(Figure 6-6)

```
//*MAIN   [ BYTES=(value[,action]) ]
          [ ,CARDS=(value[,action]) ]
          [ ,CLASS=job-class ]
          [ ,HOLD= { YES
                     NO  } ]
          [ ,IORATE= { LOW
                       MED
                       HIGH } ]
          [ ,LINES=(value[,action]) ]
          [ ,LREGION=valueK ]
          [ ,PAGES=(value[,action]) ]
          [ ,SYSTEM=system ]
```

The //*NET statement

```
//*NET option,option...
```

The //*NETACCT statement

```
//*NETACCT option,option...
```

The //*OPERATOR statement

```
//*OPERATOR message
```

The //**PAUSE statement

```
//**PAUSE
```

The //*PROCESS statement

```
//*PROCESS option
```

The //*ROUTE statement

```
//*ROUTE XEQ node
```

The /*SIGNOFF statement

```
/*SIGNOFF
```

The /*SIGNON statement

```
/*SIGNON        workn AR passw-1   passw-2   new-pass
```

Appendix B

MVS messages

As MVS processes your job, it produces many messages. Although many of them simply provide information about your job's execution, some of them represent error conditions that might cause your job to abend. Usually, MVS error messages are cryptic: In order to fully understand the problem, you must read the description of the message in an MVS manual.

Messages produced by major MVS operating system components are documented in the two-volume manual *MVS System Messages*. Most of the messages you'll encounter are described in that manual. However, there are more than 60 other manuals that also contain message descriptions from various MVS components and subsystems. For example, messages issued by the MVS utilities are documented in a separate manual, as are messages from the linkage editor. The key to locating a message's description is knowing which manual contains it. And the key to knowing which manual contains a message's description is understanding the message's format.

MVS messages can be produced in a variety of formats, but all of them begin with an identifier that you can use to look up the message in a manual. The message identifier consists of two components: a three- or four-character prefix, which identifies the MVS component that issued the message, and a serial number, which uniquely identifies the message.

The table that follows lists the message prefixes you're likely to encounter. For each message prefix, you'll find a description of the component that issued the message and the title of the manual that contains the message description. (Since IBM periodically reorganizes the message library, I don't list specific order numbers for these manuals.) This table is by no means complete; the *MVS System Messages* manual contains a similar table that's six pages long and lists more than 90 prefixes. The table in this appendix, however, includes most of the message prefixes you should encounter.

Prefix	Message source	Manual
DFH	CICS/VS	CICS/VS Messages and Codes
DFS	IMS/VS	IMS/VS Messages and Codes
DMS	PL/I checkout compiler	PL/I Checkout Compiler: Messages and Codes
DSN	DB2	IBM Database 2 Messages and Codes
HASP	JES2	JES2 Messages
IAT	JES3	JES3 Messages
IBM	PL/I optimizing compiler	PL/I Optimizing Compiler: Messages
ICB	Mass Storage System	Mass Storage System Messages
ICE	Sort/merge	Sort/Merge Programmer's Guide
ICH	RACF	RACF Messages and Codes MVS System Messages
IDA	VSAM	MVS System Messages
IDC	Access Method Services	MVS System Messages
IEA	MVS supervisor	MVS System Messages
IEB	MVS utilities	MVS Utilities Messages MVS System Messages
IEC	MVS data management	MVS System Messages
IEE	MVS master scheduler	MVS System Messages
IEF	MVS job scheduler	MVS System Messages
IEH	MVS utilities	MVS Utilities Messages MVS System Messages
IEL	PL/I optimizing compiler	PL/I Optimizing Compiler: Messages
IEN	PL/I checkout compiler	PL/I Checkout Compiler: Messages and Codes
IEV	Assembler H	Assembler H: Messages Assembler H Programming: Guide
IEW	Linkage editor/loader	MVS Linkage Editor and Loader Messages MVS System Messages
IFA	System Management Facilities	MVS System Messages
IFE	Fortran IV (H Extended)	OS FORTRAN IV Compiler and Library Messages
IFO	MVS Assembler	OS/VS - VM/370 Assembler and Programmer's Guide
IGD	SMS	MVS System Messages
IGGN	Data Facility Product	MVS System Messages
IGW	Data Facility Product	MVS System Messages
IGY	VS COBOL II	VS COBOL II Application Programming Guide
IGZ	VS COBOL II	VS COBOL II Application Programming Guide
IKF	VS COBOL II	VS COBOL II Application Programming Guide
IKJ	TSO/E	TSO/E Messages MVS System Messages
IOS	Input/Output Supervisor	MVS System Messages
IRA	System Resources Manager	MVS System Messages
IRR	RACF	MVS System Messages

Installation dependent information

This appendix provides space for you to record information that's unique to your installation, such as the accounting information you must code on JOB statements. I've duplicated the information form several times so you can record information about several systems.

Operating system

MVS/XA or ESA?   JES2 or JES3?

Information required to access the system

TSO user-id:

JOB statement accounting information:

Network access information:

DASD allocation information

Data set name high-level qualifier:

Valid generic or group names for UNIT parameter:

Eligible DASD volumes (list type and vol-ser; e.g., 3390: TSO001):

Processing classes

Job classes: SYSOUT classes:

Default: Default (MSGCLASS):

Other installation dependent information

Operating system

MVS/XA or ESA?   JES2 or JES3?

Information required to access the system

TSO user-id:

JOB statement accounting information:

Network access information:

DASD allocation information

Data set name high-level qualifier:

Valid generic or group names for UNIT parameter:

Eligible DASD volumes (list type and vol-ser; e.g., 3390: TSO001):

Processing classes

Job classes: SYSOUT classes:

Default: Default (MSGCLASS):

Other installation dependent information

Operating system

MVS/XA or ESA?   JES2 or JES3?

Information required to access the system

TSO user-id:

JOB statement accounting information:

Network access information:

DASD allocation information

Data set name high-level qualifier:

Valid generic or group names for UNIT parameter:

Eligible DASD volumes (list type and vol-ser; e.g., 3390: TSO001):

Processing classes

Job classes: SYSOUT classes:

Default: Default (MSGCLASS):

Other installation dependent information

Index

MVS TSO

Part 1: Concepts and ISPF   **Doug Lowe**

Chapter 4 in *MVS JCL* gives you a brief introduction to ISPF...cnough for you to enter job streams, submit jobs for background processing, and monitor their progress. But to take advantage of all of ISPF's features, you need to know more. So *MVS TSO, Part 1* lets you quickly master ISPF for everyday programming tasks. You'll learn how to:

- edit and browse data sets
- use the ISPF utilities to manage your data sets and libraries
- compile, link, and execute programs interactively
- use the OS COBOL or VS COBOL II interactive debugger

- process batch jobs in a background region
- manage your background jobs more easily using the Spool Display & Search Facility (SDSF)
- use member parts list to track the use of subprograms and COPY members within program libraries
- use two library management systems that support hierarchical libraries—the Library Management Facility (LMF) and the Software Configuration and Library Manager (SCLM)
- and more!

MVS TSO, Part 1, 8 chapters, 467 pages, **$32.50**
ISBN 0-911625-56-9

MVS TSO

Part 2: Commands and Procedures (CLIST AND REXX)   **Doug Lowe**

If you're ready to expand your skills beyond ISPF and become a TSO user who can write complex CLIST and REXX procedures with ease, this is the book for you. It begins by teaching you how to use TSO commands for common programming tasks like managing data sets and libraries, running programs in foreground mode, and submitting jobs for background execution. Then, it

shows you how to combine those commands into CLIST or REXX procedures for the jobs you do most often... including procedures that you can use as edit macros under the ISPF editor and procedures that use ISPF dialog functions to display full-screen panels.

MVS TSO, Part 2, 10 chapters, 450 pages, **$34.50**
ISBN 0-911625-57-7

MVS Assembler Language

Kevin McQuillen and Anne Prince

All code on an MVS system eventually gets reduced to assembler language, regardless of the language it was written in. So a basic understanding of assembler is a plus for *any* MVS programmer. That's why the first 8 chapters in our MVS assembler book present the least every programmer should know about assembler to use MVS more skillfully.

For many programmers, those 8 chapters are also the *most* they need to know. But if you want to know

more, you can read any of the remaining chapters that interest you. They cover advanced subjects like table handling, bit manipulation, translation, writing macro definitions, floating point arithmetic, disk access methods, and program design.

MVS Assembler Language, 19 chapters, 528 pages, **$36.50**
ISBN 0-911625-34-8

 Call **toll-free**   1-800-221-5528   Weekdays, 8 a.m. to 5 p.m. Pac. Std. Time

VSAM

Access Method Services and Application Programming   **Doug Lowe**

As its title suggests, *VSAM: Access Method Services and Application Programming* has two main purposes: (1) to teach you how to use the Access Method Services (AMS) utility to define and manipulate VSAM files; and (2) to teach you how to process VSAM files using various programming languages. To be specific, you'll learn:

- how VSAM data sets and catalogs are organized and used

- how to use AMS commands to define VSAM catalogs, space, clusters, alternate indexes, and paths

- how to set AMS performance options so you make the best possible use of your system's resources

- what recovery and security considerations are important when you use AMS

- how to code MVS and DOS/VSE JCL for VSAM files, and how to allocate VSAM files under TSO and VM/CMS

- how to process VSAM files in COBOL, CICS, and assembler language (the chapter on COBOL processing covers both VS COBOL and VS COBOL II)

You'll find the answers to questions like these

- How much primary and secondary space should I allocate to my VSAM files?

- What's an appropriate free space allocation for a KSDS?

- What's the best control interval size for VSAM files that are accessed both sequentially and directly?

- Do I always need to use VERIFY to check the integrity of my files?

- What's the difference between regular VSAM catalogs and the ICF catalog structure?

- When should I...and shouldn't I...use the IMBED and REPLICATE options to improve performance?

- It's easy to find out how many records are in a file's index component. But how do I find out how many of those records are in the sequence set?

- How do I determine the best buffer allocation for my files?

- What's the best way to back up my VSAM files—REPRO, EXPORT, or something else?

So why wait any longer to sharpen your VSAM skills? Get a copy of *VSAM: AMS and Application Programming* TODAY!

VSAM: AMS & Application Programming,
12 chapters, 260 pages, **$27.50**
ISBN 0-911625-33-X

VSAM for the COBOL Programmer

Second Edition   **Doug Lowe**

If you're looking for a no-frills approach to VSAM that teaches you only what you need to know to code CO-BOL programs, this is the book for you. You'll learn: the meanings of the critical terms and concepts that apply to VSAM files; the COBOL elements for handling VSAM files; how to handle alternate indexes and dynamic access; why error processing is a must; how to use the Access Method Services utility (AMS) to create,

print, copy, and rename VSAM files; how to code the MVS and VSE JCL to run programs that use VSAM files; and how your COBOL code is affected if you're working under VS COBOL II.

VSAM for COBOL, 6 chapters, 187 pages, **$20.00**
ISBN 0-911625-45-3

CICS for the COBOL Programmer

Second Edition   **Doug Lowe**

This 2-part course is designed to help COBOL programmers become outstanding CICS programmers.

Part 1: An Introductory Course covers the basic CICS elements you'll use in just about every program you write. So you'll learn about basic mapping support (BMS), pseudo-conversational programming, basic CICS commands, sensible program design using event-driven design techniques, testing and debugging using IBM-supplied transactions (like CEMT, CECI, and CEDF) or a transaction dump, and efficiency considerations.

Part 2: An Advanced Course covers CICS features you'll use regularly, though you won't need all of them for every program. That means you'll learn about browse commands, temporary storage, transient data, data tables (including the shared data table feature of CICS 3.3), DB2 and DL/I processing considerations, distributed processing features, interval control

commands, BMS page building, and more! In addition, *Part 2* teaches you which features do similar things and when to use each one. So you won't just learn how to code new functions...you'll also learn how to choose the best CICS solution for each programming problem you face.

Both books cover all versions of CICS up through 3.3. Both cover OS/VS COBOL, VS COBOL II, and COBOL/370, so it doesn't matter which COBOL compiler you're using. And all the program examples in both books conform to CUA's Entry Model for screen design.

CICS, Part 1, 12 chapters, 409 pages, **$31.00**
ISBN 0-911625-60-7

CICS, Part 2, 12 chapters, 352 pages, **$31.00**
ISBN 0-911625-67-4

The CICS Programmer's Desk Reference

Second Edition   **Doug Lowe**

Ever feel buried by IBM manuals?

It seems like you need stacks of them, close at hand, if you want to be an effective CICS programmer. Because frankly, there's just too much you have to know to do your job well; you can't keep it all in your head.

That's why Doug Lowe decided to write *The CICS Programmer's Desk Reference*. In it, he's collected all the information you need to have at your fingertips, and organized it into 12 sections that make it easy for you to find what you're looking for. So there are sections on:

- BMS macro instructions—their formats (with an explanation of each parameter) and coding examples
- CICS commands—their syntax (with an explanation of each parameter), coding examples, and suggestions on how and when to use each one most effectively
- MVS and DOS/VSE JCL for CICS applications

- AMS commands for handling VSAM files
- details for MVS users on how to use ISPF
- complete model programs, including specs, design, and code
- a summary of CICS program design techniques that lead to simple, maintainable, and efficient programs
- guidelines for testing and debugging CICS applications
- and more!

So clear the IBM manuals off your terminal table. Let the *Desk Reference* be your everyday guide to CICS instead.

CICS Desk Reference, 12 sections, 507 pages, **$36.50**
ISBN 0-911625-68-2

DB2 for the COBOL Programmer

Part 1: An Introductory Course   **Steve Eckols**

If you're looking for a practical DB2 book that focuses on application programming, this is the book for you. Written from the programmer's point of view, it will quickly teach you what you need to know to access and process DB2 data in your COBOL programs using embedded SQL. You'll learn:

- what DB2 is and how it works, so you'll have the background you need to program more easily and logically

- how to design and code application programs that retrieve and update DB2 data

- how to use basic error handling and data integrity techniques to protect DB2 data

- how to use joins and unions to combine data from two or more tables into a single table

- how to use DB2 column functions to extract summary information from a table

- how to use a subquery or subselect when one SQL statement depends on the results of another

- how to work with variable-length data and nulls

- how to develop DB2 programs interactively (using DB2I, a TSO facility) or in batch

So if you want to learn how to write DB2 application programs, get a copy of this book today!

DB2, Part 1, 11 chapters, 371 pages, **$32.50**
ISBN 0-911625-59-3

DB2 for the COBOL Programmer

Part 2: An Advanced Course   **Steve Eckols**

Once you've mastered the basics of DB2 programming, there's still plenty to learn. So this book teaches you all the advanced DB2 features that will make you a more capable programmer...and shows you when to use each one. You'll learn:

- how to use advanced data manipulation and error handling techniques

- how to use dynamic SQL

- how to work with distributed DB2 data

- how to maximize locking efficiency and concurrency to maintain the accuracy of DB2 data even while a number of programs have access to that data

- how to access and process DB2 data in CICS programs

- what you need to know about data base administration so you can design and define your own tables for program testing (this will make you a more productive and professional programmer, even if you never want to be a DBA)

- how to use QMF, IBM's Query Management Facility, to issue SQL statements interactively and to prepare formatted reports

So don't wait to expand your DB2 skills. Get a copy of this book TODAY.

DB2, Part 2, 15 chapters, 393 pages, **$36.50**
ISBN 0-911625-64-X

 Call **toll-free**   1-800-221-5528   Weekdays, 8 a.m. to 5 p.m. Pac. Std. Time

IMS for the COBOL Programmer

Part 1: DL/I Data Base Processing   **Steve Eckols**

This how-to book will have you writing batch DL/I programs in a minimum of time—whether you're working on a VSE or an MVS system. But it doesn't neglect the conceptual background you must have to create programs that work. So you'll learn:

- what a DL/I data base is and how its data elements are organized into a hierarchical structure
- the COBOL elements for creating, accessing, and updating DL/I data bases...including logical data bases and data bases with secondary indexing
- how to use DL/I recovery and restart features
- the basic DL/I considerations for coding interactive programs using IMS/DC or CICS

- how data bases with the 4 common types of DL/I data base organizations are stored (this material will help you program more logically and efficiently for the type of data base you're using)
- and more!

7 complete COBOL programs show you how to process DL/I data bases in various ways. Use them as models for production work in your shop, and you'll save hours of development time.

IMS, Part 1, 16 chapters, 333 pages, **$34.50**
ISBN 0-911625-29-1

IMS for the COBOL Programmer

Part 2: Data Communications and Message Format Service   **Steve Eckols**

The second part of *IMS for the COBOL Programmer* is for MVS programmers only. It teaches how to develop on-line programs that access IMS data bases and run under the data communications (DC) component of IMS. So you'll learn:

- why you code message processing programs (MPPs) the way you do (DC programs are called MPPs because they process messages sent from and to user terminals)
- what COBOL elements you use for MPPs
- how to use Message Format Service (MFS), a facility for formatting complex terminal displays so you can enhance the look and operation of your DC programs
- how to develop applications that use more than one screen format or that use physical and logical paging

- how to develop batch message processing (BMP) programs to update IMS data bases in batch even while they're being used by other programs
- how to use Batch Terminal Simulator (BTS) to test DC applications using IMS resources, but without disrupting the everyday IMS processing that's going on
- and more!

8 complete programs—including MFS format sets, program design, and COBOL code—show you how to handle various DC and MFS applications. Use them as models to save yourself hours of coding and debugging.

IMS, Part 2, 16 chapters, 398 pages, **$36.50**
ISBN 0-911625-30-5

 Call **toll-free**   1-800-221-5528   Weekdays, 8 a.m. to 5 p.m. Pac. Std. Time

VS COBOL II: A Guide for Programmers and Managers

Second Edition   **Anne Prince**

This book builds on your COBOL knowledge to quickly teach you everything you need to know about VS COBOL II, the IBM 1985 COBOL compiler for MVS shops:

- how to code the new language elements... and what language elements you can't use anymore
- CICS considerations
- how to use the new debugger
- how the compiler's features can make your programs compile and run more efficiently
- guidelines for converting to VS COBOL II (that includes coverage of the conversion aids IBM supplies)

So if you're in a shop that's already converted to VS COBOL II, you'll learn how to benefit from the new language elements and features the compiler has to offer. If you aren't yet working in VS COBOL II, you'll learn how to write programs now that will be easy to convert later on. And if you're a manager, you'll get some practical ideas on when to convert and how to do it as painlessly as possible.

This second edition covers Release 3 of the compiler, as well as Releases 1 and 2.

VS COBOL II, 7 chapters, 271 pages, **$27.50**
ISBN 0-911625-54-2

Structured ANS COBOL

A 2-part course in 1974 and 1985 ANS COBOL   **Mike Murach and Paul Noll**

This 2-part course teaches how to use 1974 and 1985 standard COBOL the way the top professionals do. The two parts are independent: You can choose either or both, depending on your current level of COBOL skill (if you're learning on your own) or on what you want your programmers to learn (if you're a trainer or manager).

Part 1: A Course for Novices teaches people with no previous programming experience how to design and code COBOL programs that prepare reports. Because report programs often call subprograms, use COPY members, handle one-level tables, and read indexed files, it covers these subjects too. But frankly, this book emphasizes the structure and logic of report programs, instead of covering as many COBOL elements as other introductory texts do. That's because we've found most beginning programmers have more trouble with structure and logic than they do with COBOL itself.

Part 2: An Advanced Course also emphasizes program structure and logic, focusing on edit, update, and maintenance programs. But beyond that, it's a complete guide to the 1974 and 1985 elements that all COBOL programmers should know how to use (though many don't). To be specific, it teaches how to:

- handle sequential, indexed, and relative files
- use alternate indexing and dynamic processing for indexed files
- code internal sorts and merges
- create and use COPY library members
- create and call subprograms
- handle single- and multi-level tables using indexes as well as subscripts
- use INSPECT, STRING, and UNSTRING for character manipulation
- code 1974 programs that will be easy to convert when you switch to a 1985 compiler

In fact, we recommend you get a copy of *Part 2* no matter how much COBOL experience you've had because it makes such a handy reference to all the COBOL elements you'll ever want to use.

COBOL, Part 1, 13 chapters, 438 pages, **$31.00**
ISBN 0-911625-37-2

COBOL, Part 2, 12 chapters, 498 pages, **$31.00**
ISBN 0-911625-38-0

Comment Form

Your opinions count

If you have any comments, criticisms, or suggestions for us, I'm eager to get them. Your opinions today will affect our products of tomorrow. And if you find any errors in this book, typographical or otherwise, please point them out so we can correct them in the next printing.

Thanks for your help.

Mike Murach

Book title: MVS JCL, Second Edition

Dear Mike: _____

_____

_____

_____

_____

_____

_____

_____

_____

_____

_____

_____

_____

_____

_____

_____

_____

_____

_____

_____

Name _____

Company (if company address) _____

Address _____

City, State, Zip _____

Fold where indicated and tape closed.

No postage necessary if mailed in the U.S.

BUSINESS REPLY MAIL

FIRST CLASS   PERMIT NO. 3063   FRESNO, CA

POSTAGE WILL BE PAID BY ADDRESSEE

Mike Murach & Associates, Inc.

4697 W JACQUELYN AVE
FRESNO CA 93722-9888

Order Form

Our Unlimited Guarantee

To our customers who order directly from us: You must be satisfied. Our books must work for you, or you can send them back for a full refund...no questions asked.

Name & Title _____

Company (if company address) _____

Street address _____

City, State, Zip _____

Phone number (including area code) _____

Fax number (if you fax your order to us) _____

Qty	Product code and title	*Price
MVS Subjects		
____ MJLR	MVS JCL (Second Edition)	$39.50
____ TSO1	MVS TSO, Part 1: Concepts and ISPF	32.50
____ TSO2	MVS TSO, Part 2: Commands and Procedures (CLIST and REXX)	34.50
____ MBAL	MVS Assembler Language	36.50
CICS		
____ CC1R	CICS for the COBOL Programmer Part 1 (Second Edition)	$35.00
____ CC2R	CICS for the COBOL Programmer Part 2 (Second Edition)	35.00
____ CRFR	The CICS Programmer's Desk Reference (Second Edition)	41.00
COBOL Language Elements		
____ VC2R	VS COBOL II (Second Edition)	$27.50
____ SC1R	Structured ANS COBOL, Part 1	31.00
____ SC2R	Structured ANS COBOL, Part 2	31.00
____ RW	Report Writer	17.50

Qty	Product code and title	*Price
Data Base Processing		
____ DB21	DB2 for the COBOL Programmer Part 1: An Introductory Course	$32.50
____ DB22	DB2 for the COBOL Programmer Part 2: An Advanced Course	36.50
____ IMS1	IMS for the COBOL Programmer Part 1: DL/I Data Base Processing	34.50
____ IMS2	IMS for the COBOL Programmer Part 2: Data Communications and MFS	36.50
VSAM		
____ VSMX	VSAM: Access Method Services and Application Programming	$27.50
____ VSMR	VSAM for the COBOL Programmer (Second Edition)	20.00
DOS/VSE Subjects		
____ VJLR	DOS/VSE JCL (Second Edition)	$34.50
____ ICCF	DOS/VSE ICCF	31.00
____ VBAL	DOS/VSE Assembler Language	36.50

☐ Bill me for the books plus UPS shipping and handling (and sales tax within California).

☐ Bill my company. P.O.# _____

☐ I want to **SAVE 10%** by paying in advance. Charge to my ____ Visa ____ MasterCard ____ American Express:
Card number _____
Valid thru (mo/yr) _____
Cardowner's signature _____

☐ I want to **SAVE 10% plus shipping and handling**. Here's my check or money order for the books minus 10% ($_____). California residents, please add sales tax to your total. (Offer valid in U.S.)

* Prices are subject to change. Please call for current prices.

To order more quickly,

Call **toll-free 1-800-221-5528**

(Weekdays, 8 to 5 Pacific Standard Time)

Fax: 1-209-275-9035

Mike Murach & Associates, Inc.

4697 West Jacquelyn Avenue
Fresno, California 93722-6427
(209) 275-3335

BUSINESS REPLY MAIL
FIRST CLASS   PERMIT NO. 3063   FRESNO, CA

POSTAGE WILL BE PAID BY ADDRESSEE

Mike Murach & Associates, Inc.

4697 W JACQUELYN AVE
FRESNO CA 93722-9888

Order Form

Our Unlimited Guarantee

To our customers who order directly from us: You must be satisfied. Our books must work for you, or you can send them back for a full refund...no questions asked.

Name & Title _____

Company (if company address) _____

Street address _____

City, State, Zip _____

Phone number (including area code)_____

Fax number (if you fax your order to us) _____

Qty	Product code and title	*Price
MVS Subjects		
____MJLR	MVS JCL (Second Edition)	$39.50
____TSO1	MVS TSO, Part 1: Concepts and ISPF	32.50
____TSO2	MVS TSO, Part 2: Commands and Procedures (CLIST and REXX)	34.50
____MBAL	MVS Assembler Language	36.50
CICS		
____CC1R	CICS for the COBOL Programmer Part 1 (Second Edition)	$35.00
____CC2R	CICS for the COBOL Programmer Part 2 (Second Edition)	35.00
____CRFR	The CICS Programmer's Desk Reference (Second Edition)	41.00
COBOL Language Elements		
____VC2R	VS COBOL II (Second Edition)	$27.50
____SC1R	Structured ANS COBOL, Part 1	31.00
____SC2R	Structured ANS COBOL, Part 2	31.00
____RW	Report Writer	17.50

Qty	Product code and title	*Price
Data Base Processing		
____DB21	DB2 for the COBOL Programmer Part 1: An Introductory Course	$32.50
____DB22	DB2 for the COBOL Programmer Part 2: An Advanced Course	36.50
____IMS1	IMS for the COBOL Programmer Part 1: DL/I Data Base Processing	34.50
____IMS2	IMS for the COBOL Programmer Part 2: Data Communications and MFS	36.50
VSAM		
____VSMX	VSAM: Access Method Services and Application Programming	$27.50
____VSMR	VSAM for the COBOL Programmer (Second Edition)	20.00
DOS/VSE Subjects		
____VJLR	DOS/VSE JCL (Second Edition)	$34.50
____ICCF	DOS/VSE ICCF	31.00
____VBAL	DOS/VSE Assembler Language	36.50

☐ Bill me for the books plus UPS shipping and handling (and sales tax within California).

☐ Bill my company. P.O.#_____

☐ I want to **SAVE 10%** by paying in advance. Charge to my
____Visa ____MasterCard ____American Express:
Card number _____
Valid thru (mo/yr) _____
Cardowner's signature _____

☐ I want to **SAVE 10% plus shipping and handling**. Here's my check or money order for the books minus 10% ($_____). California residents, please add sales tax to your total. (Offer valid in U.S.)

* Prices are subject to change. Please call for current prices.

To order more quickly,

Call **toll-free** 1-800-221-5528

(Weekdays, 8 to 5 Pacific Standard Time)

Fax: 1-209-275-9035

Mike Murach & Associates, Inc.

4697 West Jacquelyn Avenue
Fresno, California 93722-6427
(209) 275-3335

BUSINESS REPLY MAIL
FIRST CLASS   PERMIT NO. 3063   FRESNO, CA

POSTAGE WILL BE PAID BY ADDRESSEE

Mike Murach & Associates, Inc.

4697 W JACQUELYN AVE
FRESNO CA 93722-9888

NO POSTAGE
NECESSARY
IF MAILED
IN THE
UNITED STATES